Faith, Reason, and Theosis

ORTHODOX CHRISTIANITY AND CONTEMPORARY THOUGHT

SERIES EDITORS
Aristotle Papanikolaou and Ashley M. Purpura

This series consists of books that seek to bring Orthodox Christianity into an engagement with contemporary forms of thought. Its goal is to promote (1) historical studies in Orthodox Christianity that are interdisciplinary, employ a variety of methods, and speak to contemporary issues; and (2) constructive theological arguments in conversation with patristic sources and that focus on contemporary questions ranging from the traditional theological and philosophical themes of God and human identity to cultural, political, economic, and ethical concerns. The books in the series explore both the relevancy of Orthodox Christianity to contemporary challenges and the impact of contemporary modes of thought on Orthodox self-understandings.

Faith, Reason, and Theosis

Aristotle Papanikolaou and
George E. Demacopoulos
Editors

Fordham University Press
New York • 2023

Copyright © 2023 Fordham University Press

All rights reserved. No part of this publication may be reproduced, stored in a retrieval system, or transmitted in any form or by any means—electronic, mechanical, photocopy, recording, or any other—except for brief quotations in printed reviews, without the prior permission of the publisher.

Fordham University Press has no responsibility for the persistence or accuracy of URLs for external or third-party Internet websites referred to in this publication and does not guarantee that any content on such websites is, or will remain, accurate or appropriate.

Fordham University Press also publishes its books in a variety of electronic formats. Some content that appears in print may not be available in electronic books.

Visit us online at www.fordhampress.com.

Library of Congress Cataloging-in-Publication Data available online at https://catalog.loc.gov.

Printed in the United States of America

25 24 23   5 4 3 2 1

First edition

Contents

Introduction: Faith, Reason, and Theosis 1
Aristotle Papanikolaou and George E. Demacopoulos

PART I: THEOTIC EXISTENCE

Waking the Gods: Theosis as Reason's Natural End 15
David Bentley Hart

Does Aquinas Have the Orthodox Concept of Theosis? 37
Jean Porter

Deification as Christification and Human Becoming 72
Philip Kariatlis

Theosis as Kenosis: The Paradox of Holy Intimacy
in the Theology of Hans Urs von Balthasar 93
Carolyn Chau

Martin Luther on Faith and Union with God:
Speculations on Theosis 112
Kirsi Stjerna

Differentiation as Disfigurement: A Womanist Polemic
against the Co-optation of the Divine Essence 133
Michele E. Watkins

PART II: THEOTIC KNOWING

Revelation, Reason, and Holiness: A Wesleyan Perspective 159
William J. Abraham

The Ambiguous Meanings of Theosis in Modern and Postmodern Discourse 176
Andrew Prevot

Speculation and Theosis in Vladimir Lossky and Meister Eckhart 198
Robert Glenn Davis

Knowing through Unknowing: The Qualified Necessity of Human Reason in Dionysius 218
Peter Bouteneff

Knowing in Theosis: A Byzantine Mystical Theological Approach 231
Ashley Purpura

Deification in Evagrius Ponticus and the Transmission of the *Kephalaia Gnostika* in Syriac and Arabic 251
Stephen J. Davis

The Embodied Logos: Reason, Knowledge, and Relation 267
Rowan Williams

Acknowledgments *293*

List of Contributors *295*

Index *301*

Faith, Reason, and Theosis

INTRODUCTION:
FAITH, REASON, AND THEOSIS

Aristotle Papanikolaou and George E. Demacopoulos

Theosis shapes contemporary Orthodox theology in two ways, positively and negatively. In the positive sense, contemporary Orthodox theologians made theosis the thread that bound together the various aspects of theology in a coherent whole, but also their interpretation of patristic texts, which experienced a renaissance in the twentieth century, even in Orthodox theology.[1] One could not fail to notice how the concept of theosis saturates contemporary Orthodoxy theology in such a way that it assumes a central position. As Andrew Louth rightly describes, theosis has assumed a "place" within Orthodox theology: "What I mean by place is the way the doctrine functions in the whole Orthodox experience, including the pattern of theology. In studying the history of Christian theology, we have often paid too little attention to what I would call the pattern of theology: The mosaic, as it were, that emerges when the various doctrines of the faith are fitted together."[2] The lack of substantive theological engagement in the Orthodox world between the fall of Constantinople (1453) and the revival of Orthodox theology nineteenth-century Russia makes this convergence around theosis even more remarkable. In an age where incompatible first principles make so many theological disagreements intractable, contemporary Orthodox theology exists as a vibrant debate on the implications of a nonnegotiable grounding axiom: that God became human so that humans can become gods.

In the negative sense, contemporary theologians used theosis as a club to beat down Catholic and Protestant Christians by claiming that only Orthodox theology affirms the realism of divine/human communion. Against Protestant Christians, such a claim seemed self-evident insofar as Protestantism was reduced to forensic notions of justification; with the Roman Catholics, the condemnation was a bit trickier, especially in light of the sacramental and mystical traditions within Roman Catholicism; but in the end the Orthodox would zoom in on notions of created grace, especially in Thomas Aquinas, in order to argue that Roman Catholicism veered from the Orthodox path most essentially by denying deification. As we detailed in *Orthodox Readings of Augustine*,[3] which resulted from the first Patterson Conference hosted by the Orthodox Christian Studies Center in 2007, John Romanides traced this rejection of deification in the Latin tradition to Augustine with the claim that Augustine failed to theologically endorse the essence/energies distinction, which Romanides argued was so prevalent in the pre- and post-Nicene fathers of the Greek tradition.[4]

Happily, the idea that only the Orthodox can claim exclusive ownership of theosis has been demonstrated to be a historical fiction and part of a postcolonial Orthodox construction of the "West."[5] Admittedly, Catholics and Protestant scholars often ironically reinforced this territorialism, whether it be the Catholic manualist tradition or Harnackian notions of "Hellenization" of Christianity. Over the past few decades, however, clearer minds seem to be prevailing, as scholars across denominational divides have discovered that references to deification exist in Augustine, Anselm, and Aquinas (not to mention Bonaventure, Eckhart and the entire Catholic mystical tradition), but also in Luther, Calvin, Wesley and others in the Protestant tradition.[6] Moving toward the present, although the word "deification" would not be found in contemporary Protestant theologians, the realism of communion between the finite and the infinite, between the created and the uncreated seems to unite Friedrich Schleiermacher and Karl Barth, despite their profound differences.[7] It would also seem to unite these Protestant theologians with those Catholic theologians who initiated a rethinking of the nature/grace distinction within the Catholic theological tradition. In one sense, if contemporary Christian theology, including the emergence of various forms of liberation theology, can be seen as an extended debate on the implications of reconfiguring the nature/grace distinction, then the theme of deification has been central to Christian theology in the broadest sense for the past century. All this to argue that the debate does not really entail whether notions of deification exist outside of the Orthodox world. They do and they always have—that is a fact. The debate has really shifted to what is meant by deification and the significance of those different meanings.

Contemporary theologians did not invent these different meanings; they existed from the very beginning of Christian thought. Another by-product of the Orthodox monopoly on theosis entails the impression that it has meant only one thing throughout the ages. This homogeneous meaning was reinforced by narratives such as that by Vladimir Lossky in *The Vision of God*, which presented Greek patristic history, from the apostolic period until "the Palamite synthesis" as a singular clarification of the essence/energies distinction.[8] As Norman Russell's essential book confirms, the meaning of theosis was anything but uniform in the patristic texts.[9] *The Doctrine of Deification in the Greek Patristic Tradition* provides the most detailed and complex picture of the place and development of the concept of theosis in the Christian East, replacing the magisterial study of Jules Gross.[10]

By his own admittance, Russell covers much of the same ground as Gross. His historical trajectory begins with the cultures in which Christianity emerged, Greek paganism and Judaism, before examining the development of the concept of deification from the New Testament through John of Damascus. The climax in Russell's book is Maximus the Confessor, although he briefly examines John of Damascus in an epilogue, together with Leontius of Byzantium, Symeon the New Theologian, Gregory Palamas, and the contemporary appropriation of deification by Orthodox and non-Orthodox theologians. Russell explains in the introduction that his book goes beyond Gross in three other ways: by studying the vocabulary of deification in the Greek fathers; by clarifying the questions to which each of the Greek fathers own particular contribution to the development of the concept of deification is a response; and by illustrating the broader range of meanings of deification in the patristic tradition other than the narrow identification of deification with incorruptibility that Gross offers.

Russell names this broad range of meanings the nominal, analogical, and metaphorical. The metaphorical entails the ethical and the realistic approaches. The ethical approach involves attainment of likeness to God through ascetical endeavor; to be in the likeness of God means to possess divine attributes acquired through the imitation of Christ. In the realistic approach, deification is participation in the divine that transforms the human being. Russell cautions against interpreting these distinctions as incompatible ways of understanding deification; rather, "analogy, imitation, and participation . . . form a continuum rather than express radically different kinds of relationship."[11] These are the categories which emerge and which allow him to make sense of the broad range of meanings of deification that he discovered in the course of his exhaustive research. Russell also uses these categories to (re)construct the narrative of the development of the idea of deification in the Christian East. Beginning in the second century, especially with Irenaeus of Lyon and Clement of Alexandria, ethical and realistic approaches to deification predominate. Cyril of Alexandria begins to forge a synthesis between these approaches, which finds its climax, not surprisingly, in Maximus the Confessor. It is this synthesis that is bequeathed to the Byzantine theologians, and through them to the Russian monastic tradition. One of the most significant contributions of this book is its narration of the subtleties of Eastern Christian discourse on deification, the discovery of which is a testimony to Russell's powers of scholarly perception. In the end, the ethical and the realist approaches have enough in common to allow for the monastic synthesis that one finds in Maximus.

At least two important results emerged from Russell's study. The first consists of further marginalizing Adolf von Harnack's terribly misguided and prejudiced assessment that theosis was a "Hellenization" and, thus, betrayal of the Gospel. Harnack, an early advocate for the historical-critical method among Lutheran theologians, was an early spokesperson for the view that theosis was a Hellenistic corruption of Christian purity. As is well known, Harnack's *History of Dogma* offers a scathing critique of the gradual Hellenization of early Christianity, which he (incorrectly) concluded to be a break from the Apostolic community's original "enthusiasm" and "individualism." For Harnack, the faith of the earliest Christians gave way to institutionalization, priesthood, and—worst of all—Hellenistic philosophy. And although it is not a subject that drew much of his attention, Harnack did specifically link the patristic concept of theosis to the capitulation of third- and fourth-century Christians to Greek philosophy.[12] It is worth quoting his view in full:

> Instead of enthusiastic independent Christians, we find a new literature of revelation, the New Testament, and Christian priests. When did these formations begin? How and by what influence was the living faith transformed into the creed to be believed, the surrender to Christ into a philosophic Christology, the Holy Church into the *corpus permixtum*, the glowing hope of the Kingdom of heaven into a doctrine of immortality and deification, prophecy into a learned exegesis and theological science, the bearers of the spirit into clerics, the brethren into laity held in tutelage, miracles and healings into

nothing, or into priestcraft, the fervent prayers into a solemn ritual, renunciation of the world into a jealous dominion over the world, the "spirit" into constraint and law?

Russell rightly argues that Greek patristic understandings of deification are intertwined with a Christology that defines the person of Christ as the event of divine/human communion. Deification is the flip side of the exchange formula: God becoming human allows humans to transcend their own finitude, and this transcendence is to become like God and is only possible through a relationship with God in Christ by the Holy Spirit. This exchange formula is the common thread linking diverse patristic discussions of deification: if God did not become human in Jesus Christ, then human communion with the divine would not be possible.

Russell's second significant achievement is to perhaps, unwittingly, support current discussion on theosis, which itself is marked by differences of meaning. In other words, by deconstructing a homogeneous narrative of thinking on theosis, the past links up with the present in the sense that the current discussion stands in continuity with an already existing tradition of thinking and debate of the different meanings of the common affirmation of theosis.

Given the fact that Orthodox, Catholic, and Protestant theologians of the twentieth century appeared to identify exclusively theosis with the Orthodox Christianity, one might simply be happy with the discovery of a more ecumenical affirmation of theosis, in one form or another, throughout Christian history. Paul Gavrilyuk rightly argues that amid the newly recognized ecumenical consensus, "it would appear to be relatively uncontroversial that the ontological concepts of participation, divine likeness, and union with God are constitutive of the notion of deification." He names this the "minimalist definition" of deification.[13] An accomplishment in itself, the broad agreement on this minimalist definition, Gavrilyuk argues, should not obfuscate the differences on the details. As an example, Gavrilyuk notes how "the broader patristic context of *theosis* also presupposes certain anthropological assumptions and practices conducive to deification."[14] Even if Christian thinkers throughout the centuries affirmed a minimalist notion of theosis, they certainly did not share the patristic anthropological assumptions. Given that theosis did not quite assume in post-Reformation Protestant and Catholic theological traditions the "place" it maintained within Orthodox dogmatic architecture, does the recent rediscovery of theosis within the Western Christian traditions signal a distinctive Western understanding of deification? Is the attempt to link deification with justification a shift or stretch of the patristic meaning?

Gavrilyuk offers the most adequate framing of the recent ecumenical retrieval of deification as both the work of historical theology and "a *theological achievement*."[15] This achievement entails an ongoing willingness to keep thinking about theosis, which goes as much for the Orthodox as it does for the Protestants and the Catholics. Protestant and Catholic theologians do not simply regurgitate Luther or Aquinas, as examples, when they locate affirmations of deification in their works and attempt to connect this notion with other foundational theological principles associated with Luther and Aquinas; such an effort is to think with and beyond these theologians. It would be a mistake, however, if one did not notice the same pattern within contemporary Orthodox theologians, since contemporary Orthodox reaffirmations of theosis cannot be seen as simply repetitions of patristic sayings. All this to say that even if a minimalist definition of theosis is not quite adequate to the task demanded of theology, at least it can function as a basis on which disagreement, differences, and debate may ensue. With such a common basis, we can move past "incommensurability" language, and perhaps sees these differences as a productive stretching and shifting of the meaning of theosis.

The essays of this book are situated within this current of thinking on theosis, which consists of a common, albeit minimalist, affirmation amid the flow of differences. The lens through which theosis is interrogated is that of "faith and reason," in part because contemporary Orthodox theology identified theosis with mystical union in opposition to salvation through faith (Protestant) and theology as rational discourse (Catholic). The authors in this volume contribute to the historical theological task of complicating this contemporary Orthodox narrative, but they also continue the "theological achievement" of thinking about theosis so that all Christian traditions may be challenged to stretch and shift their understanding of theosis even amid an ecumenical celebration of the gift of participation in the life of God.

In the first section of the book, "Theotic Existence," David Bentley Hart offers a rigorous defense for the natural desire for God on the side of creation, arguing that to deny such a desire, as given by neoscholastic interpretation of Thomas Aquinas, is to deny the incarnation of the Logos, in whom is revealed nature's true end, which is nothing less than union with the divine. Jean Porter pulls the reins on the recent enthusiasm exhibited in interpretations of Thomas Aquinas that attempt to place theosis at the center of his thought. While she does not deny that Thomas has a notion of deification, it is not central to his doctrinal commitments as it is in the Orthodox tradition, revealing significant differences not simply between his notion of grace and the Orthodox understanding of theosis but also in approaches to the doctrine of God, justification, sin, and the person and work of Christ. Philip Kariatlis wades deep into contemporary Orthodox theology and asks the question whether the essence/energies distinction is/has been the only way to express the Orthodox notion of deification. He draws on the work of a lesser known but important theologian, Panayiotis Nellas, to foreground an understanding of theosis as Christification—union in the person of Christ. Carolyn Chau highlights the enigma of Hans Urs von Balthasar theology, which given Balthasar's own position on the nature/grace debate within contemporary Catholic theology, one might immediately expect theosis to be front and center. Even though the references to theosis in Balthasar are few, Chau argues that he recasts theosis as kenosis in the form of an ever-deepening love for Christ that shares in Christ's mission. Kirsi Stjerna amplifies the groundbreaking work of Tuomo Mannermaa, who argued for the compatibility of Luther's notion of justification as union with Christ in faith with patristic notions of theosis. Stjerna clarifies and modifies Mannermaa's thesis with an eye toward keeping Luther's understanding of theosis involved in the developing ecumenical conversation. Michele Watkins puts womanist and Orthodox—patristic and contemporary—theologies in conversation. By thinking theosis from a womanist perspective, she challenges typical ways of thinking theosis across denominations in terms of isolated self's relation with God and lifts up the voices of the desacralized community struggling to realize and live the promise of eucharistic divine/human communion.

In the second section of the book, "Theotic Knowing," William Abraham explores the interrelation of holiness, reason, revelation, and experience in John Wesley. He argues that the manifestation and understanding of revelation requires spiritual perception, which itself is a form of spiritual perfection or holiness. Abraham demonstrates that Wesley's understanding of this interrelation predates the insights emerging in contemporary analytical epistemology, especially in relation to the truth claims within theology. Andrew Prevot claims that theosis must be thought within the modern and postmodern intellectual traditions, in which godlikeness was not abandoned but redefined either as the surpassing of faith by reason (modern) or the infinite subversion of the relation between faith and reason. While Christian thinking on theosis in the present can learn much from the insights of modern and postmodern treatments of godlikeness, it does so toward amplifying the theological understanding of contemplative-and-active participation in the divine life, which is a surpassing-as-fulfillment of faith and reason. Robert Davis sets out to further nuance the recent correction of Meister Eckhart's thought as overemphasizing the speculative over the affective. If the recent corrective demonstrates the importance of the affective in Eckhart's thought, Davis uses Vladimir's Lossky's posthumously published study of Eckhart to recover an understanding of speculation whose scope includes a divine/human communion that is simultaneously absolute identity in Christ and the reality of relationship between the divine and the human. Peter Bouteneff explores the thought of Dionysius the Areopagite, who provided so much of the language for expressing theosis as mystical union, to refute the idea, advanced by many contemporary Orthodox theologians, that mystical theology is an experience of the divine that is arational or, even worse, diametrically opposed to knowledge-as-reason. The apophatic moment is always in dialectical tension with cataphasis, and right reasoning is necessary in the mystical ascent toward union with God. Ashley Purpura draws on the mystical writings of Symeon the New Theologian, and the liturgical reflections of Nicholas Cabasilas in order to suggest that the Orthodox tradition includes a theologically consistent way of knowing the "other" and knowing the "self," that is grounded in a relationship of theosis. This theotic way of encountering the other can provide an alternative to forms of knowing that result in diametrical oppositions or demonizations. Stephen Davis points to the lack of serious engagement with Evagrius of Pontus's understanding of deification, in spite of his centrality to the development of ascetical theology in the Christian tradition. Davis seeks to fill this gap by showing how Evagrius's use of "Holy Unity" describes the assimilation of the human being to the Holy Trinity. He also details how Evagrian notions of deification were transmitted into later medieval Syriac- and Arabic-speaking contexts and subtly written out of the Evagrian textual record. If Davis records for the reader how Evagrian notions of theosis were revised, Rowan Williams recovers the Evagrian contemplation as a rational attunement to the human and nonhuman world that is in accordance with the Logos. This reasoned responsiveness to creation is itself dependent on the passions, which if left untrained, situates our relations to "things" in the form of anger or desire rather than as eternal gift welcomed with a hospitable mind, one refashioned in the image of the Logos.

The ecumenical discussion that takes place within these pages affirms the minimalist notion of theosis as participation in the divine life. Yet the essays within the first section reveal how answering the question "what does theosis look like" is tradition-specific. The essays of the second section zero in on the relation between theosis and knowing in relation to reason. Each affirms that whatever the mystical notion of "beyond reason" may mean, right reasoning, speculation, and perception is but one manifestation of what divine/human communion looks like, especially insofar as our relationship with God shapes our seeing, thinking, and reasoning of the human and nonhuman Other. What this volume leaves unclear, admittedly, is how each of the various presentations of theosis may be challenged or stretched by the others, or what synthesis may emerge from these various individual insights. We leave it to the diligent and attentive reader to make those connections. It is, however, fitting that Michele Watkins essays straddles both sections insofar as she gives witness to the fact what we think theosis looks like will be incomplete and, quite possibly, a means to oppress if the voices of the marginalized and oppressed are not taken into account. Moreover, there is a theotic knowing that is discernible only if such voices are not simply listened to but also privileged. Even though theosis has played a significant role in the formation of various of forms of liberation theologies that have addressed issues of class, race, and sexuality, it is clear that the next volume that needs to emerge in this ecumenical revival of theosis is one devoted exclusively to marginalized perspectives of divine/human communion.

Notes

1. An example that the centrality of theosis in contemporary Orthodox theology constitutes a renaissance is the story of Nichifor Crainic, one of the leading Romanian intellectuals between 1922 and 1944, who inferred only after studying German medieval mystics in Vienna that Orthodoxy must also have a tradition of mystical theology. See Christine Hall, *Pancosmic Church: Specific Românesc Themes in Nichifor Crainic's Writings between 1922–44* (Uppsala: Uppsala Universitet, 2008), 61. See also Ruth Coates, *Deification in Russian Religious Thought: Between the Revolutions, 1905–17* (Oxford: Oxford University Press, 2019) and, Aristotle Papanikolaou, "Eastern Orthodox Theology," in *The*

Routledge Companion to Modern Christian Thought, ed. Chad Meister and James Beilby (New York Routledge, 2013), 538–48.

2. Andrew Louth, "The Place of *Theosis* in Orthodox Theology," in *Partakers of the Divine Nature: The History and Development of Deification in the Christian Tradition*, ed. Michael J. Christensen and Jeffery A. Wittung (Madison, NJ: Fairleigh Dickinson University Press, 2007), 32–44.

3. George Demacopoulos and Aristotle Papanikolaou, eds., *Orthodox Readings of Augustine* (New York: Fordham University Press, 2020).

4. Probably the most sophisticated defense of this Romanides interpretation comes from David Bradshaw, *Aristotle: East and West: Metaphysics and the Division of Christendom* (Oxford: Oxford University Press, 2007).

5. George Demacopoulos and Aristotle Papanikolaou, eds., *Orthodox Constructions of the West* (New York: Fordham University Press, 2013). See also George Demacopoulos, *Colonizing Christianity: Greek and Latin Religious Identity in the Era of the Fourth Crusade* (New York: Fordham University Press, 2019).

6. See the essays in Christensen and Wittung, *Partakers of the Divine Nature*. See also Paul L. Gavrilyuk, "The Retrieval of Deification: How a Once-Despised Archaism Became an Ecumenical Desideratum," *Modern Theology* 25, no. 4 (2009): 648, and Nikolaos Asproulis, "Eucharistic Personhood: Deification in the Orthodox Tradition," in *With All the Fullness of God: Deification in Christian Traditions*, ed. Jared Ortiz (Lanham, MD: Fortress Academic, 2021).

7. On Barth, see George Hunsinger, "The Mediator of Communion," in *Cambridge Companion to Karl Barth*, ed. John Webster (Oxford: Oxford University Press, 2000), 177–94. On Schleiermacher, we do not think it a stretch to interpret the "feeling of absolute dependence" and redemption as "God-consciousness" in terms of communion, especially in light of his conceptualization of the relation between the finite and the infinite. See *The Christian Faith*, vol. 1, trans., Terrence N. Tice, Catherine L. Kelsey, and Edwina Lawler (Louisville, KY: Westminster John Knox Press, 2016).

8. Vladimir Lossky, *The Vision of God*, trans. Asheleigh Moorhouse (Crestwood, NY: St. Vladimir's Seminary Press, 1983).

9. Norman Russell, *The Doctrine of Deification in the Greek Patristic Tradition* (Oxford: Oxford University Press, 2004). See also *Fellow Workers with God: Orthodox Thinking on Theosis* (Crestwood, NY: St. Vladimir's Seminary Press, 2009).

10. Jules Gross, *La divinisation du chrétien d'après les Pères grecs: Contribution historique à la doctrine de grace* (Paris: Gabalda, 1938).

11. Russell, *The Doctrine of Deification*, 2.

12. Adolf von Harnack, *The History of Dogma*, 3rd ed., trans. Neil Buchanan (Boston: Little Brown and Company), 1:45–46. See Mark McInroy, "How Deification Became Eastern: German Idealism, Liberal Protestantism, and the

Modern Misconstruction of the Doctrine," *Modern Theology* 37, no. 4 (2021): 934–58.

13. Gavrilyuk, "The Retrieval of Deification," 651.

14. Ibid., 652. For these anthropological presuppositions, with particular focus on Maximus the Confessor, see Aristotle Papanikolaou, "Theosis," in *The Oxford Handbook of Mystical Theology*, ed. Edward Howells and Mark L. McIntosh (Oxford: Oxford University Press, 2000), 569–85, esp. 574–82.

15. Gavrilyuk, "The Retrieval of Deification," 655.

Part I: Theotic Existence

WAKING THE GODS

THEOSIS AS REASON'S NATURAL END

David Bentley Hart

Τί γὰρ θεώσεως τοῖς ἀξίοις ἐρασμιώτερον, καθ' ἣν ὁ Θεὸς Θεοῖς γενομένοις ἑνούμενος τὸ πᾶν ἑαυτοῦ ποιεῖται δι' ἀγαθότητα; Διὸ καὶ ἡδονὴν καὶ πεῖσιν καὶ χαρὰν καλῶς ὠνόμασαν τὴν τοιαύτην κατάστασιν, τὴν τῇ θείᾳ κατανοήσει καὶ τῇ ἑπομένῃ αὐτῇ τῆς εὐφροσύνης ἀπολαύσει ἐγγινομένην, ἡδονὴν μέν, ὡς τέλος οὖσαν τῶν κατὰ φύσιν ἐνεργειῶν (οὕτω γὰρ τὴν ἡδονὴν ὁρίζονται) . . .

—MAXIMUS THE CONFESSOR

It is a source of constant vexation to me, as I am sure it must be to all of us, that philosophical theology pays such scant attention to root vegetables. Obviously, after so many centuries of appalling neglect, this is not a deficiency that can be remedied in a day; but, even so, we should not shirk such small corrective efforts as we are able to undertake. So imagine, if you will, a turnip. Imagine it set before you on a table. But imagine also that, only a few moments ago, it was not a turnip but a rabbit instead, and that I have just now magically conjured the one thing out of the other. I do not mean, I hasten to add, that I am an illusionist who has just performed a very clever trick. Rather, mine was a genuine feat of goetic sorcery, probably accomplished with the assistance of a daemon familiar. Contain your wonder. Then tell me: Have I actually transformed a rabbit into a turnip—is that logically possible—or have I instead merely annihilated the poor bunny and then recombined its material ingredients into something else altogether? Surely, it seems obvious, the answer must be the latter. It may well be that precisely the same molecules—even the same atoms—once found in the rabbit are now securely invested in the turnip; but there is nothing leporine remaining in the turnip, and neither was there any trace of rapinity (rapitude?) in the rabbit. I assume that this is uncontroversial. Very well. What, though, if instead I had transformed the rabbit not into another terrestrial organism, especially not one presumably lower in the chain of being, but had instead, so to speak, superelevated it by changing it into a more eminent kind of entity—say, an angel? Much the same question arises: has the rabbit *become* an angel, or has it again merely perished and been replaced by something else? The answer depends, I suppose, on whether one thinks there is already something angelic about rabbits (as I do, but as many do not); for, if there is no latent angelism in rabbits, even of the most purely potential kind, then again no real metamorphosis has occurred at the level of discrete substances or identities. All that has happened is that I have murdered a harmless bunny and summoned up a potentially very dangerous spiritual creature to take its place (one that may not at all approve of my callousness toward small helpless animals).

This is, of course, more or less the opposite of the Ship of Theseus conundrum. The question at issue is not a mereological or metaphysical query about whether a substantial form, individuated by its material instantiation, remains identical with itself as each of its material parts is successively replaced. Rather, it is something more along the lines of asking what continuity exists between, say, a stand of trees and a ship composed from their wood. And it seems obvious that those trees—understood as discrete substances, modes, or just relatively stable objects of deictic reference—have not become a ship but have instead ceased to exist in order that the ship might come into being. Whatever continuity persists between the trees and the ship is found only in a common substrate, at the level of sheer material plasticity, and is ultimately reducible to that pure indeterminate potency traditionally called prime matter or ὕλη. This alone remains constant across all transformations precisely because it is in itself nothing as such, and so is always absolute: *absolved*, that is, of all formal identity. It can relinquish one form in order to be subsumed into another without being itself altered because in itself it is nothing other than the abiding reality of pure possibility. There is no "thing" to be altered. At the level of actual forms and natures and determinate properties, however, nothing can ever truly become anything other than what it already is, at least potentially. A discrete substance can pass through various states proper to itself, achieve diverse stages of natural development, acquire or shed modalities or accidents implicit in its own nature. But it can never become something truly *extrinsic* to itself without ceasing to be what it was.

If, by the way, I seem to be slipping too easily and unreflectively into an Aristotelian patois, I do so without remorse. For one thing, the particular issues I want to discuss here have traditionally been couched in just such terms. More to the point, though, traditional Aristotelian language concerning the relation between potentiality and actuality seems to me merely to express what I take to be a very basic and logically impeccable modal grammar. Every specific possibility is finite; conversely, infinite possibility can never be specific. And this same elementary logical solvency can be ascribed to the whole Aristotelian language of causality, so long as one does not make the mistake—characteristic of much seventeenth-century science, with its agent and patient substances and forces—of imagining that that language concerns "causes" in the modern sense. Really, a better rendering of *aitiai* or *causae*, in the ancient or mediaeval acceptation, might be "explanations," "rationales," "logical descriptions," or "rational relations." The fourfold nexus of causality was chiefly a rule of predication, describing the inherent logical structure of anything that exists insofar as it exists, and reflecting a world in which things and events are at once discretely identifiable and yet part of the continuum of the whole. A thing's *aitiai* are intrinsic integral logical relations, not separated forces in only accidental alliance. A final cause is the inherent natural limit of a particular possibility, not an extrinsically imposed design; it is at once a thing's intrinsic fullness and its larger participation in the totality of nature. So a causal relation in this scheme is less like a physical exchange of energy than like a mathematical equation, and the final cause is like the inevitable sum determining that relation. And the logic of finality, if one grants it (as one must), tells us that the only substantial transformations that are not essentially annihilations are modifications already virtually embraced within the natural potentials of the thing transformed. There may be differing modes of leporinity, for instance, and any number of possible accidents thereof, but none of these is the condition of being a turnip. A rabbit cannot be—and therefore cannot become—a turnip, any more than a circle can be—or can become—a square.

Why is any of this important here? Principally for historical reasons. It is very easy to forget, after all, that many of the most important theological developments and movements in both Roman Catholic and Eastern Orthodox theology in the first half of the twentieth century—*ressourcement, la nouvelle théologie*, the neopatristic synthesis, neopalamism, even certain salient aspects of Bulgakov's mature thought—took shape in the same, largely Parisian intellectual atmosphere and defined themselves to a significant degree over against what was then the dominant theology of grace in Roman Catholic thought: that of the Baroque "manualist" Thomism whose institutional cry of triumph had rung out so stridently in 1879's encyclical *Aeterni Patris* but had already diminished to an asperous death rattle by the time of 1950's *Humani generis*. This was the infamous "two-tier" Thomism—or so its detractors called it—that had had no real antecedents in theological tradition much before the *de auxiliis* controversy of the sixteenth century, that had achieved preeminence only in the days of the "modernist crisis," and that was already on the way to its well-deserved demise with the publication of Maurice Blondel's *L'action* in 1893 and did not long survive Henri de Lubac's *Surnaturel* in 1946. And, until very recently, most of us thought it had been laid permanently to rest, in the deepest, dankest, and most dismal of theology's unvisited crypts. Apparently, however, someone neglected to drive a stake through its heart and cut off its head, because in the last two decades it has enjoyed a surprisingly robust reviviscence in some of the more militantly necrophile factions of traditionalist Catholicism. And so, now that the damned monster is up from its grave and spasmodically lurching about again, spreading terror among the villagers and hill folk, this might be a propitious time for Orthodox theologians to reconsider what was learned (or should have been learned) in those earlier encounters with it. (Who knows but that it will ultimately be up to them to save the occidental barbarians from themselves?)

From an Eastern perspective, the debate on the "supernatural"—epochal though it was for Catholic theology—can only seem a bit bizarre. What had become the "Thomist" position (which must be distinguished, incidentally, from any position we can confidently attribute to Thomas himself) was that a proper appreciation of the gratuity of salvation and deification can be secured only by insisting that, as the tedious formula goes, "grace is extrinsic to the nature of the creature." That is to say, human nature has no inherent ordination toward real union with God, and—apart from the infusion of a certain wholly adventitious *lumen gloriae*—rational creatures are incapable even of conceiving a desire for such union. Even the unremitting agitations of Augustine's *cor inquietum* are superadded spiritual motives that, in the current providential order of this world, happen to have been graciously conjoined to the natural intentionalities of created rational wills. But, so the claim goes, none of that need be the case. God could just as well have created a world in a state of *natura pura*, wherein the rational volitions of spiritual creatures could have achieved all their final ends and ultimate rest in an entirely natural terminus. The only longing for God such creatures would naturally experience would be an elicited velleity or abstract curiosity obscurely directed toward some original explanatory principle that might tell them where the world came from. Or, in some cases, for those who may have heard of the possibility of the beatific vision in the abstract, there might be an elicited "conditional" desire to see what it is like; but this would still not be the kind of supernatural appetite and capacity that efficacious grace might infuse in a soul. And, even then, those ungraced spirits need never discover that principle or that possible end *in itself* in order to be wholly satisfied in their rational longings, since God thus "naturally" conceived remains an object of only incidental inquisitiveness, adequately known in and through creatures. Moreover, supposedly, even in *this* world, where rational natures do bear the gracious imprint of a vocation to deification, human nature in itself remains entirely identical to what human nature would have been in a world without grace. Nature *as such* has no claim on grace, even where such grace is given, nor does it even have any awareness that such grace is desirable *unless* it is actually given. Hence the term "two-tier" Thomism: Nature is a circumscribed totality, a self-sufficient *suppositum*, while grace is a *superadditum* set, as it were, atop it, and only thereby superelevating nature beyond itself. And here too one sees the effect of a certain Thomist tendency to believe that the Fall was humanity's descent from a graciously elevated state (Eden, as it were) into the state of nature as God had created it in its integrity (including such essential features as suffering and death), as opposed to the Christian view that the Fall was the descent of humanity and the whole cosmos from an original natural created condition into an unnatural state of bondage to decay (including such accidental features as suffering and death).

Now, clearly, the two-tier picture is alien to the whole of patristic tradition—indeed, more or less antithetical to it—and probably, I think, to all of mediaeval tradition. Its rise in early modernity was the result of an accident of theological history. Thomas himself in many places, and most insistently in the *Summa contra gentiles*, asserts that *"omnis intellectus naturaliter desiderat divinae substantiae visionem*" (every intellect naturally desires the vision of the divine substance),[1] that no finite intelligible object is sufficient for human happiness because the only final end of natural human desire is the real knowledge of God,[2] and that rational mind is created specifically for the purpose of seeing God.[3] It is something of a refrain in his writings.[4] But, on the threshold of modernity, these claims became suspect, as they seemed to fall afoul of the Aristotelian principle—or, at least, of an inexplicably fashionable exaggeration of the Aristotelian principle—that, as Denis the Carthusian (1402–1471) puts it, "no natural desire can exceed natural capacity": an axiom hazily drawn from Aristotle's claim in *De caelo* (where it functions not really so much as a logical assertion as a "providential" maxim) that "had Nature endowed celestial bodies with an inclination to linear movement, she would have supplied the means for it as well."[5] There is, admittedly, a banal truism here, since a "natural" desire is necessarily determined toward a specific final cause; but how this should apply to the very special case of rational spirit is precisely the issue that the later Thomist tradition could not coherently answer because it was inhibited by a very particular understanding of grace. Cajetan (1469–1534), for instance, took it as established that, for any rational creature, "*naturale eius desiderium non se extendit ultra facultatem*," "its natural desire cannot extend beyond its own faculty,"[6] and that therefore created intellect does not naturally desire God *in se*; for it cannot aspire to an object to which the "*tota vis naturae*," "the whole power of nature," is inadequate.[7] Therefore, supposedly, it must be the case that when Thomas speaks of the natural desire for God he is referring solely to the present providential order, in which human nature has already received grace's extrinsic mark. But then, even within this order, we must still acknowledge two distinct finalities for human beings: the "supposited" natural end and the graciously "superposited" supernatural end. The "first gift" of creation and the "second gift" of deification belong to two discontinuous moments of divine largesse.

I am indifferent to whether this is the correct reading of Thomas.[8] I do, though, think it worthwhile to make a few obvious points. For one thing, as I am hardly the first to note, the principle of proportionality between natural desire and desire's ends ought not to be mistaken for a rule regarding the range of a creature's innate spontaneous powers. What is *natural* for us is not necessarily, by that token, something that we are capable of achieving for ourselves. Indeed, insofar as we are finite and contingent beings, everything "natural" about us—the very possession of any nature at all, in fact—is dependent upon some other source or power not only for its realization, but for its very existence. Thomas, for instance, drawing on Aristotle's *Nicomachean Ethics*, plainly states that certain natural inclinations can be fulfilled only through the aid of another, and that there is even a peculiar and superior nobility in those aspects of our nature that require the assistance of friends to bring them to fruition.[9] But, really, are such properties even very rare or exceptional in finite natures? Even Aristotle's celestial bodies, for instance, perpetually enact the cyclophoria of the heavens only because they are drawn ever onward from beyond themselves by the Prime Mover, to which they will never attain. In a sense, almost every natural desire—even, say, for food or for sex—is dependent for its realization on something imparted to it from beyond itself. Even those possibilities most constitutive of us as the finite beings that we are can be fulfilled only in and through the *grace* of cooperating external causes. It was perfectly natural to me, for instance, as an adult human male, to become both a husband and a father. In a sense, the fullness of my humanity—at least, as the person I happen to be—required no less of me. But I was utterly incapable of achieving that natural end without the assistance of at least two other persons. A final cause must be logically implicit in the potency it actuates, true, but not necessarily as some wholly inherent and autonomous power of expression. And there is no logical reason to claim that an end that can be achieved only by *supernatural* assistance is not, for that reason, a *natural* possibility. Indeed, if this were the case, the very concept of natural potential would be meaningless, since any finite reality's very existence is always already a possibility that has been enacted by a wholly supernatural gift of being. A potency can be thoroughly natural in itself even if proportioned to an end that the "whole power of nature" (as we know it, at least) cannot supply. There is no contradiction here. There would be a contradiction only if there were no reality at all corresponding to that natural potency, and so no real final cause implicit in it.

On the other hand—and this again brings us back to the difference between the traditional Thomistic understanding of fallenness (as a descent from a state of gracious exception from nature into one of "natural" mortality and ignorance) and the Christian view (a descent from a natural state of grace into one of unnatural corruption)—why should one assume that a wholly natural (which is also to say wholly supernatural) progress into deification lies beyond the capacity of an unfallen rational creature?[10] Why would one imagine that the capacity for the desire to see God is not also, apart from the unnatural limitations of sin and death, also the natural capacity to achieve deification? Especially if one does not make the error of thinking that such an achievement must be *either* a work of grace *or* a work of nature, but realizes instead that such a distinction is a phantom of fallen consciousness? Even in this life, after all, something of the experience of real divinizing union with God can be vouchsafed to those who are devoted to the spiritual life—ἕνωσις, *unio mystica, turiya, fanaa-fillah*—and this is evidently, however much a gift of grace, also a real capacity of human nature, when it is set free from the constraints of an unnatural limitation of consciousness. Every rational nature is already potentially infinite in its embrace of the divine nature, even if that potency can be actualized only as a kind of infinite *epektasis*.

In truth, this entire issue seems to pose a problem only if one is intent on maintaining precisely the kind of impermeable partition between nature and grace that a belief in *creatio ex nihilo* renders meaningless. Grace, to be grace, does not require a prior antithetical *suppositum* of something devoid of grace—pure nature or nature in itself—nor need it be a purely extrinsic gift at every level of its impartation; it need only be free in its entirety. Finite existence itself is always already nothing but the gracious effect of God calling creatures to himself. All those boring false dilemmas bedeviling Western theology since the Pelagian controversy—the causal priority we assign *either* to our own working out of salvation *or* to God working in us, *either* to God's foreknowledge *or* to his sovereignty in election, *either* to the creature's merit *or* to God's, and so on—are simple category errors. Between the immanent and the transcendent, or the finite and the infinite, such rivalries of agency are not even cogently conceivable. An intrinsic rational desire for God would constitute a "right" to God's grace only if our nature were our own achievement. Yes, in a sense God does manifestly owe his creatures grace, within the terms of the gift of creation; but that is a debt he owes ultimately only to his own goodness.

None of that, however, is my principal argument here. I have two very different concerns: one logical (and metaphysical), regarding potentiality and actuality, the other phenomenological (and metaphysical), regarding the necessary structure of rational volition.

As to the former, the issue is that same simple, irresoluble logical impasse with which I began these reflections. The traditionalist Thomist answer to the conundrum of how, according to its scheme, grace can be said to perfect rather than abolish human nature—how, that is, a rational creature can be transformed beyond its every intrinsic potency and given a final end wholly extrinsic to its own nature without thereby ceasing to be the creature it has hitherto been—is to assert that our nature's capacity for grace consists in a mere *potentia oboedientialis*. But this can be true only if such a potency is understood in an especially eccentric way: as, that is, a kind of indeterminate ontological plasticity, open to whatever is not repugnant to the creature's nature, and yet also somehow open to actualities genuinely extrinsic to that nature. Supposedly, this pure patiency constitutes a structural aptitude in us for grace that is, nevertheless, in no sense an inchoate possession of grace or an intrinsic disposition toward a supernatural end. This is gibberish. Far from explaining how the interval between grace and nature posited by Thomist tradition can be intelligibly closed without violence to either side of the divide, it is merely a desperate resort to the fantastic. Here we need to distinguish with absolute logical precision between, on the one hand, the potencies proper to a creature's nature and, on the other, whatever powers the creature might individually possess for making those potencies actual. Simply said, whatever is not repugnant to a finite nature is, by definition, an intrinsic possibility of that nature. If divinity is "compatible" with the humanity of a creature made in God's image, then divinity is itself an inherent possibility of humanity—an inherent *property*, in fact, even if in only potential form. That this possibility can become an actuality only by way of God's action toward the creature in no way diminishes or qualifies this truth. Before Cajetan, in fact, obediential potency was understood simply as the creature's predisposition to miraculous interventions from God, and explicitly as a predisposition that in no way violated that creature's native potencies; it referred, that is, to the capacity of any creature to be conduced by God's power to a state that is proper to its own nature but that, in the natural course of things, it could not at that particular juncture achieve on its own. For instance, God could make an old man young again without violation of his nature as a man, as youth is a natural condition for human beings, even if it is not something a man can recover by his own power once it has passed. God could make Sara bear a child well past her fertile years without in any way imposing upon her a state repugnant to her womanhood. God might make a fool wise without violence to that person's humanity, for wisdom is a natural possible state for a rational being. What the concept of obediential potential most definitely was not, however, was some hazy notion of a mysterious capacity within a creature simultaneously to remain what it is and yet also to become something truly other than itself, or to receive a nature other than its own without thereby losing its own nature. It was not, that is to say, a principle of sorcery or an abrogation of the rule of noncontradiction.[11]

Again, there is an inviolable modal grammar here that must be observed. There are only two kinds of logically conceivable potency: either the finite (formal) possibility of something in particular or the infinite (material) possibility of everything in general. In the former case, a potency is a specific predisposition to and capacity for a particular final end, and so that end necessarily determines that potency's logical structure and is already implicit in it as a real rational relation; a natural capacity for the supernatural, if conceived thus, would have to be a virtual indwelling of the supernatural in the natural. In the latter case, the potency in question is just pure possibility as such, *materia prima* as it were, intrinsically disposed to no particular end, absolved of all determinacy, persisting despite the displacement of one form by another precisely because it lacks the power to retain any formal determination in itself and so is able to relinquish one nature in order to assume another; a natural capacity for the supernatural, if conceived thus, would be impotent to preserve the form or nature it inhabits in receiving an extrinsic determination, just as the material substrate of a tree would be impotent to preserve a tree's form or nature in being subsumed into a ship. In either case, whatever is extrinsic to the creature's nature must remain extrinsic forever. And this impasse cannot be resolved by the introduction of some chimerical *tertium quid* that is neither one kind of possibility nor the other, but rather some obscure amalgamation of the two. To invoke an "obediential potential" here is to play the sorcerer's apprentice—to recite a spell, that is, in the hope that it will magically perform a task for us that we cannot accomplish for ourselves. Once again, we can become only what we are.[12] And so, if we do possess a natural desire for the supernatural, it cannot be a mere contingency of providence, superadded to our nature; the potential of theosis must always already be the very structure of our nature in any possible order of reality. And, as it happens, we do possess such a desire, and could not fail to do so without entirely ceasing to be rational agents.

Not that this has always been fully appreciated, even by opponents of the two-tier system. Even many of de Lubac's defenders seem willing to concede a modified version of the *natura pura* argument. David Braine, for instance, while rejecting the notion that there is such a thing as human nature in the abstract that would be the same reality either with or without the supplement of a supernatural vocation to union with God, still allowed for the possibility that, under the conditions of some other created dispensation, God could create a different but still rational human nature not bearing the imprint of a supernatural finality; for him, it was enough to assert that human nature as it actually exists in the present order of providence, instantiated solely in the concrete historical community of the first and last Adams, includes that finality as an objective and given fact about the world God actually created.[13] Even de Lubac himself, after the 1950 promulgation of *Humani generis*, professed perfect agreement with the encyclical, including even its rejection of the proposition that God "cannot create intellectual beings without calling and ordering them to the beatific vision." By 1965, he was arguing vigorously for a stark distinction between the first gift of creation and the second gift of the vocation to deification.[14] By the end, the only clear difference from the manualist orthodoxy in his stated opinion was a preference for speaking not of two distinct *final* ends, but rather of one end that is only *penultimate* and another that is alone truly *ultimate*. Whether this was truly his position in 1946, when *Surnaturel* was published, I cannot say, though I doubt it.[15] I suspect he stated his real view, in its purest form, in a letter of April 3, 1932, to Maurice Blondel: "How can a conscious spirit be anything other than an absolute desire for God?"[16] If, though, he truly concurred with the encyclical, so much the worse for him; because the principle that Pius XII was so eager to reject in those pages happens to be an analytic truth of reason, no more susceptible of doubt than is the principle of identity. Not even God could create a rational nature not called to deification, any more than he could create a square circle; to have received that call is precisely what it is to be a rational being. Indeed, I would go so far as to say that a spiritual creature can possess no *purely* natural end at all, not even as a penultimate station along the way, and certainly none to which a supernatural end is merely contingently or gratuitously superadded. Quite the contrary: a spiritual creature is capable of a rational desire for a natural end only within the embrace of a prior supernatural longing, and hence a spiritual creature achieves any given natural good only as already assumed into and giving expression to the supernatural Good. Any finite intention of intellect and will is possible only by way of a prior infinite intentionality. Any intellectual predilection toward a merely immediate terminus of longing can be nothing other than a mediating modality and local contraction of a total spiritual volition toward the divine. One cannot contemplate a flower, watch a play, or pluck a strawberry from a punnet without being situated within an irrefrangible intentional continuum that extends all the way to God in his fullness.[17]

Large claims, I know. But the very notion that a rational spiritual creature could conceivably inhabit a realm of pure nature, in which it could rest satisfied, and in which its only intellectual concern with God would consist in a speculative etiological curiosity *posteriorly* elicited from finite cognitions, is a logical nonsense. Those finite cognitions, to the degree they could be comprehended and then interpreted as implying further logical entailments, would have to be acts of intentionality and rational evaluation undertaken in light of an intelligibility supplied by the mind's prior preoccupation with wholly transcendental indices of meaning, and so a proleptic intentional awareness of and desire for the supernatural *in its essence* as an *intelligibile*. Neither doctrine nor metaphysics need be immediately invoked to see the impossibility of rational agency within a sphere of pure nature; a simple phenomenology of what it is we do when we act intentionally should suffice. The rational will, when freely moved, is always purposive; it acts always toward an end: conceived, perceived, imagined, hoped for, resolved upon. Its every act is already, necessarily, an act of recognition, judgment, evaluation, and decision, and is therefore also a tacit or explicit reference to a larger, more transcendent realm of values, meanings, and rational longings. Desire and knowledge are always, in a single impulse, directed to some purpose present to the mind, even if only vaguely. Any act lacking such purposiveness is by definition not an act of rational freedom. There are, moreover, only two possible ways of pursuing a purpose: either as an end in itself or for the sake of an end beyond itself. But no finite object or purpose can wholly attract the rational will in the latter way; no finite thing is desirable simply in itself as an ultimate end. It may, in relative terms, constitute a more compelling end that makes a less compelling end nonetheless instrumentally desirable, but it can never constitute an end in itself. It too requires an end beyond itself to be compelling in any measure; it too can evoke desire only on account of some yet higher, more primordial, more general disposition of reason's appetites. Even what pleases us most immediately can be intentionally desired only within the context of a rational longing for the Good itself. If not for some always more original orientation toward an always more final end, the will would never act in regard to finite objects at all. Immanent desires are always in a sense deferred toward some more remote, more transcendent purpose. All concretely limited aspirations of the will are sustained within formally limitless aspirations of the will. In the end, then, the only objects of desire that are not reducible to other, more general objects of desire, and that are thus desirable entirely in and of themselves, are those universal, unconditional, and exalted ideals, those transcendentals, that constitute being's abstract perfections. One may not be, in any given instant, immediately conscious that one's rational appetites have been excited by these transcendental ends; I am not talking about a psychological state of the empirical ego; but those ends are the constant and pervasive preoccupation of the rational will in the deepest springs of its nature, the source of that "delectable perturbation" that grants us a conceptual grasp of finite things precisely by constantly carrying us restlessly beyond them and thereby denying them even a provisional ultimacy.[18]

In fact, we cannot even possess the barest rational cognizance of the world we inhabit except insofar as we have always already, in our rational intentions, exceeded the world. Intentional recognition is always already interpretation, and interpretation is always already judgment. The intellect is not a passive mirror reflecting a reality that simply composes itself for us within our experience; rather, intellect is itself an agency that converts the storm of sense-intuitions into a comprehensible order through a constant process of interpretation. And it is able to do this by virtue of its always more original, tacit recognition of an object of rational longing—say, Truth itself—that appears nowhere within the natural order, but toward which the mind nevertheless naturally reaches out, as to its only possible place of final rest. All proximate objects are known to us, and so desired or disregarded or rejected, in light of that anticipated finality. Even to seek to know, to organize experience into reflection, is a venture of the reasoning will toward that absolute horizon of intelligibility. And since truly rational desire can never be a purely spontaneous eruption of the will without purpose, it must exhibit its final cause in the transcendental structure of its operation. Rational experience, from the first, is a movement of rapture, of ecstasy toward ends that must be understood as—because they must necessarily be desired as—nothing less than the perfections of being, ultimately convertible with one another in the fullness of reality's one source and end. Thus the world as something available to our intentionality comes to us in the interval that lies between the mind's indivisible unity of apprehension and the irreducibly transcendental horizon of its intention—between, that is, the first cause of movement in the mind and the mind's natural telos, both of which lie outside the composite totality of nature. And so the rational will's absolute preoccupation with being as a whole discloses the rather astonishing truth that the very structure of all intellection is an essential relation to God's transcendence as spirit's only possible *natural* end. As I say, for spiritual creatures, nature is experienced *as* nature only by way of a more original apprehension of the supernatural. These transcendental ends are ultimate objects of desire, after all, only in that God's transcendent goodness shines through them, and reason must love the Good.

Neither, incidentally, can that transcendental horizon be an only natural terminus of mind and will, consisting in *created* objects of rational longing, *transcendentalia ordinata* (as it were) describing just the most remote and exalted reaches of the realm of pure nature.[19] Such a notion invites only an infinite regress of final causalities, since a purely ordained object of desire still could not attract a rational nature except as illuminated by a yet more eminent end, desirable in itself. A transcendental terminus of rational yearning has its power to attract the intellect only as the splendor of God's goodness, truth, beauty, and simplicity. To desire to know the truth, for instance, is to desire that everything opaque to the understanding in experience—everything that might defy thought's overtures and importunities—progressively vanish, until mind and world together achieve perfect transparency one to the other. The mind longs from the first not only to reach, but to *become*, that divine truth that gives being to all things. It seeks, as Maximus the Confessor says, to pass beyond all finite cognitions and enter at last into a final union with its first causes in God.[20] Rational spirit, teleologically specified, *is* God; that is its horizon of final causality, because the end it seeks is the knowledge of all things in God's perfect act of knowledge, the ultimate transparency of our *scientia vespertina* to his infinite *scientia matutina*. And, again, a final cause is always a real rational relation within—and so is constitutive of—whatever efficient movement it draws into actuality. Conversely, the mind can only be moved by what is in some sense possible for it, at the very least as a rational desire. Reduced to its most primal origin and ultimate end, then—to what precedes and surpasses the empirical world, what founds and elicits the whole movement of thought in which the phenomenal world subsists—rational life is a finite participation in an infinite act of thought that is also the whole of being: the simplicity of God knowing God. And so the basis of all knowledge and intentional will is the natural desire of the creature for theosis.

I should add here, moreover, two observations. The first is that these considerations make it obvious that any meaningful distinction between the natural desire for God as the "best intelligible object" and the supernatural desire to "see him as he is" can be no more than a distinction, within a single continuous order of desire, between an imperfect and a perfect apprehension of the same end, one in which the latter is the necessary condition of the former, and most definitely not something superadded thereto. We cannot desire the best intelligible object without first and more comprehensively and more ultimately desiring the fullness of intelligibility as such and of excellence as such. I mention this because, again, much Thomist tradition inserts the division of its incommiscible tiers at precisely this juncture in the *ordo cognoscendi*, and in so doing reduces both *termini* of rational longing—God as the ultimate object of natural curiosity, God in himself as the end of supernatural desire—into arbitrary and discontinuous objects of will, apart from every intrinsically coherent rationale. The natural desire to know, thus conceived, would have no proper transcendental motive to explain it, while supernatural desire would be a bizarre saltation beyond all creaturely integrity, one that would not perfect nature, but would instead actually erase it. This way of seeing matters would disrupt the rational continuum between natural and supernatural longing quite beyond repair. In order to long for the best possible intelligible object—and thereby the ultimate explanatory principle of nature—one must first be moved by the desire for (and hence proleptic knowledge of) the direct vision of truth in itself as that which is most high: God "as he is." God (even as a mere "explanatory principle") could never be an object of natural desire if there were not already on the creature's part a more primordial consuming longing for, and constant supernatural awareness of, the knowledge of God in himself in the light of glory. And here one must assume that Thomas himself was unable to resolve the ambiguity in some of his own language. When, for instance, he considers the issue of whether the angels were created in a state of perfect beatitude, and whether then they fell from a condition of supernatural grace,[21] he is obliged to assert that they were created at first only in the state of natural beatitude, capable of perceiving God only under the conditions of their evening knowledge, knowing the Word by the similitude thereof shining forth in their own created nature, but not yet knowing the Word in the full light of glory.[22] But Thomas also knows that, if this glorious morning knowledge truly perfects the evening knowledge conferred by nature, then the latter must be intrinsically ordained to the former.[23] Yet there could be no such ordination were the latter not already the premise of the former in the real order of rational desire, as an end implicit in every movement of spirit toward any object. Nothing can be ordained to an end not implicit in its nature, and no natural end can attract a spiritual nature except as perceived in relation to the ultimate index of rational desirability. There is no natural light apart from the prior illumination of the light of glory.

And the second observation is, in keeping with the logic of act and potency unfolded above, that I do not believe that phenomenology can be sealed off from metaphysics. I do not believe in the possibility of that kind of *epochē*. To acknowledge the transcendent end presupposed by all acts of rational will is to also assert the reality of that final cause as the only possible explanation for the reality of rational existence. But for that abiding and real harmony of knowing and being, that perfect coincidence of spiritual longing and its end in the real final cause (God in himself), rational existence would be an *ontological* impossibility. It certainly could not be the invention of an inchoate will prior to the reality it posits, as that would be reducible to an infinite regress toward one spontaneity without rationale after another. A metaphysical deduction alone can account for what a phenomenological reduction discloses. A real rational relation is, of necessity, a real ontological cause (or, better, *aitia*). To recognize the shape of rational desire, then, is to acknowledge the real indwelling within rational spirit of a final cause that is nothing less than intrinsically divine.

I should add also that I do not believe that, for Christians, these issues can be decided without reference to the requirements and deliverances of revelation. And, as it happens, if one were to consider these issues purely theologically, one's deepest dissatisfaction with the traditionalist Thomist view might well follow not from any particular phenomenological reduction, but out of solicitude for the theology of the incarnation. Orthodox Christology, after all, insists not merely that there is no conflict or rivalry between Christ's divinity and his humanity, or merely that they are capable of harmonious accord with one another. Rather, it asserts that humanity is so naturally compatible with divinity that the Son can be both fully divine and fully human at once without separation or confusion, in one agent, all of whose actions are therefore at once fully human and fully divine. If our nature were not already wholly contained within the divine and the divine not already innate in us, then the incarnation of the Son would have to be either an extrinsic juxtaposition of natures "reconciled" with one another only by a kind of miraculous occasionalism, or else by way of a real change in both natures, producing a fusion or synthesis that would supplant the divine and the human alike with a new reality essentially different from either. But then Christ would be not the God-man, but rather a semidivine monstrosity: either a divine-human chimera or a divine-human hybrid. Once again, we cannot escape this problem by resorting to the vague, meaningless, modally amphibologous mechanism of manualism's version of the *potentia oboedientialis*. And, really, why should we want to do so? Do we truly wish to imagine that what the incarnation of the Logos revealed was not, at the very last, the deepest truth of rational nature, but rather only the accidental fact of a superadded impress upon that nature as vouchsafed within one particular contingent order of providence? Or that deification in Christ is the consummation not of the eternal truth of rational natures but only of one possible but logically fortuitous fate for such natures? Even if I did not regard this picture as logically incoherent, I should still find it theologically repellent.

At any rate, if nothing else, it seems clear to me that the early modern Thomist synthesis was the product of a long history of illusory dilemmas generated by false dichotomies. All too often, the debate was shaped by perceived antitheses and disjunctions where there were in reality only continuities, albeit as descried from sometimes inverse perspectives. Just as the *ordo cognoscendi* and the *ordo essendi* are one and the same continuum (as considered now from one pole, now from the other) so too perhaps are such seeming binary oppositions as nature and grace, creation and deification, the first gift and the second gift, the claims of the creature upon God and God's gifts to the creature—not to mention sufficient and efficacious grace, or the antecedent and consequent decrees of God, or any number of other oppositions that this essay has not directly addressed. And the passage from one pole to the other, rather than involving an extrinsic addition to or intrinsic annihilation of anything, should be understood as occurring only along that continuum, and as progressing only by relative degrees of intensity within an original unity. There is no abiding difference within the one gift of both creation and deification; there is only grace all the way down and nature all the way up, and "pure nature"—like pure potency or pure nothingness—is a remainder concept of the most vacuous kind: the name of something that in itself could never be anything at all. Creation, incarnation, salvation, deification: in God, these are one gracious act, one absolute divine vocation to the creature to become what he has called it to become.[24]

I should note, by the way, that I do accept some version of a principle of proportion between natural desires and their final ends; but the conclusion I draw from this principle is quite the opposite of the one reached by traditional Thomism. I take it to imply that the natural capacity of rational creatures—though it is a capacity that can be satisfied only through the aid of another—is formally and teleologically infinite.[25] Thus, as Nicholas of Cusa so acutely notes, the natural desire of spiritual creatures is ultimately oriented to God not as some kind of comprehensible quiddity, but solely as the incomprehensible infinite.[26] By its very nature, spiritual desire can never be formally teleologically finite, as the finite cannot be its own index of rational desirability. As Nicholas says, "*Quod nisi deus esset infinitus, non foret finis desidere*" (Were God not infinite, he would not be the end for desire).[27] The natural desire of spiritual creatures is nothing less, in its fullness, than an infinite intention corresponding to an infinite gift. That certainly was the conviction of Gregory of Nyssa, who would never have guessed that grace and nature might be conceived of as two opposed categories, who believed instead that human nature in its very essence is meant to becomes an ever more radiant mirror of the divine beauty and ever fuller intimacy of the divine presence, and whom I tend to trust more than just about any other theologian on these matters. From eternity, God has brought spiritual creatures into existence in the only way that such creatures could be formed: by calling them to ascend out of the darkness of nonbeing into the infinite beauty of the divine nature. To exist as a spiritual creature is simply to have heard and (from the very first instant) responded to this total vocation. Creation is already deification—is, in fact, theogony. For that eternal act—that summoning of all created natures out of the primordial darkness—is most certainly an entirely free and unmerited gift of being, imparted to those who were not and who in themselves had no claim to be; but it is also, and no less originally, the call that awakens the gods.

Notes

The epigraph is from *Ambigua* VII, PG 91: 1088C–1088D: "For what could be more desirable to the worthy than theosis, according to which God—united to Gods who have come to be—by his goodness makes everything his own? And hence this condition—born from divine contemplation and then from the elation of happiness—is rightly called delight and affection and joy: delight, on the one hand, inasmuch as it is the end of all natural activities (for this is the definition of delight). . . ."

1. Thomas, *SCG* III.57.
2. *SCG* III.50.
3. *De veritate* q. 10, a. 11 ad 7.
4. See also *In IV sent.*, d. 49, q. 2, a. 7; *ST* I, q. 12, a. 1; *ST* I–II, q. 3, a. 8; *ST* I–II, q. 113, a. 10; *ST* III, q. 9, a. 2 ad 3; *SCG* III.25; *SCG* III. 48–54; *Compendium Th.* I.104; etc.
5. Denis, *De puritate et felicitate animae* a. 56; *De caelo* II.290a.
6. Cajetan, *Commentaria in primam partem* q. 12, a. 1, n. 10. This is a classic example of the confusion of the concept of natural potency with that of an inherent and sufficient intrinsic faculty for the actuation of that potency.
7. *Commentaria in primam partem* q. 12, a. 1, n. 9. Again, the same category error as in note 6, albeit from the opposite direction.
8. I assume it is not the *sole* possible reading of Thomas at any rate, at least not by the time of the *Summa contra gentiles* and the *Compendium*. That said, I realize that there are places in Thomas's work where a certain interval of arbitrariness between God and his work in creation seems to emerge like a menacing specter from this or that shadowy corner, such as in his infralapsarian account of Christ's incarnation (*Scriptum super sententiis* III, d. 1, q. 1, a. 3; *Super primam epistolam ad Timotheum* I.15. 4; *ST* III, q. 1, a. 3), or in his seeming willingness to separate in principle the necessity of God willing his own goodness from the rationale determining the particular goodness he wills in creation (*ST* I, q. 19, a. 3 ad 4; *ST* I, q. 19, a. 4; *ST* I, q. 19, a. 10). Neither of these aspects of his thought, needless to say, is a radical departure from the tradition on his part; but, in his case, both lead to the consequent claim that God created this particular world not as the most fitting or best for revealing his nature, inasmuch as all worlds fall equally and infinitely short of his glory and so any he might create—even if it be much "better" than the world that actually exists—is a matter of pure liberty of choice on his part (*ST* I, q. 25, a. 6 ad 3). All of which is potentially quite distressing. Surely, one has to think, while it is true that there can be no best of all possible worlds in terms of some particular quantity of perfections or some Leibnizian balance between maximal beatitude and the finite conditions necessary to achieve it, it must also be the case that there is nothing truly arbitrary in the way in which God acts and reveals himself, and that therefore he creates this world precisely because it is the world of Christ, the one world whereof the incarnation of the divine Logos is the mystery hidden from the ages, and therefore the one world wherein the consummate revelation of God to his creatures occurs. Even so, none of this in itself makes it logically implausible for Thomas to have believed that any rational creature, no matter

what world that creature may inhabit, must be moved by a natural desire for union with God in order to be rational. As I say, though, it is ultimately a matter of indifference to me what Thomas's final view on the matter was, or even whether he had one.

9. Thomas, *In Boeth. de trin.* q. 6, a. 4 ad 5; *De veritate* q. 8, a. 3 ad 12; *De veritate* q. 24, a. 10 ad 1; *De malo* q. 5, a. 1; *ST* I, q. 62, a. 4; *ST* I–II, q. 5, a. 5 ad 1–2; *ST* I–II, q. 91, a. 4 ad 3; *ST* I–II, q. 109, a. 4 ad 2; *ST* III, q. 9, a. 2 ad 3; etc.

10. Thomas, for instance, will not allow that the human agent intellect, confined as it is to a kind of knowledge obtainable only through the data of the senses as converted through the phantasm, can actualize the full range of the potential intellect's patient capacity: *Compendium* I.194. But the conditions of the mortal body should not be understood as the natural conditions of the human soul.

11. This applies even to Bernard Lonergan's use of the term "obediential potential" as a sort of amphibologous median between the natural desire for limitless and unconditional knowledge and a supernaturally vouchsafed desire for "quidditative" knowledge of God in himself. It allowed him to explain how a capacity that, to all appearances, seems to be an innate intentionality toward the fullness of God could be understood as continuous with its supernatural fulfilment without wholly collapsing the distinction between the natural and the supernatural (which, as a kind of Thomist, he felt obliged to affirm). But this is simply a pointless multiplication of conceptual transitions. It is an example of what elsewhere I have called the "pleonastic fallacy": an attempt to span a qualitative disjunction by way of a quantitative accumulation of mediating principles. A creaturely obediential potential that is "natural," even if only in a restricted sense, still cannot constitute a capacity for any end that is not itself also already natural to the creature.

12. It may be worth emphasizing again, given the unfamiliarity of even the best trained Catholic theologians with some of their tradition's categories, that the issue here is the abuse of a principle, not the principle itself. I discovered when I first delivered this essay as a paper at a conference at Fordham that even many of the Thomists in the room were not entirely sure what the difficulty was. Some of those present, for instance, clearly confused *potentia oboedientialis* with a species of material potency—that is, the patiency of any "material" substrate to the actuality of an informing cause—and therefore did not see the contradiction in attempting to use it as an explanation for God accomplishing the transformation of a creature into something for which it has no natural aptitude whatsoever while somehow also not annihilating that creature as the creature it is in itself.

13. See David Braine, "The Debate Between Henri de Lubac and His Critics," *Nova et Vetera*, English edition, 6, no. 3 (2008): 543–90. See also Nicholas J. Healy, "Henri de Lubac on Nature and Grace: A Note on Some

Recent Contributions to the Debate," *Communio*, English edition, 35, no. 4 (2008): 535–64. Both Braine and Healy, despite their sympathy for de Lubac, feel constrained to defend him against the charge of having taught that human beings have a claim on God's grace by virtue of their nature. This is unfortunate, given that de Lubac would have been right to teach precisely that.

14. See Henri de Lubac, *The Mystery of the Supernatural*, trans. David L. Schindler (New York: Crossroad Publishing, 1998), 76.

15. Here I agree with John Milbank that *Humani generis* drove de Lubac toward increasingly incoherent formulations and ultimately to compromises induced by the heavy hand of the magisterium rather than by logic. John Milbank, *The Suspended Middle: Henri de Lubac and the Debate Concerning the Supernatural*, 2nd ed. (Grand Rapids, MI: Eerdmans, 2014), 8.

16. Cited in ibid., xi.

17. Even Bernard Lonergan, who should have known better, felt compelled to assert that there is "no internal contradiction" in the proposition that "a world-order without grace is possible to God and so concretely possible." Bernard Lonergan, "The Natural Desire to See God" in *Collection*, ed. Frederick E. Gowe (New York: Herder, 1967), 92. Yet, unless he coyly means a world-order devoid of rational spirit (and even then he would have been in error), his own understanding of human rational desire makes such a claim ultimately indefensible.

18. Plotinus, *Enneads* I.vi.4.

19. This solution to the issue was suggested to me by a Dominican philosopher in conversation. It is a preposterous proposition in itself, obviously, as he himself ultimately acknowledged, but it was remarkably revealing that he felt moved to venture it. On the whole, one expects Thomists *not* to flirt with nominalism's *deus absconditus*, and certainly not with a quasi-Ockhamist picture of creation as a revelation of a divine sovereignty consisting primarily in wholly arbitrary power. And yet, it seems, the Baroque Thomist synthesis is very hard to sustain in this context except by way of a certain breach between what is revealed in the necessary structure of creation and what belongs to God's own nature.

20. Maximus, *Ambigua* XV, PG 91: 1220AB.

21. Thomas, *ST* I, q. 62, a. 1–9.

22. *ST* I, q. 62, a. 1 ad 3.

23. *ST* I, q. 62, a. 7 ad 3.

24. See Sergei Bulgakov, *The Bride of the Lamb*, trans. Boris Jakim (Grand Rapids, MI: Eerdmans, 2002), 3–146.

25. Hence the need, incidentally, to reject Bernard Lonergan's distinction between the indeterminate natural desire for the whole of knowledge and a determinate supernatural desire for knowledge of God in himself—a distinction, one feels, that he maintained in his thought only somewhat *contre coeur*. The

former is not only a passive capacity or even a condition of mere openness but is also of necessity a real and unqualified intentionality toward the whole of being in all its transcendental perfections and all its infinite unity. Such an intentionality is always already a tacit awareness of its "supernatural" end as well as a natural capacity that (at least, when liberated from the unnatural conditions of sin and death) is always already adequate to the end it seeks. As anything's final cause is already a real rational relation intrinsic to that thing, and necessarily a real capacity thereof, the full supernatural knowledge of God is always already the intrinsic end of the human capacity to know anything at all intentionally.

26. Nicholas, *De venatione sapientiae*, XII.32.
27. *De visione dei*, XVI.

DOES AQUINAS HAVE THE ORTHODOX CONCEPT OF THEOSIS?

Jean Porter

According to the Greek patristic tradition, affirmed and developed by modern and contemporary Orthodox theology, the human person is capable of attaining a likeness to God so profound and complete that it can truly be identified as theosis, that is to say, divinization or deification.[1] Objectively, this transformation is made possible through the Incarnation of Jesus Christ, who realizes God's highest aims for creation and opens up the possibility that other human beings might attain, to some degree at least, the same Godlikeness and intimacy with God that Christ enjoys. Subjectively, theosis requires a disciplined and arduous way of life, grounded in the liturgy, prayers, and devotional practices of the church and disciplined through ascetical practices, through which the passions are overcome and the individual takes on divine impassibility. A select few will attain theosis itself, a Godlike state in which the individual attains the greatest possible union with God, coming to a personal, intimate knowledge of God which goes beyond reason and cannot be expressed in speech. As such, the divinized man or woman anticipates the joy of heaven and can be said to participate in the divine nature, in such a way as to become another Christ.

Since the early 2000s, a number of scholars have argued that Thomas Aquinas also teaches that the human person is capable of deification, understood in such a way as to bring him into essential agreement with Greek patristic and Orthodox thought.[2] On a first reading of relevant texts, this claim appears to be convincing. Aquinas claims that through the infusion of grace and the virtues, we receive new principles of being and action, which enable us to pursue and attain our final end of union with God (I–II 108.1 ad 2, 110.2,3).³ He describes these new principles in terms of a participation in divine nature, through which we are enabled to pursue and attain our ultimate end, union with God in the Beatific Vision (I–II 62.1, 110.2,3). Even in this life, we are brought into a relation of friendship with God through charity, which brings about a kind of participation in God's happiness (II–II 23.1). In the life to come, those who persevere will enter into the closest possible relation to God through the vision of his essence that constitutes the Beatific Vision (I 12.1). Significantly, Aquinas grounds these claims in scriptural texts that play a central role in Orthodox treatments of theosis, including, most important, 2 Peter 1:4, which claims that God has promised that we will become "partakers of divine nature."

However, as we read further, it becomes apparent that matters are more complex than we might at first have thought. For one thing, Aquinas seldom uses the Latin terms that would be most closely associated with theosis, namely, conjugations of *deificare*, and the adjective *deiformis*.⁴ He does use this language on occasion, and when he does, he does not reject or qualify it. At any rate, the relative scarcity of these terms in Aquinas's writings does not mean that he does not have a concept of theosis, or divinization, which he prefers to express in other terms. At the same time, Aquinas is careful in his use of language, and the relative absence of the language of divinization should at least raise questions about whether, and in what ways he employs the concept.

Moreover, Aquinas's concept of grace and glory differs from Orthodox conceptions of theosis in some significant ways. We will examine these differences in more detail, but for now, let me mention one which seems to me to be especially important yet often overlooked. That is, Orthodox theologians generally agree that theosis can be attained in this life. It seldom is, but the possibility shapes Orthodox expectations about the potentialities for a life of virtue and holiness, and it gives salience to ascetical and devotional practices associated with the pursuit of union with God. Within the Orthodox context, theosis represents a paradigm for the ideal Christian life and provides a touchstone for theological discourse. Aquinas, in contrast, is far more restrained in his expectations for union with God in this life. He admits, on cogent scriptural and traditional grounds, that it is possible to see God directly in this life, but he limits consideration of this possibility to the two scriptural cases, Moses and Saint Paul (I–II 175.1,3). He is aware of the patristic tradition of stages of virtue, culminating in the freedom from passions enjoyed by the purified soul (I–II 61.5). But he deals with this tradition in one article, which is effectively isolated from his extensive, Aristotelian theory of virtue. By the same token, he has little to say about ascetical practices, and so far as I can tell, he has no theology of the mystical life at all. As we will see, the paradigmatic images that shape his doctrine of grace are shaped by expectations that the life of grace is marked by progressive growth and continual struggle, rather than this-worldly fulfillment.

It is certainly the case that Aquinas's doctrine of grace has a great deal in common with the concept of theosis developed by Orthodox theologians and their patristic forbears. At the same time, even on a first consideration, there are significant differences between Aquinas and Orthodox theologians with respect both to their preferred formulations and to the place that the ideal of divinization plays in an overall conception of the Christian life. These differences do not rule out the claim that Aquinas has a concept of theosis, but at the very least they should prompt us to think more carefully about our criteria for identifying and comparing concepts of this sort.

In a recent essay on the place of theosis in Orthodox theology, Andrew Louth expresses similar reservations about attempts to find this concept in Western sources: "It has often struck me that in theology—as in other subjects—analysis of concepts can seem to miss the point in a tantalizing way, One breaks the concept down into its constituent parts and analyzes each of these parts—historically and conceptually—and then puts it all back together again, but still one seems to have missed the significance that it holds for those who value it."[5] The difficulty, he suggests, is that outsiders to Orthodox theology fail to appreciate the place that this doctrine holds in Orthodox theology more generally: "What I mean by place is the way the doctrine functions in the whole Orthodox experience, including the pattern of theology. In studying the history of Christian theology, we have often paid too little attention to what I would call the pattern of theology: The mosaic, as it were, that emerges when the various doctrines of the faith are fitted together."[6]

Louth's observation suggests a way to understand the phenomenon that confronts us as we try to compare Aquinas and Orthodox theologians on the question of theosis. As we have just noted, these theologians share the same authoritative texts, and up to a point they agree on how these texts should be read. That is hardly surprising, since these are after all Christian theologians, reading the same sacred texts and sharing, to some extent if not completely, in the same traditions of interpretation. At the same time, they agree only up to a point, and beyond that point we find deeply different views on the significance of scriptural promises of likeness to God. In other words, we can identify broad areas of agreement with respect to what Louth calls the component elements of theosis, but these are construed in different ways. Louth suggests one way of thinking about these intriguing similarities and daunting differences; that is to say, perhaps they reflect larger differences in doctrine and practice, comprising the mosaics of Eastern and Western theology. Of course, it would take us well beyond the scope of a single essay to attempt a comprehensive comparison of Eastern and Western theology. But in this case, we can identify specific differences in doctrinal commitments that go a long way toward illuminating the differences between Aquinas's conceptions of grace and glory and the Orthodox conception of theosis. The differences in question pertain to the doctrine of God and the work of Christ, and while these are of course fundamental and complex doctrines, we can focus on specific element of each which help to illuminate the subject at hand.

In what follows, I will offer an overview of Aquinas's understanding of grace and the Beatific Vision, focusing on the account developed in his last mature work, the *Summa theologiae*, and taking the Orthodox concept of theosis as a touchstone for interpreting this account.[7] In the process of doing so, I will attempt to follow Louth's advice to attend to the wider doctrinal contexts shaping the concept of theosis on the one hand, and Aquinas's concept of grace on the other.

Doctrinal Contexts

God's Engagement with the World: Creation, Nature, and Divine Energies

The doctrine of God is foundational for Christian theology, and as such it is the patrimony of the whole Christian church, East and West. For this reason we might not expect to find differences at this level that would help to contextualize the Eastern doctrine of theosis, seen in contrast to Aquinas's views on grace and glory. And yet, in some respects the Eastern doctrine of theosis is bound up with a distinctive thesis about God's existence and his relation to creatures and cannot fully be understood apart from this context. What is more, the Orthodox doctrine of God cannot be understood apart from some understanding of theosis, since one of its central tenets was spelled out in response to criticisms of the claim that the human person, through theosis, really participates in the divine nature. Thus, the doctrinal context for understanding theosis set by the Orthodox doctrine of God offers an example of the way in which this ideal has shaped the doctrine that contextualizes it.

The thesis in question was given definitive formulation in the fourteenth century by the theologian Gregory of Palamas, Archbishop of Thessalonika, in response to the argument that it is impossible for a creature to participate in the very essence of God, without actually becoming God.[8] Gregory responded by granting the premise of the argument—a creature cannot in any way attain the essence of God—while at the same time denying the conclusion, that no one can really become a partaker of the divine nature. He argued, on the contrary, that we do participate in the divine nature without thereby attaining to the essence of God. This is possible, because in addition to the processions of the Trinity, which are, so to speak, internal to God, there is also a kind of natural emanation or motion of God that is directed toward creatures and can therefore be said to be external to God. This outward motion is identified with the uncreated energies of God, which are distinct from God's essence, and yet, in view of the divine simplicity, identical with that essence. The key point is that God's actions *ad extra* communicate something more than the term of the act itself; they contain, as it were, the fullness of God's creative wisdom and love, the all-pervasive context for his discrete acts. In the words of the theologian Vladmir Lossky, "The distinction is that between the essence of God, or his nature, properly so called, which is inaccessible, unknowable and incommunicable, and the energies or divine operations, forces proper to and inseparable from God's essence, in which He goes forth from himself, manifests, communicates, and gives Himself."[9] He goes on to say that this doctrine of divine energies is the dogmatic basis for Orthodox teachings on the possibility of theosis. God's self-manifestation through the energies forms the basis, as it were, for human participation in God's nature, without requiring us to say that the divinized person attains to God's unknowable essence. This is thus a strategy for preserving both the divine/human boundary and the real, immediate union between God and his creature. Of course, it would be anachronistic to expect Aquinas to endorse the doctrine of uncreated energies as formulated by Gregory of Palamas, but it might be the case that he understands God's operations *ad extra* in a recognizably similar way. In fact, he does not. Aquinas understands God's action *ad extra* in terms of an immediate and efficacious communication of being, through which a creature comes into existence and continues in existence.[10] This is clearly a sui generis form of causality, but it resembles Aristotelian efficient causality, insofar as it involves a communication of form. More specifically, through his creative act, God communicates form together with existence— indeed, the act of creation is nothing other than the act of bringing about an informed existence, intelligible and good in itself, with its own internal principles of causality. The creature can be said to participate in God's being and goodness insofar as its existence, goodness and perfection are similitudes of God, considered as the "first and universal principle of all being" (I 4.3; cf. 6.1) But Aquinas does not say that creation communicates the substance of divine existence through the creative act. The act of creation brings about things which can be said, in their existence, intelligibility and goodness, to resemble God, but Aquinas does not say that through this act, God communicates Himself in some more comprehensive way, over and above bringing about a creature that resembles its Creator. Similarly, God is continually present to His creatures insofar as He sustains them in existence and operates in and through their causal operations (I 8.1). But this again is an exercise of God's causal power, not a communication of God's being.

The contrast between Orthodox and Thomistic doctrines of God may seem to be a matter of esoteric distinctions, having little relevance to the more practical side of theology. But as Gösta Hallonsten points out, these distinctions have far-reaching implications for the ways in which each theological option construes the relation between God and creatures, and the limits and possibilities of human assimilation to the divine:

> [The Eastern] anthropology is connected to a view of the relation between God and creation that is significantly different from that or the Latin tradition. In the East, creation from its very beginning is seen as a participation in God: hence grace cannot be separated from creation but inheres in it and potentially leads it to union with God. It is the Platonic concept of participation that is the background here. The world and human beings are seen as caused by God in the sense of formal causality, whereas in the Western view efficient causality takes its place: God and the world are distinct beings, even if the world partici-

pates in Being in an analogical sense. As a result the Eastern tradition has worked out the distinction between God's essence and energies, a distinction that makes no sense to the scholastic point of view according to which God is characterized by simplicity. Hence, philosophically speaking, the essence and existence of God coincide.[11]

Hallonsten calls attention to two points that are especially relevant to a comparison between the concept of theosis and Aquinas's accounts of grace and glory. The first of these has to do with their differing approaches to grace itself. Hallonsten observes that on the Orthodox view, God and creation are in continuity, in such a way that creation is intrinsically oriented toward full union with God. The distinction between God and humanity, in particular, is real and profound, but it does not constitute a break which needs to be repaired or bridged through special means.[12] Aquinas, in contrast, sees a fundamental gap between the natural capacities of even the highest creatures, and the attainment of full union with God.[13] Men and women cannot attain this end unless God endows them with a principle of being and action that is above nature—in other words, supernatural. It is important to realize that the limitations of nature are not due to sin, on Aquinas's view, although sin has certainly made our situation worse. Even if our first parents had not sinned, we would be unable to attain the immediate vision of God to which we are called through the exercise of our natural powers, apart from the qualitative change brought about by grace.

The second of these has to do with the doctrine of uncreated energies itself. Not all Orthodox theologians accept this doctrine, but I think it is safe to say that most do, and this way of thinking about God's creative act is central to most modern Orthodox interpretations of theosis. On this view, God's uncreated energies provide the point of contact, as it were, between God and the deified man or woman. By this means, God fully communicates Himself as active presence, even though He does not (cannot?) communicate His very essence. These uncreated energies are identified with uncreated grace. Thus understood, God's uncreated grace provides the foundation for the response of the creature, which can be construed as in itself, or as an expression of created grace. At any rate, on this view uncreated grace is prior to created grace.

Aquinas also distinguishes between uncreated and created grace, and according to some interpreters, he agrees with Orthodox theologians in giving priority to uncreated grace. Others have challenged this assertion, arguing that he gives greater priority to created grace, without which we cannot receive uncreated grace.[14] Yet the interlocutors in this debate do not take account of the fact that uncreated grace, at least, does not mean the same thing for Aquinas and Orthodox theologians. They generally acknowledge that Aquinas does not have a doctrine of divine energies, but they do not consider what it would mean to assert the priority of uncreated grace, given a very different understanding of what uncreated grace means. As we will see, Aquinas does not raise the question of the relative priority of uncreated and created grace, but he does address what I take to be a related question pertaining to the immediacy of God's presence to the beatified.

The Work of Christ

We turn at this point to a second set of doctrinal considerations that shape the Orthodox concept of theosis and its Western analogues pertaining to Orthodox and Western understandings of the significance of Christ, the relative weights given to the Incarnation and the Passion, and correlatively, the origins and significance of sin in our lives. I say "understandings" advisedly, because of course Orthodox views on these fundamental questions are as diverse and complex as the corresponding Western views. Nonetheless, we can identify two broad approaches, corresponding to Orthodox and Western theologies of the person and work of Christ. Again, Louth offers a most helpful guide:

> Deification, then, has to do with human destiny, a destiny that finds its fulfillment in a face to face encounter with God, an encounter in which God takes the initiative by meeting us in the Incarnation. . . . It is important for a full grasp of what this means to realize that deification is not to be equated with redemption. Christ certainly came to save us, and our response to his saving action and word we are redeemed, but deification belongs to a broader conception of the divine. . . . Deification is the fulfillment of creation, not just the rectification of the fall. One way of putting this is to think in terms of an arch stretching from creation to deification, representing what is and remains God's intention: the creation of the cosmos that, through human kind, is destined to share in the divine life, to be deified. Progress along this arch has been frustrated by humankind,

in Adam, failing to work with God's purposes, leading to the Fall, which needs to be put right by redemption. There is, then, what one might think of as a lesser arch, leading from Fall to redemption, the purpose of which is to restore the function of the greater arch from creation to deification The loss of the notion of deification leads to lack of awareness of the greater arch from creation to deification, and thereby to concentration on the lower arch, from Fall to redemption; it is, I think, not unfair to suggest that such a concentration on the lesser arch at the expense of the greater arch has been characteristic of much Western theology. . . .

Orthodox theology has never lost sight of the greater arch, leading from creation to deification.[15]

I have quoted Louth at some length because he brings out the complexity of the issues raised by Orthodox and Western appraisals of the significance of Christ. What we have here are two trajectories of thought, each of which is present in both Orthodox and Western theological traditions. To a considerable extent, these traditions can be distinguished by the ways in which they combine these two trajectories, and the relative weight given to one or the other. At the same time, each tradition is characterized by tendencies to minimize one or the other of the two arches. As is well known, some Western theologies are characterized by an almost exclusive emphasis on sin and redemption; correlatively, some Orthodox theologians are prepared to argue that our salvation has been accomplished through the Incarnation and consists of a union with God similar to that found in Christ. Most Western and Orthodox theologians would shy away from these extremes, but they represent tendencies which are seldom realized, and yet exercise a discernible influence on the more typically moderate positions in each tradition.

The Orthodox tradition's emphasis on what Louth calls the greater arch, from creation to deification, is clearly relevant to the concept of theosis. After all, if God created the world for the sake of deification, then the man or woman who attains theosis is the epitome of God's highest intent, second only to the Incarnation itself. Seen from this perspective, the Incarnation looks forward to theosis as its aim and fulfillment. Christ opens up the possibility of an intimate union with God, and those who attain this possibility take on the likeness of Christ. Theologians working in this tradition tend to emphasize the continuities between created nature and its fulfillment, to speculate that the Incarnation would have taken place even without the Fall, and to downplay or deny the distinction between the potentialities of nature and its supernatural fulfillment. As we have seen, these lines of thought are congruent with the Orthodox understanding of the doctrine of God and the relation between God and creation—another indication of the contextual unity of beliefs within which theosis is placed.

As Louth correctly notes, the Western tradition in contrast focuses its attention on sin, the alienation of humanity from God, and the atonement or satisfaction bought about by the work of Christ. Seen from this perspective, the Incarnation is the necessary preliminary to the Cross and Resurrection, through which Christ makes satisfaction for our sins and opens up the possibility of union with the Father—usually envisioned as postmortem union. This line of thought does not leave much room for an ideal of theosis, or some Western analogue. Western theologians tend to be very conscious of the effects of sin, and correlatively, they are suspicious of claims to exceptional holiness. Correlatively, they tend to downplay the goodness of creation, and to deny the moral and theological relevance of the natural order. All this being said, some Western theological traditions do affirm a possibility for exemplary holiness and union with God for those whose sins have been forgiven through Christ—the Wesleyan traditions provide a noteworthy example.

Where should we place Aquinas's views on the significance and work of Christ? It must be said that his Christology places him squarely within the main lines of the Western tradition. Near the beginning of his treatment of the person and work of Christ, he asserts that the Incarnation was necessary, at least in a qualified way, for the restoration of the human race (III 1.2).[16] He considers the opinion—held by his own master, Albert of Cologne, among others—to the effect that the Incarnation would have come about even if Adam had not sinned. He rejects this view on the grounds that it goes beyond what scripture says, and in matters of this sort, having to do with the providential will of God, scripture is our only reliable guide (III 1.3). Correlatively, he places great emphasis on the saving effects of Christ's passion and death, through which we are saved from sin and offered the possibility of salvation.

Yet Aquinas's emphasis on sin and redemption does not necessarily rule out an affirmation of something like theosis, to be attained on the other side of our restoration from sin. Aquinas seems to open up this possibility early in the *tertia pars*, in the context of a consideration of the appropriateness of the Incarnation. Having established that it is indeed appropriate that God should be incarnate, he goes on to ask whether the Incarnation was necessary for the restoration of human nature. He argues that it was, at least in a conditional sense, and he goes on to identify the many ways in which the Incarnation promotes the good of humanity and serves to remove evil. The fifth way in which the Incarnation promotes human good is as follows: "Fifth, with respect to the full participation in divinity, which is truly the happiness of the human person, and the end of human life. And this is bestowed on us through the humanity of Christ; for Augustine says, in a certain homily on the nativity of the Lord, 'God became a human person, in order that the human person may become God'" (III. 1.2).

On a first reading, Aquinas would seem here to endorse the Orthodox idea of theosis, at least in general terms. He approvingly quotes Augustine, who is apparently quoting Athanasius, in such a way as to imply not only a congruence of ideas, but a real—albeit indirect—point of contact between Aquinas and the Eastern tradition. Nonetheless, Louth's caution is relevant here. Aquinas does affirm the general idea that Christ enables us to share in the divine nature. However, he cites this as just one of several ways in which the Incarnation promotes human good and protects against evil, all of which are adduced to show that the Incarnation was necessary, in a qualified way, for the restoration of the human race. In the next article, he unequivocally states on scriptural grounds that the Incarnation came about for the remission of sins and would not have happened if our first parents had not sinned (III 1.3). Further on, he makes it clear that the Incarnation alone was not sufficient to free us from sin, apart from Christ's passion and death (III 48.1 ad 2). Aquinas's claims to the effect that Jesus Christ enables us to share in the divine nature must therefore be understood within the context of a well-elaborated theology of Christ's passion and death, seen as the means of our salvation. In what ways does this context shape Aquinas's claim that through the humanity of Christ, we participate in divinity?

In order to address this question fully we will need to examine Aquinas's doctrine of grace, since it is through grace that we become partakers of divine nature. We will turn to that topic in the last section. However, a few preliminary observations are in order at this point. The first and most fundamental is that according to Aquinas, grace comes to us through Christ, who has himself received a superabundance of grace, sufficient for himself and for all those who are saved through him. Yet this grace does not simply flow to us as a result of his Incarnation; rather, through his passion he merits salvation for himself and others:

> Christ is given grace not only as an individual person, but insofar as he is the head of the Church, in such a way that from him it flows out to the members. And therefore, the works of Christ are related both to himself and to his members, in the same way as the works of any person established in grace are related to himself. Now it is clear that anyone who, being established in grace, suffers for justice, merits salvation for himself. . . . Hence, Christ through his passion merited salvation, not only for himself, but for all of his members. (III 48.1)

In the same article, Aquinas goes on to say that even from his conception, the grace of Christ was sufficient in itself to merit our salvation, but we were not able to receive the benefits of his grace, so to speak, on account of certain impediments, which were removed through his passion (III 48.1 ad 2). Clearly, whatever the divinizing effects of grace may be, they do not flow spontaneously from the Incarnation. Aquinas, together with most other Western theologians, emphasizes the distance between God and the sinful human person, insists on the need for some kind of satisfaction or redemption in order to restore the breach, and correlatively reminds us that the way to salvation was opened to us through suffering and sacrifice. Seen in this context, the gift of God's grace is a costly gift, and for that very reason it offers the greatest imaginable proof of God's love and the love and humility of Christ (III 46.3).

What is more, grace considered in itself is understood within a context shaped by a deep awareness of human sinfulness, on the one hand, and a commitment to an ideal of free action as distinctively human, on the other. As we will see, Aquinas does say that through grace, we become partakers in the divine nature (I–II 110.3). And yet, when he turns from a consideration of the essence of grace to talk about the effects of grace, the effects that he identifies are the justification of the sinner and the capacity to merit salvation through one's own actions (I–II 113.1, 114.1). The emphasis here is not on grace as a state to be enjoyed in itself, but grace as necessary for one's future salvation. In one sense, Christ saves us by bestowing grace on us (I–II 108.1, III 8.1). Seen from another perspective, grace is the quality of the soul that enables men and women to envision a final state of happy union with God and to pursue that end freely through actions that are suited, through grace, for the attainment of that end (I–II 110.2,3).

Aquinas's emphasis throughout his comments on grace and merit lies on grace as a principle of freedom and action, through which we are enabled to enjoy the freedom of God's children. The ideal of freedom from sin, and freedom for a new way of life, thus come together in Aquinas's thought. We exhibit our status as adopted children of God in and through the free actions through which we hope to merit salvation (I–II 114.3).

We will return to these points in the last section. At this point, we turn to an examination of Aquinas's treatments of the light of glory and grace, each of which represents a way of being a "partaker in divine nature." It might seem logical to begin with grace, which precedes and anticipates glory. But in the ST, Aquinas's treatment of the light of glory and the Beatific Vision comes well before his treatment of grace, because these closely related topics raise fundamental issues about our knowledge of God. At the same time, the Vision represents our final happiness, the goal toward which the life of grace is directed, and for this reason Aquinas's remarks at this point anticipate his treatment of grace in helpful ways. We will accordingly follow his order of exposition, looking first at what he says about glory and the Vision, and then turning to his account of grace.

In-formed by God: The Light of Glory and Divinization

Having established that theology is a science devoted to God as its subject, and having considered God's existence and attributes, Aquinas turns in the twelfth question of the *prima pars* to a consideration of the way in which God is known by us. In the first article of this question, he poses a question which, as we have seen, was central to Orthodox reflection on knowledge of God and theosis: "Whether any intellectual creature can see God through his essence?" In sharp contrast to the Orthodox position on this question, he replies that it is indeed possible for the created intellect to attain to a vision of the essence of God. In the *sed contra*, he appeals to I Jn.3.2, "We will see him as he is," and he asserts that the claim that we cannot see God in his essence is alien to the faith and contrary to reason. Why should this be the case? He explains that the Beatific Vision encompasses the reality of God as he is in Himself and as the first cause of all created things. As such, it satisfies and perfects the intellect, which is naturally oriented toward knowing the causes of things, and in this way it fulfills the deepest desire of the will (I 12.1). If we were unable to know God in his essence, we would either be incapable of happiness, or would find our happiness in something other than God, both claims being alien to the faith; moreover, the natural desire to know the causes of things would be incapable of fulfillment, which is contrary to reason.

These are cogent arguments, but Aquinas still needs to explain how a finite, created intellect can attain to the vision of God's essence. He acknowledges that the Vision cannot be mediated through a similitude, since no finite image or likeness can encompass the full reality of God's essence (I 12.2). Much less is it possible to see God with our physical eyes (I 12.3). These arguments imply that the essence of God cannot be known through the ways of knowing that are natural and proper to us as human beings. Aquinas says as much in the next article, which argues that no created intellect can attain the vision of God through its own natural powers:

> it is impossible that any created intellect through its natural powers could see the essence of God. For cognition comes about insofar as that which is known is in that which knows. Now, knowing is in that which knows in accordance with a mode of knowing Hence, for any knower, cognition is in accordance with the mode of its nature. Therefore, if the mode of being of the thing that is known exceeds the mode of nature of that which knows, it is necessary that the knowledge of that thing be above the nature of that which knows. (I 12.4)

Aquinas goes on to develop the general argument, going through each of the levels of natural existence from inanimate objects through the angelic intellect, identifying the mode of knowing proper to each one. In every instance, cognition (or its analogues in plants and inanimate creatures) depends on some finite image or intellectual representation, generated through the senses, or discursive reasoning, or, in the case of the angels, pure intellectual apprehension. In every case, the creature's natural powers of knowing are oriented toward some finite aspect or instantiation of being. Aquinas concludes, "It is not therefore possible that a created intellect could see God through His essence, except insofar as God through His grace joins the intellectual creature to Himself, that he might be intelligible to it" (ibid.). When Aquinas says that the knowledge of God through his essence exceeds the capacities of nature, he is therefore not saying that this level of knowledge is strictly impossible, nor much less that it is repugnant to those natures, human and angelic, that are capable of attaining it in any way whatever. But he is saying that the natural powers of the rational or intellectual creature, functioning through their own proper modes of operation, cannot in any way attain to the vision of God. In the case of the human intellect, it is clear why this should be the case. The human intellect is naturally capable of grasping the forms of material things through a process of abstraction from sensate images, the phantasmata; thus, he says elsewhere that the natural object of the intellect is the quiddity, that is to say, the form grasped as informing some particular material thing (I 84.7). Clearly, God's essence cannot be represented through a particular image abstracted from his existence and represented as such in the mind. Hence, Aquinas claims that in order to see God, the creature needs a created light, by which he means a transformation of the intellect itself, enabling it to grasp God's very essence: "In order for any created intellect to see God through his essence, the essence of God itself must become the intelligible form of the intellect. Hence it is necessary that some supernatural disposition be added to it, in order that it be elevated to such a sublime height" (I 12.5). He goes on to say, "Through this light, they become *deiformes*, that is, similar to God, in accordance with I John 3.2, when he appears, we will be like him, and we will see him as he is."[17]

Clearly, for Aquinas the Vision represents a state of supreme unity with and likeness to God. It is therefore not surprising that at this point he uses the language of divinization to convey the supreme likeness to God brought about through the Beatific Vision. The term *deiformis* implies that the creature shares in some way in God's own form, becoming, as it were, similar in kind to God. This term is especially appropriate, because through the Beatific Vision, God relates to the intellect as the form through which it operates. Compare this to the natural operation of the intellect through abstraction from a phantasma of some material thing. As we have already observed, Aquinas claims that the intellect grasps the form of something through its material embodiment, as represented by phantasmata. Through this process, the form is, as it were, actualized through the intellect (I 84.2 ad 2). Given this context, Aquinas's claim that God becomes or functions as the form of the intellect through the Beatific Vision takes on a particular significance. If the intellect can be said, in a certain sense, to become what it knows in an ordinary way, it is hardly surprising that Aquinas says that through the vision, the creature takes on the very form of God.

Reading further, we see that while the language of divinization signals the greatest possible likeness to God, it also signals a boundary: "Hence, the light of glory cannot be natural to a creature, unless the creature were to be naturally divine, which is impossible. Hence, through this light the rational creature becomes *deiformis*, as was said" (I 12.5 ad 3). Of course, Aquinas does not believe that through the light of glory, the blessed soul becomes a kind of demi-God. Precisely because the beatified individual remains a creature, it stands in need of some kind of transformation, through which it is enabled to see God in his essence. This brings us to a further point.

In discussing the elevation through which the creature is enabled to see God, Aquinas consistently insists that this is a created quality of the soul. This raises the question of whether this elevation is itself a kind of similitude, a created representation of God which, so to speak, stands between the creature and God. Aquinas is aware of this worry. In the second objection to article 5, the objector claims that "if [God] is seen through some created light, he is seen through a medium. Therefore he is not seen through his essence." Aquinas responds:

> this light is not required for seeing the essence of God as a similitude, in which God is seen, but as a certain perfection of the intellect, giving it strength to attain the Vision of God. And therefore it can be said that it is not the medium in which God is seen, but that through which he is seen. And so it does not do away with the immediate vision of God. (I 12.5 ad 2)

Later in the ST, Aquinas elaborates on the distinction between the infinite God that is known and the finite act through which God is known. In I–II 3.1, he asks whether the final end of happiness is something uncreated, and he replies,

> the end can be spoken of in two ways. In one way, it is the thing itself that we desire to attain, as for example, money is the end of avarice. In another way, it is the attainment or possession, or the use or enjoyment of that thing which is desired, and in this way it is said that the possession of money is the end of avarice, and the enjoyment of something pleasurable is the end of intemperance. In the first way, the ultimate end of the human person is an uncreated good, namely God, who alone by His infinite goodness can perfectly fulfill the will of the human person. In the second way, the ultimate end of the human person is something created existing in him, which is nothing other than the attainment or enjoyment of the ultimate end. Now the ultimate end is called happiness. If therefore the happiness of the

human person is considered with respect to its cause or object, so it is something uncreated. If however it is considered with respect to the essence of happiness itself, in this way, it is something created.

I am dwelling on this point because it seems to me to be relevant to the debate over the relative priority of uncreated grace and created grace discussed earlier. We have already observed that Aquinas does not understand grace in the Orthodox sense, in terms of human participation in God's uncreated energies. He does acknowledge that we can legitimately refer to God's love or His eternal predestining will as a kind of grace. Nonetheless, for him, grace properly so called refers to something created in the soul. More specifically, as he goes on to say, grace is a habit of the soul through which it is oriented toward a supernatural end (I–II 50.2, 110.4).

All that being said, even though Aquinas does not have the specific Orthodox concept of uncreated grace, that does not mean that he does not share the commitment lying behind this concept, namely, to protect the immediacy and the intimacy of God's presence to the blessed soul. He does so by distinguishing between the infinite good that the blessed enjoy, and the finite operations which constitute that enjoyment. To put the point in another way, the transformation brought about through glory, and the actual vision enabled through that transformation, are not the means through which God is known, but the very act of knowing God, the finite side of a relationship between God and his creature.[18]

To return to the main point of this section, Aquinas describes the transformation of the soul through the light of glory as a kind of divinization, expressed by the term *deiformis*. This term is especially apt for him because through glory, as Aquinas understands it, the human soul is in some way in-formed by God. This line of interpretation is reinforced by the fact that he does not speak of other human states in these terms. He seldom uses the term *deiformis* outside I 12, and when he does, he is usually referring to the supernatural elevation of the angelic intellect (I 108.4, I–II 50.6). That is what we would expect if he associates the term specifically with the Beatific Vision.

At this point, we might be inclined to agree with those authors who argue for an essential unity between the Orthodox doctrine of theosis and Aquinas's doctrine of grace and glory. On his showing, the blessed soul attains the closest possible union with God short of the hypostatic union, a union so profound that the created intellect is in a certain sense informed by its Creator. Indeed, as we have already observed, Aquinas goes beyond Orthodox theologians by asserting that the blessed do see the essence of God. Why is the Vision not a kind of theosis?

The answer to this question is simply that the blessed in heaven are enjoying a new and distinctive kind of life. Theosis, as understood within Orthodox theology, can be attained in this life. It therefore represents an ideal state that can actually be realized in some concrete way, however rare that realization may be. As such, it provides an ideal standard by which our lives can be measured, and a state that we may hope someday to achieve. Like secular ideals of heroic virtue, it is an action-guiding ideal, even though for almost everyone it remains unrealized. For Aquinas, in contrast, supreme union with God can only be attained after death. We cannot even imagine what this state will be like, and for that reason, it is not an action-guiding ideal in the way that theosis is. Aquinas insists that everyone who is capable of free action must strive for and attain salvation through action, but these acts are guided by faith—which is precisely not vision—and directed to the final end through charity, thanks to God's grace rather than any intrinsic commensuration between our acts and their heavenly reward (I–II 114.1,3,4). On Aquinas's showing, we hope for the Beatific Vision, but the ideals that guide our lives are grounded in our understanding of God's grace.

Aquinas's remarks on the Beatific Vision are relevant to our inquiry because they represent one point at which he clearly does think of a human state in terms of a kind of divinization. What is more, this topic brings up questions about the possibilities and the limitations of human nature that are clearly relevant to everything Aquinas says about the relation between God and human persons. The most relevant point of comparison to the Orthodox concept of theosis is presented by Aquinas's doctrine of grace.

The Life of Grace and Divine Life

Our examination of Aquinas's teachings on grace will necessarily be selective because he returns to this subject many times in a number of contexts.[19] We will take our starting points from the questions directly focused on grace, placing these in the wider context of his understanding of the final goal of human life and our attainment of that final end. On this basis, we will then consider whether, and in what ways, Aquinas regards grace as a kind of divinization.

Let us begin, therefore, with I–II 110, which is devoted to "the grace of God, with respect to its essence." In the first article, Aquinas begins by asking whether grace posits something in the soul. After identifying the different senses in which we say that someone has received grace, or love, from another, he distinguishes two ways in which God loves the creature. In the first sense, God is said to love every creature, insofar as he can be said to bestow natural existence on it. In another sense, God can be said to love the creature in a distinctive way,

> according to which he draws the rational creature above the condition of nature, to a participation in divine good. And in this way, he is said to love someone simply speaking, because in accordance with this love, God simply wills the creature eternal good, which is Himself. So therefore, when it is said that a human person has the grace of God, what is signified is something supernatural in the human person, coming forth from God. (I–II 110.1)

In the next article, he goes on to develop the parallel between creation, which in a manner of speaking bestows natural existence, and supernatural elevation:

> in another way the human person is aided by the gratuitous will of God in such a way that some habitual gift is poured into the soul by God. And this indeed, because it is not appropriate that God should provide less for those whom he loves in such a way that they have supernatural goods, than he provides for creatures that he loves in such a way that they have natural goods. For he provides for natural creatures in such a way that he not only moves them to their natural acts, but he also bestows on them certain forms and powers, which are the principles of acts, so that they are themselves inclined to motions of this kind. And so the motion by which they are moved by God is made connatural and easy to creatures. . . . Much more, therefore, does he pour out certain forms or supernatural qualities on those whom he moves to attain the supernatural good of eternity, according to which they are moved by him sweetly and promptly to attain the good of eternity. And so the gift of grace is a certain quality. (I–II 110.2)

He goes on to distinguish grace from the infused virtues, in accordance with the parallel between natural and supernatural principles of action. Just as the acquired virtues are grounded in connatural rational principles and enable the creature to act in such a way as to attain its connatural end, so the infused virtues are grounded in the supernatural principles bestowed through grace, and they enable the creature to act in such a way as to attain the supernatural end of union with God. Hence, grace cannot be a virtue; rather, it is a habit of the soul itself, through which the soul is oriented toward its supernatural end. Similarly, it provides the inchoate first principles for the infused virtues, which are the operative habits of grace (I–II 110.3). Elsewhere he says that the infusion of the theological virtues, which are the operative habits of grace, brings about "a certain participation in divinity," appealing to the authority of 2 Peter, "through Christ we are given a share in divine nature" (I–II 62.1).

Aquinas thus conceives of grace as a kind of transformation, through which the spiritual form of the rational creature, together with its operative powers, is oriented toward union with God. He understands this transformation in terms that are reminiscent of Orthodox theology of theosis, and at one point, he explicitly says that this transformation is a kind of divinization. The relevant text is found in I–II 112.1, which asks whether God alone is the cause of grace. He replies,

> the gift of grace exceeds all the powers of created nature, since it is nothing other than a certain participation in the divine nature, which exceeds all other nature. And so it is impossible that some creature should cause grace. For it is necessary that God alone deify, communicating a sharing in divine nature through a certain participation of similitude, just as it is impossible that anything except fire should ignite a flame. (I–II 112.1)

Based on what we have seen so far, it is clear that Aquinas understands grace as a kind of participation in divine nature, and he is prepared to describe this participation in terms of divinization. We might conclude that Aquinas's concept of grace is fundamentally similar to the Orthodox concept of theosis.[20] But Louth's observations on the significance of context and meaning for understanding a concept such as this should give us pause. When we take account of the wider doctrinal context and the ensemble of expectations that characterize the concept of theosis, on the one hand, and Aquinas's concept of grace on the other, we find significant differences, some of which have already been noted. Let me briefly mention some of these.

We have already noted that Orthodox theologians regard theosis as a real possibility for this life. At the same time, they also emphasize that this goal normally calls for an extended period of asceticism and contemplative prayer, and it is the exemplary achievement of a few. It is therefore difficult to separate the ideal of theosis from the context of monastic life, envisioned in its highest and most exemplary forms. For Aquinas, in contrast, the bestowal of grace is the starting point for salvation, and it represents the common denominator among men and women in diverse states of life and widely divergent degrees of holiness. Of course, I realize that Orthodox theologies of grace would also acknowledge that grace is foundational and, for that very reason, widely shared. My point, however, is that Aquinas focuses on those elements of grace that are commonly shared rather than on grace as it is manifest among men and women of exceptional holiness. In contrast to those who claim that through theosis, the individual becomes another Christ, he claims that through grace, men and women are incorporated into the body of Christ—an organic and collective, rather than an individualistic way of putting on Christ (III 7.3). What is more, he identifies the effects of grace as the forgiveness of sin and the attainment of merit, in such a way as to underscore the point that grace as we experience it is responsive to our sinfulness and limitations (I–II 113, 114). It is difficult to imagine an Orthodox theologian saying that theosis is valuable and desirable because it leads to the forgiveness of sins and the attainment of merit. Finally, as we have seen, Aquinas admits that the direct vision of God, analogous to theosis, is theoretically possible in this life, but he seems to restrict this possibility to the two scriptural cases, Moses and Saint Paul (II–II 175.3, especially ad 1, 180.5). Admittedly, his views on this matter are not entirely clear, but at the very least, he does not develop a theology of the rapture that would integrate it into the wider themes of his theology. He focuses on the life of grace, and glory as the culmination of grace, and seen from this perspective, he distinctions between beginners in grace and the most spiritually advanced lose their significance in the light of the distinction between the life of grace and the Beatific Vision. Correlatively, he would never say that grace, as such, represents God's highest intention for creation. These observations suggest that the Orthodox concept of theosis and Aquinas's doctrine of grace, in spite of their formal similarities, are shaped by different doctrinal and social contexts, differences which are reflected in the concepts themselves.

Given all this, how much weight should we give to Aquinas's use of the word *deificet* to refer to the bestowal of grace? Certainly, Aquinas uses this term advisedly at I–II 112.1 He is making a point about the kind of causality—that is, divine causality—needed to bestow grace in the human soul. His argument depends on the presupposition that grace involves a participation in divine nature, and therefore it is a kind of divinization, which only a divine agent, that is to say, God, can bring about. Given this line of argument, we cannot say that Aquinas would reject the claim that through grace, men and women can be said to be divinized in some sense. But this leaves open the question of what it means, concretely, to share in the divine nature. Our initial comparison suggests that Aquinas and Orthodox theologians understand this sharing in God's nature in significantly different ways.

We should also keep in mind that however Aquinas understands divinization, this is not his preferred way of expressing the effect of grace on the human soul. The text cited above represents the only place in the ST, so far as I can determine, where Aquinas uses the language of *deificet* to refer to the bestowal of grace.[21] The relative absence of this term is all the more striking, because we would expect Aquinas to use it in order to strengthen other claims that he makes about grace and its effects. In the course of explaining how the human person is created in the Image of God, he draws on the Ordinary Gloss to establish three senses in which men and women bear the Image: through creation, re-creation, and similitude, the first applying to all, the second applying to those in grace, and the third applying to the blessed in heaven (I 93.2)[22] In contrast to those Orthodox theologians who see the Image as the starting point for theosis, Aquinas does not use this language in this context. Similarly, his basic exposition of grace as the bestowal of supernatural principles of action might suggest that grace is a kind of deification, but apart from the text cited earlier, he does not say so. Finally, his treatment of charity as friendship with God would seem to call for an appeal to deification, through which men and women are elevated to a kind of parity with the divine. But again, that is not what Aquinas says; rather, he grounds the friendship between God and the rational creature in a sharing in supernatural happiness (II–II 23.1).

How does Aquinas characterize grace? We have already observed that he identifies the justification of the sinner as one of the effects of grace, and he frequently says that grace heals or justifies (I–II 111.1,3, 113. 1, 2). He also says that through grace we are adopted, regenerated as sons of God, or adopted and promised an inheritance (I–II 110.1; 110.3; 114.3). Both sets of texts reflect the importance of sin, and the remedies of sin, in Aquinas's theological context. At the same time, the texts cited at the beginning of this section reflect what I believe to be Aquinas's most foundational understanding of grace. Grace, he says, is a certain quality of the soul, and as such it is a kind of accidental form (I–II 110.2, 2 ad 2). More specifically, grace is a habit of the soul, that is to say, a stable disposition toward a characteristic kind of existence (I–II 110.4). As an accidental form, grace does not change the essence of the soul, but it qualifies the way in which that essence is actualized. Considered within the context of the natural order, this kind of habitual disposition of the soul would be superfluous, since the soul is "the completitive form of human nature"; however, "if we speak of a superior nature, in which the human person can share, nothing prohibits the existence of some habit in the soul according to its essence, that is, grace" (I–II 50.2). As a habit of the soul, grace provides the inchoate principles for the infused virtues, which are themselves operative habits, directed toward desires and actions ordered directly or indirectly toward the final end of union with God (I–II 63.2 ad 3, 110.2,3). Elsewhere we are told that grace also provides the starting point for other habits, the gifts of the Holy Spirit, through which the human person is enabled to respond to God's guidance, in such a way as to attain final salvation (I–II 68.1).

In order to appreciate the significance of these texts, we need to look briefly at what Aquinas means by a habit. Aquinas identifies habit as one of two kinds of internal principles of human acts, the other being the potencies or faculties of the soul, including the powers of sensory and intellectual perception and the appetites (I–II 49 introduction). These principles are not unrelated, of course, since Aquinas goes on to argue that habits are best understood as stable dispositions of innate human faculties, particularly those which are immediately oriented toward action (I–II 49). Thus, a habit reflects a kind of development or formation, acquired through actions or infused by God, through which the powers of the intellect and the appetites are oriented toward certain characteristic kinds of activities (I–II 49.3). Habits are therefore perfections, in Aquinas's characteristic metaphysical use of the term. That is to say, they are actualizations of the latent potencies natural to something as a creature of a specific kind (I 4.1,3; I 5.1,3). More specifically, a habit is a kind of development of the rational creature's capacities for action, that is to say, faculties of intellect, the passions, or the will (I–II 49.3). Habits are therefore characteristically oriented toward action and defined by reference to the characteristic kinds of acts that they generate (I–II 54.2).

Seen in this context, it is apparent that when Aquinas identifies grace and the infused virtues and gifts as habits, he presents these as vital principles that presuppose and transform the principles of natural life. The kind of perfection brought about by grace goes beyond anything that human nature could achieve by its own powers, but it is nonetheless intelligibly a perfection of those powers, that is to say, an expansion and a fuller development of human potentialities (I–II 108.1 ad 2; cf. I 1.8 ad 2). As such, it enables the human person to act freely in pursuit of her own salvation, rather than being moved by God as an external agent:

> He therefore acts freely who acts from himself. Now by the fact that a human person acts from a habit appropriate to his nature, he acts from himself, since habit inclines in the mode of nature. . . . Because therefore the grace of the Holy Spirit is just like an interior habit infused in us inclining us to right operations, we freely do those things which are appropriate to grace, and avoid those which are repugnant to grace. (I–II 108.1 ad 2; cf. I–II 113.3, 114.3,4; II–II 23.2)

These and similar texts provide a context for comparing Aquinas's doctrine of grace with the Orthodox conception of theosis. Both are grounded in the claim that God enables the human person to share in the divine nature. For Orthodox defenders of theosis, this participation is ideally expressed through an exemplary, as it were, a divine way of life. Aquinas, in contrast, emphasizes the analogy between divinity and nature, seen as two principles of life and action. As we have already seen, he begins his account of the essence of grace with a comparison between God's bestowal of natural existence, and His bestowal of the principles of supernatural existence (I–I 110.2). This suggests the image of grace as a vital principle, similar in some ways to natural life. When Aquinas refers to our participation in divine nature, the key point for him is thus the communication of a form of existence which enables us to live and to act in such a way as to enter into communion with God, leading ultimately to the supreme joy of the Beatific Vision. This new form of existence may be expressed through a life of exemplary holiness, but for Aquinas that will not necessarily be the case. Even though grace is a kind of participation in divine nature, this participation can take many forms, and Aquinas does not focus his attention on what we might describe as the fullest or most exemplary instances of that participation. By implication, when Aquinas does refer to the bestowal of grace as divinization, what he means by that term is the bestowal of the divine nature, understood as a principle of life and action that may be imperfectly expressed. And the relative absence of this term suggests that while this way of speaking is not incorrect, it is not ideally suited to grace as he understands it.

Scripture and Christian tradition offer Aquinas a wide range of options for expressing the meaning and significance of grace, including a Latin version of theosis as well as images of justification, sanctification, and adoption.[23] In fact, he does not reject almost any of the traditional images that are on offer, but he interprets them in such a way as to give more weight to some, especially justification and adoption, and relatively less weight to others, including divinization. Throughout his remarks on grace, he interprets these motifs in accordance with his fundamental claim that grace is a habit of the soul, expressed through a new way of being and acting. Why should this be the case?

Louth would remind us at this point that in order to appreciate the significance of Aquinas's conception of grace, seen both in relation to theosis and on its own terms, we need to place it in a wider context of beliefs and practices. We have already considered some of the ways in which concepts of theosis and grace may have been shaped by different approaches to the doctrine of God and the work of Christ. At this point, it will be helpful to return to these, in order to reflect further on the significance of Aquinas's doctrine of grace.

In the first section of this essay, we saw that Aquinas, in contrast to medieval and contemporary Orthodox theologians, does not have a notion of divine energies, which provide a medium for a human encounter with God. At the same time, he does have a conception of God as existing without limit or qualification, implying that God is supremely intelligible (I 14.2, 16.5; cf. I 12.1). This claim, taken together with scriptural and philosophical views on the final end and ultimate perfection of the human person, lead him to claim that the human person can see the essence of God. At the same time, he understands this state in such a way as to render it fundamentally inconsistent with the mode of existence proper to us in this life, dependent as we are on images grounded in the senses for rational understanding. In effect, he rules out the possibility of attaining supreme union with God in this life, as a corollary of the strong claims he makes for the possibility of union with God in the next life.

Aquinas's doctrine of God has shaped his understanding of grace in another way. We noted above that according to Hallonsten, the different approaches to the doctrine of God that characterize Orthodox and Western theology have given rise to different construals of the relation between divine and natural principles of action. Broadly speaking, Orthodox theologians tend to see a continuum between natural and divine principles of action, whereas Western theologians are more likely to emphasize discontinuities between God and creation. Aquinas's doctrine of grace, like his account of glory, fits within this broad template. As we have already seen, he claims that through grace we are oriented toward a final end that exceeds our natural capacities and can be attained only through supernatural principles of action. Elsewhere he makes it clear that the gap between our natural capacities and our supernatural end is not due to sinfulness alone; even integral human nature, untouched by sin, would not be adequate by itself to attain the final end of union with God to which we are called (I–II 109 2, 4, 5).

Aquinas's Christology, and correlatively his construal of grace seen in connection with Christ, are deeply shaped by the conviction that Christ came among us to free us from sin. As we have seen, he does not rule out the possibility that God might have become human if we had never sinned on general theological grounds, but he rules out this line of speculation on scriptural grounds. Aquinas has a great deal to say about the different aspects of Christ's redeeming work, culminating in his passion and death. For our purposes, the most immediately relevant of these have to do with Christ's grace and merit, seen in relation to our own grace and ultimate salvation.

Aquinas affirms that Jesus Christ is fully human and fully divine, in accordance with the ancient dogma of the church. Yet he also claims that the human soul of Jesus is informed by habitual grace (III 7.1). He offers three reasons for this claim: The first is that Jesus's soul is uniquely close to the Word of God, and for that reason, it is open, in an unsurpassed way, to the influx of grace. Second, and perhaps more surprisingly, Aquinas claims that in order to attain the supreme knowledge and love of God proper to him, the natural powers of Jesus's soul must be elevated through grace; here we see further confirmation of the point that for Aquinas, even sinless human nature is incapable, through its own innate powers, of attaining full union with God. Finally, Aquinas observes that the grace of Christ, who as a man is mediator between God and humanity, is meant to overflow to others. In the next question, Aquinas returns to this latter point. Jesus Christ, as Head of the Church, is in a sense the source of grace for all those who are saved through him, and Aquinas emphasizes the point that the grace that is proper to Christ as an individual is the same as the grace proper to him as head of the church (III 8.5). As we have seen, he also claims that through his grace, the man Jesus merits salvation for himself and others through his passion and death on the Cross (III 48.1)

Aquinas clearly agrees with Orthodox defenders of theosis that Jesus Christ is the meeting point between God and humanity, and correlatively, that the life of Christ is the template for what we can become through him. However, Aquinas interprets this key point in such a way as to emphasize the humanity, rather than the divinity of Christ. We draw near to God by sharing in the grace of the man Jesus, who is himself full of grace, and as such is the means through which we receive grace. Through grace, we participate in the body of Christ, relating to Jesus as the members of a body to its Head (III 7.3). We are enabled to merit salvation through our own free actions, just as Christ merited salvation for us through his sacrificial death—although Aquinas insists that we are unable, without grace, to merit what he calls the first grace (I–II 114.3,5). Aquinas's emphasis throughout these remarks falls on the ways in which men and women, in their humanity, are enabled through grace to act in accordance with the prompting of the Holy Spirit, in solidarity with Jesus Christ and the many members of his body. It is not surprising, given this context, that he associates grace with adoption, since it is through grace that we are enabled to enter into the inheritance of Jesus Christ (I–II 114.3).

The body of Christ, as Aquinas understood and experienced it, is closely tied to—although not strictly identical with—the Catholic Church of his time. This suggests a third context within which to understand Aquinas's concept of grace, namely, the lived experience of the Church as he and his contemporaries would have known it. Aquinas, like nearly every other Western theologian at this time, associated grace and the Christian life with a sacramental system that attempted to provide clear markers for inclusion and reintegration into the Church.[24] Whatever we may think of this system and the theology associated with it, in practice, it was an inclusive system, and it had the effect of democratizing grace, as it were. It was very easy to become a Christian—most people crossed that line as infants—and thanks to a system of private confession and penances, sinners could be reintegrated into the community on less harsh terms than would have been the case in earlier times. For these reasons, the Christian community as Aquinas and his interlocutors experience it is a very mixed assembly, including some men and women of exemplary holiness, but also including very many who are clearly well disposed but still worldly or beset with temptations. Yet given the terms of Aquinas's theology of grace, all of these, with the important exception of those who had committed grave sins, are living lives of grace and infused virtue. This implies that practically speaking, the life of grace can look very imperfect indeed.

When we turn to Aquinas's theology of grace and his moral theology with this context in mind, we clearly see that he is well aware of the realities of continuing weakness and struggle among those who have received grace. This is apparent in the overall structure of his moral theology, which carefully distinguishes between minimal standards for virtue and the ideals of holiness and directs attention to the virtues of ordinary Christian life, as lived in the marketplace, the courtroom, the social world of dinner parties and festivals, and even the marriage bed II–II 77–78; 67–71; 141.6; 153.2). At one point, he explains why those who receive infused virtue can find it harder to be virtuous than those whose virtues have been acquired through effort, and at another point, he explains how even those who are naturally foolish can practice infused prudence (I–II 65.3 ad 2; II–II 47.14). He is careful to distinguish mortal sins, which are to be avoided at all costs, from venial sins, which are an inevitable part of everyone's life (I–II 86.1).

In short, Aquinas's emphasis, in speaking of grace, falls on the human side of the new relation between the rational creature and God. That, I would suggest, offers another reason why the language of divinization might seem inappropriate in this context—not incorrect, but not ideally suited for conveying what he wants to say about the life of grace. Aquinas does acknowledge that God makes us godlike through grace, but he leaves open the question of what that might mean in terms of Christian experience. The church is full of men and women who hope and reasonably believe that they have grace, but they hardly feel godlike, nor do they see many divine individuals around them. By the same token, Aquinas's context helps to explain why he thinks of grace as a kind of vital principle, a form to be understood through analogy to the natural forms of creatures, especially living creatures. Living things grow and develop; they may flourish, or they may be stunted or malformed in some ways; they may sicken and decline, only to revive. Life can be cultivated, nourished, and protected, or it can be neglected, starved, and endangered. The dynamics of the life of grace as Aquinas understands it look very much like the dynamics of natural life, marked by growth from infancy to maturity, and even at its best, fragile and in need of care.

So far, we have focused on Aquinas's concept of grace as seen within the context of what might be called the ordinary Christian life. I am suggesting that this context shapes Aquinas's concept of grace in a fundamental way. For him, grace is centrally and paradigmatically responsive to and expressed through the lives of men and women who experience struggles, setbacks, and also growth throughout their lives. But is this really a complete account of what Aquinas has to say about the life of grace and its completion in glory? What does he have to say about those who attain a closer union with God through extraordinary holiness or contemplation? To what extent would a consideration of the exemplary cases alter our reading of his remarks on grace?

In order to address these questions, we need to look more closely at what Aquinas says about what we might call exemplary or outstanding forms of Christian life. I have already noted that he does not appear to have a theology of mysticism at all. He does discuss different forms of what we might call manifestations of divinity, such as prophecy or speaking in tongues, which he identifies as "graces freely given"—that is to say, graces bestowed for the sake of the community. As such, these gifts do not, in themselves, render the recipient pleasing to God, or much less God-like (II–II 172.4).

We have already observed that Aquinas acknowledges that two individuals did see the essence of God in this lifetime, namely Moses and Paul, through what is traditionally called rapture (II–II 175.1,3; cf. I 12.11, II–II 180.5). Aquinas takes care to explain how this experience is like, and unlike, the final vision of God, but he does acknowledge that given these examples, we must admit that it is possible to see God in this life. At the same time, it would seem that these are exceptional cases, reflecting the special status of Moses and Paul as the professors, as it were, of the Old and New Covenants, respectively. What is more, rapture is not a state that can be attained through progressive stages of asceticism and holiness. It involves a kind of suspension of natural processes of perception and cognition, and for that reason it can only be brought about through divine initiative. Aquinas even reminds us of the violent connotations of the word *raptus*, to underscore the point that this is an exceptional experience, outside the natural order of things (II–II 175.1). While he does not rule out the possibility that others might experience the rapture, he does not discuss this possibility, in such a way as to incorporate it into a range of options for living a Christian life, nor does it play a key role in his theology.

Aquinas devotes considerable attention to the contemplative life, considered in comparison to the active life, which is lived out through the practice of the cardinal virtues (II–II 179.1). Contemplation in this context is to be understood in its primary sense as the intellectual consideration of God as first truth and secondarily the consideration of other truths seen in relation to God (II–II 180.4). It is thus the act of the highest and most characteristically human power, the intellect, directed to the highest object, God. As such, it is simply speaking the highest kind of life, and what is more, it anticipates the happy contemplation of the blessed (II–II 182.1). So far, it might seem as if the contemplative life might be described as more visibly God-like than the life of the ordinary Christian.

On closer examination, however, it is apparent that the contemplative life as Aquinas understands it does not represent a way of life that is different in kind from that of any other wayfarer. The contemplative comes to know God through processes of human reasoning, elevated through faith and motivated by charity (II–II 180.1, 5, especially 5 ad 2). This knowledge begins with the consideration of sensate particulars and is grounded in phantasmata, some of which are supplied directly by God through faith (I 12.13). Clearly this way of knowing God is different in kind from that enjoyed through the rapture, or much less the Beatific Vision, and Aquinas says as much (II–II 180.5). Contemplation is said to offer a foretaste of future happiness insofar as the act of contemplation stems from charity, in virtue of which it merits the reward of heaven (II–II 180.1, 182.2). Contemplation as Aquinas understands it plainly resembles philosophical reflection more than it does mystical union with the divine. What is more, the contemplative life is not so sharply distinct from the active life as we might imagine. The practice of the cardinal virtues, which is inextricably bound up with the active life, serves as a preparation for the contemplative life, and contemplation itself can provide a starting point for active works, such as teaching. Indeed, it would seem that both ways of life can be pursued together or brought together as stages of one lifetime (II–II 182.3,4). In short, the life of the contemplative is not different in kind from that of any other wayfarer. Aquinas's treatment of it does not affect his overall sense of the dynamic character of the life of grace, and the need to speak of it in terms that reflect its temporal and mutable character.

Theosis and Grace

Does Aquinas have a concept of divinization, essentially similar to the Orthodox concept of theosis? By now it will be apparent that the answer to this question will depend on what we take to be the key respects in which Aquinas's doctrine of grace might be compared to theosis and how much similarity is enough to justify a claim of fundamental agreement. Aquinas uses the language of divinization in reference to both the glory of the blessed and the grace of the wayfarer, and on this basis, we are justified in saying that he has a concept of divinization. Furthermore, his accounts of grace and glory do share certain salient features with the Orthodox conception of theosis, most notably, the fundamental conviction that through Christ we partake in the divine nature.

Yet when these points of agreement are placed within the wider contexts of the accounts of theosis and grace, respectively, it becomes difficult to maintain that Aquinas's doctrine of grace is essentially the same as the Orthodox concept of theosis. What is more, when we take account of the significance of theosis and grace, seen in light of their respective theological contexts, it becomes apparent that these reflect two significantly different approaches to the doctrine of God, the status of creation and nature, the salience of sin, and the person and work of Christ. We have also seen that the concepts of theosis and grace reflect two different social settings, as it were, and correspondingly different expectations about the real possibilities for attaining a divine ideal in this life. Given all these considerations, I do not believe that we can say that Aquinas has the Orthodox conception of theosis, or at least, it does not appear in the *Summa theologiae*. Furthermore, while he does not reject the claim that grace is a kind of divinization, this is not his preferred way to characterize grace. He is more likely to speak of grace as justification or adoption, and he understands it in terms that emphasize analogies between grace and the principles of life.

Recent work on theosis and potential Western analogues has been motivated, at least to a considerable extent, by a desire to find points of contact between Orthodox and Western theologies, in service of a broader ecumenical agenda. At the same time, at least some Orthodox theologians have been less than enthusiastic about recent attempts to find a concept of theosis in classical Western theologies. It is difficult to do so without westernizing the concept, in such a way as to lose sight of its distinctiveness and its wider significance. I take that to be Louth's point, and it should be clear by now that I agree with him. The same can be said about Aquinas's doctrine of grace, which cannot be separated from distinctively Western ways of construing divine/human relations, the realities of sin, and the salvific work of Christ. At any rate, ecumenical dialogue need not begin with points of agreement; it can also take its starting point from a respectful acknowledgment of difference. My hope is that this essay will make a contribution to an ecumenical conversation on the distinctive yet mutually enriching ways in which Orthodox and Western theologians approach the topics of theosis and grace.[25]

Notes

1. In addition to the authors cited in the notes following, my understanding of the Orthodox concept of theosis is indebted to Daniel B. Clendenin, "Partakers of Divinity: The Orthodox Doctrine of Theosis," *Journal of Evangelical Theological Society* 37, no. 3 (September 1994): 365–79; Paul L. Gavrilyuk, "The Retrieval of Deification: How a Once-Despised Archaism Became an Ecumenical Desideratum," *Modern Theology* 25, no. 4 (October 2009): 647–59; Archimandrite George, Abbot of the Monastery of St. Gregorios on Mount Athos, *Theosis: The True Purpose of Human Life* (Mount Athos: Holy Monastery of St. Gregorios, 2006); Jean Meyendorff, *St. Grégoire Palamas et la mystique orthodoxe* (Paris: Éditions du Seuil, 1959); and Aristotle Papanikolaou, *Being with God: Trinity, Apophaticism, and Divine-Human Communion* (Notre Dame, IN: University of Notre Dame Press, 2006). The treatise by Archimandrite George is especially illuminating, because it is written for a popular audience; anyone who thinks that academic discussions of theosis, divine energies, and related topics have no practical interest will be disabused of that view upon reading this book.

2. One of the first, and certainly one of the most influential defenses of this claim is A. N. Williams, *The Ground of Union: Deification in Aquinas and Palamas* (New York: Oxford University Press, 1999). Subsequently, Luke Davis Townsend offered a series of corrections and expansions of Williams's work, while affirming her basic thesis, in "Deification in Aquinas: A *Supplementum* to *The Ground of Union*," *Journal of Theological Studies* 66, no. 1 (April 2013): 204–34. Daria Spezzano offers a helpful overview of recent discussions of theosis in Aquinas in her *The Glory of God's Grace: Deification According to St. Thomas Aquinas* (Ave Maria, FL: Sapientia Press of Ave Maria University, 2015), 1–16. At the same time, she distinguishes her project from theirs: "it is not my intent to support a claim that Thomas's teaching on deification is (or is not) the same as the Eastern doctrine. Rather, I seek . . . to understand how the teaching on deification functions internally to Thomas's theology" (15).

3. All references to the *Summa Theologiae* are incorporated into the text, and all translations are my own.

4. This point is generally acknowledged. In order to locate Aquinas's uses of the terms deificare and deiformis, I relied on Roy J. Deferrari, *A Lexicon of St. Thomas Aquinas Based on the Summa Theologica and Selected Passages of His Other Works* (Washington, DC: Catholic University of America Press, 1948).

5. Andrew Louth, "The Place of *Theosis* in Orthodox Theology," in *Partakers of the Divine Nature: The History and Development of Deification in the Christian Tradition*, ed. Michael J. Christensen and Jeffery A. Wittung (Madison, NJ: Fairleigh Dickinson University Press, 2007), 32–44, at 32–33.

6. Ibid., 33.

7. Townsend rightly observes that a study focused on the *Summa Theologiae* cannot claim to represent the trajectory of development of Aquinas's thought on a subject; see "Deification in Aquinas," 208. However, this approach has the advantage of allowing for a critical study of Aquinas's position as developed in one integrated work, which furthermore represents his mature views on the subject. Townsend offers a comprehensive survey of Aquinas's treatment of divinization throughout his career (210–27). This survey makes it clear that Aquinas is aware of the language of deification and comments on it at some length, especially when it is pertinent to some text on which he is commenting. It is not so clear, at least to me, that Aquinas's use of the language of deification in his earlier works reflects a concept of deification essentially similar to theosis. At any rate, the relative scarcity of the term *deificare* in the ST, as compared to earlier works, may suggest that as Aquinas's thought developed, he found the image of deification to be less appropriate for expressing the meaning of grace than other traditional images.

8. For good discussions of Gregory of Palamas's work and its significance, see Meyendorff, *St. Grégoire Palamas*, 111–32, and Williams, *The Ground of Union*, 102–27.

9. Vladimir Lossky, *The Mystical Theology of the Eastern Church* (Cambridge: James Clarke and Co., 1957), 90; the whole chapter "Uncreated Energies" (67–90) offers a very helpful treatment of a difficult topic.

10. It would go well beyond the scope of this paper to discuss Aquinas's doctrine of creation in detail. However, it seems clear that he understands the act of creation in terms of a kind of efficient causality, implying an efficacious communication of form; as he says at I 44.4 ad 4, "God is the efficient, exemplary, and final cause of all things." Exemplary causality should be understood here as equivalent to formal causality. Aquinas has already explained that God creates in accordance with divine ideas, which he interprets as the forms of things, which, so to speak, preexist in the mind of God (I–II 15.1). At the same time, we cannot read back from the forms of things to knowledge of the divine

essence; we can say only that creatures resemble God insofar as they are existing beings, whereas God is pure act (I 4.3) Finally, God is the final cause of things, insofar as he is the principle for existence and perfection (I 6.1).

11. Gösta Hallonsten, "*Theosis* in Recent Research: A Renewal of Interest and a Need for Clarity," in Christensen and Wittung, *Partakers in the Divine Nature*, 281–93 at 286.

12. However, according to Meyendorff, Palamas also distinguishes between the knowledge of God attained, or claimed, by philosophers, and the supernatural knowledge of, and union with God attained through Jesus Christ; *St. Grégoire Palamas*, 112.

13. Aquinas returns repeatedly to this point, and we will consider it in more detail. The key text for understanding the distinctions that he draws, between God's creative act and His supernatural elevation, and between the necessity for grace for integral and corrupted human nature, is I–II 109, on the necessity of grace. He first asserts the comprehensive necessity of grace for both sinless and corrupted humanity at 109.2.

14. Both Williams and Townsend defend the priority of uncreated grace; see *Ground of Union*, 87–89, and "Deification in Aquinas," 228–31. For a thoroughgoing, and in my view convincing response, see Richard Cross, "Deification in Aquinas: Created or Uncreated?" *Journal of Theological Studies* 69, no. 1 (April 2018): 106–32.

15. "The Place of *Theosis* in Orthodox Theology," 34–35.

16. According to Aquinas, the Incarnation was not strictly necessary for the reparation of the human race, because "For God, through his omnipotent power, would have been able to restore the human race in many other ways" (III 1.20) However, he goes on to say, the Incantation was necessary in the sense of offering a better, more appropriate way of restoring humanity.

17. Cross offers an insightful account of Aquinas's understanding of the Beatific Vision in "Deification in Aquinas," 116–19.

18. Cross makes a similar point; see "ibid., 118–19.

19. Strictly speaking, it is inaccurate to speak of grace in this way without qualification. Aquinas distinguishes between two kinds of grace: *gratia gratum faciens*, and *gratia gratis data* (I–II 111.1) Through the former, the individual is joined to God, in such a way that, if she preservers, she will attain salvation. The latter includes all those special gifts, such as prophecy, which are given to the individual for the sake of preparing others to receive grace in the first sense. Unless otherwise indicated, all references to grace in this essay should be understood as *gratia gratum faciens*.

20. If I have understood her correctly, Williams interprets Aquinas in just this way. While she recognizes that Aquinas uses the word, *deificet*, very rarely in the ST, she takes this term to provide the key for interpreting his reference to

participation in divine nature. That is why she assumes that Aquinas and Gregory of Palamas have essentially the same understanding of participation in divine nature; see *Ground of Union*, 34–39. As Hallonsten points out, this is precisely what would have to be argued, in order to sustain her line of interpretation; "*Theosis* in Recent Research," 286. Townsend offers a more detailed analysis of deification as Aquinas understands it, but he also assumes that the language of deification provides the key for understanding the language of participation; see "Deification in Aquinas," 227–34.

21. Spezzio cites three other texts in which Aquinas refers to the deification of individuals, namely II–II 184.5, 188.2 obj.1, and III 79.8; *The Glory of God's Grace*, 7. In each case, the reference to deifying occurs within a quotation and plays no role in the argument of the article itself. Aquinas also says that the flesh of Christ is deified through union with the Word of God (III 2.1 ad 3).

22. To a considerable degree, scholastic appropriation of patristic thought was mediated through glosses on scripture compiled from patristic writings, particularly the comprehensive gloss produced by the school of Anselm of Laon at the beginning of the twelfth century that came to be known as the Ordinary (that is, the standard) Gloss. For a comprehensive account of the formation of the Gloss and its later significance, see Beryl Smalley, *The Study of the Bible in the Middle Ages* (Notre Dame, IN: University of Notre Dame Press, 1964; a reprint of the 1952 Blackwell edition), 46–65.

23. Hallonsten makes a similar point, distinguishing among a theme of theosis, which is widely shared among most Christian authors; theosis as connected to a specific anthropology; and a comprehensive doctrine of theosis as including the whole plan of salvation; see "*Theosis* in Recent Research," 287. I would prefer to speak of images or motifs, but I agree with the basic point that references to theosis or deification do not necessarily reflect a comprehensive doctrine.

24. Of course, Orthodox Christianity is also deeply rooted in sacramental and liturgical practices, and the attainment of theosis is frequently linked to faithful practice of the rites of the Church. For Aquinas and his contemporaries, however, the sacraments were understood and practiced in a context of rapid social change and institutional innovation, which gave salience to the ways in which they are linked to status within the community. Aquinas's juridical understanding of the sacraments is clearly evident in his discussion of the character bestowed by a sacrament, which he understands to be a certain active or passive power, to do or receive something in the Church; see III 63.1,2.

25. An earlier version of this essay was presented at the Fourth Patterson Triennial Conference, "Faith, Reason, Theosis," at Fordham University, New York, on June 5, 2019. I am deeply indebted to those present for invaluable comments, and I would also like to thank two readers for the press for their helpful suggestions.

Deification as Christification and Human Becoming

Philip Kariatlis

> It is no longer I who live, but Christ who lives in me.
> —Galatians 2:20

The doctrine of deification, theosis, which has typically enjoyed a central place in the Eastern Orthodox tradition, especially in the way it has informed the related understandings of soteriology and spirituality respectively,[1] has, in more recent times, also experienced a kind of resurgence in contemporary Christian thought more broadly. This has largely been due to the promising phenomenon of ecumenical receptivity, a fresh approach to dialogue that has seen different Christian denominations seeking to respond to contemporary challenges in a spirit of shared exploration. The endorsement of theosis as an appropriate term encapsulating the entire economy of salvation can be seen, for example, in the growing number of publications in this area, from within not only Eastern but also Western theological traditions.[2] Undoubtedly, this broader interest has brought with it new and variegated perspectives, the result of which has been a richer and more nuanced understanding of deification.

Within the Eastern Orthodox tradition, this ongoing interest in deification has also given rise to other distinct perspectives. And so, whereas in the past the concept of deification was almost exclusively presented from within an essence/energies distinction framework, other writings, more recently, have attempted to present a more person-centered—or prosopocentric—approach. Accordingly, representatives from the first school—most notably

Vladimir Lossky and Giorgios Mantzaridis—would, on the whole, concur in seeing deification in distinctly Palamite terms, namely as participation in the uncreated energies of God. The latter understanding, however—of which some adherents would include Panayiotis Nellas, John Zizioulas, Aristotle Papanikolaou, and John Behr—understand deification, generally speaking, in more personal terms, as union with Christ or correlatively as humanity's sonship with God. Notwithstanding these discernible distinctives—which have incidentally become the cause of some debate within Orthodox scholarship—for neither school has deification ever signified any connaturality or fusion with God; namely, neither approach has ever identified deification with the ancient Greek philosophical notion of apotheosis.[3] Both groups would assert that humanity's ultimate deified state—whatever this may look like—while real, will in no way ever extinguish the radical otherness between creator and creature. Furthermore, recurrent emphases in deification theologies reveal an understanding which gives preeminence to the divine gift-dimension of this renewed theotic existence. Lossky, for example, captures this fundamental aspect when he defines deification as humanity's movement "to become by grace . . . that which God is by nature."[4] Beyond the clear depiction of deification as a graced existential reality, Lossky also identifies, in this instance, its dynamic quality, which presupposes an ongoing receptivity on the part of humanity. In tracing the meaning of deification in some of the earlier church fathers, John McGuckin concludes in the same vein: "in all Christian conceptions of the notion [of deification], the divine initiation and priority is always at the basis of the creaturely ascent."[5] Last, and indeed most important, a hallmark of both approaches has been their reliance on the Athanasian adage, "God became human so that the human person may become God [by grace],"[6] and therefore their Christocentricity. In this "admirable exchange [*admirablile commercium*]"[7] deification is presented as the logical consequence of the incarnation. Yet, even though Christ is at the center of both approaches, there are distinct emphases. More concretely, it could be said that whereas for the first school it is Christ's incarnation which makes deification—namely participation in the energies of God—possible, for the second, Christ's theanthropic existence is not simply the decisive presupposition for deification but more than that, its ultimate end, namely humanity's "hypostatic union with the divine Logos in Christ."[8]

In light of the distinct or, perhaps more correctly, complementary views briefly presented, this essay will examine the extent to which a plausible case can be made for deriving an understanding of deification, not primarily from within an essence/energies distinction framework—as has traditionally been the case—but rather from one focusing on humanity's union with the incarnate Son of God, the crucified and exalted Christ resulting in humanity's "Christification" [Χριστοποίησις]. Arguably, a pioneering proponent of this consistently Christ-centered approach has been Panayiotis Nellas. In coining the term "Christification" for deification, Norman Russell argues that Nellas "returns to a more biblical focus,"[9] shedding light on many Pauline expressions, some of which would include being "in Christ," "with Christ," and "united with Christ." As such, closer attention to Nellas's contribution will show that this second approach to deification, as also reflected by its other adherents, far from being novel in its desire to want to work beyond an essence-energy framework is, on the contrary, a faithful reflection of and in concert with the Christian tradition as a whole. Indeed, Nellas's understanding is marked by a radical inclusivity that brings together both the anthropological and economic aspects of this doctrine, resulting in a wonderfully positive understanding of the human person. More specifically, Nellas's understanding also merits ongoing attention to the extent that it sheds light on what it means to be human. Thus, far from only implying humanity's ascent and union with God, resulting in human beings becoming "gods by grace," a Christologically conditioned understanding of deification, indeed one formulated from within a Chalcedonian framework—as Nellas does—would also give preeminence to deification's human aspect. Consequently, in this understanding, to be deified would also imply becoming truly human as God intended humanity to be. Yet this latter dimension of deification as "human becoming" has for the most part received little attention.[10]

Deification as Christification

Central to Nellas's treatment of deification is the broad framework in which he places this concept. For him, deification is not principally an antidote to humanity's transgression from sin, but rather the fulfilment of God's initial creative act. Citing from Ephesians 1:4–11—"he chose us in him before the foundation of the world . . . to gather up all things in him [Christ]"—he sees deification from its widest scope, namely, as the crowning moment of God's entire creative economy, and more so, as the very reason for the creation of the world *ex nihilo* in the first place.[11] Andrew Louth expresses the same idea when he writes that deification ought to be seen, "in terms of an arch stretching from creation to deification, representing what is and remains God's intention."[12] Indeed, according to Nellas, failing to account for salvation in this way leads "to a mutilation and distortion of the truths of faith, the content of the spiritual life and the various dimensions of the Church."[13] In a clearly definitive way, therefore, Nellas presents salvation and more specifically deification as a process in which God is involved from the very beginning of the creation of the world, for the purpose of bringing about humanity's gradual transformation and ultimate unity to himself. More specifically, he understands deification as an invitation on the part of God, or more correctly a "command" issued to humanity "to transcend the limited boundaries of creation and to become infinite," that is, "god-like."[14] Accordingly, in seeing the creation of the world as the place *par excellence* for the unfolding narrative of God's salvific plan for the world, he highlights a unifying link between cosmology—or indeed, *protology*—and deification—eschatology—where deification is seen as the fulfilment of God's initial creative act. This point is explicitly made in the following excerpt from his main work *Deification in Christ*: "Christ is not the result of an act of Satan. The union of the divine and human natures took place because it fulfilled the eternal will of God."[15] He takes an unequivocally clear stance that the Incarnation would have taken place even if humanity had not sinned. Indeed, from the very beginning, the world was created so that it could be united to God, in this way necessitating Christ's coming to complete this unity between God and the world irrespective of sin. Accordingly, Christ did not simply redeem humanity *from* the reality of sin and the effects of the fall, but more important, as noted by Nellas, he completed the pre-fallen nature of humanity by opening it up, through Christ, *into* the divine and eternal life of God. Christ's coming therefore was nothing less than the fulfillment of the eternal will of God. This all-encompassing dimension of deification is succinctly captured in the following: "Christ accomplishes the salvation of man not only in a negative way, liberating him from the consequences of original sin, but also in a positive way, completing his iconic, prelapsarian being."[16] Consequently, the hypostatic union of divine and human accomplished in Christ, becomes the very foundation upon which God's pre-eternal plan for the deification of humanity becomes possible.

Coupled with this radical broadening of soteriology's parameters, Nellas understands deification not only as a divinely bestowed *gift* of unity with

Christ, but also in terms of the human adventure—or human response—involved, relating to its actualization. And so, for him, deification becomes synonymous with Christification, namely a kind of human refashioning which results not only in human persons becoming more Christlike, but more so genuinely incorporated into Christ. In this way, far from being an *ephhapax* event, deification, according to Nellas, needs to be understood in more dynamic terms, in which the human person is progressively enabled to become conformed to the incarnate Logos. The theological basis for this is his understanding of the scriptural concept of "image," that divine potentiality innate within finite human persons making possible their transcendence to divine infinitude. Without in any way abolishing the ontological gap between the Son of God and humanity,[17] it is the divine image within each person, namely this, "element of the divine" that makes possible humanity's union with the incarnate Logos. Bringing together two biblical texts on the concept of "image" more specifically, from Genesis and Colossians, the former presents the human person as having been created in the image of God, the latter Christ specifically. Nellas concludes that it would be more correct to see humanity as having been created "in the image of the Image"[18] and consequently "ordered" to become Christlike. Here Nellas is simply following the early patristic tradition that understood the human person as an image of Christ. Accordingly, he succinctly writes: "the real anthropological meaning of deification is Christification."[19] In his treatise *On the Incarnation*, for example, Saint Athanasius wrote that God: "bestowed [on humanity] a grace which the other creatures lack—namely, the impress of his own image, a share in the reasonable being of the very Word himself."[20] And Saint Irenaeus before him noted: "For I made the human person in the image of God and the image of God is the Son, according to whose image was man made; and for this reason he appeared in the last times, to render the image like himself."[21] Having received this divine gift, which opens up the way into a radically new graced existential reality, humanity needs to strive at the same time to make this gift a reality. This idea is summed up in the following: "Christ, as the highest realisation of man, naturally constitutes the goal of mankind's upward journey, the beginning but also the end of history."[22] In order to be made whole, the human person, Nellas writes, "must put on 'the image of the heavenly man' who is Christ (1 Cor 15:49) in order to attain 'to the measure of the stature of the fullness of Christ' (Eph 4:13)."[23] Quoting Nicholas Cabasilas, he concludes, "it was not the old Adam that was the model for the new, but the new Adam for the old."²⁴ This dynamic vision of deification as Christification is beautifully encapsulated in the following: "Through correct knowledge and the free exercise of love, man can be raised in Christ from being "in the image" to being the Image itself."²⁵ In a radically explicit manner, therefore, the full extent of Christification is underlined which, according to Nellas, results in human beings called to become nothing less than "christs" with a small "c." Far from signifying a mere moral external identity, Christification, for Nellas, is understood as real participation in the hypostasis of Christ. Having identified a dynamic understanding of deification as Christification, Nellas turns his attention to shed further light on the full extent of this unity of humanity with Christ.

Nellas's distinctly Christological framework for understanding deification results in his explicit proposition that humanity's unity with God needs to be situated on the hypostatic—and not energetic—level. For Nellas, it was the hypostatic union of the divine and human accomplished in Christ which constitutes the foundation of humanity's deification. And so, by extension, Nellas's Christ-centered vision of deification leads him to affirm that deification ought to be understood as participation in the hypostasis of Christ rather than in God's uncreated divine energies. Zizioulas subsequently furthers this idea.²⁶ Papanikolaou does as well.²⁷ Nellas argues that human persons "enhypostasised in the Logos become capable of being raised up into an 'image' [namely Christ]."²⁸ In this understanding, Nellas argues that the faithful are united to Christ by being incorporated into his hypostasis—namely, members of his body united to Christ, their head. In its theological discourse on deification as humanity's unity with God, twentieth-century Orthodox scholarship usually identified three distinct levels of unity, "unity according to essence [ἕνωσις κατ' οὐσίαν]," "unity according to hypostasis [ἕνωσις καθ' ὑπόστασιν]," and "unity according to energy [ἕνωσις κατ' ἐνέργειαν]." It understood deification as taking place on the third level. This became the interpretative key for understanding deification in the Eastern Orthodox tradition in this time. According to Lossky, for example, who was largely responsible for championing the Palamite language of "divine energies" to speak about the real possibility of union with God, argued that the saints' experience of deification, presented more often than not in terms of light, was a specific reference to their vision of God's uncreated energies, and not his essence. He wrote, for example: "God is called light . . . not according to his essence but according to his divine energies."²⁹ And for Lossky, even in this illumined state, God, for the human person, remains beyond light, or in the words of the Areopagite cited by Lossky, "an experience of dazzling darkness of hidden silence."³⁰ Elsewhere Lossky is more explicit: "God lives absolutely inaccessible insofar as his essence is concerned and cannot be the object of knowledge or vision even for the blessed and the angels, to whom the divine being is revealed and has become knowable in his uncreated and deifying energies."³¹ Lossky argued that if humanity's union with God was on the level of essence, then human beings would be gods by nature which they are clearly not.³² Wanting to affirm the possibility for real union with God without compromising God's transcendence, Lossky believed that the distinction in unity between the essence and energies within the Godhead made possible the prospect of deification language without this leading to any pantheistic apotheosis. In this way, he believed that he was able to affirm humanity's real union with God while at the same time preserving God's inexhaustibility and transcendence. In concert with most Orthodox scholars, therefore, Lossky interpreted 2 Peter 1:4 as the possibility, graciously bestowed by God, for human persons to become partakers of God's uncreated energies.

Nellas, on the other hand, while not outrightly rejecting the conceptual understanding of deification as unity in the energies of God, sees this as only an initial step leading to unity in Christ. "Union according to energy," he notes, "is preparatory to hypostatic union; it is the union of communion of a betrothal."³³ Consistent with Nellas's person-centered approach, Papanikolaou succinctly notes that "personhood is the goal; the means are the energies of God."³⁴ Accordingly, having situated deification from within the context of a theology of 'image' and having identified it with Christ, he is now able to further explain that deification is nothing less than participation in the hypostasis of Christ. He thus writes that the ultimate purpose of deification for the human person is to be "enhypostasised in the Word . . . becoming the body of the Word."³⁵ It is the hypostatic union, therefore, which overcomes any separation between God and humanity leading to the latter's deification. In agreement with Nellas, Zizioulas also notes, "It is, therefore, precisely at the hypostatic level—the *hypostasis* of the Son—that *theosis* is realized through our adoption *by grace* (= in the Spirit) as sons in the Son."³⁶ Deification understood as Christification—in which the human person is called to become united to the hypostasis, or person of Christ—Nellas contends, reflects the scriptural vision of the spiritual life: "We know that union with Christ was defined by Paul, in an unequivocal and irrevocable manner, as the essence and purpose of the Christian life."[37] Further on, he explains in more detail citing certain key Pauline references: "to be made whole, [the human person] must put on 'the image of the heavenly' man who is Christ (1 Cor 15:49), in order to attain 'to the measure of the stature of the fullness of Christ' (Eph 4:13)."[38] For Nellas, it is Christ's condescension that makes possible humanity's union with Christ. He writes:

> Prior to the hypostatic union of the divine nature with the human, man even before the fall was anterior to Christ, a fact which means that even then, in spite of not having sinned, man had need of salvation, since he was an imperfect and incomplete "child." . . . Human nature could not have been completed simply by its tendency; it had to attain union with the Archetype . . . as long as human nature had not received the hypostasis of the Logos it was in some way without real hypostasis—it lacked real "subsistence" . . . The realisation of man as a truly completed "saved" being took place with the birth of Christ.[39]

Here Nellas emphasizes that the deification of humanity required the hypostasis of the Logos, becoming in this way the archetypical model for humanity and providing for its "true ontological content,"[40] namely, a Christlike form. Nellas is very clear that participation in Christ is only possible because of his faithfulness from the beginning to be united and formed in us, the result of which is humanity's recreation. In juxtaposing the experience of deification with ontology and more than mere moral assimilation (*imitatio Christi*), Nellas plainly asserts a real union effected by Christ, one in which "the most crucial and fundamental oppositions—those which are ontological, and therefore unbridgeable according to philosophy—are removed; the circle is squared."[41]

A further dimension relating to Nellas's understanding of the dynamic of Christification is the ecclesial framework in which he places humanity's communion with Christ. If Christification concerns being incorporated into Christ, then it is quite simply that it is within the context of the church that this becomes a concrete possibility. Indeed, for Nellas, the church is nothing less than Christ in actuality. He is quite explicit in this regard: "the blessed flesh of the Lord is none other than the Church. The "dominical body" . . . constitutes the place . . . in which salvation becomes concrete."[42] It follows that the church, as the living presence of Christ among his people, is the place *par excellence* in which Christ can be encountered.[43] In contrasting human persons' physical birth from that of their spiritual birth, Nellas poignantly identifies the extent of humanity's unity with Christ. He notes that whereas a child's birth into the world necessarily implies a separation between mother and child, humanity's spiritual birth, on the other hand, involves an inseparable connection with Christ. He writes, "Communion with our physical progenitors is no more than an image of true communion. Real communion is communion with Christ. . . . A marvellous synthesis thus takes place in which each person is unique and self-determining yet simultaneously an inseparable member of the body of Christ, functioning with the functions of Christ."[44] In this case, Nellas not only highlights the inextricable link between Christ and the *ekklesia* but also brings to the fore a more pervasive and interpenetrating dimension of fellowship in which the faithful are said to "identify" with Christ to such an extent that their actions are considered to be those of Christ. Elsewhere and on a similar note he argues that the church is "the perpetual marriage in space and time of the Creator with creation. . . . Through this unconfused mingling in Christ of created with uncreated nature, the created is subsumed into the flesh of Christ, is rehabilitated sacramentally, is transformed, becomes the body of Christ and lives as such."[45] It is for this reason that he sees the church as a constitutive element of Christification. Consequently, within the church, the innumerable possibilities for Christification become a reality enabling the "body" of the faithful to become one with Christ, their "head." Consequently, for Nellas, the church becomes a foundational premise for Christification insofar as it is the topos in which the faithful throughout the centuries can continue to be incorporated into Christ.

Christification as Human Becoming and Rationality's Renewal

Having affirmed a real union with Christ on the hypostatic level and its realization for the faithful throughout time within the context of the church, Nellas is equally clear that, in this transformative dynamic toward Christification, the anthropological dimension remains; more correctly it becomes its true self. Nellas argues that humanity's quest toward Christification, namely, this "mingling and mixing with God,"[46] also reveals what it means to be human. Born in Christ and united in him, human beings become truly human because of Christ who, as "the concrete realization of true humanity"[47] reveals the meaning of true humanity. According to Nellas, "the Lord inaugurates a new human ontology, and Christ constitutes the real progenitor of a new humanity."[48] This quest toward human becoming is patterned after Christ who through the incarnation, cross and resurrection revealed the true meaning of humanity. "The Saviour," Nellas writes, "was the first and only person to show us the true humanity which is perfect in manner of life and in all other respects."[49] It follows that for Nellas, Christ becomes not only the bridge uniting the human person to God but also the fulfilment of our human becoming. The quest toward Christification is equally a quest of human self-discovery. Enhypostasised into Christ, Nellas highlights that humanity "finds in Him its truth, its integral wholeness, its health and its current mode of functioning which stretches out to infinity."[50]

Indeed, for Nellas there can be no integral understanding of humanity without reference to Christ: "Looked at from the ontological point of view, this means that he is not yet a full and true man, and this is precisely because union with God is not some additional element but actually constitutes man. For a man to be a man he must become that which he was created to be."[51] In this way, human beings discover, in Christ, their ultimate end. Nellas is very clear in emphasizing that in Christ, "is revealed . . . the full development and activation of the faculties and functions of man."[52] Far from being a mere moral appropriation of Christ, salvation is ontological to the extent that it completes the person, otherwise, according to Nellas, "Christ would not have been something essential to man."[53] This Christologically conditioned anthropology is reminiscent of Saint Irenaeus, who in asking a series of rhetorical questions explicitly connects deification with human becoming. He asks: "How, then shall he be a god, who has not as yet been made a human?"[54] In the same way that the patristic tradition often used different analogies to shed light on this dynamic—most often the image of iron being cast into fire—so too does Nellas, relying on Cabasilas, explain this aspect of Christification as human becoming by relating it to the development of a fetus in a mother's womb: "Nature prepares the foetus, all through its dark and nocturnal life . . . and when it has been fashioned and formed here, it is thus born as a perfect man."[55] In presenting this life as the groundwork for humanity's true becoming in the age to come, Nellas understands the latter as the place where the human person is incorporated into Christ, and in so doing becomes a "true human person."[56]

Along the same lines and relying upon Saint Ignatius of Antioch, Behr points out that only in death is a human being "born into life receiv[ing] the pure light and strikingly be[coming] a human being in the state of Christ."[57] It follows that in this life human beings await their true birth, anticipate true life, and look forward to becoming genuinely human.

One further significant dimension of Nellas's understanding of Christification with respect to human becoming is its rational aspect. United to Christ, the incarnate Logos, human persons become truly rational, *logikoi*, enabling the reintegration of all faculties previously scattered and in conflict.[58] The etymological synonymity, in this case, between the Greek words for "reason" (λόγος, together with its cognate λέγω) and "gathering" (σύλογος, συλλέγω) should be noted. In Nellas, there is no contrariety between reason and salvation, as was often thought to be the case in twentieth-century Orthodox theology. In this way, experience and rationality are brought together, where the latter is viewed to be an integral part of the soteriological purview. While the theotic state, for Nellas, is explained in terms of life in Christ, this is no way excludes human rationality; on the contrary, its renewal is presupposed. Quoting Saint Athanasius, Nellas observes, "as our own reason (*logos*) is an image of the true Logos of the Son of God, so the wisdom that has been created in us, whereby we possess the power to know and to think, is likewise an image of his true Wisdom; and so by virtue of our human wisdom we are capable of receiving the Wisdom of the Creator."[59] Thus, far from standing in opposition, human reason is inseparably linked to Christification—and more broadly, deification—in which the former must learn to act in concert with divine wisdom, since Christ illumines the intellect as well. To conclude that human rationality is otherwise not assumed and saved in Christ, let alone spurned, would be nothing short of Apollinarianism. The early church's rejection of Apollinarianism, however, with the famous "that which is not assumed is not healed" signified "the fundamental justification of reason and thought"[60] in the Christian life. Baker succinctly sums this up: "The person of Jesus and his work, in all its absolute singularity, forms the keystone around which the whole rational structure of the cosmos and history is ordered and unified, the *Logos* in which all the *logoi* subsist."[61] For this reason, in no way does Nellas disparage humanity's quest for human knowledge. On the contrary, he writes, "the progress of man in scientific knowledge is not an arbitrary or fortuitous matter. Human knowledge develops because development is an intrinsic element of it. Human knowledge is driven by its own nature to raise itself up to the totality of knowledge."[62] The destiny of the human person in Christ is therefore to be raised to the level of supreme wisdom. It is at this point that Nellas underscores the indispensability of the church's sacraments and the ascetical struggle more generally, as the means by which this refashioning of all the human faculties take place, uniting and bringing them into alignment with the Logos.

The Gift and Living Out of Christification

If Christification, as we have seen, is a term Nellas uses to underline the reality of humanity's profound unity with Christ by which the human person becomes truly human, then the means and process by which this is actualized and personally realized within the context of the *ekklesia* is humanity's participation in the sacramental life of the church and one's ascetic struggle more generally. Quite simply, for Nellas, the sacraments, especially those of baptism, chrismation and eucharist, are the gracious means provided by the church which make possible a life in Christ to the extent that these make "the economy of the Saviour actively present once again."[63] In theologically reflecting on the sacraments in general, Nellas argues that it is more correct to view Christ as the primary sacrament, since it is He who "is refracted and becomes concrete and active within time through the sacramental mysteries"[64] in this way making himself available in actuality. Nellas understands the ascetical dimension, on the other hand, as the personal appropriation and living out of the sanctifying gifts bestowed by the church through the sacraments enabling the process of Christification. Put another way, whereas the sacramental mysteries are the gifts equipping a person toward Christification, the ascetical struggle, equally importantly, constitutes the journey toward the goal of unity with Christ. Accordingly, participation in the sacramental life of the church together with one's ascetical struggle are considered basic presuppositions for Christification. In setting the necessary groundwork that theologically brings Christification and the sacraments into a correlative relationship, Nellas briefly turns his attention to examine the particular sacraments of baptism, chrismation, and the eucharist. Baptism for Nellas is the first step toward Christification, since through this sacramental mystery the human person is spiritually reborn by being enhypostasized into the body of Christ, the church, and thus united with him in a most intimate way. And together with the sacrament of baptism, Nellas highlights the salvific significance of the eucharist.[65] Here Nellas wants to underscore, in the strongest possible way, that in partaking of the body and blood of the risen Lord, the faithful receive the whole Christ in reality and are therefore joined in a most profound and deep union with him. He writes, for example: "Here the union with Christ is complete and full. The whole person in all its dimensions, with all its psychosomatic senses and functions, is joined in a deep union with Christ, is transformed and christified."[66] For Nellas, therefore, baptism is the initial gift making Christification possible; the eucharist is the fulfillment of the initial gift. In this way, going further, he can identify Christ with the eucharist: "the eucharist is Christ."[67] Underscoring the reality of Christ in the eucharist, he is also able to write a little further on: "The historical body of Christ, as it lived, died and rose again, and as it shines glorified at the right hand of the Father, is found in reality on the altar and is offered to the faithful as a meal."[68] In this context, the Christification of the human person is therefore complete to the point, according to Nellas, that the faithful are also able to affirm, like Saint Paul in his letter to the Galatians, that "it is no longer I who live, but Christ who lives in me" (Gal 2:20). In reflecting further on the transformation of the bread and wine into the body and blood of Christ, Nellas notes that unlike the food that is consumed on a biological level, which is taken up by the physical body and transformed into sustenance for the body's survival, in the case of the eucharist, far from being *transformed*, on the contrary, it *transforms* believers into the body of Christ.[69] Quoting Cabasilas, he writes, "our food, whether fish or bread or any other kind of nourishment, is changed into human blood, into the person who consumes it. But in this case quite the opposite happens. The bread of life himself changes the person who feeds on him, transforms him and assimilates him to himself."[70] Nellas is concerned to demonstrate that Christification, in this case, is not so much humanity's ascent to God as it is Christ's descent down to, and union with, the communicant, wherein "all the human functions [are] transformed into functions of Christ."[71] In this way, far from understanding the saving effects of the eucharist in a metaphorical way, for Nellas, Christ's profound union with the faithful is interpreted in a genuinely literalist way.

As in the case of his understanding baptism, what is missing in Nellas's understanding of the eucharist for Christification is again the dynamic character of this sacrament, namely its gift-goal dimension. While the eucharist truly manifests the presence of Christ, it necessitates at the same time a calling for the faithful to make the fullness of this gift a reality. Namely, understood as the gift *par excellence* of *koinonia* with Christ, the eucharist is equally a calling for the faithful to grow in fidelity toward the goal of such unity, the fullness of which will only be experienced in God's future kingdom where Christ will truly be everything to everyone (cf. 1 Cor 15:28).[72] To be fair, Nellas does include within his vision of Christification a dynamic element, evident most clearly in his brief discussion on asceticism. Accordingly, Nellas notes that gifted with the grace of the church's sacraments more generally, the human person is equally called to strive to appropriate their saving effects in the living out of these through an ascetical predisposition. He maintains that the spiritual life involves essentially the gradual alignment of all that the human person thinks and does toward Christ. In this sense, Nellas is clear that while the sacraments actualize the Christification of the human person, they do so through ascetical struggle, which for him ultimately signifies learning to "live the life of love."[73] Without discussing the necessary relationship between sacramental theology and ascetical struggle at length, because he presumably takes this for granted, he turns his attention to offer a corrective to the ascetical ideal. Here Nellas first points out that all ascetical practices find their true meaning only to the extent that they point to Christ. Seen in this more positive light, asceticism, according to Nellas, has little to do with the renouncement of human potentialities in order to acquire the more so-called spiritual, and more to do with their alignment to Christ. He notes, for example: "This union and the subsequent change of the biological dimensions and functions of man into functions of the body of Christ, does not take place through the destruction of the former but through their transformation."[74] In reflecting further on the way in which human potentialities need to be reeducated and not eradicated, Nellas continues in this positive way by noting two essential requirements: first the study of the works and life of Christ, and second the constant reminder of the human person's dignity, or what he calls a "theocentric humanism."[75] The former, he argues, leads to a realization of God's "frenzied love"[76] for the human person, while the latter acts as a reminder for human persons to remain true to their essential being. Moreover, not only is his vision of the means toward Christification a positive one, but it is also more inclusive. Irrespective of diversity with regard to the way different members of the church may live their life—some as leaders, he points out, others as monastics or as lay members—the calling according to Nellas is one and the same, namely, "the concentration of the thoughts on Christ"[77] realized through prayer. Consequently, for Nellas, the sanctifying gifts of the sacraments, together with Christ-centered ascetical practices—prayer being at the forefront to the extent that it concentrates the mind on Christ and offers all things to Him—constitute a kind of road map leading to Christification.

In an attempt to explore the teaching of "deification," a term that received growing receptivity in twentieth-century discussions on soteriology, largely prompted by modern ecumenical conversations, the task was taken up to examine specifically the theological appropriacy of the concept of Christification, confident of its indubitable biblical underpinnings and congruity with the Christian tradition as a whole. This chapter invariably focused much of its attention on examining this incontrovertibly Christ-centered approach to theosis from one of its pioneering proponents within the Orthodox world of twentieth-century theology, Panayiotis Nellas. The significance of such an undertaking, especially from within the perspective of the Eastern Orthodox tradition, is all the more essential because Christification has typically been and continues to be overshadowed by more customary essence/energy distinction discourse. Five key aspects of his teaching concern his approach to Christification: (1) Its all-compassing nature, which brought together not only different Christian doctrines but also a vision that radically broadened the soteriological purview to include God's entire salvific economy outside and beyond the framework of the sin of Adam; (2) its emphasis on the dynamic or "synergetic" character of Christification, which integrated Christ's indwelling with that of humanity's active receptivity to the transformative grace of becoming the very image of Christ; (3) the assertion that humanity's unity is not simply on the "energetic" but rather on the hypostatic level, where humanity is said to be "enhypostasised" to the Logos, a teaching clearly consistent with the scriptural worldview; (4) the ecclesial framework in which Christification takes place, since the church was shown to be nothing less than the abiding presence of Christ in the world; and (5) the understanding of Christification as a process through which the person became truly human. It was here that we saw a further harmonization between Christification and human reason.

Quite simply, for Nellas, precisely because Christification and "human becoming" were shown to be intimately connected, then human reason—a constitutive element of the human person—necessarily also awaited its renewal, transformation, and Christification. Along with the patristic tradition, Nellas did in fact identify a link between the Logos (Λόγος) and a rational human being (λογικός). A consideration of these constituent elements of Nellas's understanding of Christification naturally led to an examination of Nellas's sacramental theology and ascetic worldview to the extent that these were seen as the means through which the process of Christification could be progressively actualized in the life of the faithful. These brought about a radically new mode of functioning, which was nothing less than a grace filled and Christ-centered mode of being. To be sure, in his presentation of Christification, Nellas captured a small snippet of God's inexhaustible and unfathomable love for the human person—and the world at large—where Christification became, a way of explaining humanity's origin and structure leading human persons to stand in awe and thanksgiving at the fascinating and tremendous mystery that God is, but equally importantly their ultimate destiny to become "christs" by grace. Nellas's comprehensive vision of deification therefore offers the world today a vision of life as "life in Christ," empowering it to live as Christ—through loving and serving as Christ—in this way, becoming one with Christ.

Notes

1. While deification was a central teaching in the patristic tradition, it needs to be admitted that it was only in the latter part of the twentieth century that this was reclaimed in the Eastern Orthodox tradition, especially with the rediscovery of the teaching of Saint Gregory Palamas and the *Philokalia*. John Meyendorff's renowned *Study of Gregory Palamas* (London: Faith Press, 1964) was instrumental in this regard, as was Georgios Mantzaridis's *Deification of Man: St Gregory Palamas and the Orthodox Tradition* (Crestwood, NY: St. Vladimir's Seminary Press, 1984). Interestingly, Russell contends that on the Orthodox side, renewed interest in Palamite studies during the twentieth century was a reaction to a less than favorable publication that appeared in the *Dictionnaire de théologie catholique* (1931) by the Roman Catholic scholar Martin Jugie, who had argued that Palamas's teaching on the essence/energy distinction was fundamentally wrong. See Norman Russell, *Fellow Workers with God: Orthodox Thinking on Theosis* (Crestwood, NY: St. Vladimir's Seminary Press, 2009), 14. In his seminal study on deification, Gross wrote, for example: "from the fourth century the doctrine of divinization is fundamental for the majority of the Greek fathers. It forms a kind of center of their soteriology." Jules Gross, *The Divinization of the Christian According to the Greek Fathers*, trans. Paul A. Onica (Anaheim, CA: A&C Press, 2002), 271.

2. In his contribution to the *Oxford Handbook of Systematic Theology* on salvation, Fiddes, for example, is quite clear in stating that the concept of deification "is increasingly taking a central place in all modern systematic theology." Paul S. Fiddes, "Salvation," *The Oxford Handbook of Systematic Theology*, ed. John Webster, Kathryn Tanner, and Iain Torrance (Oxford: Oxford University Press, 2007), 176. See also Paul Gavrilyuk, "The Retrieval of Deification: How a Once-Despised Archaism Became an Ecumenical Desideratum," *Modern Theology* 25, no. 4 (2009): 647–59. In "Deification in Contemporary Theology," *Theology Today* 64 (2007): 186–200, Roger E. Olsen offers an insightful survey of the different understandings of deification in both the Eastern and Western traditions, introducing the main proponents whose works are usually cited in relation to this concept.

3. Even though *apotheosis* may have, at first glance, been thought to correlate with the notion of "deification," the Eastern fathers, according to McGuckin, were careful to dissociate themselves from this understanding. He notes: "Deification (Greek: *theosis, theopoiesis*) was a bold use of language, deliberatively evocative of the pagan acclamations of *apotheosis* (humans, especially heroes, great sages, and latterly emperors, being advanced to the rank of deity) although that precise term was always strictly avoided by Christian writers because of its fundamentally pagan conceptions of creatures transgressing on divine prerogative: a blasphemous notion that several of the ancient Hellenes themselves . . . found worthy of denunciation." John A. McGuckin, "The Strategic Adaptation of Deification in the Cappadocians," in *Partakers of the Divine Nature: The History and Development of Deification in the Christian Traditions*, ed. Michael J. Christensen and Jeffery A. Wittung (Grand Rapids, MI: Baker Academic, 2008), 95.

4. Vladimir Lossky, *Orthodox Theology: An Introduction* (Crestwood, NY: St. Vladimir's Seminary Press, 1989), 72.

5. McGuckin, "Strategic Adaptation," 95.

6. Saint Athanasius, *On the Incarnation,* 54. PG 25.195B. Before him, Saint Irenaeus wrote: "in his immense love he became what we are, that he might make us what he is [*qui propter immensam suam dilectionem factus est quod sumus nos, uti nos perficeret esse quod est ipse*]." *Adversus Haereses* 5 praef. PG 7.1120B.

7. An expression, according to Louth, often found in the Latin fathers. Andrew Louth, "The Place of *Theosis* in Orthodox Theology," in Christensen and Wittung, *Partakers of the Divine Nature*, 34.

8. Panayiotis Nellas, *Deification in Christ: The Nature of the Human Person*, trans. Norman Russell (Crestwood, NY: St. Vladimir's Seminary Press, 1987), 33.

9. Russell, *Fellow Workers with God*, 47.

10. Like Nellas, Behr more recently has underscored what could be called the human aspect of deification. See John Behr, *John the Theologian and His Paschal Gospel* (Oxford: Oxford University Press, 2019), 194–244.

11. Panayiotis Nellas, "Redemption or Deification? Nicholas Cabasilas and Anselm's Question 'Why Did God Become Man?'" *Sourozh* 66 December (1996): 11.

12. Louth, "The Place of *Theosis*," 35.

13. Nellas, "Redemption or Deification," 11.

14. Following the patristic tradition, Nellas speaks not only of the human person's "obligation" to become Christlike (*Deification in Christ*, 28) but that humanity "has received the command to become a god" (30).

15. Ibid., 37–38.

16. Ibid., 39.

17. Nellas is very clear in this regard: "The natural and essential difference between created and uncreated nature is fathomless and unbridgeable." Nellas, "Redemption or Deification," 15.

18. Nellas, *Deification in Christ*, 24.

19. Ibid., 39.

20. Saint Athanasius, *On the Incarnation*, 3, trans. and ed. A Religious of C.S.M.V. (Crestwood, NY: St. Vladimir's Seminary Press, 1993), 28.

21. Saint Irenaeus, *On the Apostolic Preaching*, 22, trans. John Behr (Crestwood, NY: St. Vladimir's Seminary Press, 1997), 53–54.

22. Nellas, *Deification in Christ*, 35.

23. Ibid., 24.

24. Nellas, "Deification or Redemption," 16. See also Nicholas Cabasilas, *Life in Christ*, 6.12 Eng: "It was for the new human being (ἄνθρωπος) that human nature was created at the beginning, and for him mind and desire were prepared. . . . It was not the old Adam who was the model for the new, but the new Adam for the old. . . . Because of its nature, the old Adam might be considered the archetype to those who see him first, but for him who has everything before his eyes, the older is the imitation of the second. . . . To sum it up: the Savior first and alone showed to us the true human being (ἄνθρωπος), who is perfect on account of both character and life and in all other respects." Nicholas Cabasilas, *The Life in Christ* 6.12, trans. Carmino J. deCatanzaro (Crestwood, NY: St. Vladimir's Seminary Press, 1974), 190.

25. Nellas, *Deification in Christ*, 114.

26. See John Zizioulas, *Communion and Otherness: Further Studies in Personhood and the Church*, ed. Paul McPartlan (London: T&T Clark, 2006), 31n51: "*Theosis* is not simply a matter of participating in God's glory and other *natural* qualities, *common to all three persons of the Trinity*; it is also, or rather above all, our recognition and acceptance by the Father as his *sons* by grace, *in and through our incorporation into his only-begotten Son by nature*. . . . As to the fear, expressed by certain authors, that this may lead to the absorption of our personal particularities by the *hypostasis* of the Son, this is totally excluded in an

understanding of personhood as *communion in otherness*, according to which . . . personal union does not preclude, but on the contrary generates, otherness and particularity. This allows us to speak of Christ as *one* and *many* at the same time (*polyhypostasity*), i.e., of Christ not as an individual but as a *body*, the Church, in which alone *theosis* can be realized."

27. Aristotle Papanikolaou, "Divine Energies or Divine Personhood: Vladimir Lossky and John Zizioulas on Conceiving the Transcendent God," *Modern Theology* 19, no. 3 (2003): 357–85. See, for example: "Thus the significance of the union in Christ is not the communication of divine energies, but becoming a 'son' of God by transforming one's hypostasis through a relationship identical with that of the Son. Christ is the 'one' and the 'many' in whom our *hypostases* are not merged or absorbed, but transfigured, or rather reconstituted in the relationship which Christ has with the Father. It is within this relationship that the human person becomes, or exists eternally as a unique and unrepeatable being" (369).

28. Nellas, *Deification in Christ*, 36–37.

29. Vladimir Lossky, *Vision of God*, trans. Asheleigh Moorehouse (Crestwood, NY: St. Vladimir's Seminary Press, 1983). 160–61.

30. Vladimir Lossky, *The Mystical Theology of the Eastern Church* (Crestwood, NY: St. Vladimir's Seminary Press, 1976), 27. See Saint Dionysius the Areopagite, *Mystical Theology*, 1.

31. Lossky, *Vision of God*, 12.

32. Lossky, *Mystical Theology*, 69–70.

33. Nellas, "Redemption or Deification," 16.

34. A. Papanikolaou, "Divine Energies or Divine Personhood," 370.

35. Nellas, "Redemption or Deification," 13. Nellas argues that this teaching which for him is found in Cabasilas is in no way in conflict with the Palamite teaching of divine energies. On this, he specifically writes: "Kavasilas was in complete agreement with Palamas, but at the same time he brought the apostle Paul's terminology back to the forefront of theology and, taking it further, interpreted deification as true and real Christification." Nellas, "Redemption or Deification," 13.

36. J. Zizioulas, *Communion and Otherness*, ed. Paul McPartlan (London: T&T Clark, 2006), 31.

37. Nellas, "Redemption or Deification," 13.

38. Nellas, *Deification in Christ*, 24.

39. Ibid., 38.

40. Nellas, "Redemption or Deification," 18.

41. Ibid., 20.

42. Nellas, *Deification in Christ*, 113.

43. Nellas repeatedly depicts the church as the presence of Christ among the faithful. Elsewhere, for example, he writes: "God who before the incarnation

was "without house" as far as creation was concerned, now finds a created place in which to sojourn and dwell." Nellas, *Deification in Christ*, 145.

44. Ibid., 118.
45. Nellas, *Deification in Christ*, 143.
46. Ibid., 116.
47. Ibid.
48. Ibid., 112.
49. Ibid., 113. John Behr argues along the same lines: "Christ himself . . . is the first human being, strictly speaking, of whom Adam was but a foreshadowing." Behr, *Irenaeus of Lyons: Identifying Christianity* (Oxford: Oxford University Press, 2013), 171.
50. Nellas, *Deification in Christ*, 124.
51. Ibid., 116.
52. Ibid., 136.
53. Ibid.
54. *Adv. Haer.* 4.39.2. PG 7.1110B.
55. Nellas, *Deification in Christ*, 117. Elsewhere, Nellas makes the same point by directly quoting from Cabasilas: "Man hastens towards Christ by his nature, his will and his thoughts, not only because of his divinity, which is the goal of all things, but because of his other nature as well. He is the fulfilment of human love" (132–33). Furthermore, relying on Cabasilas, Nellas compares the unity that is realized with the world, overcoming any separation between God and humanity, to a perfume bottle when affected by the perfume, enables it to by enjoyed by its surroundings, so too, Christ's deified human nature joints God with the world. "The assumed matter, the Lord's body, henceforth functions for the rest of creation as 'chrism.' What happens, explains Kavasilas, is akin to that which occurs in the case of a phial containing perfume. When the sides of the phial are in some way changed into the contents, then instead of separating the perfume from the surrounding atmosphere they enable it to pervade it. 'Similarly, when our nature is deified in the Saviour's body, there is nothing which separates the human race from God.' Flesh was deified and human nature received God Himself as its hypostasis" (141–42).
56. Ibid., 117.
57. Behr, *John the Theologian*, 197.
58. Nellas, *Deification in Christ*, 25.
59. See Saint Athanasius, *On the Incarnation* 3. PG 25:101B: "In his own image, He made them, having also give to them a share in the power of his own Logos, so that having the Logos like a shadow [ἵνα ὥσπερ σκιᾶς τινας ἔχοντες τοῦ Λόγου καὶ γενόμενοι λογικοί], and having become rational, they might be able to remain in a state of blessedness, living truly the genuine life of the saints in paradise." Nellas, *Deification in Christ*, 28.

60. See G. Florovsky, "Revelation, Philosophy and Theology," in *Creation and Redemption* (Belmont, MA: Nordland Press, 1976), 48.

61. Matthew Baker, "'Theology Reasons' in History: Neo-Patristic Synthesis and the Renewal of Theological Rationality," Θεολογία 4 (2010): 111.

62. Nellas, *Deification in Christ*, 28.

63. Ibid., 143. Nicholas Denysenko offers an insightful study of the sacramental dimension of Cabasilas's work *The Life in Christ*, one that Nellas is reliant upon in his discussion of the sacraments and their relation to Christification. Denysenko, "*The Life in Christ* by Nicholas Cabasilas: A Mystagogical Work," *Studia Liturgica* 38 (2009): 242–60. Ladouceur also understands Nellas's vision of spiritual life in terms of "a process of Christification through the progressive realization of the full implications and benefits of the three principal sacraments." Paul Ladouceur, *Modern Orthodox Theology* (London: T&T Clark, 2019), 320.

64. Nellas, *Deification in Christ*, 142.

65. Cf. also Dumitru Stăniloae, *The Experience of God: Orthodox Dogmatic Theology; The Sanctifying Mysteries,* trans. Ioan Ioniță and Robert Barringer (Brookline, MA: Holy Cross Orthodox Press, 2012), 5:73: "If chrismation gives power to develop the new life in Christ received through baptism, it is through the eucharist that this life is perfected with Christ and the church."

66. Nellas, *Deification in Christ*, 127.

67. Ibid., 129.

68. Ibid., 129–30.

69. Ibid., 127–28.

70. Ibid., 128.

71. Ibid., 129.

72. For a more detailed analysis of this dynamic aspect of the Eucharist, see Philip Kariatlis, *Church as Communion: The Gift and Goal of Koinonia* (Sydney: St Andrew's Orthodox Press, 2011), 79–136.

73. Nellas, *Deification in Christ*, 145.

74. Ibid., 122–23. Elsewhere Nellas notes: "These functions are called to be purified and changed, to be filled with the Spirit of God and to function in a new manner closely attuned to the functions of the body of Christ. This will take place, not through the abandoning of these functions, but through a specific process of change and transformation which harnesses the work of man to the grace of God" (147).

75. Ibid., 145.

76. Ibid., 132.

77. Ibid., 134.

THEOSIS AS KENOSIS

THE PARADOX OF HOLY INTIMACY IN THE THEOLOGY OF HANS URS VON BALTHASAR

Carolyn Chau

Theosis, or divinization, is not a term that pervades the theology of Balthasar, even as his eschatology, most would agree, is all about participation in divine life.[1] Jonathan Ciraulo, and others, note the curious absence of the language of theosis from Balthasar's work, especially given the extent to which Balthasar drank from the wells of the Greek Fathers. According to Ciraulo, Balthasar is more focused on Ignatian *indiferencia*, and this, if anything, comprises the content of Balthasar's conception of theosis.[2] Deirdre Carabine also demonstrates various ways in which Balthasar transforms the Patristic concept of eschatological deification, from substantialist and ascent-focused models of theosis to existential and descent-oriented models of theosis.[3]

However, it has also been proposed that a theology of deification is in fact an organizing "inner logic" in Balthasar's corpus that may be traced from his theological aesthetics to his other works.[4] Indeed, in *The Eschatology of Hans Urs von Balthasar*, Nicholas Healy shows that "the end" is for Balthasar "creation taken into the divine life by means of sharing in the one hypostatic union of Christ."[5] We may say, then, that while the language of theosis is not prominent in Balthasar's writings, Balthasar's theology does include a rich conception of what it means to share in divine life, one that shifts divinization from the way it had been traditionally understood in Eastern theology toward a more scriptural vision that ties it inextricably to kenosis, the doctrine of Christ's descending, self-emptying love, and to *mission*, the act of being sent by God to the world. I will propose that Balthasar's Ignatian emphasis on mission is, indeed, Balthasar's unique specification of theosis.

To understand what theosis looks like in the thought of Balthasar, we will consider how the *analogia entis* and the Ignatian emphasis on mission conspire to recast theosis as kenosis.[6] We will see how theosis for Balthasar is not a straightforward return to God based on exemplary assent of faith or refinement of reason, but an ever-deepening love of Christ, being so moved by Christ as to take on his "mind," his existence of total obedience, self-surrender, and prayer such that one comes to share in his cross and in his descent; to share, in a word, his mission. Through these reflections we will argue that, paradoxically, we are nearest to God, and participate most in the life of God, as we allow ourselves to be moved outward from the heart of God into the world, in mission, remembering, at the same time, that all of creation is "in God," that all takes place in the *diastasis* between the persons of the Trinity. As we explore the paradox of theosis as kenosis and as mission, we will consider the attendant paradoxes of activity and receptivity and knowing and unknowing in the experience of becoming ever more intimately embedded in the life of God.

Theosis Challenged

Before proceeding to articulate the way in which the shape and content of theosis is, for Balthasar, kenosis, we consider Balthasar's critique of the traditional doctrine of divinization. In his essay "The Fathers, the Scholastics and Ourselves," Balthasar observes that the desire to "ascend to God, to become like God" has, since the Fall, contained within it a perversion of the genuine religious impulse, namely, "a revolt against the Creator, a disowning of the nature in which man was placed and created: the earthly, physical-psychic, communal, spatial-temporal existence."[7]

Without accusing the church fathers of being wrong about divinization, Balthasar does seek to correct what he sees as an excess or latent problem in the fundamental metaphysics of the patristic thinkers. "Spiritualization, Balthasar writes, is the basic tendency of the patristic epoch."[8] Neoplatonism, with its belief in a participatory and, ultimately, an emanationist ontology, understands the world as coming out of God, and so, in the end, returning to God through a reversal of the descent into materiality. Union with God is premised on a rejection or shedding of materiality, the nature that is not God, who is spiritual. The problem with this, for Balthasar, is that doing away with the very nature of human nature to attain God, is precisely the way to elude intimacy with God, for there can be no union where the difference between God and humanity is destroyed. Difference implies distance, *diastasis*, which is the condition for the possibility of unity.

Yet Balthasar acknowledges that the fathers do not, in the end, fall into a denial of the ever-greater difference between God and man, resisting at various turns any pantheism in their philosophy. They acknowledge that "all 'divinization' is only a participation from grace and never a fusion of nature." They are saved from falling into actual, thoroughgoing spiritualization and pantheism by "an authentic Christian shyness before the ineffable God who dwells beyond all seeing and grasping, the knowledge of God's eternal otherness and thus of his overpowering and ever-greater darkness even in the midst of his light."[9] The patristic sensitivity to divine mystery protects the analogical structure of their theologizing.

The scholastics, typically following the lead of Aristotle over Plato, refine further the basic "law of Christianity," of the fundamental ontological difference between Creator and creature, by embracing nature on its own terms. Thomas, Balthasar says, is the theologian of "nature": nature that is self-subsistent created being that enters into a relationship of participation in God, a relationship where mutual otherness is preserved. Thomas coins the principle, "The nearer a creature stands to God, the more it is capable of moving by virtue of its own powers."[10] This development guards against spiritualization but can fall into its own error of rationalism through overstating the role and capacity of reason, even as Thomas names the goal of human nature and life in terms of its supernatural end.[11]

Finally, as a capstone, the moderns discover the concrete and the individual, and recognize, according to Balthasar, the centrality of the personal, such that they also realize that God as personal God can only be known in and through divine self-disclosure. Revelation is the "personal self-disclosure of the divine majesty."[12] We, as creatures, must then receive and respond to this personal revealing in the here and now, in obediential response to the positive law or 'particularity' of divine revelation. The full recognition of God's presence to and in the worldliness of the world is achieved such that modernity has as its defining contribution to clarifying the law of Christianity that we meet God in the world, in history. In other words, modernity helps to underscore the concreteness of the concrete *analogia entis*, Jesus Christ; it embraces history and emphasizes that it is this world into which Christ has come, specifically, and it is in this world that we must follow him and find him in all things. Balthasar pauses to note how far we have come from a patristic notion of divinization, as he conceives of it: "And in this encounter [the creature] is told that he cannot 'divinize' himself by setting aside his nature. That can only happen, should it occur, on the basis of the permanent level of this nature."[13] That is, the ontological foundation of human nature, the revelation of Jesus Christ and our receptivity to it, is necessary for divinization.

Balthasar ends the essay by stating, essentially, that theosis, properly considered, is kenosis. Theosis is realizing that God is in the world, and we are invited to participate in God's descent in the world so as to sanctify it with love, and thereby, to share in the life of God.

Centrality of the *Analogia Entis*

For Balthasar the true way to strive to reach the "divine home" must be based on the most fundamental truth of God and creature: "God is God." We, "to the very marrow of [our] existence," are not God.[14] So, as the creature comes nearer to God and becomes more "similar" to him, Balthasar states, the dissimilarity must always appear as the more basic, as the "first truth."[15] Balthasar's famed emphasis on the *analogia entis* or the analogy of being, learned from his teacher, Erich Przywara, runs through his corpus as a key metaphysical commitment, and his understanding of how human beings share in the life of God abides by this principle. Whether in pointed dialogue with Karl Barth or not, Balthasar was always emphatic about the way in which, as per the Fourth Lateran Council, any similarity between God and humanity is always encompassed within an ever-greater dissimilarity. Accounts of divinization that ignore this basic truth and understand deification as a spiritualization or a rationalization that does away with human nature, or as an "absorption into divinity," to quote Carabine, are distorted understandings of what it means to achieve union with God or to share in his nature.

Theosis in Balthasar

In contrast to substantialist conceptions of deification that portray the end goal as the transformation of human nature into divine nature theosis is, for Balthasar, graced, Christological, pneumatological, trinitarian, eucharistic, ecclesial, and Marian. Much of this he learns from Maximus the Confessor. As Rowan Williams puts it, for Maximus,

God's *kenosis* of love, his *ekstasis* from his own nature in becoming human must be answered by human love and human *ekstasis* into the divine life . . . in a characteristic expression of Maximus, the human destiny is to become by grace what God is by nature (e.g. Amb. Liber. 1308B). And this is achieved by the indwelling of the Spirit, who realizes in us the sonship of Christ (ibid. 1345–1348).[16]

For Balthasar, too, becoming divine can only happen through grace. We do not come to participate in divine life through mere human spiritual practice or excellence, or through the general evolution of the human over the course of a life. Rather, theosis is a gift bestowed by a gracious God who invites us into his triune life of love by giving us his own Spirit, who enables us to live the life of the obedient, self-surrendering Son in our own unique human existence.

Grace enables us to live a Christological existence. Balthasar draws heavily on Maximus's conception of Christ as the fulfillment of humanity.[17] It is Maximus who, following the Christological controversies, utilizes the idea of mode of being (*tropos*), to further crystallize the achievement of Chalcedon. Tropos answers the question of *how* and *who* a being is, rather than simply *what* a being is. In the Incarnation, the Word has taken on a human nature, which remains fully human in essence, while taking on a new mode of existence, the mode of obedience, prayer, self-surrender.[18] Just as there is no confusion or separation of the two natures in the one subject of Christ, because Christ's unity lies in his personal existence, "where freedom, love and being are one,"[19] so, in deification, there is no blending or mixture of human and divine essences in creatures: "'Synthesis,' not 'confusion' is the first structural principle of all created being"[20] as well. Rather than a two-natures Christology that holds the natures in parallel and theosis as a return to the origin of divine being, then, attending to the category of Christ's mode of existence in Maximus means that theosis is about existing in Christ (*en Christo*), fully divine and fully human, and, in the concreteness of bodies and time, receiving a new mode of human existence, which we call mission. Christ is the concrete analogy of being, and mission and identity coincide perfectly in Christ alone. In and through Christ we participate analogically in the eternal, self-giving processions of the divine Godhead.

It should be clarified, though, that being "in Christ" is not simply a moral description; while we cannot talk of a mixture of essences, Balthasar will side with Augustine that Christ is not simply an example, but a sacrament. Expounding on the difference between Pelagius and Augustine and the metaphysical correctness of the latter's position, Balthasar writes, "Pelagius is satisfied with man's practical, 'ethical' approximation to Christ and with the presence of the Spirit that implies.' But an ethicism of this kind cannot stand without being linked to the ontic problem of the God/creature relationship and particularly that between infinite and finite freedom."[21] Divine freedom for Balthasar is the guarantor of human freedom: "Only in God's freedom can a human being find his 'exemplary identity.'" Christ is the sacrament of God who makes divine life present and invites us into divine life. Just as the divine and human natures exist in active circumincession in the person of Christ, so too, by analogy, human freedom can only be fulfilled in divine freedom. Indeed, Maximus succinctly portrays man's ascent within God's correlative descent in Christ.[22] We "become divine" as we are "inserted into" Christ's life of descending, self-giving love.

This "insertion into Christ," and hence the life of God, happens through the Spirit. When we allow the grace of the Spirit to take all that is "not-love" out of ourselves and fill it with the total self-giving, self-surrendering love that is God, we come to share in divine life. The Holy Spirit is the gift who enables us to be wholly conformed to the self-emptying Son, whose being is his mission. Participation in the processions of the divine persons is through a Christoform existence of prayer made possible by grace, faith, and the Holy Spirit. Prayer is the mode of total receptivity, and it is the mode of Christ's existence and time.

In a passage from his classic work *Prayer*, Balthasar underscores the gracious, trinitarian underpinnings of experiencing life in Christ and knowledge of God:

> We would never come to a knowledge of the triune life in Jesus Christ, not even on the basis of the "objective" elevation we have received in the "state of grace" (assuming that such a "state" could exist in pure objectivity), unless we had also been participants, from all eternity, in the subjective relationship of the incarnate Son with his heavenly Father in the Holy Spirit. If grace is also given by all three Persons in unity, it follows that grace gives us a participation in their threefold nature. In faith—and not in open sight—we are drawn into this threefold nature as a result of our meeting and fellowship with the Son on earth. From a strictly theological point of view, therefore, our

"seeing, hearing and touching of Jesus Christ, the "Word of life," mediates to us a knowledge (veiled, no doubt, but absolutely true and objective) of the triune life of God. Grace is our mode of sharing in this life; it therefore endows us with the appropriate subjective faculty so that, with the certainty of faith, we can see the trinitarian side of the phenomenon of Christ as the object of our contemplation. It is an essential, indeed it is the cardinal activity of Christian prayer to unfold this implicit faith knowledge, faith's "seeing, hearing and touching," in an ever-new seeking and finding. It does this precisely at the point where the incarnate Son, in complete openness, faces the Father in the Holy Spirit. Only in this way can the purpose of God's becoming man be fulfilled. That purpose is that God's inner nature and life should be opened up to us, should become familiar to us, and that we should experience with our very being, and hence also with our minds and senses, what it means to say that God is love.[23]

Balthasar leaves little doubt that we can indeed come to know the inner life of God. We come to a knowledge of the triune life of God through our encounter with Christ. Moreover, Balthasar says, we come to know the Trinity in Christ because we have been "participants, from all eternity" in the life of the Trinity. What does this mean? For Balthasar all of creation exists in the "space between," the *diastasis* between the Son and the Father. That is, the entire drama of time and history is a participation in the eternal Triune drama which God himself makes possible through the Incarnation. All creation, including time, exists in the kenotic space between the Father and the Son bound together by the Holy Spirit.[24] The initiative and the condition for the possibility of sharing in divine life is, therefore, from God and God's grace.

Faith then draws us into the life of God, in and through our encounter with the living Christ. Prayer is thus critical as the experience of holy intimacy with God cultivates faith; in prayer we receive the privilege of sharing in the relationship between the Son and the Father, of facing the Father, as the Son does, in the Holy Spirit. This divine life which is ours by grace, and not by nature, is, Balthasar says, an experience of truly knowing, "seeing, hearing, and touching" the Lord.[25] We know God with the certainty of faith, though we do not possess a complete knowledge of God. In fact, knowledge of God is not possessive at all but personal.

Balthasarian theosis radicalizes what we mean by knowing, the knowledge of God, and "rationality" by anchoring "faith knowledge" in the inner life of God, and clarifying that such knowledge is a personal knowing, knowing through encounter and communion rather than detached observation and analysis. The truth of the drama between God and humanity, the truth of salvation history as Balthasar sees it, is that Love is not something to behold, only, but something to be experienced and shared. For Balthasar, knowing God is not a matter of propositional knowledge but personal, intimate knowledge, communion. As Matthew Moser puts it, "Love itself is understanding." Faith enables us to perceive God and to reason in a fulsome way, rather than in a truncated, mind-centric conception of rationality. "Eternal life is essentially a communion of persons, and the paradoxes of unity and difference, and knowledge and mystery, are best engaged at the level of personal communion. In particular, the notion of God's abiding incomprehensibility in the eschaton, so dear to the Orthodox tradition, will become clearer in light of the structure of what we can call 'personal knowing.'"[26] That is, in knowing God, and, according to Balthasar, God reveals himself to us completely—Christ is not a partial revelation but a full revelation of divine glory—we must recognize that we know God as mystery, for to know in the personal sense is to perceive and to appreciate the unfathomable depths of the other as other, to revel in their mystery. Balthasar does not believe that God's ungraspability means there is more to God than we are given. To quote Carabine, "The 'dazzling darkness of divine beauty is not that which remains inaccessible to human understanding, but the splendour of the love of God,' which gives itself without remainder."[27] Yet, the more we "know" God in the sense of personal knowing, the more aware we are of God's being as mystery.

Faith helps to bring us closer to the divine, and it helps us to see how little we "know." As Nicholas Healy points out, knowledge also always has an element of unknowing—Balthasar elaborates this in *Theologic I*; another way of putting this is that unknowing is constitutive of any knowing. To truly "know" in a nonmonological way requires that the mystery of being remain itself in its difference. We know only as we allow ourselves to participate in a dynamic encounter with the other, and refrain from subsuming the other under our own knowledge structures. To know, then, involves an absence of knowledge and a trust that 'builds a bridge' over that absence of knowledge. And so, faith as a form of trust, we may also say, is crucial to the knowing process. It spurs us on in our journey to greater understanding and communion.

In contrast to a Kantian framework that maps out the limits of reason to make room for faith, Balthasar portrays faith and reason in a kind of symbiotic relationship that also involves paradox, namely: as we grow in intimacy with God, our reason helps us to recognize how deeply we are not God, and faith propels us to pursue closeness and likeness to God nonetheless.

We have often heard it said that the saints, those whose lives share most in God's own holiness, who live out of the divine pleroma of love, are the very ones who are most conscious of their sinfulness and distance from the Holy One. Balthasar's account of participation in the life of God seems to illuminate this idea: approaching ever closer to divine goodness brings with it an attunement to the incomparable perfection of God. The saints who approximate better than anyone the concrete *analogia entis* show with their lives of total availability to divine will their recognition of the ever-greater dissimilarity. The awareness is a faith-guided rationality, a rationality that is keenly conscious of "God's uniqueness and incomparability, with a reverence that nevertheless refrains from 'turning into an inhibiting fear which would refuse the proffered intimacy.'"[28] The awareness is a revelation-informed wisdom that holds the mean between reverence that falls into a sense of guilt-ridden unworthiness and a presumptuous faith that elides the difference between God and creature.

Theosis is, then, a dynamic process involving a paradox of nearness and distance between God and creature. Rather than seeing the world as remote from the Godhead, Balthasar understands Christ as the inner principle of all that is real, that Christ is "nearer to me than I am to myself"; by the same token, all that has any reality at all is "in Christ." The process of divinizing transformation is allowing God who *is* in all to *be* in all, and recognizing at the same time that all *is* in God and enabling all to *be* in God. This is the path and the task that human freedom is called to undertake. As Brendan McInerny has pointed out, deification is a process that moves in two directions: we become incorporated into divine life, and God is "incorporated" into all of creation.[29]

We become participants in the life of the Triune God and God is all in all through Christ and the work of the Holy Spirit, present at creation, the Incarnation, the crucifixion, and the Eucharist. Each is a form of universalization and concretization of Christ's presence in the world. Paradoxically,

Christ reveals most fully the glory of God in the world on the cross, when he is, it seems, furthest, most abandoned by the Father. For it is here that Christ is completely united to the Father through the person of the Holy Spirit, whose love holds them through the most terrible tearing asunder for the sake of love.

It is the Holy Spirit who enables Christ's bodily presence to be given to us in time, in the Eucharist. The Eucharist is the privileged point of access to divine grace, Christ's ongoing gift of self to us made possible through the "liquefying" action of the Holy Spirit.[30] That is to say, the Spirit universalizes Christ's action in the world in and through the concrete giving and receiving of Christ's body. More than any other human experience, the Eucharist is God's tangible gift of self to us in the present. Balthasar states, "Our participation in the Incarnation actually becomes deeper and deeper and more and more effective, because the divine realm never discloses itself to us except in the self-offering of Christ's flesh and blood" (6:53–57).[31] It is in the Eucharist that we are invited, by Christ's *ek-static* gift of self to thereby make our own *ek-static* gift of self to God and to God's creation in response. Healy highlights Balthasar's ongoing emphasis on the reality of God's self-gift: God does not withhold God's substance in the mediation of Christ to us, and this is evident, above all, in the Eucharist. In the Eucharist, Christ gives all of who He is to us, and we receive all that He is and give all of who we are back to Christ. For the Eucharist may also be considered the epitome of the nuptial mystery of the unity between Christ and the church.[32] This is what it means to say that there is a concrete reciprocal exchange between persons in the liturgy of the Mass. Indeed, the sacraments in general introduce us to the Christological mode of life—through them we encounter Christ and receive "the possibility, given . . . in faith, of becoming like him who became man."[33]

In addition to the mediation and agency of Christ and the Holy Spirit, the church plays a role in human subjects becoming persons "born from above." Beyond the incomparable way in which the church offers the presence of Christ in the Eucharist, the church more generally effects a transformation in persons such that they become expropriated for ecclesial mission, for participation and service in Christ's own life and mission. Balthasar calls this becoming a theological person, *homo ecclesiasticus*, and person *tout court*. What he means is that the life of eternal self-giving love that is the Holy Trinity becomes the very life of those who allow themselves to be "taken into service" by the Holy Spirit in and through the church. Such an "ecclesial person" can be said to be divinized insofar as her life is now lived completely in Christ, outside of herself, for love of God and neighbor. Her life is formed and conformed to the mission and destiny set out for it by God and is expressed in the ongoing life of kenotic prayer and action that define it. She is no longer her own master, but the one whose life is given for others for the fruitfulness of ecclesial life, mission, and ultimately, the mission of Christ. This process of becoming truly human in and through the Church is another way of talking about divinization in Balthasar, for Christ's mission, the acting area, is a "personal and personalizing area."[34] We are most "divine" when we become the persons we are called in Christ to be. Thérèse of Lisieux, who worked so hard to enter into the mysteries of Christ's life and to allow Love to fashion her existence in every mundane manner, is an example of such personalization.[35] Theosis is thus also Marian, since Mary exemplifies total openness and receptivity to divine love and divine will, particularly with her *fiat*, and this receptivity shows how she lives *en Christo*.[36]

Theosis as Kenosis

We thus come upon the key paradox of holy intimacy in Balthasar's conception of theosis: we are most united with God, most a part of the divine mystery of love when we are sent out by God on mission. It is in taking the stance of kenosis, of self-giving, of self-surrendering love, and allowing ourselves to be expropriated in service of God, the church, and the world, that we experience most deeply the holy intimacy of being adopted children of God, that we realize most what it means to be born of God, through the work of the Spirit.

As Christ's own kenosis in his Incarnation, death, and descent into hell shows us, we must be in the "heart of the world," in the "far country," to truly participate in divine life, to know the joy of divine, total self-giving love. Dwelling in Christ and allowing Christ to dwell in us leads to divinization that appears as the glory of God revealed in the form of a person. For Balthasar, a person is not the same as a conscious subject. Balthasar famously criticizes the way in which there has been widespread and repeated conflation in modern discourse of individuality, individuation, being a conscious subject, and personhood. In contrast, Balthasar holds that the term "person" ought to be reserved for the one who becomes who they are *in Christ*, for a *theological* person, for one who lives completely for God and allows their divinely ordained call to express itself in their life and whose life is therefore a mission.

> If grace grants us a share in the divine nature (2 Pet 1:4), and if this elevates and transfigures the created image into a similitude, it follows that the person thus endowed with grace must participate in the triune life in ways that are ever new and ever more profound.... However, it is not simply that the *imago* is a foundation on which heaven builds the *similitudo* in an entirely different style: rather, it is created man, as the conscious subject that he is, who is given his true purpose in the divine, triune life. In that trusting self-surrender to God that we call the faith that hopes and loves, and which Christ performed on earth in an exemplary way, as our prototype (Heb 12:2), man both transcends himself and lives in Christ, or allows Christ to live in him: "It is no longer I who live, but Christ who lives in me; and the life I now live in the flesh I live by faith in the Son of God, who loved me and gave himself for me" (Gal 2:20). Loving, vibrant faith is the factor that assimilates us to Christ—"that Christ may dwell in your hearts through faith" (Eph 3:17)—which entails the indwelling of the "We" of the Trinity also (Jn 14:23, and so forth).[37]

Grace and self-surrendering faith together make us true sharers in divine life. As Christ, "our prototype" is most divine when he is "made sin" for us on the cross, and in hell, confronting the sin in the heart of the world with love, likewise, in faith and love we are called to enact our mission through receiving it from the Father.

Following Christ to share in divine life means that deification for Balthasar is also Christification. If deification is Christification, we may say that it involves the further paradox of receptivity as the deepest form of activity, for Christ's mode, "Christ's time," is one of pure receptivity.[38] Christ in his human existence chooses at every moment, only that the will of the Father be done. His stance is one of attention, waiting, but never anticipation. Anticipation, Balthasar notes, is precisely the attitude of one who resists time, who tries to leap over it, or get around it, whereas Christ is the one who, in his humanity, lives time fully and thus redeems it. The paradox of Christ's receptivity and his "faith": he is nearest to God, he *is* God, and yet he walks as a man in time, without anticipation. In this way, the way of receptive obedience, Christ makes real all that exists in history, by fashioning everything in and through humility and love.

Similarly, the more receptive we are, the more efficacious our lives; the nearer we are to Christ, the more we live in the mode of receiving, as Christ, in faith, receives from the Father. In this ongoing act of receptivity, we realize God's ever-greater power as love (or divine power as love), working in us. In receiving the will of God to love, in loving, we participate in the divine transformation of the world. We make space for the life of Christ and the Spirit to increase in us and to flow through us to our neighbor.

We can say, then, that kenosis is not a "bottoming out" of theosis, but the full extent of theosis. To become divine is to descend as God descends into the world, into its muck and misery. As such, kenosis can look really difficult in the present moment, it can involve suffering, and being present to suffering. It leads us to, in a word, solidarity. And, as we deepen the love between creatures through deepening the love between God and humanity, we nurture and embody ever more the communion that characterizes the life of the Triune God.

Balthasar's reframing, however, of theosis as kenosis is not without challenges or contentions. Some may wonder why Balthasar's account of theosis is not substantialist, since that would seem to be a more thoroughgoing expression of a kenotic God, namely, God giving God's very being to creatures. Given Balthasar's emphasis on the kenotic character of deification, it may seem reasonable to ask why he resists the move to assert that God gives his very essence to humanity, and that in theosis, human beings partake substantially in the divine nature itself. Would this not be the meaning of what it is to make a total gift of self to another? Balthasar's nonsubstantialist though ontologically real account of theosis goes back to Balthasar's understanding of the line that must not be crossed theologically, that of the analogy of being. Humans must remain human and God remain God for there to be true relationality, intimacy, and communion. Relationality, intimacy, and communion can only exist among separate people. The similarity or likeness of creature to God, even in deification, always exists within an ever-greater dissimilarity; otherwise the reality of the creature would be threatened, and the creature's freedom would be crushed. Balthasar is committed to an understanding of God as valuing creation as creation in its irreducible difference.

Another way to address the question is to probe what it means to even speak of God's essence outside of God's love. That is to say, one cannot speak of a preexistent essence before God's love, as God's essence is already relational and communal; for this to remain true, the creature cannot be sublated into divine being, even in theosis. True kenosis is the self-gift that, according to Nicholas Healy, involves also the making of space for the freedom of the other to give in return. Healy thus discusses the possibility of receptivity in God to the self-gift of the creature. This of course gives rise to concerns about divine impassibility and immutability and whether the doctrine of divine immutability is undermined by such a radical proposal. Does theosis mean that God must be receptive to finite being? The question has received treatment by scholars who make a compelling case for the view that for Balthasar receptivity to created being does not imply any lack or need by God of creation, but is part of God's being as love, an extension of divine perfection.[39]

A criticism of theosis as kenosis that comes from a different direction is that of those who oppose kenosis as a universally viable stance for all human beings. Many feminists and advocates for other marginalized persons have criticized Balthasar for his exaltation of kenosis as the fundamental pattern of Christian existence, arguing that kenosis is not a viable option for those who have no self to empty. Some, such as Sarah Coakley, have tried to counter this view.[40] It remains important in such a dialogue to be clear about what Balthasar actually means by the term. Kenosis is not so much a matter of emptying oneself for others; it is rather about understanding one's life and one's being as a gift for all, and standing out, in the radiance of divine love, as a witness to that love. This is not the same as self-destructive, self-abhorrent abnegation, but is instead a testimony to one's own being as God's beloved and God's intimate friend, called to live and to love as God lived and loved, with a capacity to give new life to others.

Others may find Balthasar's account of theosis unappealing depending on the degree to which one is Thomistic or Palamite on the issue of human participation in divine knowing. According to Healy, Balthasar is an interesting position of mediation in the comparative positions of Aquinas and Gregory Palamas on the nature of divine knowing and human participation in divine life.[41] The question of what actually occurs in theosis has long been a debate about what manner and to what degree God and humanity, respectively, are involved in the process. If Aquinas is right, there is a participation in the being of God through the creature's creaturely capacity to know, as elevated by the *lumen gloriae*. While the light of glory is not the created intellect as such, it may be said to be created light that helps adapt the created intellect to receive that by which we know God's essence.

Thus, it is not God who does all the work of rendering us one with him, but a true engagement of the created human intellect in knowing God.

If Palamas is correct, it is not possible for the creature to attain to God in this manner, for God is the one who is beyond human knowing. Humans can know the divine energies, but the essence of God is unknowable. Moreover, whatever makes union with God and knowledge of God possible must come from the side of God as God alone can divinize. Thus, it must be uncreated grace that brings about theosis, and while there is correspondence between God's essence and God's energies, they are not the same. For Palamas, there is no room for created grace to act in such a way as to make possible a participation in God's inner life.

Balthasar, Healy argues, in contrast to both of these positions shows how Balthasar wishes to maintain the robust distinction between God and creature *and* preserve the capacity of the creature as creature to be truly active in the process of participating in the life of the triune God. He does this through his unique narration of what participation consists in, namely, life in Christ, the concrete *analogia entis*, through reception of God's own being in the Eucharist, opening oneself to the Holy Spirit, who then allows one to be in Christ and enact one's mission in the world, which includes an ongoing act of total self-surrender to the will of God, an obedience to the divine call at every moment, and giving oneself as gift for the life of the world, as Christ does. Interestingly and paradoxically, it is from being most intimately grounded in the triune life of God that one can extend oneself toward that which is most not like God, that which is most forsaken, tragic, broken. This is the kenotic pattern of theosis for Balthasar, the missionary, descending, existential pattern of participation in divine life.

Participation as Mission

Theosis is, then, for Balthasar, a participation in the processions of the Godhead through responding to one's call to mission, and becoming, thereby, analogically speaking, a person in Christ. Theosis is realizing that God is in the world, and we are invited to participate in God's descent in the world so as to sanctify it with love and, thereby, to share in the life of God. Theosis as kenosis means obedience, mission, and living in the mode of praise, reverence, and service as we receive the gift of adopted childhood and friendship from the Lord. The Son took on the form of a servant, and through Him, through living in Him, we are called in our servanthood, to be sons and daughters of God.[42]

We are called to be expropriated for true personalization and freedom, for the more we become *personae Christi*, the more we share in the life of God, the more we are who we are. With the understanding that all are "in" Christ, the movement toward true human freedom is, in Balthasar's theology, an allowing of ourselves to be expropriated, by grace, and appropriated, so to speak, by the Holy Spirit, who moves us ever more into Christoform existence. A Christoform life is one in which action is mission and mission the expression of ongoing, ceaseless prayer, a life that is one with the perichoretic self-giving love that we call the Trinity.

We can thus see how Balthasar shifts the terms of classical theosis rather dramatically in several ways. Whereas some patristic discussions of theosis centered on essences, Balthasar's account emphasizes the way in which participation in divine life crucially involves and respects human freedom. Balthasar expounds the way in which divine freedom invites human freedom into the divine dance of love through the attraction of divine glory and the gift of divine grace. Balthasar's account offers salutary warnings against possible conceptions of theosis that may seem to describe divinization as a kind of human achievement, elevation, and victory; in contrast, he focuses on the element of receptivity to and humility before the divine will. There is nothing self-aggrandizing about theosis in Balthasar; however, it is not gratuitous self-abasement, either. Rather, it is the glory of love that triumphs in Balthasar's account of divinization, the thoroughgoing credibility and integrity of divine love that, true to its form, gives itself to humanity and receives enrichment too, from finite, broken creatures. Finally, theosis as kenosis reveals that love takes the form of service, not power as might. It is not an increase in human noetic capacities in an impersonal sense, but an ability to love, and to be in communion in a way that exceeds all human imagining.

Notes

1. See Brendan McInerny, "Sharing in Triune Glory: Balthasar's Theological Aesthetics and Deification," *Cithara* 52, no. 1 (2012): 50–64; Jonathan Martin Ciraulo, "Hans Urs von Balthasar's Indifference to Divinization," in *Mystical Doctrines of Deification: Case Studies in the Christian Tradition* (London: Routledge, 2019), 165–85; Anthony Cirelli, "Form and Freedom: Patristic Retrieval and the Liberating Encounter between God and Man in the Thought of Hans Urs von Balthasar," PhD diss., Catholic University of America, 2007;

Chris Hadley, "The All-Embracing Frame: Distance in the Trinitarian Theology of Hans Urs von Balthasar," PhD diss., Marquette University, 2015.

2. See Ciraulo, *Mystical Doctrines*.

3. See Deirdre Carabine, "The Fathers: The Church's Intimate, Youthful Diary," in *The Beauty of Christ*, ed. Bede McGregor and Thomas Norris (Edinburgh: T & T Clark, 1994), 74–91.

4. See McInerny, "Sharing."

5. Nicholas J. Healy, *The Eschatology of Hans Urs von Balthasar: Being as Communion* (Oxford: Oxford University Press, 2005), 188.

6. A book on this topic was published after the original manuscript of this chapter had been submitted. See Sigurd Lefsrud, *Kenosis in Theosis: An Exploration of Balthasar's Theology of Deification* (Eugene, OR: Pickwick Publications, 2020) for a monograph-length treatment of this topic, which corroborates and expounds in more fulsome way the argument sketched here.

7. Hans Urs von Balthasar, "The Fathers, The Scholastics, and Ourselves," *Communio* 24 (1997): 353.

8. Ibid., 375.

9. Ibid., 377.

10. Ibid., 381.

11. Further, "On this foundation the (Platonic) order of grace is constructed without any longer undermining the foundation itself. For since grace is no longer a pneumatic *substance* (as it is in the murky anthropological "Pneuma" of the patristic period) but a modification (even if an unheard of one) of the natural substance (an *accidens*), all participation in a unification with God can be viewed from now on as a simultaneous perfection and crowning of the "naturality" of nature." Ibid., 382.

12. Ibid., 387.

13. Ibid., 389.

14. Ibid., 354.

15. "Balthasar always emphasizes the need to guard against delusions regarding the human spirit's adequacy in its ascent toward God and to reject the illusion of any kind of identity between creation and God according to nature. He insists on the "gift" quality of God's descent to the world in mercy and grace and he favors Gregory's [of Nyssa's] common insistence on it." Hadley, "The All-Embracing Frame," 31.

16. Rowan Williams, *The Wound of Knowledge: Christian Spirituality from the New Testament to Saint John of the Cross* (London: Cowley Publications, 1991), 132.

17. Carabine, "The Fathers," 82.

18. See Mark L. Yenson, *Existence as Prayer: The Consciousness of Christ in the Theology of Hans Urs von Balthasar* (New York: Peter Lang, 2014), and

Mark A. McIntosh, *Christology from Within: Spirituality and the Incarnation in Hans Urs von Balthasar* (Notre Dame, IN: University of Notre Dame Press, 2000).

19. Balthasar, *Cosmic Liturgy: The Universe According to Maximus the Confessor* (San Francisco; Ignatius Press, 2003), 260.

20. Yenson, *Existence as Prayer*, 45.

21. Balthasar, *Theo-drama: Theological Dramatic Theory*, vol. IV, *The Action*, trans. Graham Harrison (San Francisco: Ignatius Press, 1994), 379–80.

22. Hans Urs von Balthasar, *Theo-drama: Theological Dramatic* Theory, vol. II, *Dramatis Personae: Man in God*, trans. Graham Harrison (San Francisco: Ignatius Press, 1990).

23. Hans Urs von Balthasar, *Prayer*, trans. Graham Harrison (San Francisco: Ignatius Press, 1986), 178–79.

24. See Hans Urs von Balthasar, *A Theology of History* (San Francisco: Ignatius Press, 1994), for an elaboration of this idea.

25. Mark McInroy clarifies the relationship between nature, grace, and the spiritual senses thus: "We are destined to have physical and spiritual perception, even if we cannot attain that destiny by our own natural powers. The spiritual senses are received from 'outside,' to be sure, but they are also used 'spontaneously.' The spiritual senses become the human being's *own* in that they are used in an active response to the grace that is granted to him or her." See McInroy, *Balthasar on the Spiritual Senses: Perceiving Splendour* (Oxford: Oxford University Press, 2014).

26. See Healy, *Eschatology*, 179.

27. Carabine, "The Fathers," 87.

28. Balthasar, *Dramatis Personae: Man in God*, 401.

29. McInerny, "Sharing," 61. Note that the distance of alienation between God and creatures due to sin is not what we are talking about here. For an in-depth look at the various ways in which diastasis functions in the theology of von Balthasar, I recommend Chris Hadley's dissertation on the topic.

30. Healy, *Eschatology*, 195.

31. Balthasar, *Theo-Logic: Theological Logical Theory*, vol. III, *The Spirit of Truth*. trans. Graham Harrison (San Francisco: Ignatius Press, 2005), 75.

32. Healy, *Eschatology*, 195–200.

33. Balthasar, *Theology of History*, 97.

34. Balthasar, *Theo-Drama: Theological Dramatic Theory*, vol. III, *Dramatis Personae: Persons in Christ*, trans. Graham Harrison (San Francisco: Ignatius Press, 1992), 248.

35. McIntosh, *Christology from Within*, 23–24.

36. Ciraulo's article on Balthasarian theosis as Ignatian indifference expounds on how theosis is also Marian for von Balthasar.

37. Balthasar, *Dramatis Personae: Persons in Christ*, 528.

38. Balthasar, *Theology of History*, ch. 1.

39. See O'Hanlon, *The Immutability of God in the Theology of Hans Urs von Balthasar* (Cambridge: Cambridge University Press, 1990).

40. See Sarah Coakley, "Kenosis and Subversion: On the Repression of 'Vulnerability' in Christian Feminist Writing," in *Powers and Submissions: Spirituality, Philosophy, and Gender* (Oxford: Blackwell Publishers Ltd, 2002), 3–39; Aristotle Papanikolaou, "Person, *Kenosis,* and Abuse: Balthasar in Conversation with Feminist Theology," *Modern Theology* 19, no. 1 (2003): 41–65; Carolyn Chau, "'What Could Possibly Be Given?': Towards an Exploration of Kenosis as Forgiveness—Continuing the Conversation between Coakley, Hampson, and Papanikolaou," *Modern Theology* 28, no. 1 (2012): 1–24; Jennifer Newsome Martin, "The 'Whence' and the 'Whither' of Balthasar's Gendered Theology: Rehabilitating Kenosis for Feminist Theology," *Modern Theology* 31, no. 2 (2015): 211–34; Annie Selak, "Orthodoxy, Orthopraxis, and Orthopathy: Evaluating the Feminist Kenosis Debate," *Modern Theology* 33, no. 4 (2017): 529–48.

41. See Healy, *Eschatology*, 169–79, for an excellent discussion of the created/uncreated grace debate.

42. Simone Weil, *Gravity and Grace* (Lincoln: University of Nebraska Press, 1997): "Falling toward the heights . . . what grace, raised to the second degree, causes us to be raised as we fall further?"

Martin Luther on Faith and Union with God

Speculations on Theosis

Kirsi Stjerna

Martin Luther's "faith vision" provides a constructive window to his justification language and its resonance with the Eastern Orthodox teaching of theosis. The foundation for the reflection is in the late Finnish Luther scholar Tuomo Mannermaa's (1937–2015) pioneering thesis on the compatibility of Luther's view of justification as a union with Christ in faith with the patristic vision of theosis and the idea of participation in God.[1]

The aim here is not to provide radically new arguments or documentation on the matter but to clarify the case Mannermaa originally made and to offer a slight shift in approach to further suggest the value of the ongoing ecumenically promising theosis conversation and keeping Luther involved in that.[2] The focus, however, is on faith in Luther's theological language and imagination.

Faith Language with Luther and Theosis?

Martin Luther's central theological interest was the dynamics of the God/human relationship. Existentially, he sought from the Scriptures for sources of hope to counter the spiritual—and probably psychological—anxiety (*Angst*) he felt. With life-changing insights from Paul's letters to the Romans and the Galatians in particular, he found grounding for both eschatological hope and the parameters for life here and now in God and in a restored relationship with God.[3] To borrow the expression of the Lutheran theologian

Paul Tillich, Luther named the ground of being and all that it entails—security, orientation, hope, responsibility, and happiness—in God.[4]

The reformer developed a particular "faith language" about the transformation he personally experienced and that he, as a preacher and a teacher, sought to explain to others. Not a scientific formula with proofs, not aiming at poetic or symbolic expression, faith language for Luther is a particular dialect about reality, one with a theological premise. The word *faith—fides, die Glaube*—is pivotal in his theological language and particularly in his "justification grammar," with which he describes the promised restoration of God/human relationship on the basis of "faith alone."[5]

Luther's understanding of justification by faith alone has been interpreted as a divine act of a human being "made right" with God, to use the language of Alister McGrath and Gerhard Forde, notable English-speaking interpreters of the doctrine. That is, a justified person is considered forgiven, righteous, and thereby worthy of a loving relationship with the God of grace and justice.[6] Faith in such a logic is deemed a gift, which is a fundamental starting point for Lutheran theology and for Lutheran statements on justification and the premises of a God/human relation; the foundation is a gift, something that is gifted to the human being, and that has God as the subject and the source.

From a human perspective, from the point of the recipient of this gift, faith can be experienced as a form of trust.[7] The word seems—albeit falsely—to imply passivity. Namely, faith in Luther's justification grammar represents the opposite to any human effort or conscious decision or saving knowledge. In that regard, faith as trust in God's action entails passivity in that the human being is solely the recipient and not the doer. At the same time, faith is the most active word in Luther's theology. That faith "does" what happens in justification for and to and in the human being deserves renewed attention, and it is an important factor in considering the different dimensions of justification.

For Luther, it appears, it is less important to define the content of the justifying faith in detail while the emphasis is on what is said "with" it: to point to the gift nature of salvation—that is, the redeemed human/God relationship and all that comes with that—versus something human beings could earn, manufacture, cause, or choose by themselves. This emphasis that is traditionally referred to as "forensic" language underscores the *extra nos* nature of grace and justification as a form of forgiveness from guilt and judgment, and it allows the word faith to remain quite passive or abstract. In this case, the "what" of justification also may seem ambiguous in terms of its real impact on and in the person's being and existence.

Whereas the forensic emphasis has dominated Lutheran theological discourse, for Luther himself this was just one dimension of what happens in justification. Justification also induces or "effects" a reality change in terms of the perspective and the existential condition human beings can expect. This is typically named as the "effective" side of justification. In both forensic and effective languages about the justification in Luther's argumentation, faith is instrumental; faith is the key to each argument Luther makes about justification, and it opens up a vista to imagine the new reality justification brings about.[8]

The Mannermaa Thesis

Tuomo Mannermaa has stimulated vigorous discourse in Luther scholarship with his corrections on how Luther's doctrine of justification should be understood.[9] Reading Luther's interpretation of Paul's letter to the Galatians, he made startling discoveries on how the meaning of justification by faith had been watered down in post-Luther conversations whereas the reformer himself had taught something quite radical about the reality change that occurs: in justification human beings are united with God, because of and in Christ. The meanings of such an argument had not been perused until Mannermaa's discovery awakened a dormant topic in Luther scholarship.[10]

The context for Mannermaa's findings is relevant to note. During his engagement in the 1970s in an ecumenical conversation between Finnish Luther scholars and Russian Eastern Orthodox theologians who actively teach theosis, his task was to peruse Luther's lectures on the Galatians, a central text for Luther's justification theology, and explicitly to look for possible connecting points between the traditions. Both a complicating and a rewarding factor is the history of the sources available for such a study, namely, Luther left two sets of interpretation: first, his early lectures were printed in 1519 in one of the most illuminating texts regarding his first reformation insights; second, he returned to lecture on Paul's letter again, and this work was printed in 1535.[11]

Whereas the latter "is typically called Luther's 'large' commentary," Mannermaa's colleague and collaborator Simo Peura suggests that "there are reasons to consider Luther's 1519 commentary an exposition of his early theology. It expresses his love for Pauline theology."[12] In 1531, after his personal life had changed significantly upon marriage, Luther uttered in few words his affection toward the letter to the Galatians: 'The epistle to the Galatians is my epistle, towards which I feel trust, my Käthe von Bora.'"[13]

Mannermaa's initial work focused on the later lectures from 1535. As said, his mission was to explore if there were any openings in Luther's theology that would give fruitful conversation points between Lutherans and Orthodox Christians. In his own words, he aimed "to look for a theological motif in the Lutheran concept of Christian faith which would be analogous to the notion of divinization and could thus serve as a point of contact with Orthodox theology."[14] In this situation he made a significant discovery that is still causing reverberations among the interpreters of Luther: he found evidence from Luther's own words to argue that a central teaching of Luther is that in justification, because of Christ's work, human beings actually participate in God. Specifically, with Luther's language about "Christ being present in faith," the idea of participation deserves further exploration. Mannermaa dared to propose that the concept of theosis could work to describe the reality change the justifying faith promises and effects, in Luther's understanding.[15]

Peura on Mannermaa

Mannermaa's suggestion of theosis as compatible with Luther's teaching of justification as a union in faith was initially tested, supported, and expanded by his colleague Simo Peura,[16] whose original work focused on the idea of theosis with Luther and specifically in the earlier Galatians lectures; the agenda for his research was to test and seek evidence from Luther's earlier works toward the theosis argument or note the possible evolution in the reformer's central argumentation about justification. In his introduction to the new (revised) English translation of Luther's earlier lectures on the Galatians, Peura describes the turning point.[17]

Mannermaa discovered "in Luther's theology a heretofore neglected emphasis on the real, reality-altering presence of God that occurs along with the act of imputation, in which the believer is made righteous and thus one with God." In other words, in his interpretation of Luther's language, Mannermaa maintains that Luther gives equal emphasis to both the "forensic" and the "effective" sides of righteousness, to how justification means both being declared forgiven before God and being made holy in a personal union with God. He demonstrates that, for Luther, justification has real effects, that Christ the Redeemer does not operate only for us but also in us. "The depth of Luther's theology of justification by faith cannot be appreciated fully without coming to appropriate conclusion about what it means in reality when Christ comes to live in us and makes us one with God—and thus, in a sense, gods."[18]

Further, Peura writes on the impact of these arguments: "If Mannermaa's attention to what is traditionally called the 'effective side of righteousness' is already controversial, even more so is his suggestion, or rather thesis that the idea of divinization, theosis, is a central part of Luther's theology and particularly of the doctrine of justification. Mannermaa states that the concept of participation in God (theosis) is inherent *in all* [emphasis mine] of Luther's theology." Peura clarifies about the terms used: "As synonym for the term theosis, which he does use here explicitly, Luther speaks frequently of 'God's indwelling' or 'inhabitation' in the human being (e.g., WA 4:280, 2–5; WA 3:106, 14–15). The focus in Luther is not on what a human becomes but on what is done 'to' the human being and what this means to the human being in relation to God: deification is about participation in god, the focus being on God's act."[19]

Mannermaa's thesis has proven controversial, with no end in sight in debating the philosophical grounding of his claims. Ambiguity remains in discerning whether the union would imply a "substantial" or "relational" reality change. Obviously caution is in order when even attempting to apply an Eastern term with its specific uses and means to a sixteenth-century Western thinker's work, especially when he does not explicitly and frequently use the specific term. One way to address this is to pause with Luther's imagination of the "union in faith" language and consider how he understands specifically faith's operations in justification and do this clearly against his *coram Deo/coram hominibus* framework, allowing elasticity with the speculations regarding what this all means, ontologically speaking.[20]

Regardless of how the mechanics of the mystery are understood, Luther is quite clear with his expectation that in faith, which is completely divine, a person becomes God via participation in *unio personalis*, and this means becoming filled with God.[21] Faith is the agent for the union.

On Luther's Vocabulary

Luther uses a particular vocabulary for his doctrine of justification and for viewing the human beings' justified-by-faith reality. There are specific terms that offer a crucial framework for considering the idea of theosis vis-à-vis his theology of justification.

Luther presumes an intertwined dual reality for the human existence, one that can be approached philosophically and that offers a particular spiritual lens: Human lives are lived in two realities, *coram Deo* and *coram hominibus*. In the former, human beings are recipients of "alien holiness" (*iustitia aliena*), which is granted by God, and which makes them completely holy and righteous. In the latter, human beings are a work-in-progress, experiencing the fermentation of "proper righteousness," a person's "own" righteousness.[22]

The word "sanctification" could be applicable but the word has been shunned in much of the Lutheran discourse, for theological reasons: with sanctification, one could mean an anticipated progress of a human beings becoming holy in varying degrees, which is a common teaching in other types of religious discourse, but which would clash with the fundamental Lutheran insistence on grace not being experienced or consummated in degrees and shades, an idea that would compromise the notion of human beings' equal standing as recipients of grace.

A different expression features what is Luther's emphasis in teaching grace and holiness in justification: *simul iustus et peccator*. One of Luther's pivotal insights with the scriptures with respect to his own spiritual experience was that a human being is, always, simultaneously both holy and a sinner. Instead of expecting a progress of improvement or different shades of holiness, with the *simul iustus et peccator* premise, Luther describes a reality of the existence of a human being with all the fragility and faltering, while underscoring that the overarching reality is that of grace and holiness already received in full effect, the source of which is only and solely God.[23] In this view, the human beings are freed from efforts to sanctify or save themselves. There is significant freedom to be experienced in this relief of ontological magnitude.

How this works in Luther's theological imagination is that in justification human beings are purged from the sin's damning effect, so that even if they are not free from sin as long as they are breathing, they are free from the sin's most devastating impact, which is the eternal death and separation from God of life. The sin stays as part of human life as a chronic condition, but it is not a terminal condition; life eternal wins. Luther writes "This [faith] is an infinite righteousness, one that swallows up sins." The sins must be swallowed, otherwise human being could not be one with Christ. Faith does this, as the divine agent. At the same time, faith has another important function as trust: Luther says, "who trusts in Christ is attached to Christ, is one with Christ, having the same righteousness as he."[24]

Given what Luther says about sin, what does it mean that a human being receives Christ's righteousness? If the word *righteousness* describes God's way of being, nature, "essence" (not in a substance-meaning but in terms of who and how God "is" in relation to humans), then it means that human beings receive from the "essence" of God. Furthermore, when Christ's righteousness becomes "ours," everything Christ has becomes "ours." (This, Luther reminds, is the blessing promised to Abraham first in Genesis 12:3: "and in your seed [Christ] shall all the nations be blessed.")[25] The most important conclusion Luther makes is this: Christ's righteousness becomes our righteousness and all that he has, rather, he himself, becomes "ours." This happens through faith, "in the righteousness of Christ my God which becomes ours through faith and by the grace and mercy of God."[26]

In justification, therefore, human beings receive not only a "freed" status but also are made into something new: in justification, a person is imputed with the Holy Spirit who brings the gifts of Christ to the life of the human beings who remain in their flesh and mortality. In this tension, human beings are aware, on some level, of the divine expectations and could be crushed with the awareness of not being able to meet them; the dominant chord in the justified life, however, is the promise that "regardless" of this condition, a person is free in the larger sense and is gifted with the life eternal that comes with the personal union with the divine, the source of life.

In other words, the famous observation that human beings are *simul iustus et peccator* speaks of this dual reality: human beings enjoy, on the one hand, 100 percent holiness and forgiven status in their *coram Deo* existence; yet, on the other hand, they cannot expect to be free from sin and all that it brings along, while still in this life. This struggle shows in human beings' *coram hominibus* relations and different dimensions of life as experienced in its finitude and brokenness in the company of other saint-sinners.[27]

Faith is the language for Luther to talk about what could be called a "holiness reality," and faith is the word that explains the dynamics of and the rationale for the fundamental change that can be expected to occur in human existence with the justification. Faith language allows Luther to name the real work and gift of Christ—Luther's passionate concern in his theologizing—in effecting the holiness and righteousness, which is gifted to human beings for their benefit without their own merit, effort, or doing; this is what alien righteousness, *iustitia aliena*, refers to.[28]

These conclusions lead back to the theosis question: Could the justified reality be described as participation in the divine reality as in the meaning of theosis? The answer could be affirmative, when looking at how Luther explains the effect faith has in this regard.

Faith as Divine Action

A few words are in order of the meaning of the word *faith* for Luther.[29]

The word *faith* for Luther is an active verb because of Christ; faith is a verb and Christ is the subject of the verb. When speaking of the justifying faith, Luther refers primarily to the faith that relies on Christ as the subject of human life and a divine presence that involves the individual's ultimate being and promises a transformation in the life that ensues from this personal encounter. Luther expresses this with his statement *in ipsa fide Christus adest*.[30] With this insight Luther names that faith is about and rooted in Christ's person and work, that faith is about Christ's real presence and action, without ceasing, for the benefit of the individual—and, thereby, the entire humanity, starting from the individual's transformation. Luther develops his arguments on the basis of his reading of Paul's letter to the Galatians and statements there, such as "Christ lives in me" (Gal 2:20) and, furthermore, believes for me.[31]

The justifying kind of faith, thus, is about a Godly action that not only corrects the relationship but also brings a divine reality to the existence of the human being, or, in other words, draws human being into the realm of the divine. Naturally, a question arises with the words divine reality about how God "is" and how God's essence is understood in human terms, which is not the primary concern here. In *Two Kinds of Righteousness*, Luther asks, "What is this faith that justifies" and answers, that such a faith is called "the righteousness of God." The faith that justifies is about God and God's action. Further, he writes, "In many passages of the Psalter, faith is called 'the work of the Lord,' 'confession,' 'power of God,' 'mercy,' 'truth,' 'righteousness.' All these are names for faith in Christ, rather, for the righteousness which is in Christ."[32]

This short quote points to Luther's fundamental point that the justifying faith does not originate from a human being, that it is not about a particular "content" or desire or will, but rather it points to what all Christ, in his person and through his work, brings to the existence of the human being. With faith language Luther points out what happens in justification, by faith, through faith, and in faith: that Christ arrives and unites one to God via divine participation. Faith is the key to imagine how the divine participation happens.

Luther writes on this from varied angles and in different texts. The following statement demonstrates Luther's logic:

> But *it is through faith that the heart and the name of the Lord cling together* (cf. Rom 10:17). Faith, however, comes through the word of Christ. . . . Therefore, just as the name of the Lord is pure, holy, righteous, true, good, etc., so, if it touches, or is touched by, the heart (which happens through faith), it makes the heart entirely like itself.[33]

For this, sin needs to be negated. The word heart calls for attention: on the one hand, Luther's *extra nos* emphasis on the saving power coming from outside the person underscores the ontological way that God's Word works via Christ for the human being. On the other hand, the word heart points to the embodiment of the promise, the personal internal impact of the grace in the human being. The saving grace does not remain *extra nos*; faith makes sure of that.

> Thus it comes about that for *those who trust in the name of the Lord all sins are forgiven, and righteousness is imputed to them* "*for your name's sake*, Lord" (Ps 25:11), because this name is good. This does not come about because of their own merit, since they have not deserved even to hear of it. But *when the heart has thus been justified through the faith that is in God's name, God gives them the power to become children of God* (John 1:12) by immediately pouring into their hearts God's Holy Spirit (Rom 5:5), who fills them with God's love and makes them peaceful, glad, active in all good works, victorious over all evils, contemptuous even of death and hell. Here all laws and all works of laws soon cease; all things are now free and permissible, and the law is fulfilled through faith and love.[34]

Becoming Christ's siblings and inheritors with Christ is a major status change for humans, altering their position in God's kingdom. This is a mystery, hard for human beings to comprehend or believe. And yet, believe it one must.

> Behold, this is what Christ has merited for us, namely, that the name of the Lord (that is, the mercy and truth of God) is preached to us

and that whoever believes in this name will be saved. Therefore, if our conscience troubles you and you are a sinner and are seeking to become righteous, what will you do? . . . *See to it that your heart or recall the name of the Lord, that is, that God is righteous, good, and holy; and then cling to this, firmly believing that God is such a One for you. Now you are at once such a one, like God. But you will never see the name of the Lord more clearly than you do in Christ.* There you will see how good, pleasant, faithful, righteous, and true God is, since God did not spare God's own Son (Rom 8:32). *Through Christ God will draw you to God's self.*[35]

Luther's point is consistent: this is all God's doing; all human beings can do is to trust it.

Without this righteousness it is impossible for the heart to be pure. That is why it is impossible for the righteousness of human beings to be true. . . . This is a *righteousness* that is bountiful, freely given, firm, inward, eternal, true, heavenly, *divine*; it does not earn, receive, or seek anything in this life. Indeed, *since it is directed toward Christ and his name, which is righteousness, the result is that the righteousness of Christ and of the Christian are one and the same, united with each other in an inexpressible way.* For it flows and gushes forth from Christ, as he says in John 4. "The water that I shall give them will become in them a spring of living water welling up to eternal life." Thus, it comes about that just as all became sinners because of alien sin, so *by alien righteousness all become righteous*, as Rom. 5:19 says: "As by one person's disobedience many were made sinners, so *by the righteousness of one human being, Christ, many are made righteous.*"[36]

Luther draws his evidence from the scriptures, and his consistent reminder is that with his justification language he is advising his readers of the meaning of Christ for the believers.

This is the mercy predicted by all the prophets; this is the blessing promised to Abraham and to his seed. . . . First hear that "Jesus" means salvation and that "Christ" means "the anointing of mercy"; then firmly believe this unheard-of salvation and mercy, and *you will be justified.* That is, believe that Christ will be your salvation and mercy, and beyond all doubt Christ will be.[37]

Apropos, in another text, a sermon aid, Luther expresses the same convictions a bit more deliciously, using an image of cake: "Christ is reflected in the same way as the sunlight is reflected in the water or in a mirror, and He lets Himself shine in our hearts. So we will be glorified, from glory to glory, so that we grow daily and get to know the Lord more and more clearly. Thus we are transformed and glorified into His very image, so that we become one cake with Christ (*das wyr alle eyn kuche werden mit christo*). We cannot make this happen by our own strength; God, who is the Spirit, must do it."[38] This is about as concrete an expression of the depth of the union as Luther can imagine, that human and divine become one like in a "Kuchen," a pastry, where all "ingredients" are needed for the right form and taste.

Faith That Unites with Christ

"Indeed, since it is directed toward Christ and his name, which is righteousness, the result is that the righteousness of Christ and of the Christian are one and the same, united with each other in an inexpressible way."[39] This statement from Luther reminds of his logic: when he speaks of the union of God and human, he is explaining the impact of Christ in human life and human-God relations. The word *righteousness* refers to the transformation entailed in justification, which is his key teaching, and one that involves the active role of faith.

As noted earlier, Mannermaa elaborated on the essential connection between Christ and justification. The participation idea would not have a grounding without pointing back to Christ and Christ's effect. There is a reason why Luther speaks of the participation in God specifically as a union with Christ, and not around or without Christ. Because of his beliefs in what all Christ is and does as a savior, he therewith names justification as an actual reality change from a doomed sinner to a "wholly" justified and holy person. This holiness pertains to the reality that is in effect in relation to God, *coram Deo*. Alien righteousness is the word to describe the source of this holiness that comes from outside of human being's own equipment or aptitude and connects human being essentially with the divine. Christ is the connector, in his being and doing, and because of Christ, it is feasible to speak of a reality change.

Mannermaa has amply demonstrated how for Luther the reality change in justification is rooted in Christ's person and nature: Luther does not separate Christ's person and work (*persona* and *officium*) but considers Christ himself *in toto*, his person and his work, as the Christian righteousness, i.e. faith righteousness. In faith Christ is *realiter* present and acting—*in ipsa fide Christus adest*—and therewith his whole person and work comes "to" and "for" the existence of the human being. Christ is both the *favor* and the *donum*, inseparably and without mixing (per Chalcedonian Christological language about Christ's two natures).[40]

This means, not only is Christ's sacrifice considered "for" the benefit of the sinners, in declaring them forgiven, but the incarnate, crucified, resurrected Christ is received as the new subject of the human life. The former action of Christ causes a change in human beings' ontological/existential situation and relationship with God, granting them a new, "freed" status as a forgiven beloved of God. The latter action, ongoing, promises a change in the existence and reality of the human being. This Luther describes with the language of a "happy exchange" (*fröhliche Wechsel*), from the foundation of Chalcedonian definition of how it is possible for human and divine to not only interact but be united while distinct.

Mannermaa stresses the role of faith and the subject of Christ in this mystery that is logical in Luther's justification doctrine. He significantly augments the meaning of faith for Luther. First of all, it can be concluded, faith is divine work. In faith, human beings partake in God's *essence*—even possessing something of the essence of God (*olemus* in Finnish). This is purely and only Christ's doing: Christ and faith belong together, when human beings are considered. Christ is both the object of faith, and the subject present and acting in faith that works for the human beings' benefit; Luther calls this *fides Christo formata*.[41] Christ being the *donum*, the gift, who dwells within the person, he can (like none else) lead one to divine participation, to real union with God.[42]

For this argumentation to make sense, it needs to be reckoned that this is faith language. Luther proposes specifically a faith vision for the human reality.[43] This is the realm of faith where human knowledge and faculties like reason are helpless, given (Luther's premise of) the devastating impact of original sin that has stripped human beings from many good things.

Reason's Lies, Faith's Reality: Being Loved

Speaking of human faculties: because of the fall, and the unavoidable reality it brings along, on their own, human beings are at loss and lost, not finding God or themselves in proper relation with God. Not even the highest of human faculties, reason, could facilitate that. Even if human "reason has a quality akin to godlike majesty,"[44] Luther makes it clear, that reason has serious limitations, only amplified in the post-fall reality.

Hans Grosshans has shed light on how Luther considers the reason's realm: "Reason, for Luther, is a faculty of the human soul and therefore a part of nature. It is bound to the created world, to time and space. When it respects its own limitations, it fulfills its God-given vocation. When it overextends itself beyond the empirical world, reason gets it wrong. Reason is woefully inadequate, even stubbornly sinful, in religious and spiritual matters. For Luther, reason deployed in religion always misses the true God and ends up constructing idols of its own fabrication."[45]

It is worth noting that regardless of all the negative things said about what negative things Luther said about reason, the reason has its due place in Luther's theological imagination. This is so particularly when considering how a person is expected to live in the finite, temporal world.[46] It just is not the prime mover or the final word, rather it is a vehicle within limited parameters. Luther also warns that human beings should not believe what their reason tells them about themselves or about God and about the reality between the two. Post-fall, the reason speaks with the mouth of the devil that damns people and leads them to despair, further enhancing the gulf the sinner feels between oneself and God.

In other words, reason will never lead a person to God, reason will never hold the right mirror in front of the despairing individual, reason will never let the person to see (the ultimate) reality and the human *telos* as it is in God's design. Quite the contrary: reason operates within human standards and limitations and human beings' vision is clouded and filled with lies about the existence. Given the reality of sin in mortal life, human beings are prone to see themselves as not loved by God. Reason cannot give the vital information about God's love for human beings; the recognition and experience that a human being is loved, and the transformation that ensues, is beyond reason's comprehension. Something else is needed: faith.[47] And not just any kind of faith, but "faith that is a living daring confidence in God's grace."[48]

In his *Bondage of the Will* (1525) Luther speaks of the dynamics between God and the human and how God's true being remains hidden for the human being who needs faith to see as God truly is. He reminds of the vitality of faith in this regard and of what is the highest degree of faith: to believe that God is merciful.[49]

For Luther, faith gives the proper lens to see human reality through the eyes of God. Faith allows human being to know God as God is in relation to the individual: God is mercy and God is love, and human beings' true and God-intended relation to this God is that of being beloved and freed. In other words, when approaching life with faith, human beings can see themselves through God's eyes—through the eyes of faith—as a beloved of God. This is the specific meaning of faith, or its impact:[50] a restored love relationship with God, and thereby a new orientation to and grounding in reality in its many dimensions.

Not just Mannermaa but other theologians have observed the idea of participation in Luther and the still insufficiently explored interconnectedness between faith and love. For instance, Gerhard Ebeling's thoughts on this are helpful; he does not speak of theosis but of participation.[51] "For faith has to do with God. But one cannot speak of God without ascribing to him power over all power. Faith means *participation in this omnipotence of God*, because it is faith and nothing else which ascribes to him this power. If faith did not do this, it would not be done, and this power would be denied to God." Furthermore, when approaching life with faith, human beings can see themselves through God's eyes—through the eyes of faith—as a *beloved* of God. This is the specific meaning of faith, or its impact: a love relationship with God.

Ebeling writes further, "This is the power of faith, that in virtue of God's love it comes to [hu]man and remains with him [her], which simply means that [hu]man has a different relation to God, the world, and him[her]self. In what way different? One could simply say, in that he [she] knows that he [she] is loved. For faith comes from and goes to being loved."[52]

Resonating with Mannermaa's and Ebeling's interpretations of Luther on faith's impact in human life, Reformation scholar Denis Janz concludes: "Faith, ultimately, is the ability to understand and accept ourselves as the objects of God's love. This, Luther thought, is the key to finding happiness in life."[53] Denis Janz's conclusion shows the existential promise of Luther's basic theological discovery: "In the final analysis, faith is for Luther the confidence that, because *we are objects of an infinite and unconditional love*, the negativities of human existence can have no finality or ultimacy for us: fear, despair, death, and all troubles have been conquered." In other words, "faith is a living daring confidence in God's grace."[54]

On Christ's Righteousness Becoming "Ours"

As has become clear by now, in Luther's view, faith is crucial in resetting the human beings' vision of their worth as God's beloved and of their grounding in hope. But even more so, faith not only sets the vision right but significantly alters the human existence: faith unites human being with God, in ways that only divine faith can.

Faith is pivotal for Luther's doctrine of justification and the union idea, for which he also uses the word *dwelling*: Christ intimately dwells in faith. It is this kind of faith that justifies because it takes hold of Christ and already means the presence of Christ.[55] It is the Christ-in-faith dwelling, which is more than the person having faith in Christ, that brings about a reality change: in faith, world ends and the divine begins.[56] Mannermaa reminds that this is the realm of theology; theologians' work is done with this kind of faith and naming reality as it truly is, not being fooled by how things may appear to human eyes.[57] In this light, the concept of theosis is not far removed or alien to Luther's central theological convictions, especially when the term is understood to imply a transformation on the deepest level and with the broadest of ramifications.

On the basis of Luther's fundamental theology of justification, faith offers an experience and orientation for life that promises to be transforming, not just for the individual but also to those around her, love becoming the consequence expressed in "mighty deeds of faith," as Gerhard Ebeling articulates.[58] The expression of a reality change has a solid grounding in Luther's thought and involves the existence beyond the individual to the life shared on this earth and experienced in multiple relations.

To conclude, for Luther, importantly, the word *faith* is a verb: (1) It names a specific divine action in the restoration of the God/human relation; faith brings about both the forensic and effective impact of justification. (2) It points to the changed status, existence, and orientation of human beings and how they experience their "justified" reality as a result of this divine action from the position of a faith vision, or faith orientation. (3) It expresses the human reception of this gift as a trust that "it is so."

In other words, faith effects a reality change and alters the human perception of the new reality: faith offers a Godly view on the Godly reality human beings, as justified, are already part of, even if it does not necessarily appear like that to the human eye. Faith allows human beings to trust and therewith "see" with the eyes of faith that the current reality is interwoven with another reality, the eternal kind.

By unfolding the meaning of faith in Luther's theology, Mannermaa has opened new perspectives to the promise of Luther's theology, spirituality, and philosophy in light of contemporary conversations. The language of participation and union and dwelling points to the transformative impact of faith in the human being's situation and relations and brings attention to the core of Luther's discovery of faith as an actual reality-changing agent—with Christ. Luther can thus return to conversations with theologians who speak of theosis as a "normal" and to-be-expected reality.

As an interim conclusion, we could say that for Luther, the justifying faith is about a perspective, it is a kaleidoscope, it is a vision that is gifted to human beings who by the nature of being created finite, and as sinners, cannot see the reality as God does. A faith lens is the only chance, in this life, to see the design and the telos for human beings through God's eyes.

Christ is the lens, Christ is the reason, Christ is the subject of this "knowing." Christ is the content of the justifying faith, Christ is the reason for what this faith does, namely: it unites one with God. What follows from that is expressed in Luther's quoting Paul: "I live, though not I, but truly *Christ lives in me*," and Ephesians 3:17, "that Christ may reside in your hearts through faith."[59]

Notes

1. See Tuomo Mannermaa, *In Ipsa Fide Christus Adest: Luterilaisen ja Ortodoksisen Kristinuskonkäsityksen Leikkauspiste* (Helsinki: Missiologian ja Ekumeniikan Seura, R.Y., 1980). The work is available in German and English also. In the following, most of the references draw from the English translation, *Christ Present in Faith: Luther's View of Justification*, trans. Kirsi Stjerna (Minneapolis: Fortress Press, 2005), with the understanding that more people can have access to that than the original Finnish edition.

2. Mannermaa's work has fueled several dissertations, monographs, and articles; see Risto Saarinen's listing of the materials produced in Finland and review of the context of Finnish Luther studies before and after Mannermaa, https://blogs.helsinki.fi/ristosaarinen/luther-studies-in-finland/ and https://blogs.helsinki.fi/ristosaarinen/z5/. See also Antti Raunio, "Martin Luther in Finland and the Baltics," in *Oxford Research Encyclopedia on Martin Luther* (Oxford: Oxford University Press, 2017). See also the bibliography, compiled by Kirsi Stjerna, in Mannermaa, *Christ Present*.

3. Martin Luther's famous *Rückblick* can be read in his "Preface to the Latin Works," 1545, in *The Annotated Luther*, ed. Hans J. Hillerbrand, Kirsi I. Stjerna, and Timothy J. Wengert (Minneapolis: Fortress Press, 2015–2017), 4:489–503.

4. Of the many works of Paul Tillich, his *Courage to Be* (New Haven, CT: Yale University Press, 1952) would serve as a fitting reference with these questions. On Luther's discoveries, struggles, and elaborations, Susan Karant-Nunn offers a fresh take in *The Personal Luther: Essays on the Reformer from a Cultural Historical Perspective* (Leiden: Brill, 2017). For a critical biography, see Volker Leppin, *Martin Luther: A Late Medieval Life* (Ada, MI: Baker Academic, 2017), and Heiko E. Obermann, *Luther: A Man between God and the Devil* (New Haven, CT: Yale University Press, 1989).

5. For a historical look into Luther's development as a reformer and his theological insights and spiritual outlook, *The Annotated Luther* offers the essential Luther texts to consult. Volume 1, for example, includes *On the Freedom of a Christian* and *Ninety-Five Theses*; volume 2 includes *Two Kinds of Righteousness*, *Large Catechism*, and *On the Bondage of the Will*; and volume 6 contains several of Luther's exegetically oriented texts, such as his interpretations on Paul's letters to Romans and Galatians and his expositions on the Psalms.

6. Among others, Alister E. McGrath and Gerhard Forde have written on Luther's justification of faith from the perspective of "being made right" with an emphasis on the forensic dimension of justification. See Alister E. McGrath, *Iustitia Dei: A History of the Christian Doctrine of Justification*, 3rd ed. (New York: Cambridge University Press, 2005), and Gerhard Forde, *Justification by Faith: A Matter of Life and Death* (Eugene, OR: Wipf and Stock, 2012).

7. Luther scholar Robert Kolb suggests "trust" as the synonym for faith with Luther.

8. For different views on Luther and justification, see, e.g., Veli-Matti Kärkkäinen's discussion in *One with God: Salvation as Deification and Justification* (Collegeville, MN: Liturgical Press, 2004) and Else Marie Wiberg Pedersen's contribution in "Luther and Justification," in *Dialog: Journal for Theology* 25, no. 2 (June 2017): 133.

9. See Mannermaa, *In Ipsa Fide Christus Adest*. See also Mannermaa, *Kaksi rakkautta: Johdatus Lutherin uskonmaailmaan* (Helsinki: Juva, 1983), translated into English by Kirsi Stjerna, *Two Kinds of Love: Martin Luther's Religious World* (Minneapolis: Fortress Press, 2010).

10. On this debate and on the approaches, Mannermaa explicitly challenges Karl Holl, Heinrich Bornkamm, Emanuel Hirsch, Hanns Rückert, Erich Seeberg, and Erich Vogelsang, among others, and critically engages the tradition he is building on (e.g., Wilhelm Maurer, Lauri Haikola). See Mannermaa's "Introduction" to *Christ Present*, 1–9; also the editor's introduction, xiv–xv.

11. Martin Luther, *In epistolam S. Pauli ad Galatas Commentarius ex praelectione D. Martini Lutheri collectus* (1535), WA 40/I and WA 40/2; LW 26 and 27. The 1517 lectures can be found in LW 27, 151–410 and WA 2, 445–618; the 1535 lectures in LW 26, 1–461 and 40/I, 40–688 and 40/II, 1–184.

12. For contextual information on Luther's Galatians lectures—the lectures he gave from October 27, 1516 until March 13, 1517—and the process of their completion for publication in 1519, see Peura's "Introduction" to *Lectures in Galatians*, in *The Annotated Luther*, ed. Euan Cameron (Minneapolis: Fortress Press, 2017), 6:535–41.

13. Ibid., 541.

14. Mannermaa, *Christ Present*, 3. For the description of the original research situation for Mannermaa, see vii–xix.

15. "Sic ut Christus sit obiectum fidei, imo non obiectum, sed, ut ita dicam, in ipsa fide christus adest" (WA 40/1 228, 33–229, 15–18). LW 26:129.

16. As a personal note, Simo Peura and I were Tuomo Mannermaa's doctoral students in different years. Upon his graduation, Peura became Mannermaa's assistant at the Ecumenical Department of Helsinki University's Theological Faculty; when during Mannermaa's research leave Peura took his role as the Professor of Ecumenics, I had the honor of stepping in as an interim assistant. Until recently Peura served as the Bishop of Lapua, Finland.

17. Simo Peura, *Mehr als ein Mensch? Die Vergöttlichung als Thema der Theologie Martin Luthers von 1513 bis 1519* (Mainz: Philipp von Zabern, 1994). See also Peura's introduction and annotations for the 1519 Galatians lectures in Cameron, *The Annotated Luther*, 6:535–41.

18. Stjerna, xii. Mannermaa's argument is discussed in ibid., 6:548: "From the inner logic of justification, it is decisive that Christ and human being become united through faith. The *unio cum Christo* idea originates from Paul and is quite prevalent in medieval theology. When one with Christ, the Christian participates (*participet*) in God's 'being' and names, that is, in God's righteousness and grace. The idea of participation in divine nature has biblical roots (2 Pet 1:4). The concept of participation appears frequently in Luther's theology. In his *Large Catechism*, when explaining the third article of the Creed, Luther emphasizes the meaning of the church in generating this Christ-oneness: when the church proclaims the gospel and distributes the sacraments, a faith is born in us and we become participants in the Christ-treasure" (Peura in ibid., 6:548n23).

19. Stjerna, in Mannermaa, *Christ Present*, xii.

20. Mannermaa's choice of terminology when describing the union and the transformation it causes has evoked reactions and criticism for philosophical ambiguity. For reflection and explanation of Mannermaa's choice to first use the word "ontic" (*onttinen* in Finnish) and later "ontological," see *Christ Present*, 95n14.

21. Ibid., 42, 45. "Union is a permanent condition for the Christin's participation in Christ's righteousness." At the root of this is Luther's idea of alien righteousness. Peura in Cameron, *The Annotated Luther*, 6:550n30.

22. A succinct synopsis of Luther's justification doctrine can be found in Simo Peura's "Introduction" to Luther's *Lectures on Galatians* 2:15–16, in Cameron, *The Annotated Luther*, 6:535–41, esp. 539–540. "To Luther, justification is both about (1) a person's sins being forgiven and Christ's righteousness being imputed (imputation), and (2) the person being made righteous (iustum facere). The Christian thus becomes a child of God and received the infusion of Christ's Holy Spirit" (6:548n25).

23. See Luther's 1519 *Two Kinds of Righteousness*, ed. Else Marie Wiberg Pedersen, in Stjerna, *The Annotated Luther*, 2:9–24.

24. Ibid., 15.

25. Ibid., 14, 15. Luther quotes Romans 8:32, Luke 22:27, and Romans 1:17, as well as Genesis 12:3 and Isaiah 9:6 to make the point about the promise of Christ to become entirely "ours."

26. *Two Kinds of Righteousness*, in Stjerna, *The Annotated Luther*, 2:15.

27. See, e.g., in *Lectures on Galatians* 2:15–16, in Cameron, *The Annotated Luther*, 6:542–55. See also *Two Kinds of Righteousness* in Stjerna, *The Annotated Luther*, 2:9–23, on Luther's terms alien and proper righteousness. See LW 26:129; WA 40/I:228–30–239, 15.

28. See, e.g., Simo Peura's "Introduction" to Luther's *Lectures on Galatians* 2:15–16, in Cameron, *The Annotated Luther*, 6:535–41: "Luther consistently rejects any ability of human beings to collaborate or assist in their own salvation by meeting the expectations of God's law. . . . True righteousness thus does not arise from human efforts; rather, righteousness is granted from above, descending to humans from heaven. It is founded on grace and received by faith, and these are what make a Christian one with Christ. Faith means participation in Christ and in Christ' righteousness." "From this union with Christ flow the many aspects of justification. For Luther, justification means both being declared righteous and being made righteous. The former is holistic in character, whereas the latter is completed in this life only in part. Justification effects a change in a Christian, so that one, at least momentarily, does good deeds freely and without coercion" (539). The theme of freedom in faith and bondage in servitude in love Luther elaborates shortly after in his *On Freedom of a Christian* (1520), see Wengert, *The Annotated Luther*, 1:67–119.

29. A fundamental study on Luther's idea of faith can be found in Gerhard Ebeling, *The Nature of Faith*, trans. Ronald Gregor Smith (London: Collins, 1961), 119.

30. "Sic ut Christus sit obiectum fidei, imo non obiectum, sed, ut ita dicam, in ipsa fide christus adest." WA 40, 228, 33–229, 15.

31. "I have been crucified with Christ and I no longer live, but Christ lives in me. The life I now live in the body, I live by faith in the Son of God, who loved

me and gave himself for me." (NIV Gal. 2:20.) See more on Luther's treatment of Galatians 2 to articulate his view of how human being is saved with the Christ-centered righteousness rather than with futile attempts to rescue herself, in *Lectures on Galatians*, in Cameron, *The Annotated Luther*, 6:542–55.

32. *Two Kinds of Righteousness*, 1519, quoted in ibid., 2:15.
33. *Lectures on Galatians*, in ibid., 6:549–51. Emphasis added.
34. Ibid.
35. Ibid.
36. Ibid., 549–50.
37. Ibid., 549–51.
38. Luther's *Predigt* (1522) WA 10/3:425, 13–25, quoted in Mannermaa, *Christ Present*; also in *Luther's Works*, Church Postil I, ed. Benjamin T. G. Mayes and James L. Langebartels (St. Louis, MO: Concordia Publishing House, 2013), 75:217.
39. Luther, *Lectures on Galatians*, in Cameron, *The Annotated Luther*, 6:549.
40. Mannermaa, *Christ Present*, 13–30.
41. Ibid., 18, 7, 22.
42. Ibid., 19.
43. Ibid., 27. Luther talks about darkness of faith, not seeing, on the one hand, and on the other, how this gift/Christ/faith takes hold of Christ, regardless. See Cameron, *The Annotated Luther*, 6:546–47n20, on how human beings experience God's alien work and their *redactio ad nihilum*.
44. LW 34:137; quoted in Hans-Peter Grosshans, "Luther on Faith and Reason: The Light of reason at the Twilight of the Word," in *The Global Luther: A Theologian for Modern Times*, ed. Christine Helmer (Minneapolis: Augsburg Fortress Press, 2009), 173–86. "Reason is part of God's good creation. Luther's fourth thesis admits reason's divine origin: 'And it is certainty true that reason is the most important and the highest in rank among all things and, in comparison with other things of this life, the best and something divine.'" LW 34:137, *Disputation Concerning Man*, quoted in Grosshans, 180, who also points out Luther's conviction expressed in his Large Catechism: "I hold and believe that I am God's creature, that is, that he has given me . . . all my sense, my reason and understanding."
45. "Luther's sharp criticism of reason as it relates to true religion and the true God is behind his famous condemnation as a 'whore who sells itself to anyone . . .'" Grosshans, *Luther*, 175.
46. See Jennifer Hockenberry Dragseth, *The Devil's Whore: Reason and Philosophy in the Lutheran Tradition* (Minneapolis: Fortress Press, 2011).
47. Grosshans, *Luther*, 181. Relationship with God cannot be comprehended with reason. "Faith alone is the vehicle and instrument by which the human person is related to the triune God. Only by faith can the human being apprehend God's

self-giving and self-revealing essence in Jesus Christ. The human person is given faith to connect to God in a relationship with God. Reason is, thereby, freed by faith from any illusions of attaining God on its own capacity. Once freed from the aeterna, reason becomes the vehicle and the instrument by which human beings are related to all the temporalia (coram hominibus)" (ibid., 181.)

48. LW 35:371; Cameron, *The Annotated Luther*, 6:469.

49. "Hence, in order that there may be room for faith, it is necessary that everything which is believed should be hidden. It cannot, however, be more deeply hidden than under an object, perception, or experience which is contrary to it." "Thus, when God makes alive, God does it by killing; when God justifies, God does it by making human beings guilty." Stjerna, *The Annotated Luther*, 2:178. "Thus God hides divine eternal goodness and mercy under eternal wrath, God's righteousness under iniquity. This is the highest degree of faith, to believe God is merciful when saving so few and damning so many, and to believe God to be righteous when making us necessarily damnable" "If, then, I could by any means comprehend how this God can be merciful and just who displays so much wrath and iniquity, there would be no need of faith. As it is, since that cannot be comprehended, there is room for the exercise of faith when such things are preached and published, just as when God kills, the faith of life is exercise in death." Ibid., 2:178–79.

50. Ebeling, *The Nature of Faith*, 133.

51. Ibid.

52. Ibid., 137.

53. Denis Janz, "Back to Hell and Back," *Encounters with Luther*, ed. K. Stjerna and B. Schramm (Louisville, KY: Westminster John Knox Press, 2016), 53, 29.

54. LW 35:371, in the reading of Denis Janz, ibid., 26.

55. Mannermaa, *Christ Present*, 57, 67.

56. Ibid., 36.

57. Ibid., 53. See also *Heidelberg Disputation*, in Wengert, *The Annotated Luther*, 1:67–119, for Luther's arguments for the parameters and reality of theological work and the task to call the "thing" what it is.

58. WA 17, 2. 98; Ebeling, *The Nature of Faith*, 137. In a similar vein, Ebeling writes, "This is the *power of faith*, that in virtue of God's love it comes to man and remains with him, which simply means that man has a different relation to God, the world, and himself. In what way different? One could simply say, in that he knows that he is loved. For faith comes from and goes to being loved . . . much more takes place; on this basis of faith being loved comes liberation from self-love. . . . He is therefore free to love his neighbour. But all this—freedom from self-love, freedom to love one's neighbor—is the consequence, not the cause. They are mighty deeds of faith, not faith itself. As Luther says, 'Faith is the doer, and love the deed' (WA 17, 2; 98)" (ibid.).

59. *Two Kinds of Righteousness*, in Stjerna, *The Annotated Luther*, 2:15, quoting Galatians 2:20.

Differentiation as Disfigurement

A Womanist Polemic against the Co-optation of the Divine Essence

Michele E. Watkins

In the modern theological imagination, there has been no logic more destructive to human flourishing than the Western world's fictive conception of whiteness as an essential and divine property of sacrality. Therefore, a conversation about the relationship between faith, reason, and theosis should query what we are to do when reason is corrupted. More specifically, what is the task of Christian theology when Western rationality becomes a form of reasoning to propagate and justify the absurd? Georges Florovsky's neopatristic synthesis encourages Orthodox theologians to trust and use the witness of the Greek Church Fathers as a "permanent category of Christian faith, a constant and ultimate measure or criterion of right belief."[1]

Paul L. Gavrilyuk rightly observes that Florovsky's focus on recovery of what the Greek Fathers intended to convey without modern influence was shaped by his humanistic drive to make an impact within history.[2] This chapter furthers Florovsky's aim, yet is distinct by nuance of his neopatristic synthesis with womanist interpretative theory, which interrupts the cacophony of white male perspectives on theosis, or divine/human communion, with a deliberate recognition of how patriarchal privilege has muffled the prophetic voice and liturgical action of women within the tradition and how white supremacist ideology has silenced the sacramentality of nonwhite Christian witness. A womanist interpretative approach to the neopatristic synthesis affords the tradition with a hermeneutic to expose and deconstruct the assumed nontruth constructed by the modern Western world—namely the absurdities of race, gender, and caste that have taken the act of the differentiation of humanity to the destructive end of its disfigurement.

Whiteness as a Theological and Methodological Problem

To understand whiteness as both a theological and methodological problem, it is critical to deconstruct the modern Christian imagination with particular attention to its disfiguration of theology to *desacralize* black humanity. From this point, the modern Western world's differentiation of humanity through disfigurement in light of Black American women's experience of social suffering will be referred to as *desacralization*. I formally define desacralization in another work as the "systematic process of divestment that involves a series of intentional actions and steps taken to socially construct particular bodies in the secular and sacred imagination as contemptuous symbols of desecrated existence."[3]

White colonists collectively used the Abraham/God covenant narrative and the Hamitic myth to create a God-image for America that gave God the face of the white male slaveholder who required and sanctioned the enslavement of Africans.[4] In the white American Christian imagination, Africans were the descendants of Ham cursed by God through the mouth of Noah and condemned to servitude. In addition to a racialized biblical hermeneutic, theologian James W. Perkinson accounts for the preexisting and the modern caricature of Blackness and how such an illustration of Blackness was used to create whiteness as a soteriological category. Perkinson argues that color symbolism combined with the increase in Muslim conquests in the Middle Ages collectively created "soteriological anxiety" among Europeans.[5] Perkinson argues that this soteriological anxiety of Europeans informed their appropriation of both biblical narrative and Christian theology, particularly John Calvin's interpretation of the elect and predestination wrought this whitening of divinity, spiraling the spiritual and material damnation of Black men and women.[6] Whites became the elect and Black people were those whom "God had given over to their reprobate minds" (Rom 1:28). Through this immoral seizure of theology and bodies, American Christianity reintroduced a strand of Christian Gnosticism that provided theory and practice for Christians to again become estranged to human embodiment.[7]

To qualify the analogous relationship between American Christianity and Christian Gnosticism, the work of Christian theologian J. Kameron Carter and his book *Race: A Theological Account* helps us understand how both American Christianity and Christian Gnosticism both affirm heretical claims related to the inseparable nature of the person and work of Christ. Carter argues that the early denial of Jesus' humanity by Christian Gnostics of pre-Nicene Christianity was driven to a large degree by anti-Semitism within Greco-Roman thought. Carter's analysis is of great value for the argument I formulate here, for in his examination of Ireneaus of Lyon's *Against Heresies* (*Adversus haeresus*) Carter notes that how the problem of "ethnic reasoning" in second-century Gnostic thought shaped Irenaeus's grasp of what was at stake in his fight against Valentinian Gnosticism. Carter contends that Irenaeus understood this Christological controversy to be "a struggle over the meaning of the body both individually and as a sociopolitical arrangement" that had dire implications on how the person and redemptive work of Jesus were to be valued within the Christian faith.[8] Carter utilizes Ireneaus's perspective on Gnostic thought in light of the problem of ethnic prejudice and identifies the fight of Christian abolitionists against antiblackness in modern Christian thought to be a correlative phenomenon and threat against orthodoxy.

American Christianity in its weddedness to white supremacy participates, then, in the tradition of Christian Gnosticism in at least three ways. First, it denies the divine consubstantiality of Jesus with the whole of creation that is inclusive of the black humanity. Second, it negates the hypostatic union of Christ which John Zizioulas describes metaphorically as the "bridge" by which God crosses over "the gulf of otherness by affecting the changeable and adjustable aspect of being" and thus brings the holy Trinity in communion with creation.[9] Third, it denigrates the sacramentality of the bodily suffering of Jesus when it depreciates the sacramental witness of the social suffering experienced by nonwhite persons and communities.

The Anti-Eucharistic Dimension of American Christian Gnosticism

In *Communion and Otherness*, John Zizioulas clarifies the connection between faith and the rejection of narcissism as a part of "the eucharistic ethos" when he states:

Whatever exists or happens is given to us by a person. "Every house is built by someone (= a person), and he who built everything is God" (Heb. 3.4). Faith does not spring from a rational conviction or from a psychological experience, but from the ethos of attributing everything to a personal cause. Whatever we are or have is attributed to an *Other*—not to Self or to nature. And since everything, including our being, is a *gift*, we cannot but assume a giver behind everything. This is the eucharistic path to faith.[10]

Rendering the experiences of the racially and gendered dispossessed castes visible in Christian theology engenders a more profound demonstration of commitment to "the eucharistic ethos" that John Zizioulas astutely observes as that which gives rise to faith. Gnosticism has been a problem for the Christian faith since the birth of the Church. American Christianity's perpetuation of Gnosticism in its propagation of whiteness as divinity can be understood with the help of Greek patristic thought as anti-eucharistic. Through its denial of the sacramentality of the *other*, American Christianity debases the embodied nature of Christ in favor of the embodiment of whiteness and degrades the Christian faith by further denying the relational ontology of the body of Christ. As Gregory of Nyssa keenly notes, "for only evil brings degradation." Gregory goes on to describe in *The Great Catechism* humanity's "contracted fellowship with evil."[11] For Gregory, the sociability between humanity and evil resulted in a degenerative μεταμορφόω, or metamorphosis, whereby the nature of humanity became disfigured and, thus, established the need for Transfiguration.

How are we to understand this μεταμορφόω, or metamorphosis in light of American Christianity and its strand of Gnosticism? In this respect, it is important to understand American Christianity's practice of differentiation as disfigurement as not only Gnostic but also as an attempt to further estrange humanity from itself and the transformative power of Transfiguration. In other words, disfiguration is not only what the Transfiguration is not, but it also operates within and against the eucharistic body in order to undermine the power of the Transfiguration. The cost of humanity's association with evil is the inheritance of the condition, in part, of its progenitor which according to Gregory is "the disease of the love of rule, that primary and fundamental cause of propension to the bad and . . . all the wickedness that follows.[12]"

Twentieth-century Christian theology, Orthodoxy included, inherited a tradition that perpetuated white superiority that came as a result of the allure of ideological and colonial power. The fixation with white supremacy resulted in the erasure of black humanity within the eucharistic body in its failure to directly address American Christianity's white supremacist form of Christian Gnosticism in any substantial way. Evidence of whiteness as a methodological problem in the field of theology can be found in the dissonant presumption that only the white, European, and or Euro-American experience is the only human experience worthy of critical examination. One of the only meaningful readings of theosis for today is an understanding of divine/human communion that is rooted in the experiences of those most impacted by the modern Western world's deluded narcissism. Orthodox discourse on theosis must then disinherit itself in its methodology as well as its theology. Orthodox thought refined through its inclusion and adoption of a womanist methodology affords an opportunity to usurp this false narrative by making the social histories and narratives of the *desacralized* to be featured prominently in its discourse on theosis.

Such adoption is vital for embarking upon a subversive meaning-making of theosis by doing Orthodox theology from a "Black" perspective. As the late Christian theologian James H. Cone clarified, "Being black . . . has very little to do with skin color. To be black means that your heart, your soul, your mind, and your body are where the dispossessed are."[13] Womanist methodology invites Orthodox thought to venture deeper into the reality of the dispossessed because it is emergent and reflective of Black women's experiences of survival, resistance, and moral agency expressed over and against a logic of oppression to improve the quality of life for themselves and their communities.

Demonarchy and a Womanist Theorization of Evil

A survey of the work of womanist theologian Delores S. Williams and her identification of the concretization of whiteness as a social evil in the lives of Black women with the specification in her concept of demonarchy constitutes the first step in exposing and refuting the practice of differentiation through disfigurement. Williams's concept of demonarchy problematizes the notion of redemptive suffering that is valorized within Orthodox conceptions of theosis. The discussion of demonarchy rids the necessity of redemptive suffering as an essential part of entering into communion with the divine and situates the discussion of divine/human communion toward a more liberative interpretation. Second, after interrogating the elevation of race as a social evil antagonistic to divine/human communion and the problem of redemptive suffering, readers are invited to consider theosis from a non-European axiology by considering the character of Sethe and the striving of her neighboring community in Toni Morrison's novel *Beloved*. I utilize Sethe and her community from Toni Morrison because their experience evokes the memories and histories of Black American women and other "dispossessed" communities. It is because of this resonance that Sethe and her community collectively serve as an effective channel connecting the experiences of the desacralized with the themes of contemplation and eucharistic community that is conceptualized in the Greek patristic and Orthodox doctrine of theosis.

For Williams, the cooption of reason by the modern Western world begins with "white racial narcissism." She defines it as follows: "White racial narcissism indicates a malfunction in the American national psyche that can ultimately lead the culture to self-destruct or can lead the powerful racially narcissistic group to genocide members of a less powerful racial group. One way of dealing with white racial narcissism in the culture is for the victimized group to stand against the powerful, racially narcissistic group in a permanent posture of self-defense."[14] Williams identifies this elevation of race in the form of "white racial narcissism" as the social evil at the core of Black women's experience of oppression. It is the ideological culprit undergirding the concretization of the demonic in Williams identification of the concretization of the demonic in lives of Black women as demonarchy. She defines this as "the demonic governance of Black women's lives by white male and white female ruled systems using racism, violence, violation, retardation, and death as instruments of social control."[15] At the heart of Williams's description of demonarchy is her aim to articulate the powers and principalities that oppose the spiritual life of Black women and their communities; particularly, the misappropriation of resources for living that results in both the social death and physical death of Black life. In her womanist commitment to the survival and wholeness of an entire people, Williams is concerned about the materiality of salvation or the lack thereof when it comes to Black women and their communities.

Williams's theorization of evil as demonarchy hinges upon her critique of redemptive suffering within Western Christian soteriology. Utilizing her engagement with the Jewish tradition of Yom Kippur, she argues, "Jesus conquered sin in the wilderness, in life" as opposed to accomplishing human salvation through death.[16] In Williams's delegitimization of suffering as a divinely sanctioned aspect of the human experience, we note one of the most significant areas within which womanist theology charges renderings of theosis to be meaningful in a modern context by ridding itself of its ubiquitous and death-dealing commitment to assert the redemptive nature of suffering. We find some intervention in the Orthodox thought of John D. Zizioulas, who problematizes the "idealizing" of suffering without consideration of the defects within nature (inclusive of a "condemned" human nature) that cause suffering.[17]

According to Williams, a womanist approach to salvation should be directed to remove surrogacy by way of the cross as a criterion for imaging redemption and to cast down Western traditions constructions of divine surrogacy due to pay Satan for the return of humanity (Origen), punishment for sin, or the restoration of divine honor (Anselm). Salvation is found in the provision of survival skills to conquer the threat of death.[18] Williams suggests that the idealization of suffering within a cross-centered soteriology has left the suffering of Black women invisible, unliberated, and infinite for centuries while withholding the resources for their survival and healing from the oppression of racists and patriarchs.[19] Well, one might ask, what are the resources Black women have utilized to aid in their survival and improvement of their quality of life? This leads me to the constructive arm of the essay that makes use of Black women's literary tradition, which is a key feature within womanist methodology. The practice holds Black women's literary tradition to be a critical resource for theological meditation, particularly for those whose experiences have been largely rendered as invisible with the Western Christian tradition.

The use of Black women's literary work helps us to formulate a way of describing with particularity and accuracy how Black women and other desacralized communities operate within their innate divinity to resist and exorcise the demonarchy on a structural level. More specifically in relation to the objective of this work, Black women's literary work can prove vital in the development of an understanding of theosis that counteracts the way that whiteness serves as a methodological problem in the field of Western monotheism.

An Antidemonarchal Approach to Divine/Human Communion

To explore theosis toward an antidemonarchal aim—namely, to resist and exorcise white hegemonic governance of Black and other marginal communities—requires engagement of what womanist pastoral theologian Carroll Watkins-Ali describes as "cognate resources indigenous to the cultural context" of the dispossessed.[20] Ali argues that sources that situate a dominant culture's experience as normative lack both the capacity and authority to be adequate wellsprings for members of minoritized and marginal communities to interpret their cultural experiences.[21] What, then, are the most efficient cultural resources that speak to the experiences of those who have been forced to endure the destructive impact of the sacralization of white racial narcissism in America? The most efficacious sources are those fashioned by the oppressed for the oppressed and generated out of their desire for healing or reconciling their fragmented identity of being under the threat of nonbeing. Within Black women's literary tradition, exemplified here by Toni Morrison's novel *Beloved*, theologians can find an efficacious repository of both fiction and nonfiction narratives that stretch our theological imagination beyond the contours of white Western theological imagination.

Beloved conjures the past for both the reader and characters, for individuals and an entire formerly enslaved community, to heal, embody and share love in a more approximate way that mirrors the love of God, and live out the fullness of their emancipation not in negation of their heritage and struggle but affirmation of their survival. *Beloved* provides its best offering as a meditation on the sacraments as valued and understood by Morrison herself, who converted to Catholicism at the age of twelve.[22] The Catechism of the Catholic Church defines the sacraments as "efficacious signs of grace instituted by Christ and entrusted to the Church, by which divine life is dispensed to us."[23] The Catechism also describes the communion of the sacraments, which is a significant statement concerning our purpose here: "The communion of saints must be understood as the communion of the sacraments."[24] *Beloved* offers a literary illustration clarifying, specifically for the Black community, mimesis, penance, and reconciliation with both the living and the ancestral community as requisites of divine/human communion. In the context of desacralized bodies that have been wounded after bearing the cross of enslavement, the wounded body of Christ is intimated and grants prominence to the Eucharist. According to the Catechism, the Eucharist is "the sacrament of our salvation."[25] Within the Catholic Church, salvation is mediated through the sacraments and the failure to fully engage the sacraments on the terms in which Christ instituted them results in a perpetually wounded and broken community.

Morrison's tapestry alternates literary genres within one work that reflects the complexity of Black life that carries historical fiction, tragedy, horror, the fantastical, and the romantic. As a work of historical fiction, the novel depicts the truth of chattel slavery and its indelible impact of the psychic and material realities of the formerly enslaved. Readers are enthralled in the fantastical wherein the formerly enslaved are to confront the embodiment of the horrors of their past that escapes the confinement of their memory banks. Within the relational dynamic between the characters, there is a quadrilateral of intimacies that exist between mother-daughter, wife-husband, sister-sister, and self-God. Morrison encapsulates her novel where the plot is centered on a failed love relationship between mother and daughter reflective of a whole community's struggle to live into the freedom that self-love and intercommunal love provides.

Though Morrison situates the novel during the historical period of Reconstruction in 1873, the use of narrative voices the memory and impact of enslavement disrupt the present tense. The writer dedicated her novel to the more than sixty million Africans who died in the Middle Passage, whose number remains uncountable in favor of economic goals of colonialism and imperialism.[26] The overall spirit of the work enables the reader's experience of the ongoing haunting. The sacrifice made by Black people in the Middle Passage described in *Beloved* includes the murder of the innocent, mass displacement, and separation of families.

Beloved and Black Women's Experience of Desacralization

Morrison depicted the horror and cruelty of slavery as well as the path to enlightenment and love through the prism of the lived experience of her main character, Sethe. In order to gain an accurate picture of who the character Beloved is within the context of the literary work, it is important to begin the theological analysis with the foremost consideration of Sethe, the novel's main protagonist. Sethe is a formerly enslaved woman committed to her family as a wife, mother, and daughter-in-law. Like others in her community, Sethe is a survivor of chattel slavery whose escape resembled that of Harriett Jacobs in the sense that its success involved reliance on the secrecy of unknown persons, the benevolence of white women, boat transportation North, camouflaged shelter found in forests and swamplands, and the entrustment of the well-being of their children in the care of grandmothers.

The reader meets Sethe terrorized by the traumatic experiences of enslavement, and specifically what I identify here as desacralization. Morrison uses a series of flashbacks, monologues, and soliloquies to establish continuous reflection on particular psychologically devastating and emotionally disturbing events in Sethe's life. Morrison uses ironic language such as naming the plantation in Kentucky from which Sethe fled as "Sweet Home" as a means of summoning the reader's consciousness of the hypocrisy of American slavery and culture. For the enslaved and the desacralized that were regarded as lower than animals, the plantation was a land of untold horrors. Sweet Home is the setting in which Sethe endures the first of these particular traumatic events highlighted here. In conversation with Beloved, Sethe begins to remember their intimate moments and quality time together, but a beautiful memory fades to dark when it is overshadowed by her recollection of a specific day that she and Beloved were together and she overheard the iniquitous conversation Schoolteacher was having with his students. Sethe recalls:

> I couldn't help listening to what I heard that day. He was talking to his pupils and I heard him say, "Which one are you doing?" And one of the boys said, "Sethe." That's when I stopped because I heard my name, and then I took a few steps to where I could see what they was doing. Schoolteacher was standing over one of them with one hand behind his back. He licked a forefinger a couple of times and turned a few pages. Slow. I was about to turn around and keep on my way to where the muslin was, when I heard him say, "No, no. That's not the way. I told you to put her human characteristics on the left; her animal ones on the right. And don't forget to line them up." I commenced to walk backward, didn't even look behind me to find out where I was headed.[27]

Sethe shares this story hoping Beloved might understand the degradation constitutive of enslavement—an experience she hoped to prevent her daughter from ever experiencing. For Sethe, this degradation meant the denial of Black humanity and the sexualized violence to which Beloved would have been forced to endure had she been captured by Schoolteacher and taken back to Sweet Home.

The second experience of desacralization Sethe experiences involves Schoolteacher and his nephews acting out on their reduction of her (and enslaved women in general) to an animal, yet still an object of their sexual perversion. Sethe is haunted by yet another memory that occurred on the day of her planned escape, chronicling her experience:

> "I had milk," she said. I was pregnant with Denver but I had milk for my baby girl. I hadn't stopped nursing her when I sent her on ahead with Howard and Bulgar. . . . Anybody could smell me long before he saw me. And when he saw me he'd see the drops of it on the front of my dress. Nothing I could do about that. All I knew was that I had to get my milk to my baby girl. Nobody was going to nurse her like me. Nobody was going to get it to her fast enough, or take it away when she had enough and didn't know it. Nobody knew that she couldn't pass her air if you held her up on your shoulder, only if she was lying on my knees. Nobody knew that but me and nobody had her milk but me.[28]

To the dismay of the reader, Sethe goes on to describe her sexual assault by Schoolteacher and his nephews. Sethe testifies to Paul D.:

> After I left you, those boys came in there and took my milk. That's what they came in there for. Held me down and took it. I told Mrs. Garner on em. She had that lump and couldn't speak but her eyes rolled out tears. Them boys found out I told on em. Schoolteacher made one open my back, and when it closed it made a tree. It grows there still.[29]

Annie-Paule Mielle de Prinsac and Susana M. Morris acknowledge how Morrison uses metaphors and images to elucidate depraved conditions under which enslaved African were forced to endure or perish. Prinsac and Morris make special mention of the signification of a "mother's milk" as contextualized in the previous quotation and suggest that it serves as a "metonymic symbol of mother-child love, which is declined in all the tenses: the milk the child has had, has, will have, or dream of having, missing milk, denied, stolen milk."[30] This analysis helps the reader understand Morrison's use of figure of speech here in which the life force that nurtures Black women's progeny is not explicitly named as such but it is described as "milk." For an enslaved mother to testify against those who have sexually assaulted her and have stolen her resources, however empathetically engaged by their white mistress, is anathema punishable by the shedding of blood. This is the risk of exposing the inhumane and detestable work of demonarchy.

Unbeknownst to Sethe, Paul D. responds by attributing her husband Halle's sudden mental illness to his probable witnessing of her sexual assault. Paul D. tells her: "I never knew what it was that messed him up. That was it, I guess. All I knew was that something broke him. . . . But whatever he saw go on in that barn that day broke him like a twig."[31] His testimony bears witness to the destructive consequences that Black women's sexual violation had on their partners and intimate relationships.

Sethe's experience recounts how desacralization as a contextual feature of chattel slavery also operates as an embodied consciousness out of which the "sacralized" or culturally deified not only besieges Black women's embodiment and reduces it to something between an animal and an object but also robs the desacralized Black female body of its resources to sustain and nurture Black life. This is the crime against God, Black women and men, and the sacred community. It is a form of patricide/matricide in which demonarchs attempt to usurp the divine to remake Black bodies in their image.

Through the eyes and thoughts of Sethe, Morrison depicts the personal grief of this former enslaved woman and mother and tragedy while maintaining the link with the overall Black community and ancestors. Within the historical reality of Black people, Sethe experiences and copes with her drama evoked by the murder of the baby.[32] "When the four horsemen, a schoolteacher, one nephew, one slave catcher, and a sheriff" came to enforce the Fugitive Slave Law of 1851 on Sethe and her children, she commits infanticide to protect her daughter from the tragedies of enslavement.[33] This is the third experience of desacralization that Sethe endures.

The infanticide was Sethe's utilization of her restricted agency. It was the demonstration of her power and authority as a mother within a context that did not allow her to be human, let alone a mother. The infanticide signifies on the hermeneutics of sacrifice that requires spilled blood to atone for sin and to have an abundant life. This conviction is fallacious when placed in conversation with the experiences of Black women who have made sacrifices to recover the power stolen from them. The hermeneutics of sacrifice that demands the shedding of blood is deceptive in this regard because it gives the false impression that the smeared blood on the doorposts of the oppressed will allow death to pass them by. However, within the context of demonarchy, the blood of the desacralized is an invitation for more violence. The infanticide portrays how these sacrifices are made out of love for themselves and their children and have life-giving or death-dealing consequences.

American slavery did not afford Sethe the opportunity and power to shape and direct the life of her child, but she did utilize her power to take it. Her power is expressed in an extreme form because of the denial of power in the context of enslavement is sacral larceny.[34] Motherhood is a sacred office and vocation because of how the Triune God communes with creation, nurtures creativity, and it is the office out of which the Infinite chooses to materialize its vitality. Enslavement placed overwhelming limitations on how an enslaved woman could commune with and nurture her children. Enslavement constructed a cultural, social, economic, and theological technology that worked as a matrix of divestment of that which is honored as sacrosanct to manufacture what Charles Long terms "empirical others" whose experiences were rooted in the absurd meaning of their bodies.[35]

Naming Sethe's experience of desacralization helps to contextualize the psycho-emotional violence that chattel slavery enacted against Black women's humanity. The tragic reality is while Beloved is a fictional depiction of the complex and continually subjugated lives of formerly enslaved persons, it is remarkably close to the experiences that historian Sowande Mustakeem documented in her work *Slavery at Sea*. Sethe is one of the millions of enslaved African women who were raped, beaten, persecuted, victimized, and forced to live in a state of extreme fear and distress. As Mustakeem notes, millions did not survive the journey from the shores of Africa to the "terror at sea."

Beloved and Ancestral Mimesis

Beloved represents the "Sixty Million or more," who were murdered during The Middle Passage. Morrison comments on Beloved's identity with the following words: "[Beloved] is a spirit on one hand, literally she is what Sethe thinks she is, her child returned to her from the dead . . . She is also another kind of dead which is not spiritual but embodiment . . . a survivor from a true, factual slave ship."[36] Beloved's simultaneous existence in both the physical and spirit worlds emphasizes the African tradition of linking life and religion in esoteric and practical ways. Thus, Sethe's understanding of the world grounds in the cultural and religious beliefs of Africans concerning communalism, mother's rights, and the continuum between the dead ancestors and unborn spirits.[37] In parallel with Jesus Christ's abasement and death on the cross, Morrison describes American slavery and the unspoken homage paid by Africans. The infanticide that Sethe commits reflects the helplessness and despair of enslaved and formerly enslaved Africans. It is so extreme that it calls forth the fantastical.

Beloved is in part the reincarnational presence of Sethe's murdered child nicknamed "crawling already." Morrison does not assign "crawling already" a formal name, yet the unnamed presence is fitting because Beloved is also in part the reincarnational presence of the ancestral community who did not survive The Middle Passage. These ancestors are reborn, emerging out of the birth canal of a stream as "old soul(s) seeking reunion with the community."[38] The purpose of their collective reincarnation is to correct the ancestral amnesia of the community. The deaths of the enslaved ancestral community have not been properly mourned, remembered, and taken up into the future by those who survived. Where there is ancestral amnesia, the mimetic offering within the Eucharist celebration is incomplete, decontextualized, and corrupted through the sin of forgetfulness and disregard for the sacramental witness of the blood that was shed and is added unto Christ's afflictions.[39]

Beloved is the host for the ancestors. Sethe, though she is happy at the return of her deceased daughter, becomes their scapegoat to garner the recognition they had been denied. Beloved's violence against Sethe is the expression of the resentment of a child murdered by their parent and the bitter indignation of a cloud of witnesses whose sacramental witness is never fully acknowledged. Beloved, though now embodied, is still "full of a baby's venom" and attempts to strangle Sethe while with her in the Clearing.[40] Beloved should be regarded not as a mere apparition to be exorcised but as one instead to be seen, recognized by her mother and mothering community whose care she was denied, and properly mourned as a single collective consisting of the ancestral martyrs she embodied. The reincarnation of the ancestral martyrs is an assertion of ancestral personhood and human sacrality.

One of the main interventions made on behalf of Sethe and her community is found in the stabilizing presence and influence of her mother-in-law,

Baby Suggs. On a personal level, Baby Suggs tended to Sethe's physical and spiritual wounds. She encourages Sethe to transform her pain into understanding and love.

> "Lay em down, Sethe. Sword and Shield. Down Down. Both of em down. Down by the riverside. Sword and Shield. Don't study war no more. Lay all that mess down. Sword and Shield."[41]

Baby Suggs is the pastoral voice to Sethe and the community. Her voice proclaims love is the counterforce against internalized hate and oppression that robs individuals and communities from its life-giving potential. Womanists have often lifted Baby Suggs's sermon given in the Clearing in which she preaches a holistic doctrine of self-love as well as love for others—a love that cares for the spirit as well the Black body.

In this respect, Baby Suggs promotes contemplation of sacred worth that is fruitful through "deeply loved embodiment" to find relief and communion with the ancestors, community members, and places self-love at the core of communalism. A Christian womanist reading of the text might argue that the Baby Suggs in her efforts to assist in the healing and wholeness of her community represents the liberative work of Christ. She is the face of a womanist Black Christ. Through the voice of Baby Suggs, Morrison embeds the religious inspiration and practices that have enabled African people to overcome that destructive part of their history maintaining their cultural values, dignity, and morals. It is largely due to the death of Baby Suggs that the life-affirming ministry to the formerly enslaved is entrusted to the whole community.

The first generation is represented in Sethe's youngest daughter, Denver who makes supplication to the community to intervene. Out of her plea for help, one of the priestesses in her midst would carry her grievance to the altar of the community of women who understood Sethe's emotional world, but not her infanticide. As Baby Suggs taught them to wail and cry, a cluster of women in the community formed outside of Sethe and Denver's home to intercede on their behalf. The significance of this ritual of healing and intercession resonates with the thought of African religionist Malidoma Patrice Somé, who stresses the importance of grief in his work *Ritual: Power, Healing, and Community*: "Humans must feel grief and be able to express it sincerely in order to free the dead spirit. . . . A singular expression of grief is an incomplete expression of grief. A communal expression of grief has the power to send the deceased to the realm of the ancestors and to heal the hurt produced in the psyches of the living by the death of a loved one."[42]

The healing of the community cannot happen through one person. A Christian engagement of this principle acknowledges the necessity of the whole body of Christ for healing to manifest. Somé furthers our understanding of communal grief and what ensues when this goes unaccomplished when he states: "Any isolated, individual effort to perform ritual that requires community effort will only result in having the departed one come back as a ghost."[43] Beloved expresses a cadre of emotions that holds she and the other ancestral martyrs hostage between the two worlds. In one instance, she is lying on Sethe's lap and softly caressing her neck in search of her mother's diamonds. In another instance, she is strangling her mother.

Somé shares that human emotions can be positive if addressed or become negative and detrimental if these feelings are disregarded.[44] One of the ways that human emotion can be dishonored is through the absence of proper funeral and burial rites. Somé adds this specification: "An unweaned baby who dies does not get this kind of ceremony," and the consequence is that "the dead are stranded between worlds."[45] The community responds to this opportunity to participate in the healing of their sister and community through what Monica A. Coleman describes as "creative transformation," which she defines as a way of "making a way out of no way" through the process of discerning and acting upon the call of Christ in particular situations where it is necessary to challenge the destructive behaviors at work to affirm the life-giving and redemptive incarnation of God in the world.[46] Coleman describes the process of creative transformation as a form of salvific activity in the world that is activated by way of communities embodying the teaching and healing practices of Jesus's ministerial vision.

The Eucharistic Community and Its Divining Power of Solidarity

Human participation in the saving work of Christ is constitutive of transubstantiation, which is consistent with the doctrine of theosis that presumes divine/human consubstantiality as the dynamism within the divine economy. The dynamism of divine/human consubstantiality within the divine economy is lived out through the partaking of the divine nature made real, tangible, and meaningful in the recapitulation of Christ's ministry of compassion through the community's "ministry of compassion" and healing.[47]

Through the clustering of these women who dared to face the past while at the same time humbled themselves to reclaim their exiled sisters, a community was allowed to step out of their disappointment and resentment and into a new future with one another through creative relationality. The invocation provided through their many yet unified voices were enough to conjure up infiltrating holiness that would loosen Sethe's hold on the past so that she might be reconciled to her community. With Sethe reconciled back to the body, a community was fully able to embody redemption through what M. Shawn Copeland refers to as "Eucharistic solidarity." Copeland writes:

> Our daily living out, and out of, the dangerous memory of the torture and abuse, death and resurrection of Jesus Christ constitutes us as his own body raised up and made visible in the world. As his body, we embrace with love and hope those who, in their bodies are despised and marginalized, even as we embrace with love and forgiveness those whose sins spawn the conditions for the suffering and oppression of others.
>
> Eucharist solidarity challenges us in living out the implications and demands of discipleship.[48]

Copeland's words are descriptive of the transformation that occurred for Sethe and is entitled to all who find themselves subject to suffering at the hands of the destructive influences that entrap them. As the thirty women gathered around Sethe's home and sewed themselves together to embrace Sethe and Denver with an emancipatory hope, the marginalization of their bodies and the dejection of their spirits were interrupted. The formation of the body of Christ by the community of women was an extension of forgiveness to Sethe and itself. Through the intercession of these women, Sethe was presented with a chance to finally forgive herself, and this was a salvific opportunity for her. Where there is the assurance of salvation, condemnation no longer has a foothold to establish itself in the lives of individuals. Like Beloved, it ceases to function as a terrorist in our lives. The power to successfully contend with the destructive structures of death and sin is the freedom-bound discipleship to which Copeland's suggestive notion of Eucharist solidarity exemplifies and is assumed in the exercise of creative relationality.

As Copeland poignantly mentions in her work, "solidarity affirms life."[49] One can add: Communal dissension negates life. The disposability of Black bodies and the pessimism regarding the nature of Black life erodes communities because of this lack of solidarity, fragmenting the body, further inhibiting it from being a mode of transformative healing for its members. However, we come to understand what happens when community members choose to embody Eucharistic solidarity by engaging a process of creative transformation through relationality.

For Sethe in Morrison's *Beloved*, through the intervention of her daughter Denver and her community, the soul of the daughter whom she killed along with the cloud of ancestral martyrs who also did not survive, are recognized and communally grieved that they might transition and no longer effect discord. Healing is made manifest through the eucharistic community. The restoration of community for those that have endured fragmentation through the power of the Holy Spirit is the restorative work of divinization. Divinization, then, involves the transformation of individuals as well as the whole community. To echo Zizioulas's astute observation in the last chapter, gleaned through his study and engagement of the pneumatology of Basil of Caesarea, "There is no true being without communion. Nothing exists as an 'individual,' conceivable in itself. Communion is an ontological category."[50] Zizioulas argues that it is the ecclesial community that "hypostasizes" an individual according to the being of God, and this is why the Church, itself, not lone individuals, is the image of God.[51] Furthermore, he clarifies that the very foundation of the Church's existence is "the work of Christ and the Spirit in history."[52]

Zizioulas describes the work of salvation as the "new birth." He is careful to note the presence of the Son in what would otherwise be described as the paracletic work of the Holy Spirit in building communion among human beings or koinonia. With nostalgia appropriate for a patristic theologian, Zizioulas esteems the early church's practice of the Eucharist as a communal practice in which the people of God gathered to manifest, or image God as a collective.[53] Zizioulas regards the Eucharist as the link that connects the early church to the historical Christ and the means of grace through which the Holy Spirit in its distinction is called down from on high to open up history and time for the proleptic inclusion of the Second Coming of Christ.[54] Through the sacramental invocation of the Spirit, the church can become the manifestation of the Trinity through the exercise of God's will to be in *schesis*, or relationship with humanity as a collective body that commits to image God.

According to Zizioulas and other Orthodox theologians, there is a dimension to Eucharistic community that invites individuals to share in the communal life of the Triune God through the Spirit and the engendering of koinonia through remembrance, witness, and testimony. Here we find an affirmation of the part of the filioque clause that witnesses to the prominence of the Spirit in the redemptive work of Christ. The Spirit of God is key to identifying divine activity in creation and formative in our regeneration. Sharing in this regeneration as a communal body is the relational reality of the Church as a Eucharistic community that is the work of God through the Spirit that invites us to witness and partake in faith, hope, and love.

M. Shawn Copeland reminds us that this work of God through the Spirit comes with a particular kind of moral witness, which is that of solidarity and full alignment with the ministry and teachings of Jesus coupled with the embodiment of the mystical body of Christ. Copeland comments that it is only really through this form of solidarity that the restorative work of Christ is accomplished, for it is the marked body of Christ that is exclamatory in this regard. Employing the marginal/God dialectic, Copeland describes divine unanimity with the marginalized as follows:

> If the cries of the victim are the voice of God, then the faces of the victims are the face of God, the bodies of the victims are the body of God. The anguish of the victims of history and the demands of authentic solidarity plead for the presence of the supernatural in the concrete. The history of human suffering and oppression, of failure and progress, are transformed only in light of the supernatural . . . if each and every human person is a part of the whole of interpersonal relationships that constitute human history, then we, too—each one of us—shall be transformed.[55]

Authentic solidarity as a means of transformation involves what womanist ethicist Emilie Townes describes as the transition of the marginalized populace from "victim to change agent."[56] In her proposal of a womanist social ethic of justice, the concretization of the divine occurs through the participation of the oppressed in the resurrection of Christ as a continuous interventionist metaphysical reality. Townes employs womanist writer Audre Lorde's delineation between pain and suffering in her theo-anthropological ecclesiastic realized eschatology. According to Lorde, the pain of the marginalized can be used as a tool for transfiguring one's reality while suffering is a recurrent experience of living through pain to what seems no end.[57]

Townes uses Lorde's portrayal of pain in contrast to suffering to relate the crux of the resurrection of Christ and humanity's participation therein, which is that through Christ's defeat of sin and death came the elimination of what she distinguishes as "true suffering."[58] It is important for the oppressed redeemed in Christ to know "true suffering" is the oppressively constant existence of pain without access and deployment of the theological virtues of faith, hope, and love, that reduces life on this side of consciousness and the hereafter to nonbeing. It is for this reason that Townes provides the disclaimer that in order to engage in the work of liberation, one must dedicate themselves to a life of resistance to the ontological violence that evil imposes upon the oppressed which is "the denial of the right of being."[59]

The ontological violence comes in the form of coercive attacks against what Papanikolaou identifies as the thematic character of the Trinity, which includes freedom, irreducibility, love, relationality, and personhood.[60] The untruth exclaimed through the evils of racism, heterosexism, and class/caste exploitation is "othered" bodies are not a part of the image of God and therefore are not entitled nor should be imagined to be capable of participating in the divine life. The survival and thriving of "othered" and marked bodies are subject to the discretion of the demonarchs. Often the results of these attacks show up in a far more degrading form than dehumanization, such as the acceptance of the poisonous deception that one is limited in freedom, unidentifiable and insignificant in the creation, replaceable, and without the capacity to image the divine. The end of Morrison's *Beloved* illustrates this. Paul D. cannot seem to convince Sethe that she is her "best thing."[61] On a macro level, within communities of the desacralized, individuals wrestle with acceptance and recognition of their innate divinity before they can engage in process of spiritual striving toward greater participation in the life of God.

Divine creativity is paradoxical in that within the pain and torment of enslavement that began at the point of capture, enslaved Africans experienced great agony in no longer being able to claim their embodiment for themselves, but this agony is creatively transformed into a shared emotive tool out of which to build communal solidarity. Within the creative building of community out of the transformation of pain, the desacralized exposes the condemnation of blackness as an unequivocal untruth because through the power of the Holy Spirit and the cooperation of human will, the corporate body of the formerly enslaved images God and affirms their sacred participation within the being of God.

Theosis and Moral Agency

In the final analysis, a womanist refined Orthodox understanding of theosis is a perspective that holds the expression of moral agency by the dispossessed toward their survival, self-reclamation, and flourishing over and against the social evil of racial narcissism to be sacred participation within the being of God. Theosis cannot be understood fully and be consequential in a culture of structural oppression without attention to how the Spirit operates in and through the eucharistic community to be a restorative and redemptive practice of faith when the cognitive approach to understanding ontology is skewed by a deluded consciousness of the self and the *other*. For a community that has been desacralized by the modern Western world's fictive conception of whiteness as an essential and divine property of sacrality, theosis as a holistically redemptive experience counteracts against demonarchy and any other form of evil that seeks to perpetuate the disfigurement of humanity. Using cultural resources such as Toni Morrison's *Beloved* to stretch our imagining of theosis in modern society, divine/human communion is shown to require radical self-love, mimesis, penance, and reconciliation with both the living and the ancestral community. This work also demonstrates that when Orthodox theologians are invited to privilege the voices of the dispossessed and thus disinherit itself from American Christian Gnosticism, then it can renew its commitment to the Transfiguration, which necessitates the divining of theological discourse itself.

Notes

1. Georges Florovsky, "The Ethos of the Orthodox Church," *The Ecumenical Review* 12, no. 2 (1960): 187.

2. Paul L. Gavrilyuk, *George Florovsky and the Russian Religious Renaissance* (Oxford: Oxford University Press, 2014), 262–63.

3. Michele E. Watkins, "A Sacralization to be Fostered: Democratic Womanism as a Construal of the Doctrine of Theosis" (PhD diss., Garrett-Evangelical Theological Seminary, 2017), 45–46.

4. See Sylvester A. Johnson, *The Myth of Ham in Nineteenth-Century American Christianity: Race, Heathens, and the People of God* (New York: Palgrave MacMillan, 2004), 41–44, 47.

5. James W. Perkinson, *White Theology: Outing Supremacy in Modernity* (New York: Palgrave MacMillan, 2004), 58–62.

6. Ibid., 59.

7. J. Kameron Carter, *Race: A Theological Account* (Oxford: Oxford University Press, 2008), 107.

8. Ibid., 11.

9. John D. Zizioulas, *Communion and Otherness* (London: T&T Clark, 2006), 11–12, 24.

10. Ibid., 97–98.

11. Gregory of Nyssa, *The Great Catechism*, V, in *Select Library of Nicene and Post-Nicene Fathers of the Christian Church*, ed. and trans. Philip Schaff and Henry Wace (Grand Rapids, MI: Eerdmans, 1954), 472 and 482.

12. Ibid., 493.

13. James H. Cone, *Black Theology, Black Power* (Maryknoll, NY: Orbis Books, 1969), 151.

14. Delores S. Williams, *Sisters in the Wilderness: The Challenge of Womanist God-Talk* (Maryknoll, NY: Orbis Books, 1993), 88.

15. Delores S. Williams, "The Color of Feminism: Or Speaking in the Black Woman's Tongue," *The Journal of Religious Thought* 43, no. 1 (1986): 52.

16. Delores Williams, "Re-Imagining Jesus," 1993 Re-Imagining Conference Audiotapes (Apple Valley, MN: Resource Express, 1993), album 1, tape 3-1b.

17. Zizioulas, *Communion and Otherness*, 63.

18. Williams, *Sisters in the Wilderness*, 164.

19. Ibid., 166.

20. Carroll A. Watkins Ali, *Survival and Liberation: Pastoral Theology in African American Context* (St. Louis, MO: Chalice Press, 1999), 110.

21. Ibid., 113.

22. Toni Morrison, "'I Regret Everything': Toni Morrison Looks Back on Her Personal Life," interview by Terry Gross, NPR, April 20, 2015.

23. *Catechism of the Catholic Church*, 2nd ed. (Washington, DC: United States Catholic Conference, 2006), sec. 1131.

24. Ibid., sec. 950.

25. Ibid., sec. 1359.

26. Toni Morrison, *Beloved* (New York: Vintage Books, 2004), 336.

27. Ibid., 222–23.

28. Ibid., 19–20.

29. Ibid., 20.

30. Annie-Paule Mielle de Prinsac and Susana M. Morris, "Toni Morrison," in *Icons of African American Literature: The Black Literary World*, ed. Yolanda Williams Page (Santa Barbara, CA: Greenwood, 2011), 276.

31. Morrison, *Beloved*, 81.

32. Angela DiPace, "Toni Morrison's *Beloved*: "Unspeakable Things Unspoken" Spoken," *Sacred Heart University Review* 14, no. 1 (1994): 46.

33. Morrison, *Beloved*, 182.

34. Here I am providing a theological interpretation of Morrison's note of the denial of motherhood and the "outrageous" show of power that Sethe displays.

35. Charles Long, *Significations: Signs, Symbols, and Images in the Interpretation of Religion* (Philadelphia: Fortress Press, 1986), 80, 211.

36. Toni Morrison, *Conversations with Toni Morrison*, ed. Danielle Taylor-Guthrie (Jackson: University Press of Mississippi, 1994), 247.

37. Sharon P. Holland, "*Bakulu* Discourse: The Language of the Margin in Toni Morrison's *Beloved*," *LIT* 6 (1995): 89–100.

38. Barbara A. Holmes, *Joy Unspeakable: Contemplative Practices of the Black Church* (Minneapolis: Fortress Press, 2004) 59.

39. Colossians 1:24.

40. Morrison, *Beloved*, 113–14.

41. Ibid., 105.

42. Malidoma Patrice Somé, *Ritual: Power, Healing, and Community* (New York: Penguin Books, 1997), 74.

43. Ibid., 85.

44. Ibid., 87.

45. Ibid.

46. Monica A Coleman, *Making A Way Out of No Way: A Womanist Theology* (Minneapolis: Fortress Press, 2008), 89–90.

47. *Catechism of the Catholic Church*, sec. 1506

48. M. Shawn Copeland, *Enfleshing Freedom: Body, Race, Being* (Minneapolis: Fortress Press, 2010), 126–27.

49. Ibid., 101.

50. John D. Zizioulas, *Being as Communion: Studies in Personhood and the Church* (New York: St. Vladimir's Seminary Press, 1997), 18.

51. Ibid., 19.

52. Ibid.

53. Ibid., 20–21.

54. Ibid., 22.

55. Copeland, *Enfleshing Freedom*, 101–2, emphasis mine.

56. Emilie M. Townes, *Womanist Justice, Womanist Hope* (Atlanta: Scholars Press, 1993), 195.

57. Audre Lorde, "Eye to Eye: Black Women, Hatred, and Anger," *Sister Outsider: Essays and Speeches* (Freedom, CA: Crossing, 1984), 171–72.

58. Ibid., 195.

59. Ibid., 200.

60. Aristotle Papanikolaou, *The Mystical as Political: Democracy and Non-Radical Orthodoxy* (Notre Dame, IN: University of Notre Dame Press, 2012), 99.

61. Morrison, *Beloved*, 322.

Part II: Theotic Knowing

REVELATION, REASON, AND HOLINESS

A WESLEYAN PERSPECTIVE

William J. Abraham

John Wesley did his work in philosophy and theology on horseback. It is not in the least surprising, therefore, that his contribution to the theology and to the epistemology of theology and that of his heirs in the manifold history of Methodism has not been taken seriously outside its own in-house institutions. Even there, its contribution more often than not lies dormant. As one Presbyterian wag once quipped, "Talking to Methodists about theology is like talking to a bunch of immature teenagers." I have no desire or interest in admitting to or embracing even a soft inferiority complex. Wesley and Methodism represents a whole new configuration of Primitive Christianity that stretches back through Anglicanism to crucial figures in the East like Ephraim the Syrian and Pseudo-Macarius; and it reaches forward through revivalism, the Holiness Movement, Pentecostalism, and post-Pentecostalism to form one of the most vibrant constellations of Christianity in the contemporary world. Hence, it cannot be fitted neatly into the horizons of classical forms of Catholic Christianity or classical forms of magisterial Protestantism.[1] It has in fact a rich legacy of philosophical and theological material, not least in its contributions to dogmatic theology in the nineteenth century. For the most part these remain unknown and underdeveloped precisely because they do not fit the ruling paradigms of the big brothers and sisters in the history of Christianity. Regrettably, Methodists themselves have aided and abetted in this development by dismissing the work done in the nineteenth century as a form of arid scholasticism.[2]

John Wesley, the crucial founder of the tradition, has been understood in a host of ways. I once interviewed for a job (which happily I did not get) where the person who did get it let slip over tea and biscuits that John Wesley was a bigot. It was an awkward moment, but I did nothing to relieve his embarrassment. More seriously, Wesley has been seen as an Anglican revivalist, a folk theologian, a *via media* between Eastern and Western Christianity, and a reasonable enthusiast.[3] For my part, he is best seen as an ascetic theologian, that is, as a theologian of the Christian life. His own favored terminology is that of practical divinity, but we should not be misled by this.

One way to see what he is doing is to note that his canonical *Sermons on Several Occasions* is a fascinating handbook of spiritual catechesis that divide neatly into three units.[4] There is an opening set of fifteen sermons that wrestle with issues related to becoming a Christian; then comes a middle set of thirteen sermons that deal with what it is to be a Christian as delineated in the Sermon on the Mount in Matthew; the last unit of sixteen sermons deals with how to stay a Christian and thus wrestles with a network of issues bookended by the temptation of antinomianism and the hazards of wealth. Hence, while he has a host of essays that deal head-on with what we can rightly identify as revelation, reason, and experience, his treatment of these themes arises in, with, and through his exposition of ascetic theology as worked out by his incessant reading and by acute observations of folk coming to voluntary, conscious faith for the first time. Central to his vision of the Christian life is his commitment to a doctrine of Christian Perfection, a doctrine which brings us within earshot of the language of theosis. For Wesley Christian Perfection was the ultimate goal of the Christian life; it is precisely this emphasis that sets him apart from the standard versions of magisterial Protestantism. It also pulls him into the orbit of the Eastern traditions.

The themes of holiness, revelation, and reason are important to our discussion. These in turn will need to be located into a wider vision of epistemology for the connection to his doctrine of perfection to be intelligible and minimally plausible. It is much more compelling than is generally assumed, and it fits neatly into his vision of divine revelation understood as a polymorphous action on the part of God and into his vision of reason as a capacity to perceive and reason about divine revelation. It also has significant epistemological payoff when related to more recent developments in epistemology. As we proceed, I shall take the liberty of leaving aside at times the precise language Wesley himself used and render it in my own voice.[5]

Realized Eschatology and the Phenomenology of Christian Experience

At the outset, we should beware of our natural inclination to dismiss the language of Christian perfection. Wesley did not believe in some kind of sinless or comprehensive perfection, say, in word, thought, and deed. He was drawing on an earlier usage that came naturally to him as a student of church history. Moreover, speaking of Christian perfection was but one way to capture what was at stake. Thus, we could readily substitute, as Wesley does, a whole range of other concepts: entire sanctification, perfect love, holiness of heart and life, purity of heart, restoration of the image of God, and the like.

One way to think of what Wesley was seeking to delineate is to see it as at one and the same time as a vision of realized eschatology and a phenomenology of spiritual development. Thus, his vision of Christian perfection insisted that in the arrival of God's kingdom brought about by the Son and the working of the Holy Spirit, it is possible in this life to gain victory over evil. He has in mind here a vision of sin as a voluntary transgression of a known law of God rather than sin as original sin, a moral and spiritual state inherited from Adam. Put in more positive terms, Christians do not need to live morally defeated lives; by the grace of God through the inner working of the Holy Spirit, it is really possible to love God and to love our neighbors as ourselves. Given that it is a matter of grace, there is no room for boasting; given that the Holy Spirit causally brings about this transformation, there is no room for Pelagianism. What is at issue is the promise of God in salvation mediated through the ordinary and prudent means of grace made available in the church. God's kingdom has been inaugurated through the incarnation and the gift of the Holy Spirit; promised in that inauguration is the possibility of radical transformation of human agents wherein they come to enter into and then exercise the love that is at the very heart of the Triune God. So much for the realized eschatology.

As to the phenomenology of spiritual development, think of his proposal this way. Initially, the problem of sin for Wesley and for most of his converts focused on the problem of guilt. How can a sinner find the pardon and forgiveness for one's sinful actions? At this point Wesley came to rediscover the radical liberty dramatically captured in the doctrine of justification set forth by Martin Luther and enshrined in the Articles of his own Anglican tradition. This was something of a surprise given his earlier commitment to the view that salvation was by grace—but one became worthy of that grace by works of piety and mercy. It was the encounter with Luther that liberated him from this incoherent and destabilizing doctrine. However, this was but one aspect of the problem of sin; the other aspect was the challenge of the power of sin, the tendency to fall back into the old sins that were constitutive of life before justification and its natural correlative, new birth by the Spirit. This is where we find the psychological observation that generally the new believer was so preoccupied with the problem of guilt that he or she was not even aware of this deeper dimension of the human predicament. Wesley's solution to this was to point out the need for a kind of second conversion, analogous to the first conversion that focused on the problem of guilt. Such a conversion often correlated with a profound crisis of loss, including the loss of children or the crisis of failure in ministry.[6] As the language of entire sanctification suggests, it also generally involved a profound reorientation requiring a meta-choice in which one's life was now entirely at the disposal of God. This kind of choice was renewed in the remarkable covenant service that became a hallmark of Methodist liturgical life before it became a dead letter across the years.

Wesley works out the parallels between justification and entire sanctification in his famous sermon "The Scripture Way of Salvation,"[7] written in 1765 when he was at the height of his powers. He is working here from acute psychological observation of those he was spiritually directing; happily, he does not turn this contingent observation into a causal necessity. However, there is a fascinating underground history to this observation that shows up in the Holiness Movement and that is picked up in early versions of Pentecostalism where teachers develop a two-stage doctrine of the Christian life that shifts from the language of entire sanctification to that of baptism in the Holy Spirit. Contemporary treatments of that issue, namely, baptism in the Holy Spirit, reflect difficulties that are already visible in Wesley. The pertinent issue is how to map a rich variety of theological concepts (justification, new birth, the witness of the Holy Spirit, baptism in the Spirit, and the like) on to the vicissitudes of person-relative experience. There is much work to be done in this domain, work that is crucial for any critical, contemporary appropriation and development of Wesley and the classical theological literature of Methodism.

There is also a very different reception of Wesley's vision of Christian perfection that shows up in the Social Gospel and that in turn explains in part why Methodists have been naturally drawn to versions of liberation theology. In this instance the optimism of grace and its moralistic imperatives are taken into the public arena and worked out in conversation with developments in Christian socialism as developed in England and Germany and more recently in Latin America. The latter obsession shows up in the twentieth century when Methodists become fascinated by various forms of liberation theology.[8] There is also much work to be done in this domain in the wider arena of a theology of politics, even though the conversation has tended to be much too partial and dogmatic in content and resources. For his part, Wesley is best seen as a Burkean in his theology of politics.[9]

So much for a brief exposition of a Wesleyan perspective in the neighborhood of theosis. What is on offer is less an ontology of human transformation and more of a combination of a version of realized eschatology and a psychology of spiritual development. How might any of this relate to treatments of revelation, and reason? Let me take this up by touching on how these themes begin to play out in Wesley.

The Appeal to Divine Revelation

We can begin with Wesley's skepticism about classical natural theology, represented by the standard proofs for the existence of God. The problem here was not so much the logical problems of soundness and validity and more the fact that these did not secure either spiritual stability or intellectual assurance. What bothered Wesley in the 1730s was his lack of assurance in the face of death. Natural theology was useless on this front; it did not resolve the problem of sin and guilt. It was the Moravian missionaries who rattled him to the foundations of his very being on this score. Here were these Christians who could sing hopeful and joyful hymns when there was the danger of their being drowned at sea on their way to the New World. Their teachers challenged him as to where he stood before God, and the best he could muster was a weak expression of hope. This set him back to a study of scripture and the early Anglican theological tradition where he had to come to terms with the need for repentance, with faith in Jesus Christ as the point of access to salvation, and with the possibility of the assurance of the forgiveness of sins here and now. Coming to faith in Christ was accepted as instantaneous, as was the experience of new birth, as was the witness of the Holy Spirit to be a child of God, as was the reception of power to lead a life of genuine holiness.

The Moravians supplied him with a kind of package deal which included assurance of the love of God and the transformation of his moral endeavors. This almost immediately came under strain because Wesley, after his famous Aldersgate experience, found at times he still had doubts and was far from leading a life of holiness.[10] It took him a lifetime to sort all this out both theologically and epistemologically. Given that reason in terms of conventional natural theology failed, he was now forced to think though the epistemology of his commitments. On the one hand, this happened because of his own fierce intellectual curiosity; and, on the other hand, because a host of critics accused him of "enthusiasm," that is, illusory claims to knowledge of God through immediate inspiration or through subjective experience of the divine.

We might capture some of the central moves he makes in this way. His position as a whole might well be presented as a complex articulation of a vision of divine revelation. Consider revelation as a polymorphous concept. Agents reveal themselves in with and through various actions. Think of farming. One farms by planting crops, breeding cattle, reading weather reports, checking market trends, cleaning out pigsties, and the like. Or consider another polymorphous action, teaching. One teaches by giving lectures, grading exams, responding to preceptorial papers, conducting seminars, and so on. Farming and teaching are not actions that one does after one performs these networks of action; farming and teaching supervene on these actions. Likewise with revelation. Hence God reveals himself (his nature and his purposes) by creating and sustaining the universe, by speaking within in conscience, by communicating through chosen prophets and apostles, by enacting his mighty acts in Israel, and supremely by coming in the incarnation in the Son. We are not here dealing with arguments from neutral premises or arguments to the best explanation; we are dealing with various divine actions perceived by the human agent straight off, so to speak. It is a matter of perception of the divine rather than inference to the divine from various phenomena.

The Appeal to the Witness of the Holy Spirit

It was one subset of divine actions that became critical to Wesley after his Aldersgate experience, namely, our perception of the witness of the Holy Spirit wherein we cry "Abba Father" as the Spirit bears witness with our spirits that we are children of God (Rom 8:15–16). On the divine side we have the action of divine testimony: the Holy Spirit bears witness to the love the Father has toward us as made visible to us in the actions of the Son in incarnation and atonement. Think of it as a divine voice within, but a voice that either reminds us or brings home to us the significance of what Christ has done for us. On the human side, the relevant action is that of perception of that action, that is, conscious awareness of the love of God for us as given to us through the working of the Holy Spirit.

This vision of the witness of the Holy Spirit is to be distinguished from two other ways of construing this language. First, the inner witness is not some kind of testimony that tells us which books belong in the canon of scripture, a position adopted, for example, by John Calvin. Second, it is not some kind of inference derived from perceiving the fruit of the Spirit in our lives, a position developed by Jonathan Edwards. The crucial metaphor is that of witness or testimony, that is, discourse drawn from the law courts. A witness gives testimony to that which they know; so, in this case the Holy Spirit who knows the mind of God gives testimony to the love that God has for us. That love in turn has supervened on the action of the Son in incarnation and atonement. Hence the testimony works in, with, and through the preaching of the Gospel (and equivalent media like scripture or other printed media); and the appropriate response to that preaching is faith or trust (*fiducia*) in the promises of God heralded in the Gospel. However, the witness in turn to be effective requires appropriate recognition on the part of the recipient. Here the relevant language is that of perception. One becomes consciously aware of that testimony as a basic act of perception. Exactly the same analysis emerges if we deploy the other metaphor that shows up in the Pauline text that became the central site of exposition, namely, that of the language of "Abba," the language of a child that becomes aware of the love of her Father for her personally.

In both cases, the intentional object of awareness and perception is that of one's pardon and acceptance by God made known in Christ's person and work. Moreover, Wesley is assuming and bringing to his experience the wider doctrinal heritage of the church hammered out in the patristic material and expressed in terms of the canonical doctrine of the Trinity. He is not thinking in terms of nineteenth-century liberal Protestant theology, which focused, say, on some kind of generic experience of absolute dependence on the Whence of the Whole, as developed by Schleiermacher. Nor is he thinking in terms of standard forms of mystical experience that show up on the literature on mysticism, even though he was intensely interested in this material.

Wesley's discourse is rooted in and formed by the wider faith of the church mediated to him in the Anglican tradition. Wesley benefited enormously in this context from the penetrating apologetic work carried out by figures such as Bishop Butler, who defended the truth of the Christian tradition against the deistic attacks of the late seventeenth century. In addition to this tailwind, he lived in a world where there still existed a confessional form of Anglicanism, confessional universities at Oxford and Cambridge, and even a confessional state. The standard picture of the eighteenth century as a bastion of Enlightenment thought needs extensive correction at this point.[11]

Even so, Wesley's vision is a radical one, as radical as the one that shows up in Saint Symeon the New Theologian.[12] Furthermore, Wesley at times, proposes that this kind of assurance applies not just to the intentional object of forgiveness and reconciliation; it also applies to assurance of having experienced nothing less than the Christian perfection that he considered the goal of the Christian life here and now. However, my sense is that Wesley never really pursued this with any care; it was quietly dropped from the tradition as a whole. Perhaps he had his hands full dealing with his doctrine of assurance as applied to forgiveness, not least because what he affirmed to be the case failed to fit with the more complex experiences of Christian believers formed in the Methodist tradition.[13]

My central claim, then, is that Wesley's epistemology can initially be cast in terms of a vision of divine revelation, a vision that has buried within it an account of the spiritual senses that is essential to its content. Thus, he has picked up the important point that divine revelation requires appropriate perception on the human side. One perceives the divine in creation and in Christ; one hears the word of God given to the prophets; one becomes consciously aware of the testimony of the Holy Spirit in one's heart; one sees the sanctifying work of the Spirit in the lives of the saints. Divine revelation without spiritual perception is ineffective; spiritual perception without divine revelation is empty. Such perception of the divine is neither infallible nor comprehensive. It is not comprehensive because it leaves room for essential mystery; it is not infallible because there can be malfunction with respect to the spiritual senses, just as there can be malfunction with respect to the physical senses.

I have already indicated that this vision raises fundamental questions about the relation between perception and the concepts in which we articulate our perceptions. I have also suggested that there are interesting instantiations of some of Wesley's claims, not least, in Saint Symeon the New Theologian. I have not raised the obvious lacuna of how his account is to be integrated into a vision of assurance which rests on authorized absolution given either through the office of priesthood or through a general rendering of absolution given to the gathered congregation. We might state this as the challenge of integrating the charismatic with the institutional (terms much too crude and disjunctive, of course), a challenge that is acutely present in the life and work of Saint Symeon.[14]

The Challenge of Subjectivism

Let me stick to our agenda here and touch initially on one epistemological question that crops up. One that Wesley himself faced is this: How can we secure the epistemic credentials of the inner witness of the Holy Spirit? Is this not a form of subjectivism? What do we do with wayward claims that are delusional? Wesley pursued three lines of response to this challenge.

First, he insisted that the inner witness of the Holy Spirit is confirmed by the fruit of the Spirit that emerges on the other side of such experience.[15] Thus, the internal witness was only genuine if accompanied by the external witness of the Spirit in producing virtue and goodness. I think that the form of argument here is that of informal or tacit inference of the kind developed by Jonathan Edwards. Those who have received the witness of the Spirit show the marks of the Spirit in terms of love, joy, peace, and the like. We observe these marks of the Spirit. Therefore, we have confirmation of the inner working of the Holy Spirit.

Second, Wesley readily deployed a vision of the spiritual senses in which the spiritual senses were to be considered on a par with our reliance on our physical senses. In this he was an empiricist in the tradition of Aristotle rather than of Locke, who argued that you either do or do not trust your senses. There was no evidence beyond this bedrock appeal; you either did or did not trust your senses. To be sure, sin has harmed the reliability of our spiritual senses; however, through the work of the Spirit these were either healed if they were damaged or re-created if they had been destroyed. However, they were to be seen as reliable unless their doxastic outputs were rendered false by relevant evidence. Put differently, the beliefs that arose from spiritual perception could be defeated by further evidence; thus, the failure to exhibit sanctity defeated the claim to have experienced the inner witness of the Holy Spirit.

Third, all claims to have perceived the inner witness of the Spirit are to be governed by the truth about God given in scripture. Thus, the content of scripture operates as a check on what can be asserted about the inner witness of the Holy Spirit. Put in the language I have just used, scriptural teaching could and should defeat any claim that was based on the outcome of the spiritual senses. At this level Wesley took a traditional line on the causal origin of scripture in terms of divine dictation and a correlative doctrine of scriptural inerrancy. Thus, scripture secures an infallible foundation for faith that teaches clearly that the inner witness of the Holy Spirit is underwritten by scripture in that it is clearly taught within scripture itself. More generally, scripture underwrites the epistemological claim that one can and should rely on one's spiritual senses. We see here how Wesley's view of divine revelation as delivered in scripture governs all claims to have rightly perceived all other claims to divine revelation.

I mentioned earlier that at one stage Wesley tried out the proposal that just as one could have awareness of the inner witness of the Holy Spirit with respect to forgiveness, so one can and should expect to experience the inner witness of the Holy Spirit with respect to Christian perfection. However, I dismissed this as a marginal element that died from lack of attention. I also think that it is radically mistaken, in that this claim is defeated by the testimony of those who exhibit exceptional holiness. To express the issue summarily, it is a hallmark of those who exhibit conspicuous sanctity that they insist on the depths of their own sin and their utter reliance on divine grace. This is not in the least surprising in that deep union of God reveals the distance of human agents from God as sinners and thus heightens the sense of divine generosity and divine assistance in the efforts to lead a life of holiness.

Holiness and Epistemology

I now want to look at two ways in which we might explore the significance of holiness in terms that are explicitly epistemological in provenance. One way to think of this is to look on the relevant phenomena as instantiations of conspicuous sanctity. At this point we touch in a direct relation between theosis broadly conceived and the justification of Christian belief. So let me unpack what is at stake.

We all know that many folk come to faith because of exposure to the lives of the saints who live among us. They come across a figure like Archbishop

Dimitri of Dallas; or they come to know someone who loves the unloved to a degree that is astonishing. Are we dealing here with merely emotional and psychological phenomena that have no intellectual or cognitive impact or contact? Wesley rejected this analysis. What happens is that folk who are attentive find this strange and anomalous. Thus, they begin looking around for an explanation. So, they consult the saint, or they read relevant biographical materials and discover that the explanation that invariably shows up in the first-person perspective is that any goodness arises because of divine grace. It is action of God that explains the phenomena not the actions of the human agent. Indeed, as I have already noted, the greater the degree of sanctity, the greater the insistence that the agent is the worst of sinners and that any goodness discerned is to be attributed to divine grace.

Drawing on Wesley, consider the following comment:

> The beauty of holiness, of the inward man of the heart which is renewed after the image of God, cannot but strike every eye which God hath opened, every enlightened understanding. The ornament of a meek, humble, loving spirit will at least excite the approbation of all those who are capable in any degree of discerning spiritual good and evil. From the hour men begin to emerge out of the darkness which covers the giddy, unthinking world, they cannot but perceive how desirable a thing it is to be thus transformed into the likeness of him that created us. This inward religion bears the shape of God so visibly impressed upon it that a soul must be wholly immersed in flesh and blood when he can doubt of its divine original.[16]

Here is the argument that is informally in play in this comment. Suppose we ask: How come such conspicuous sanctity exists? The saint replies: "It is not of me; it is entirely the work of grace." This is a causal explanation of the relevant phenomena. So now we ask: Why should we accept this explanation? The crucial response is that we should accept this explanation prima facie in the absence of a better explanation. Why? Because we have to take seriously the agent who makes these avowals as to its proper origin. At this point we have two options. Either the saint is lying or the saint is misinformed. The first option is out of the question for we are dealing with a person of conspicuous sanctity, and such folk do not generally lie. The second option is questionable because the saint has prima facie privileged access to the truth of the causal factors at work in the origination of sanctity. At this stage the critic must try and provide a better, competing explanation. And that is a tall order precisely because there are no obvious alternative explanations immediately available.

The second way in which a Wesleyan perspective touches on epistemological issues related to conspicuous sanctity is this. The relevant concept at this stage is that of the proper function of our spiritual senses. We noted earlier that sin causes our spiritual senses to malfunction. Wesley went so far as to say that things are so bad after the Fall that human agents are by nature atheists. They have no knowledge of God and no fear of God, and God is systematically absent from their thoughts. The obvious correlative judgment is that the activity of God in sanctification heals our spiritual senses. Initially, our spiritual senses need to be repaired or even re-created (Wesley wobbles on these alternatives). Pressing the issue further, we can surely say that as we are purified in thought, word, and deed we are in a better position to see and understand the truth about God and about ourselves. Put in scriptural terms, the pure in heart see God. As in the case of the argument from conspicuous sanctity, we have here the platform for further and deeper reflection on the relation between theosis broadly conceived and significant warrants for our claims about God. In the first instance, we have a case of an argument to the best explanation; in the second, we have not an argument but a claim represented by the practice of perception.

Both these claims can readily come across as radically odd in the ears of contemporary theologians. This is certainly the case of an argument to the best explanation; the very idea of theological discourse as providing an explanation of anything is enough to evoke stares of incomprehension. Put more formally, it will be said that we have misunderstood the grammar of theological discourse. The appeal to perception is less likely to provoke stares of incomprehension in that most theologians are unaware that there has long been an appeal to the language of spiritual senses in the Christian tradition. Even so, it is easy to miss the epistemological significance of talk about perception of the divine. I think that both the stronger and weaker expressions of incomprehension stem from a failure to come to terms with the dramatic changes in analytic philosophy over the last hundred years. So let me now provide the relevant context for making better sense of the claims that have arisen in my exposition of Wesley.

A Helping Hand from Analytic Philosophy

We can think of the development in Anglo-American analytic philosophy in terms of three phases. In the first phase, there was an all-out attack on the intelligibility of theological discourse represented by the logical positivists so ably represented by A. J. Ayer.[17] Reacting against the idealism of figures like F.H. Bradley and building on the work of G. E. Moore and Bertrand Russell, Ayer resurrected the empiricism of Hume and presented Hume's arguments against all forms of theism in terms of a theory of meaning. Religious discourse was not verifiable by sense experience; hence it could be used to make assertions about God or about divine action. Theological claims could not be true or false; hence theology really had no place in the university.

In the second phase, theologians and philosophers sympathetic to religion tried to provide space for theology by appeal to the principle that usage secured meaning. The principle of verification was meaningless on its own terms (it could not be verified by sense experience); it was usage that determined meaning; and, clearly, religious language must have meaning because it was and is used across space and time. So maybe religious discourse was a form of disguised moral discourse; or it operated by means of disclosure situations; or it had its own unique logic and grammar known to insiders if unintelligible to outsiders. In time, none of these options proved acceptable. Each proposal failed to make actual sense of religious discourse as ordinarily used. More important, there is no such phenomenon as religious usage of language; in religion we use language to perform a host of logically distinct practices, say, making assertions, praying, asking questions, performing baptisms, giving reassurance, and so on. By the late nineteen sixties it was patently clear that the veto on theological truth claims had been either undermined or lifted. In theology we make assertions; the debate is closed.

Phase three both broke new ground and retrieved earlier work by tackling the crucial question of how theological claims were to be justified. In England we had the seminal work of Basil Mitchell, followed by the rigorous and full-scale efforts of Richard Swinburne. In North America we had the emergence of Reformed epistemology brilliantly developed by Alvin Plantinga and Nicholas Wolterstorff. In time this work became so diverse and fertile that it became necessary to invent a new subdiscipline that bridged the divide between philosophy and theology and is now identified as the epistemology of theology.[18] It is not an exaggeration to say that phase three constitutes a revolution not just in philosophy of religion but in philosophy more generally.[19]

Regrettably, this work remains on the margins of much contemporary work in Christian theology. Many theologians continue to take up the challenge of the justification of their claims by historically focused mining of this or that great figure in the history of theology, reaching for help, say, in Pseudo-Dionysius or Evagrius or Nicholas of Cusa, in order to find a way to defend the intelligibility and truth of Christianity in the context of modernity and postmodernity. It is not always clear whether they are offering a regional epistemology that works in the case of theology or a universal epistemology that works in the case of any claim to truth. It would be foolish to ignore such proposals; there is, indeed, epistemic wisdom buried in the work of our predecessors. However, in the end such proposals are unlikely to engage critically or harvest fruitfully the gains that have been made over the recent work in epistemology that is pertinent to sorting through debates about the justification of Christian beliefs, however they may be formulated.

One of the deep surprises of research on John Wesley is that in his own inimitable way he has captured some of the most important insights that have surfaced within recent work in the epistemology of theology. What I have sought to delineate is that he grasped two of those crucial insights.

First, theological proposals do indeed offer explanations for states of affairs in the world. Thus, in looking for an explanation for the existence of conspicuous sanctity, Wesley is rightly noting that by speaking of this originating in divine grace, he is explaining this phenomena in terms of the causal activity of God. It is God and not we ourselves that has brought about conspicuous sanctity. This is an entirely respectable kind of explanation that explains states of affairs in terms of the action of an Agent. We fail to see this either because we harbor pious but underdeveloped views on what theological discourse can genuinely mean, or because we are still taking in the unwashed laundry bequeathed to us by the hostile attacks on theology that were the standard position of a generation of philosophers schooled in the revised version of empiricism developed with such panache by Ayer and his cohorts. No doubt, some may be prevented from being persuaded because they also entertain classical conceptions of God as Being or Being-beyond Being that provide a veto on construing God as an

Agent. However, this move involves at the very least a massive question-begging enterprise that fails to come to terms with the natural discourse of the Gospel and the scriptural traditions.

Second, theological proposals can naturally draw on the whole tradition of the spiritual senses that show up here in the ruminations of Wesley. He is surely on the right track in claiming that growth in grace and sanctity, that struggling with sin and evil in our lives, are important elements in the healing of our spiritual senses. The pure in heart see that God is not a mere pious platitude. It draws attention to the possibility of perception of the divine in creation, in the history of Israel and in Christ, in conscience, in the lives of saints, in our hearts, and the like. Clearly there is much work to be done in sorting through how best to think of perception of the divine and in dealing with the challenges it evokes.[20] However, it is surely obvious that perception of the divine readily provides grounds for believing various theological proposals to be true rather than false. There is no need to claim some kind of infallibility for our perception of the divine, not even when canvassed by the saints of the church. It is enough to speak of *prima facie* reliability, to speak of rational certitude rather than absolute certainty. Thus, in very broad terms, we can begin to see the obvious connection between sanctification and ascertaining the truth about God.

In closing, it is important to highlight the limitations of these arguments in securing the truth claims of Christianity. In and of themselves, they will not be enough to achieve that kind of goal. Thus, we will also need to appeal to the critical place of divine revelation in reaching the full contours of Christian belief. However we integrate the diverse resources for grounding the deep claims of theology, we are likely to fail in this endeavor if we ignore the considerations I have picked up from this foray into the work of John Wesley.

Notes

1. See William J. Abraham, *A Very Short Introduction to Methodism* (Oxford: Oxford University Press, 2019).

2. The only text that provides a rich overview is that of Robert E. Chiles, *Theological Transition in American Methodism 1790–1935* (Nashville, TN: Abingdon Press, 1965), who provides a tendentious, Barthian account of the tradition and it representatives. For an important recent study see Kevin M. Watson, *Old or New School Methodism?* (New York: Oxford University Press, 2019). A first-rate overview is to be found in Jason E. Vickers, "American

Methodism: A Theological Tradition," in *The Cambridge Companion to American Methodism* (Cambridge: Cambridge University Press, 2013), 9–43.

3. The standard biography is that of Henry D. Rack, *Reasonable Enthusiast: John Wesley and the Rise of Methodism* (London: Epworth Press, 2002).

4. John Wesley, *Sermons on Several Occasions* (London: Epworth Press, 1944).

5. For extended treatments of the material I deploy here, see my "Christian Perfection," in William J. Abraham and James E. Kirby, eds. *The Oxford Handbook of Methodist Studies* (Oxford: Oxford University Press, 2009), 587–601; William J. Abraham, *Aldersgate and Athens: John Wesley and the Foundations of Christian Belief* (Waco, TX: Baylor University Press, 2010).

6. This element is well brought out in the work of Elaine Heath in her work on Phoebe Palmer, the nineteenth century Holiness theologian and leader. See *Naked Faith: The Mystical Theology of Phoebe Palmer* (Eugene, OR: Wipf & Stock, 2008).

7. "The Scripture Way of Salvation," in Albert Outler, ed., *The Works of John Wesley, Sermons II* (Nashville, TN: Abingdon Press, 1985), 155–69. This sermon does not show up in Wesley's canonical sermons; it is not entirely clear how it is to be integrated with his strong emphasis on growth in grace to be found there.

8. I stumbled into this when I was a graduate student at Oxford in the 1970s and saw the introduction of liberation theology into the highly influential Oxford Institute of Methodist Studies, which meets at Oxford every four years. I attended a fascinating session with James Cone and later found that the pervasive influence of Latin American liberation theologians sidelined, for example, the much more traditional voices from, say, Singapore. The footprints were still visible at the last meeting of the Institute in 2018.

9. For details see the much-neglected work of Theodore R. Weber, *Politics in the Order of Salvation, Transforming Wesleyan Political Ethics* (Nashville, TN: Kingswood Books, 2001)

10. For a brilliant treatment of what happened at Aldersgate, see Richard Heitzenrater, "Great Expectations," in his *Mirror and Memory* (Nashville, TN: Kingswood Books, 1989).

11. See the revisionist work of J. C. D. Clarke, *English Society 1660–1832* (Cambridge: Cambridge University Press, 2000).

12. I know of no evidence of the influence of Saint Symeon on Wesley. However, a comparison of the two will readily reveal amazing overlapping by way of emphasis. Thus, both make faith, hope, and love the heart of Christianity as embodied in human existence and both insist on a very robust doctrine of assurance through the work of the Holy Spirit.

13. The trouble with Wesley's doctrine of assurance insofar as it maps on to Christian experience shows up emphatically in the life and work of Borden Parken Bowne in the nineteenth century. Seen his treatment of the issue in his *The*

Christian Life: A Study (Cincinnati: Curts and Jennings, 1899). Bowne is too readily dismissed as a facile expression of liberal Protestantism. His efforts to negotiate the challenges that emerge more generally in the nineteenth century are fascinating and should be read with appropriate sympathy.

14. See H. J. M Turner, ed., *The Epistles of St Symeon, The New Theologian* (Oxford: Oxford University Press, 2009).

15. In the canonical sermons Wesley devotes two sermons to the challenges presented by his interpretation of the inner witness of the Holy Spirit.

16. "Upon our Lord's Sermon on the Mount, IV," in Albert Outler, ed., *The Works of John Wesley, Sermons I* (Nashville, TN: Abingdon, 1984), 531.

17. Ayer's *Language, Truth, and Logic* (London: Victor Gollancz, 1936) became the landmark text that sought to undermine the cognitive meaning of theological discourse.

18. See William J. Abraham and Frederick D. Aquino, eds., *The Oxford Handbook of the Epistemology of Theology* (Oxford: Oxford University Press, 2017).

19. The change in fortune has more recently led to the development of analytic theology where the resources of analytic theology are now explicitly brought to bear on the themes and challenges of theology proper.

20. Two especially important treatments are William P. Alston, *Perceiving God: The Epistemology of Religious Experience* (Ithaca, NY: Cornell University Press, 1991), and Caroline Franks Davis, *The Evidential Force of Religious Experience* (Oxford: Clarendon Press, 1989).

The Ambiguous Meanings of Theosis in Modern and Postmodern Discourse

Andrew Prevot

In contemporary intellectual culture, the idea of becoming divine—the idea of theosis, whether always called by this name or not—suffers from numerous ambiguities. Many of these ambiguities derive from the innovative and distorting ways that this idea has been employed in modern and postmodern philosophy.[1] Christian theology needs to discern how best to express a Christian understanding of theosis today in an intellectual milieu shaped by such modern and postmodern philosophical reinterpretations. This is the constructive theological task that I take up in this essay. In addition to certain early Christian and eastern Christian traditions with which the idea of theosis is most often associated, I also consider certain Western Christian (so-called mystical) traditions from the Middle Ages onward, which, thanks to their knowledge of the Dionysian corpus and their debts to Christian Platonism more broadly, also entertain the idea of becoming divine and significantly influence its modern and postmodern receptions.

The particular focus of this volume, namely the question of how theosis stands in relation to faith and reason, helps to clarify some of the ambiguities in contemporary discourse. Classical accounts from various Christian traditions claim that theosis surpasses reason and faith insofar as it empowers one to know God in a way that is so intimate and sublime as to be incomprehensible to ordinary reason and distinguishable from the more obscure ways of knowing that are proper to faith. Yet these same Christian traditions teach that theosis remains deeply connected to reason and faith. As the highest wisdom, theosis not only exceeds but also fulfills the aims of reason. As the highest love, it immerses one in the very mysteries of trinitarian self-gift that faith proclaims. Classically, theosis is not a process by which reason surpasses faith and claims a divine status for itself, as some modern philosophers would have it. Nor does theosis supply the sort of subversive alternative to both reason and faith that some postmodern philosophers would like it to offer. Much depends, therefore, on how one understands the surpassing vis-à-vis reason and faith that theosis is said to accomplish. Although not devoid of productive insights, modern systems of rationalistic idealism and postmodern literatures of excess largely misconstrue the nature of this surpassing.

Questionable shifts also occur through modern and postmodern ideas about the conditions that make theosis possible and the effects that are supposed to follow from it. In short, whereas classical Christian accounts hold the economic Trinity, the ascetical life of the believer, and the sacramental life of the church to be indispensable conditions for theosis, modern and postmodern philosophers tend to view the conditions of theosis as more or less inherent in human nature, whether this is construed in terms of a capacity for transcendental reason (in modernity) or as the self's auto-affective vitality and relationality with the other (in postmodernity). In the extreme, such naturalization of theosis inverts it and reduces it to its very opposite: an idolatrous worship of the creature in place of the Creator. Regarding the anticipated effects of theosis, classical, modern, and postmodern accounts agree that these effects will be both contemplative and active. However, the contemplative takes on an increasingly psychological meaning and the active an increasingly political meaning as one moves closer toward the present. More than ever before, the idea of becoming divine engenders discussion of how such divinization bears on the pathos of each individual life and on the prospects for social transformation. Contemporary theology seems poised to appreciate some of these psychological and political developments while continuing to question whether modern and postmodern treatments of the meaning of theosis are at least somewhat complicit in a host of cultural maladies such as individualism, imperialism, secularism, racism, sexism, and nihilism.

How Does Theosis Stand in Relation to Reason and Faith?

Cruciform, Affective, and Dialectical Motifs

The relationship between faith, reason, and theosis can be clarified to some degree by distinguishing three ways—namely, cruciform, affective, and dialectical—in which theosis may be thought to surpass reason and faith but in which the relationship is actually more complicated. First, the mystery of the cross goes beyond what reason, of a certain sort, can tolerate. A Hellenistic philosophical theology that affirms God's omniscience, incorporeality, and impassibility would hardly predict such an event and could be forgiven for not comprehending it. Yet the apparent foolishness of the doctrine of a crucified savior also represents, according to Paul, a path to a higher wisdom.[2] Moreover, as Athanasius's *On the Incarnation* and subsequent Christological treatises demonstrate, this wisdom admits of some reasonable, theological elucidation.[3] This central Christian mystery does not invite a surpassing of reason and faith but rather a surpassing of mere pagan philosophical reason in order to advance to the wisdom of faith, which in antiquity is still considered a kind of philosophy.[4]

Is the cross a path of theosis? Some sources emphasize that following Jesus to Golgotha is a way for Christians to share not immediately in his divinity, but in his humanity. Hadewijch, for instance, argues that in order to win the favors of Christ's divine love and experience its full fruition one must first consent to be human with him and to take up his cross in one's daily struggles. She argues that cruciformity *humanizes* us. For this reason, it must be distinguished from divinization in any strict sense. Nevertheless, sharing in Christ's crucified humanity remains for Hadewijch an indispensable route toward the eventual enjoyment of Christ's divinity and thus part of the process of theosis in a broader sense.[5] Something similar might be said about John of the Cross's dark nights, where a cruciform experience of divine purgation prepares one for the spousal intimacy of divine union.[6] In short, according to these sources, theosis incorporates the way of the cross in the form of an active or passive asceticism ("passive" meaning that God has taken over the purgative process). This asceticism may be characterized in part as the proper activity of reason subjecting and ordering the unruly passions, and in this respect at least some sort of practical reason may have a significant role to play in the embodiment of the wisdom of the cross. Yet the life of faith, in the sense of discipleship, is more to the fore in such sources.

A second way that theosis may be thought to surpass reason and faith turns on a family of distinctions between terms such as intellect and will, knowledge and love, spiritual sight and spiritual touch, and so on. Some Christian thinkers argue that in order to reach the heights of divine union, the illuminative activities of the mind must give way to the fierier movements of the heart. Consider the final chapter of Bonaventure's *Itinerarium* as just one example.[7] Now, this characteristically Franciscan teaching is far from a universal position in the Christian tradition, and it is often counterbalanced (as it is in the Dominican thought of Thomas Aquinas and in the Orthodox hesychastic tradition) by the idea that theosis encompasses both cognitional and volitional dimensions of the soul.[8] Nevertheless, Bonaventure's *Itinerarium* does indicate one way that theosis may involve some distancing from reason and perhaps from faith as well, namely through feeling or the will. The question of faith's status in such an affective form of theosis hangs on whether one takes faith to be more nearly an intellectual virtue congruent with reason or a volitional disposition of trust akin to love.

A third way that theosis may be thought to surpass reason and faith is arguably the most decisive one for the future, problematic trajectory of this idea. For the sake of convenience, I shall call it "dialectical" (though this name has possible meanings I do not intend in this context). Here I use the word "dialectical" very specifically to refer to a way of construing the meaning of theosis that focuses on a radical suspension of the creaturely conditions of the soul and a total influx or uncovering of the divine nature within it. This dialectic seems, at first blush, to surpass reason and faith absolutely insofar as they are finite activities of the thinking and believing creature for which the creature, now united with the infinite God, would no longer have any use. But matters are more complicated for a number of reasons.

First, perhaps reason and faith will be surpassed at the soul's innermost site of maximal union with God (the soul's center, apex, or ground) but remain operative at other, more mundane levels of the soul's commerce. Something such as this occurs in Julian of Norwich's *Showings*. She posits a radical unity of substance between God and the soul in Christ and at the same time insists on the need to continue reasoning and believing with the church, on the assumption that she remains a composite creature of substance and sensuality in need of continual reform.[9] Meister Eckhart might employ his favorite grammatical tool, the *insofar as* construction, in order to argue similarly that insofar as I am just, I am divine, because justice is a property of the divine nature, while making room for the important caveat that insofar as I am not purely just, there are other aspects of my existence which are not divine and need to be disciplined through reason and faith.[10] Therefore, even in the context of a theosis that is dialectically construed—that is, a theosis in which the finite is negated and the infinite affirmed—the conditions of a corruptible creaturehood can and must be approached from other angles which show that they have not been simply abolished.

Another consideration is that the God with whom one is dialectically united may be the very God of one's faith, not an abstract infinity but the triune God disclosed in sacred scripture and church teaching. This is quite clear in the Seventh Dwelling Places of Teresa of Avila's *Interior Castle*.[11] Even if the act of faith (*fides qua*) were surpassed by a mode of knowledge and love so intimate as to no longer require it, the content of faith (the *fides quae*, that which was believed) could become all the more salient, because now this content would be seen and touched and lived interiorly in an approximately plenary manner. If in theosis faith and hope pass away and there is only love, as Paul seems to suggest, this divine love would nevertheless remain that which one had believed in and hoped for all along, only now experienced with an all-consuming fullness and vibrancy that could not have been anticipated. Whether through a glass darkly or face-to-face, it is the same love.[12] The apparent surpassing of faith that a dialectical account of theosis seems to imply is, therefore, far from a simplistic negation.

Sorting out what happens to reason in a dialectical account of theosis is somewhat more daunting. On the one hand, reason finds itself thoroughly surpassed. Following the path of Dionysius's *Mystical Theology*, the mind is uplifted into a contemplative silence beyond affirmation and denial, beyond similarity and dissimilarity, beyond all of the typical discursive devices normally used to categorize perceptible and conceptual things.[13] On the other hand, this very way of describing an intellectual ascent beyond reason may be attributed to the influence of Neoplatonic philosophy and its abstract speculations regarding the dynamic constitution of the many and the one. In the hands of Eckhart, the infinite divine ground which might at first seem to surpass reason turns out instead to be the very essence of reason (or perhaps of intellect, if a distinction is warranted between these two). There is a way in which Eckhart's philosophical thinking on this point is more audacious even than René Descartes's, since for Eckhart the central argument is not merely *I think, therefore I am* but *insofar as I think and exist, I am divine*.[14] Although Marguerite Porete's *Mirror of Simple Souls* is not particularly affective in its rhetoric and imagery, she does differ from Eckhart insofar as she associates her dialectical account of theosis not with her personified character of Reason but with her personified character of

Love. Porete is clear that this Love has its own intellect.¹⁵ Nevertheless, her love-based dialectical theosis seems less vulnerable than Eckhart's to a distortive rationalistic interpretation.

Modern and Postmodern Variants of These Motifs

Such a rationalistic interpretation of theosis reaches its high point in the modern tradition of the "metaphysics of spirit" that Hans Urs von Balthasar associates especially with the three titans of German idealism: Johann Fichte, Friedrich Schelling, and G. W. F. Hegel. These modern philosophers identify their own transcendental consciousness with the infinite subjectivity of divine spirit. Exploiting a dangerous possibility latent in Eckhart's dialectical thought, they attribute a divinizing power to reason itself.¹⁶ Hegel, for his part, does grant that the content of Christian faith, including especially the trinitarian event of the cross, represents, as well as any historical faith might, the dialectical relation of the infinite and the finite which is the truth of philosophy. Nevertheless, he contends that reason's method of comprehending this truth is the only sure way for consciousness to reach the absolute. Hegel thus reverses the direction of the cruciform strategy of surpassing. His meditation on the cross leads him from faith to the supposedly higher wisdom of reason, not the other way around.¹⁷ Hegel's resistance of Friedrich Schleiermacher's turn toward religious feeling shows both that Hegel is not attracted to an affective account of deification and that this affective approach finds its own modern reconfigurations in the liberal Protestantism that Schleiermacher inaugurates. Above all, Hegel builds his modern doctrine of theosis on a rationalistic revamping of Christian mysticism's traditional dialectics. He takes the reason of the philosopher—not the faith or love proclaimed by the Christian tradition—to be the means by which the absolute becomes manifest in and through its antithesis. At first, this approach to theosis might seem to come at the expense of a real appreciation for human finitude, passion, and materiality. However, the dialectical tables are easily turned when the reason of a human mind provides their axis, and it may in fact be the divine that finds itself debased. Balthasar suggests as much when he concludes that Hegel's thought is only a short step away from the atheism of a Karl Marx or Friedrich Nietzsche.¹⁸ As William Desmond puts the point: "Hegel gives us a counterfeit double of God." Hegel's is an "erotic absolute," a product of human spirit's striving for mastery of self and other.¹⁹

Some Christian commentators on Hegel do offer a more sympathetic reading. For example, while acknowledging some problems with Hegel's totalizing ambitions, Rowan Williams charitably interprets Hegel's dialectical philosophy as a form of nondualistic thinking resonant with the apophatic theology of John of the Cross, Vladimir Lossky, and Christos Yannaras. Williams appreciates Hegel's emphasis on the doctrine of incarnation, Hegel's affirmation of the theological importance of dynamic social processes in history, and Hegel's (perhaps surprising, but in any case underappreciated) references to an ecstatic divine love.[20] Although Williams's argument discourages any immediately dismissive response to Hegel on the part of Christian theologians interested in theosis, it does not eliminate Balthasar's and Desmond's grounds for worry, which have been echoed and developed in a different way in Cyril O'Regan's studies of Hegel's Gnostic distortions of Christian narratives.[21]

With the dangers of Hegel in view, Christian theologians may be inclined largely to agree with the postmodern complaint that German idealism misconstrues theosis by identifying it so thoroughly with reason. On such grounds, theologians may justly appreciate Martin Heidegger's critical account of the ontotheological constitution of metaphysics and his confrontation with modern technocracy, even though his own mythopoetic ontology leaves much to be desired.[22] Nevertheless, theologians must also recognize that postmodern philosophers exploit a dialectical account of theosis in other ways that are similarly problematic. That by virtue of which the creature loses itself and becomes divine—or vice versa—is no longer called "reason" in postmodern texts but rather "life" or "otherness." The vitality and alterity of human experience are not only thought to surpass reason. They also function like the reason of modern philosophy insofar as they appear to carry thought beyond both the act of faith and its content. The content of faith might not be dismissed entirely, just as Hegel does not entirely dismiss it, but it is interpreted in terms of the life and otherness that it represents, and thus not straightforwardly on its own theological terms.

According to the postmodern phenomenologist Michel Henry, who has recently garnered some appreciative scholarly attention,[23] the transcendental self's auto-affection—its experience of itself as a touching, feeling, and living thing—manifests the very essence of the divine. Henry argues that scripture and phenomenology equally support the claim that there is a transcendental unity of each living thing with divine life itself. For Henry, theosis is a process of becoming aware of this already given unity, and this can be done with or without faith, simply by contemplating the fact that one is alive. In this way, Henry integrates an affective surpassing of faith and reason with an Eckhartian dialectical argument, which holds that insofar as I am *x* (in this case, living), I am divine.[24]

Michel de Certeau moves in a different direction in his postmodern studies of Christian mysticism and his broader heterological project. Without neglecting the content of Christian faith, he interprets it in terms of the otherness that it represents, an otherness that appears as an enticing or disruptive force in various historical, cultural, and institutional spaces. To be clear, for Certeau one is not divine simply because one is othered in such spaces. Indeed, as a Lacanian, he thinks of the divine not as something one possesses but as something one perpetually lacks—a never attainable, infinite object of desire—and in this sense there is no real doctrine of theosis in Certeau's work. Before death there is only ceaseless mourning and longing. Nevertheless, one's otherness enables one to function in the sorts of subversive, incomprehensible ways that the divine would function in similarly structured circumstances, and in this respect one's otherness may indicate a practical kind of divine likeness.[25] Certeau's account of alterity as a discourse which names the nonsystematizable practices of the human and the divine resonates with Jacques Derrida's similarly de-theologizing suggestion, informed by his readings of Emmanuel Levinas and Søren Kierkegaard, that "every other is wholly other" (*tout autre est tout autre*).[26] For such postmodern thinkers, otherness enacts a theosis not of divine substance and presence but of divine performance, style, and ethical injunction. Even if there is an explicit denial of God, as there is in Georges Bataille's Nietzschean *Atheological Summa*, there may still be a kind of "atheosis" that surpasses reason and faith for the sake of a nondivine transcendence or excess with notable cruciform, affective, and dialectical features. Bataille's reading of Angela of Foligno exemplifies this possibility.[27]

Some postmodern feminist philosophers divinize women's subjectivity by interpreting women's vitality and alterity as signs of an inherent or emergent divine status. The chapter called "La Mysterique" in Luce Irigaray's *Speculum of the Other Woman* is a crucial text in this regard. Irigaray argues that the feminized soul's abyssal ecstasies of torment and *jouissance* identify it with Christ crucified and transform it into "God."[28] She puts the word "God" in scare quotes to emphasize its questionability. Grace Jantzen's book *Becoming Divine* draws on Irigaray to contend that the act of faith is unnecessary. What matters for the theosis of women is recognizing that their subjectivity already has the power to exhibit divine characteristics of fruitfulness and life-giving relationship with others.[29]

The importance of such feminist interventions should not be underestimated. Throughout the Christian tradition the idea of theosis has been construed in patriarchal terms, whether this means presupposing a male subject of mystical ascent (as on the exclusively male Mount Athos) or attributing stereotypically feminine characteristics to this subject regardless of whether its physical sex is male or female, that is, characteristics such as receptivity, emotionality, and submissiveness to a masculinized depiction of divine power (as one finds in the *Song of Songs* commentary tradition). To uphold the idea that theosis is a gift meant equally for women and men, a gift that does not discriminate based on gender but rather calls each precious human life to the same unfathomable experience of divine union, it is necessary not only to resist androcentric and gender essentialist features of the Christian tradition but also to offer positive accounts of a deifying divine presence at work in real women's lives. At their best, Irigaray and Jantzen do just that.

As a Christian theologian, my only worry about their works is that, like those of Heidegger, Henry, Certeau, Derrida, Bataille, and other postmodern thinkers, they transpose theosis into a faith-bracketing, philosophical register that does not thoroughly accommodate it. Something crucial is lost in such transpositions. Their affirmations of life and otherness are commendable and illuminating. Indeed, with enough theological circumspection these affirmations may be appreciated as potentially beneficial developments of the doctrine of theosis. Nevertheless, the fact remains that these postmodern philosophers theorize divine becoming in atheological ways that dramatically alter its meaning.

The Conditions and Effects of Theosis

Questions of Nature and Grace

The gravest problem shared by modern and postmodern philosophers alike is their "naturalization" of the conditions of theosis. They suggest in different ways that certain formal structures of human existence—independent of the practice and content of Christian faith, though this content may be mined for anthropological insights—provide a sufficient basis for whatever sort of theosis they desire. The human can become divine, or at least something like the divine, by embracing its capacity for reason, on the one hand, or its vitality and alterity, on the other. There is no need for the saving work of the economic Trinity (that is, no need for this saving work if it is understood as a real happening and not a mere representation of logic's inescapable movement from thesis to antithesis to synthesis or human flesh's excessive oscillations between suffering and pleasure). There is no need to receive the sacrament of baptism and participate in the mystery of Eucharistic communion, and hence no need for the church. Certain ascetical requirements remain in the form of disciplining the mind to think philosophically and disciplining the body to live relationally. Yet these epistemological and ethical requirements may do little to alleviate Christian theological doubts about whether the most salubrious forms of wisdom and right relationship are likely to emerge from a version of theosis which, at bottom, appears to be self-glorifying.

Should it be so easy to say that I am divine? Should we not tremble at such a thought, confess our lowliness and failings, and offer all honor and glory to the Father, Son, and Holy Spirit who give their life to be shared in such an extraordinary manner? If theosis ceases to be an ecstatic doxology that carries the creature into union with its trinitarian source on the wings of praise and adoration, then, regardless of certain stylistic similarities and material borrowings, it is no longer theosis in a proper sense but something else. It is the creature finding satisfaction in itself and in its admittedly mysterious powers or vulnerabilities. It is a finite nature feigning self-sufficiency by secularly repackaging certain modes of transcendence which the Christian tradition, by contrast, receives and names as grace. Christian theology attributes theosis, not to mere reason, life, or otherness, but to a historically operative divine love, reigning from all eternity, which takes flesh in Christ and gathers together a Spirit-filled community of believers called to holiness.

The fact that certain features of human nature seem to imitate this grace should not be surprising to theologians who accept Karl Rahner's well-known contention that there is no such thing as "pure nature."[30] The only nature that concretely exists is one that is always already graced—and, one must add, deeply marred by sin. The graced character of nature accounts for its ability to reflect theosis in a rich abundance of different forms, including those of modern and postmodern philosophy, whereas the corrupting power of sin upon nature accounts for the ways that these philosophical discourses rationalistically, vitalistically, or heterologically turn certain cruciform, affective, and dialectical features of theosis against the very God that made theosis thinkable in the first place by giving this incomprehensible mystery to the world as a sheer grace. The problem is not that the gift of divinization, which inchoately permeates human existence thanks to the incarnation of the Word and the historical movements of the Spirit, generates countless imperfect analogues and replicas. The problem is that many modern and postmodern imitations of theosis forsake their divine source, neglect the mystagogical practices and communities of worship which have historically prepared believers to be drawn into it, and thereby fundamentally misconstrue the meaning of this greatest of all possible gifts. In the final analysis, the love of God is replaced by the creature's admiration of itself. I am not claiming that such admiration is wrong. There is much to admire in a graced nature even if one does not recognize it as graced. My claim is only that such admiration is no substitute for the love of God.

Some theologians might suggest that such modern and postmodern deviations prove that the doctrine of theosis is too risky to be sustained, at least in exoteric teaching. Their reasoning might be that in traditional texts, such as Dionysius's *Mystical Theology*, union with God is not an experience meant to be discussed with everyone but rather a secret, esoteric knowledge meant only for the few who are prepared to receive it. Perhaps the pitfalls of modernity and postmodernity reveal the wisdom behind Dionysius's secrecy. Yet I cannot embrace this line of reasoning because I actually do appreciate modern and postmodern efforts to expand the reach of the idea of theosis and thereby overcome any unnecessary and detrimental elitism. Why not pursue deification for all? Is not God's love boundless and infinitely merciful, ever seeking out the lost? The obvious challenge in such a project will be to retain the Christian theological meaning of the discourse, without which it becomes something considerably different. To meet this challenge, I suggest that it would be best for theologians not to discard the doctrine or to hide it from view but rather to disambiguate it by studying its classical sources and contemporary variants simultaneously, as I have been attempting to do throughout this essay.

The scholarly labor of historical retrieval is an essential part of the effort to disambiguate the idea of theosis. To restore a clearer sense of its meaning, contemporary theologians need to reexamine the trinitarian, sacramental, and ascetical conditions for theosis which are widely attested in some of its earliest formulations. Jeffrey Finch illustrates this possibility in his reading of Athanasius's teachings on deification in the context of the Arian controversy. Finch summarizes Athanasius's logic in this way: "The redeemed cannot be made participants in the divine life of the Holy Trinity through incorporation into the Son [that is, the redeemed cannot be divinized] if the Son himself had been divine only by gratuitous participation [that is, if the Arians were correct to deny the Son's divine nature]." As Finch reconstructs it, Athanasius's anti-Arian polemic does not argue *for* the doctrine of theosis but rather argues *from* it to the idea that the Son is truly divine. For Christian theologians today, this premise of Athanasius's argument has the added value of clarifying, *pace* modern and postmodern interlocutors, that theosis is made possible not merely by certain conditions of human nature but by the saving action of God occurring through Christ. In other words, the same premise can now help Christians navigate a new historical moment of doctrinal crisis, in which the disputed question is no longer merely about the divinity of Christ but about the divinity of divinization itself. Athanasius bears witness to the early church's unambiguous views on this latter question, which I dare say were so unambiguous that the question would hardly have been conceivable to him. Clearly, he would claim, theosis is a work of the Trinity.

Finch's analysis proves helpful in another way by demonstrating that, for the patristic tradition, just as for modern and postmodern philosophers, the human creature does not do nothing in the process of deification. However, *what* the creature does is fairly specific, and there is an ecclesial setting for such practices. According to Athanasius, merely thinking, living, and relating as a human being are not sufficient means to prepare one for theosis. He presupposes that "the divine-human exchange of the incarnation must be appropriated to each individual through the obedient imitation of Christ's ascetical practices [which involve the overcoming of sin and the development of virtue] and by reception of the sacraments [including especially Baptism and Eucharist]."[31] Union with God therefore traditionally requires an arduous struggle for self-discipline and holiness, which is assisted by a church that unites and transforms its members by means of the waters of rebirth and the communal breaking of bread.

Such trinitarian, ascetical, and sacramental conditions of theosis are also evident in Cyril of Alexandria, Maximus the Confessor, and Teresa of Avila, to name only a few.[32] This is the consistent teaching of the premodern Christian tradition regarding the particular factors which make it possible for human beings to let their nature be renewed and remade in God's image.

The basic meaning of theosis (whether named as such or not) is more or less continuous across these disparate sources. It refers to a transformative gift of union with the triune God that is administered through an ecclesial practice of faith. For Christians of both East and West, the doctrine of theosis does not imply that there is a divine likeness so inherent in and constitutive of human nature that there would be no need for anything else. On the contrary, it explicitly holds that fallen human nature needs to be transfigured by wondrous divine actions—above all the action of God taking on human flesh—and that this normally happens for each individual through communally mediated strivings for virtue, wisdom, and sanctity. A Rahnerian account of a universal offer of divinizing grace, which is grounded in the core Christian belief in a God of infinite love, may lead some theologians (and I am among them) to question whether explicit sacramental participation is strictly necessary for theosis to occur in every conceivable case. But even on such a Rahnerian account, the acquisition of virtue and, above all, the unitive action of the Trinity *ad extra* would remain nonnegotiable conditions. Keeping these foundational elements in view helps one distinguish a mimetic discourse of theosis that has been compromised by a process of philosophical naturalization from a more reliable doctrine of theosis that remains faithful to its original meaning as a Christian theological experience of grace.

Changing Views of Contemplation and Action

Although, as I have just argued, God is the primary agent of theosis, the human creature also participates in it in many ways. Sometimes this participation is parsed in terms of contemplation and action, theory and practice, the interior life of the mind and the exterior life of the body, or some other similar pairing. This twofold contemplative-and-active participation of the creature may be understood as both a condition for theosis (that is, something without which it would not occur, as noted earlier) and as its principal effect (that is, how the gift of divinization becomes manifest or what differences it makes to the one who receives it). The question for the Christian tradition and its modern and postmodern reception is not whether theosis becomes recognizably efficacious through transformed ways of thought and life but how precisely to characterize such effects. In the passage to modernity and postmodernity, the methods of description have become increasingly psychological and political. Although theologians may be skeptical of such developments insofar as they may betoken anthropocentric, experientialist, or pragmatist reductions of the meaning of theosis, I would suggest that greater attention to the personally introspective and socially impactful effects of theosis could be a very good thing if these are understood in the context of the creature's contemplative-and-active participation in what is essentially a saving work of the Trinity.

Denys Turner is troubled by a certain psychological turn in modern Christian mysticism which he traces back to John of the Cross's descriptive account of the "experiential feedback" of divine union. Turner contends that the modern problem of "experientialism" arises when such descriptions of experiential feedback are mistaken for the substance of mystical theology, which is more properly the dialectical oneness with God taking place beyond both perceptible and conceptual consciousness. Turner's argument helpfully warns against the contemporary trend, evident at least since William James, of reducing the meaning of theosis to an extraordinary type of religious experience which I might undergo if I am fortunate enough to be a mystic.[33] But suppose one does not mistake the experiential effect for the transcendent mystery. Would it not be worthwhile to study both with as much precision as possible? As Turner acknowledges, there is a difference between taking psychology to be definitive of theosis and paying close attention to the figuratively "interior"—that is, affective and cognitive—manifestations of theosis. Given this distinction, one need not read the sixteenth-century Discalced Carmelite Doctors as merely foreshadowing a subjectivist deterioration of the mystical tradition, as Turner does. One can also, in line with Constance FitzGerald and Joann Wolski Conn, work to recover John and Teresa's simultaneously theological and psychological insights about the mysteries of impasse, torment, and ecstatic joy.[34]

For psychoanalytic postmodern philosophers, the temptation may be to explain away any divine transformation by attributing the supposed experiential evidence of it to certain psychodynamic properties of a fragile, desirous ego, which wants to make an impossible return to the womb and restore its lost "oceanic" feeling. However, interestingly, Julia Kristeva does not favor this route in her *Teresa, My Love*. This remarkable text, both novel and treatise, instead explores certain positive therapeutic insights in Teresa's writings and praises her for providing corrections to the psychoanalytic traditions of Sigmund Freud and Jacques Lacan.[35] A theologian reading Kristeva's book can appreciate her investigation of the psychological aspects of Teresa's contemplative life while resituating them in a more traditional theological understanding of theosis.

The question of a political meaning of theosis may understandably cause some alarm among observers of a modern epoch that has witnessed untold destruction and cruelty at the hands of rulers feigning a godlike sovereignty, that is, implicitly espousing a modern doctrine of theosis, not of reason but of the will. The Hobbesian dream of a dictator with the absolute powers of a deity—a nightmare revived by Carl Schmitt's *Political Theology* and exemplified by the most violent tyrants of the twentieth and twenty-first centuries—must be sharply differentiated from the sorts of political thinking and conduct which may result from a true participation in the divine life offered through Christ. If the rationalism of Hegel is perilous, a Hobbesian voluntarism proves to be even more so, because even the insufficient restraints imposed by Hegel's philosophical ambitions of logical coherence and systemic completeness are removed, and society is left at the whims of an unrestrained will. Such a voluntarist pretense of godlikeness is, in fact, demonic, as the genocidal rage of the Third Reich unspeakably demonstrates.[36] This point is made in another way by Michele Watkins's discussion of the false divinization of racial whiteness in connection with Delores Williams's account of "demonarchy."[37]

In various ways, both Jürgen Moltmann and John Zizioulas suggest that a pneumatologically accented social trinitarianism might be a key to specifying the political form of genuine deification, namely as a graced communitarian existence.[38] This is an attractive possibility for a number of reasons, both theological and political. With respect to theology, it overcomes the false impression that theosis is an individualistic doctrine, merely about the spiritual journey of an individual soul, as if such a journey could occur in isolation from others. It draws on the liturgical life of the church and certain teachings about the community-building work of the Holy Spirit that are sometimes underappreciated by Western Christians to argue that grace is a constitutively relational happening. The Christian Platonic emphasis on the divine one is counterbalanced by a celebration of trinitarian multiplicity and *perichoresis*. Politically, this approach counteracts the antisocial habits of both would-be authoritarian leaders and self-obsessed subjects. It underscores the need for political communities of hospitality, interdependence, and solidarity (perhaps like the audience of Baby Suggs's sermon in the Clearing from Toni Morrison's *Beloved*).[39]

While endorsing such theological communitarianism, I also submit that it works best when supplemented by the dramatic, martyrial image of believers so consumed by the love of God and so distressed by the way the current social order of things rejects it, that they are willing to risk and lose their lives in a political struggle for a divinely transfigured world. In addition to the ideal of a loving community, contemporary theology needs a politically conscious hagiography that highlights the socially impactful struggles of the deified. I am thinking of saints such as Archbishop Oscar Romero, whose witness to Christ represents, as well as any historical witness might, what theosis looks like in an oppressive political context. The martyred Jesuit theologian Ignacio Ellacuría wrote that "with Monseñor Romero God passed through El Salvador."[40] I read this statement as a claim about Romero's theosis. The deified in the public square are not those pretending to be gods and amassing wealth and power for themselves but rather those who have been totally undone and remade according to the humble yet courageous pattern of Jesus.

Another witness who might be mentioned in this regard is Sojourner Truth. As a young slave girl (originally named "Isabella") who knew no life outside of slavery, she viewed her masters as gods and surrendered herself to their often cruel, sexually abusive treatment. This condition of spiritual and physical subjection took a new form after her emancipation from slavery, when she fell under the influence of a misogynistic, charismatic cult leader ("Matthias") who styled himself an incarnate god and taught that "everything that has the smell of woman will be destroyed" because it "is full of all deviltry."[41] For the first four decades of her life, Isabella suffered greatly from the violent actions of pseudo-Christian slaveholders and counterfeit millenarian prophets who made false claims to deification, suggesting that their supposed access to divine power and authority gave them the right to control and manipulate others' lives at will. Her oppressors are poignant representatives of a Schmittian sort of demonic "political theology," which naturalizes theosis in a particularly dangerous way by equating it with a man's sovereign will. In part, therefore, Isabella's story demonstrates the extraordinary psychological and political stakes of getting the idea and practice of theosis right in a white supremacist, sexist culture where it so often goes horribly wrong. If the *Narrative of Sojourner Truth* ended here, it would only offer an important lesson about what divinization is *not*.

However, by the grace of God, Isabella's story does not end at this miserable point. Gradually, a healing relationship with the Trinity emerges and grows in her prayer life. She receives mystical visions of the almighty Creator and of Jesus as an intimate friend, visions which convince her that she is not meant to be enslaved. After the collapse of Matthias's "kingdom," she receives another mystical experience on the feast of Pentecost. The Holy Spirit calls her to a new way of life as a true prophet of God's goodness and mercy. In response to this new vocation to holiness, Isabella changes her name to "Sojourner Truth."[42] As a *sojourner*, she remains very much a fragile human being, a pilgrim wandering the world, continually searching, longing, and striving. But as *truth*—that is, insofar as she is now also a vessel of the divine wisdom that has come to her through the indwelling presence of the Holy Spirit (an Eckhartian type of argument)—she is really and truly divine, albeit by participation. God now speaks and works through her, just as God spoke and worked through Marguerite Porete, Teresa of Avila, and so many others. This presence does not belong to any of the false gods that afflicted Isabella but rather to a true and living deity, a source of infinite love, strength, and peace. This presence is not identical to her innate subjectivity (as it would be for some modern and postmodern philosophers). Rather, this presence is the indwelling of a divine other who loves her. It is the Trinity revealed in the economy of salvation, now received into her traumatized but healing heart.

This divinization empowers her to be an extraordinarily influential abolitionist and feminist activist, both in her day and in our own. Her example is cited by Kimberlé Crenshaw's groundbreaking formulation of the critical legal theory of "intersectionality," a theory that has since moved beyond law to transform discourses across the humanities and social sciences, compelling them to seek the liberation of all people, including poor Black women and other frequently forgotten persons marginalized by multiple overlapping oppressions.[43] Sojourner Truth is an icon of what theosis looks like within the intersecting, violent political realities of our modern and postmodern world. The soothing experiential feedback of her practice of contemplation empowers her to struggle for a new political reality of communitarian grace. If God passed through El Salvador in Oscar Romero, God also passed through the United States in Sojourner Truth. Theirs are the real, human faces of theosis. Their examples inspire a contemplative-and-active practice of Christian faith that does not abandon the world in an escapist flight toward eternity but rather fights in and for the world with the tender guidance of eternity. Together they prove that deification, in a right and proper sense, really can make a major, recognizable difference not only in individual lives but also in the lives of entire intergenerational societies.

The Stakes of a Disambiguated Theosis

Are modern and postmodern naturalizations of theosis reflective of a narcissistic individualism, which encourages each person to view him or herself as a little god? Are they complicit in a world-destroying imperialism, which occurs in intersecting white supremacist and misogynist forms that mimic divine sovereignty without a trace of divine compassion (Schmitt)? Are they uncritically beholden to an atheistic secularism, which has no further need for God or for the church and blithely dismisses the experiences of those who are devoted to these realities? Are they vulnerable to a terrifying encroachment of nihilism, which either instrumentalizes the murderous history of the world for the sake of a supposedly absolute system of knowledge (Hegel) or fetishizes the lacerations perpetrated by this history as means for evading conceptual control (Bataille)? Although these questions are stated rather pointedly, and although they are certainly not applicable in every case, since distinctions need to be made between various modern and postmodern proposals, they are meant to provoke some much-needed reflection, particularly about thinkers such as Schmitt, Hegel, and Bataille, whose problematic theories I have noted. The dangers indicated in this litany of questions are real.

But so too is the promise of revitalizing a Christian theological understanding of theosis as a mystery of contemplative-and-active participation in divine life, which surpasses reason and faith only while fulfilling their deepest aims. In addition to the ascetical training of the mind and will which modern and postmodern philosophers retain in various respects, a theological doctrine of theosis requires a particularly Christian form of asceticism defined by discipleship, that is, following Jesus. To recover their own best understanding of theosis, Christians must remember the trinitarian economy of salvation and affirm it as an unsurpassable gift. The divinizing grace of the Trinity is made accessible in crucially important (though not exclusive) ways through the ecclesial celebration of Baptism and Eucharist as sacraments which unite believers in the body of Christ and bless them with the superabundantly loving presence of the Holy Spirit.

In view of such trinitarian grace, the excessive qualities of the wisdom of the cross, the fiery passions of the sanctified heart, and even the dialectical closeness of Creator and creature in the innermost depths of the soul need not cause Christians to fret, as if all the troubles of modernity and postmodernity followed automatically from such cruciform, affective, and dialectical features of their own tradition. These features must simply be given a proper theological interpretation.

Nor should Christians be afraid to incorporate new insights from modern and postmodern treatments of theosis, particularly regarding its connections to transcendental reason, auto-affective life, ethically obligating alterity, psychotherapeutic practice, and the liberative transformation of society. Provided that Christians do not forget the gracious conditions that make theosis possible and provided that they remain cognizant of the ambiguities that plague its modern and postmodern receptions, they are free to investigate the full range of its contemporary significance and wholeheartedly affirm what is good in it. When in doubt, a critical hagiography of Christian saints and witnesses may be a sure guide. Once disambiguated, theosis ought not be an occasion for fear but rather for hope—hope, namely, that another world is possible.

Notes

1. Other ambiguities pertaining more to the ecumenical Christian broadening of the idea of theosis than to its reception in modern and postmodern philosophy have been discussed by Gosta Hallonsten in "*Theosis* in Recent Research: A Renewal of Interest and a Need for Clarity," in *Partakers of the Divine Nature: The History and Development of Deification in the Christian Tradition*, ed. Michael J. Christensen and Jeffrey A. Wittung (Madison, NJ: Farleigh Dickinson University Press/Rosemont Publishing, 2007), 281–93.

2. 1 Corinthians 1:17–25.

3. Athanasius, *On the Incarnation*, trans. John Behr (Yonkers, NY: St. Vladimir's Seminary Press, 2011), sections 21–27.

4. Gregory of Nyssa, *The Life of Macrina*, in *Lives of Roman Christian Women*, trans. Carolinne White (New York: Penguin Books, 2010), 22–48, at section 5.

5. Hadewijch, "Letter 6," in *The Complete Works*, trans. Mother Columba Hart, O.S.B. (Mahwah, NJ: Paulist Press, 1980), 56–63.

6. John of the Cross, *The Dark Night*, in *The Collected Works of St. John of the Cross*, trans. Kieran Kavanaugh, O.C.D., and Otilio Rodriguez, O.C.D. (Washington, DC: ICS, 1991), 358–457.

7. Bonaventure, *The Soul's Journey into God*, in *Bonaventure: The Soul's Journey into God, The Tree of Life, and The Life of St. Francis*, trans. Ewert Cousins (Mahwah, NJ: Paulist Press, 1978), 110–16.

8. A. N. Williams, *The Ground of Union: Deification in Aquinas and Palamas* (New York: Oxford University Press, 1999), 73, and *The Art of Prayer: An Orthodox Anthology*, ed. Igumen Chariton of Valamo and Timothy Ware, trans. E. Kadloubovsky and E. M. Palmer (London: Faber and Faber, 1997), 181–98.

9. Julian of Norwich, *Showings*, trans. Edmund Colledge, O.S.A., and James Walsh, S.J. (Mahwah, NJ: Paulist Press, 1978), ch. 54 of The Long Text.

10. Meister Eckhart, *The Book of "Benedictus": The Book of Divine Consolation*, in *The Essential Sermons, Commentaries, Treatises, and Defense*, trans. Edmund Colledge, O.S.A., and Bernard McGinn (Mahwah, NJ: Paulist Press, 1981), 209–39, at 229.

11. Teresa of Avila, *The Interior Castle*, trans. Kieran Kavanaugh, O.C.D., and Otilio Rodriguez, O.C.D. (Mahwah, NJ: Paulist Press, 1979), 172–96.

12. 1 Corinthians 13:12–13.

13. Pseudo-Dionysius, *The Mystical Theology*, in *The Complete Works*, trans. Colm Luibheid (Mahwah, NJ: Paulist Press, 1987), 135–41.

14. Eckhart, "Sermon 48," in *The Essential Sermons*, 197–98, and Denys Turner, *The Darkness of God: Negativity in Christian Mysticism* (New York: Cambridge University Press, 1999), 153–59. See also René Descartes, *Discourse on Method* and *Meditations on First Philosophy*, 4th ed., trans. Donald A. Cress (Cambridge, MA: Hackett, 1999).

15. Marguerite Porete, *The Mirror of Simple Souls*, trans. Ellen L. Babinsky (Mahwah, NJ: Paulist Press, 1993), ch. 12.

16. Hans Urs von Balthasar, *The Glory of the Lord: A Theological Aesthetics*, vol. 5, *The Realm of Metaphysics in the Modern Age*, ed. Brian McNeil, C.R.V., and John Riches, trans. Oliver Davies et al. (San Francisco: Ignatius Press, 1991), 546–90.

17. G. W. F. Hegel, *Lectures on the Philosophy of Religion: The Lectures of 1827*, ed. Peter C. Hodgson, trans. R. F. Brown, P. C. Hodgson, and J. M. Stewart with H. S. Harris (New York: Oxford University Press, 2012), 152–88. See also Hegel, *The Science of Logic*, trans. George Di Giovanni (New York: Cambridge University Press, 2010), 29.

18. Balthasar, *The Glory of the Lord*, 5:590–96.

19. William Desmond, *Hegel's God: A Counterfeit Double?* (New York: Routledge, 2017), 6.

20. Rowan Williams, "Hegel and the Gods of Postmodernity," 25–34, at 31–32, and "Logic and Spirit in Hegel," 35–52, at 42, in *Wrestling with Angels: Conversations in Modern Theology*, ed. Mike Higton (Grand Rapids, MI: Eerdmans, 2007).

21. Cyril O'Regan, *The Heterodox Hegel* (Albany: SUNY Press, 1994) and *Gnostic Return in Modernity* (Albany: SUNY Press, 2001).

22. Martin Heidegger, "The Onto-Theo-Logical Constitution of Metaphysics," in *Identity and* Difference, trans. Joan Stambaugh (Chicago: University of Chicago Press, 2002), 42–74, and Andrew Prevot, *Thinking Prayer: Theology and Spirituality amid the Crises of Modernity* (Notre Dame, IN: University of Notre Dame Press, 2015), 37–69.

23. Joseph Rivera reads Henry in line with the Christian mystical tradition, particularly the legacy of Augustinian interiority, in his *The Contemplative Self after Michel Henry: A Phenomenological Theology* (Notre Dame, IN: University of Notre Dame Press, 2015), 219–35. See also Jeffrey Hanson and Michael R. Kelly, eds., *Michel Henry: The Affects of Thought* (New York: Continuum, 2012).

24. Michel Henry, *The Essence of Manifestation*, trans. Girard Etzkorn (The Hague: Martinus Nijhoff, 1973), 310–22, and *Words of Christ*, trans. Christina Gschwandtner (Grand Rapids, MI: Eerdmans, 2012).

25. Michel de Certeau, *The Mystic Fable: The Sixteenth and Seventeenth Centuries*, vol. 1, trans. Michael B. Smith (Chicago: University of Chicago Press, 1992).

26. Jacques Derrida, *The Gift of Death*, trans. David Wells (Chicago: University of Chicago Press, 1995), 82.

27. Georges Bataille, *Inner Experience*, trans. Leslie Anne Bolt (Albany: SUNY Press, 1988), 101–57, and *Guilty*, trans. Bruce Boone (Venice, CA: Lapis Press, 1988), 11–17.

28. Luce Irigaray, *Speculum of the Other Woman*, trans. Gillian C. Gill (Ithaca, NY: Cornell University Press, 1985), 191–202.

29. Grace M. Jantzen, *Becoming Divine: Towards a Feminist Philosophy of Religion* (Bloomington: Indiana University Press, 1999), 77–99.

30. Karl Rahner, "Concerning the Relationship between Nature and Grace," *Theological Investigations*, vol. 1, trans. Cornelius Ernst, O.P. (London: Darton, Longman, & Todd, 1961), 297–317.

31. Jeffrey Finch, "Athanasius on the Deifying Work of the Redeemer," in *Theosis: Deification in Christian Theology*, ed. Stephen Finlan and Vladimir Kharlamov (Cambridge: James Clarke, 2006), 104–21, at 104 and 110.

32. Daniel A. Keating, *The Appropriation of Divine Life in Cyril of Alexandria* (New York: Oxford University Press, 2004), 54–143; Elena Vishnevskaya, "Divinization and Spiritual Progress in Maximus the Confessor," in *Theosis*, 134–45; and Rowan Williams, *Teresa of Avila* (London: Bloomsbury, 2003).

33. Turner, *The Darkness of God*, 226–73. See also William James, *The Varieties of Religious Experience: A Study in Human Nature*, ed. Martin E. Marty (New York: Penguin Books, 1982).

34. Constance FitzGerald, "Transformation in Wisdom: The Subversive Character and Educative Power of Sophia in Contemplation," in *Carmel and*

Contemplation: Transforming Human Consciousness, ed. Kevin Culligan, O.C.D., and Regis Jordan, O.C.D. (Washington, DC: ICS, 2000), 281–358, and Joann Wolski Conn, *Spirituality and Personal Maturity* (Mahwah, NJ: Paulist Press, 1989).

35. Julia Kristeva, *Teresa, My Love: An Imagined Life of the Saint of Avila*, trans. Lorna Scott Fox (New York: Columbia University Press, 2015). See also Sigmund Freud, *Civilization and Its Discontents*, trans. James Strachey (New York: Norton, 2010), and Jacques Lacan, *Encore: The Seminar of Jacques Lacan, Book 20, On Feminine Sexuality: The Limits of Love and Knowledge, 1972–1973*, ed. Jacques Alain-Miller, trans. Bruce Fink (New York: Norton, 1998).

36. Carl Schmitt, *Political Theology: Four Chapters on the Concept of Sovereignty*, trans. George Schwab (Chicago: University of Chicago Press, 2005), and Joseph J. Bendersky, *Carl Schmitt: Theorist for the Reich* (Princeton, NJ: Princeton University Press, 1983).

37. See Michele Watkins, "Differentiation as Disfigurement," in this volume.

38. Jürgen Moltmann, *Trinity and the Kingdom*, trans. Margaret Kohl (Minneapolis: Fortress Press, 1993), 191–222, and John Zizioulas, *Communion and Otherness: Further Studies in Personhood and the Church*, ed. Paul McPartlan (New York: T&T Clark, 2006). See also Aristotle Papanikolaou, *The Mystical as Political* (Notre Dame, IN: University of Notre Dame Press, 2012).

39. For a communitarian vision of theosis that connects Zizioulas with Baby Suggs, see Watkins, "Differentiation as Disfigurement," in this volume.

40. Cited in Jon Sobrino, S.J., "Monseñor Romero's Impact on Ignacio Ellacuría," in *A Grammar of Justice: The Legacy of Ignacio Ellacuría Today*, ed. J. Matthew Ashley, Kevin Burke, S.J., and Rodolfo Cardenal, S.J. (Maryknoll, NY: Orbis, 2014), 57–76, at 57.

41. Sojourner Truth, *Narrative of Sojourner Truth: A Bondswoman of Olden Time, with a History of Her Labors and Correspondence Drawn from Her "Book of Life"; Also, a Memorial Chapter*, ed. Nell Irvin Painter (New York: Penguin Press, 1998), 18, 22, 56, and 64.

42. Truth, *Narrative*, 44–45 and 68.

43. Kimberlé Crenshaw, "Demarginalizing the Intersection of Race and Sex: A Black Feminist Critique of Antidiscrimination Doctrine, Feminist Theory, and Antiracist Politics," *University of Chicago Legal Forum* (1989): 139–67.

Speculation and Theosis in Vladimir Lossky and Meister Eckhart

Robert Glenn Davis

The study of Christian mysticism over the last thirty years has treated with suspicion any sharp distinctions between "intellectual" and "affective" paths to union with God in the medieval West. Largely this has been a welcome and necessary correction to longstanding scholarly typologies of mystical texts into "speculative" and "affective" or "experiential" varieties.[1] Charlotte Radler has pointed to the ways in which nineteenth- and twentieth-century scholarship on Meister Eckhart imposed on his thought, and on so many subsequent approaches to medieval Christian mysticism, this dichotomy between speculative and affective mysticism.[2] The former is characterized as male-dominated, learned, philosophical, and intellectual, where the latter is largely the province of women, simple and unreflective, devotional, and experiential. Scholars have challenged this dichotomy from a number of angles—Amy Hollywood, Sara Poor, and Patricia Dailey, for instance, have all illuminated the literary and theological complexity of supposedly "experiential" writings of medieval women such as Hadewijch of Antwerp, Mechthild of Magdeburg, and Marguerite Porete.[3] And Radler and Bernard McGinn have demonstrated the centrality of love and affective language to Eckhart's own mysticism, challenging the assumption that being and intellect were the most important categories of Eckhart's thought. Far from a work of cold speculation privileging the solitary and sovereign intellect, Eckhart's mysticism is alive with the passion of divine/human relation.[4]

I want to suggest here that the misreading of Eckhart that scholars such as McGinn and Radler have worked to correct is based less on a privileging of the speculative aspects of his thought over the affective, than it is on a misconstrual of the very nature of scope of the role of "speculation" in his thought. As Jeffrey Hamburger has observed, medieval theories and applications of *speculatio* differed in consequential ways from modern notions of speculation drawn largely from nineteenth-century German philosophy.[5] As an example of the modern concept Hamburger cites Martin Jay's definition of speculation as "the rational perception of clear and distinct forms with the unclouded eye of the mind."[6] This modern conception of speculation excludes the mediation of images and is defined against corporeal vision. By contrast, Hamburger observes, for medieval theorists *speculatio* was a process connecting the outer to the inner (in, for example, Bonaventure's *itinerarium* from the apprehension of physical bodies to the contemplation of the eternal being and goodness of God).[7] The retrojection of a modern, dualistic concept of speculation onto medieval mystical texts has thus resulted in the dichotomy of speculative mysticism and *Erlebnismystik* or *Gefühlmystik*, where the latter is defined as taking embodied, affective experience or feeling, rather than intellection, as its point of departure.[8]

If German identitarian concerns imprinted scholarship on Western mysticism with a valorization of intellectual or speculative mysticism over a putatively anti-intellectual spirituality of divine/human relationship, the reverse image can be observed in modern constructions of the Greek and Russian Orthodox tradition. Here, to recur to the broadest caricature, a Western tradition, shaped by Augustinian individualism and Latin scholasticism, contrasts unfavorably with the Dionysian, apophatic, and Trinitarian mystical theology of the Eastern church. Vladimir Lossky's 1944 *Mystical Theology of the Eastern Church* stands out, though not alone, in creating and popularizing this vision of the Eastern tradition.[9] Scholars working in the Orthodox, Catholic, and Protestant traditions have interrogated and historicized the polemical mutual construction of Orthodox and Western theological traditions, often in a spirit of engaged ecumenism.[10]

In his unfinished but still monumental study of the theology of Meister Eckhart, *Théologie négative et connaissance de dieu chez Maître Eckhart*, Vladimir Lossky surfaces a nondual conception of speculation that nevertheless resonates with his contemporary philosophical and theological aims.[11] For Lossky, Eckhart's mysticism was deeply relational not in spite of its speculative nature but precisely as a result of it. Lossky shows how the category of "speculation" can exceed and differ from "rationalism" or "intellection." The language and metaphors of speculation expressed, for Lossky, the simultaneous possibility of both complete union without distinction and real relationship between human beings and the divine. For Lossky, in fact, deification is the name for this seemingly paradoxical reality of *becoming divine* which is at the same time *divine/human communion* (as Aristotle Papanikolaou has proposed to translate theosis, thus emphasizing the relational character of this dynamic).[12] In Lossky's great, unfinished study of Eckhart's thought, begun as his dissertation under Etienne Gilson, the language of speculation—of mirroring and imaging—is central to Eckhart's account of the analogical relation of God to the human person, made possible in Christ and fulfilled in human beings through the deifying grace of the transfiguration. For Lossky, to characterize the divine/human communion as speculative is to affirm simultaneously the absolute identity of the human person with Christ and the ongoing reality of relationship between them. Here I want to situate Lossky's reading of Eckhart within a broader framework of certain nineteenth- and twentieth-century interpreters, from Franz von Baader to Rudolf Otto.

As is well known, the modern career of Meister Eckhart began when, in the nineteenth century, he assumed paternity for the great tradition of German speculative idealism and marked the moment when the German spirit began to break free of the strictures of Catholic scholastic dogma. This appropriation of Eckhart for German nationalist pride, of course, reached its nadir in the 1930s and 1940s with the Nazi celebration of Eckhart as the great vindicator of the so-called Nordic race.[13] But as Cyril O'Regan demonstrates in a recent survey of Eckhart's nineteenth-century German reception, debates about the character of Eckhart's mysticism were not just about Germanness but also constituted theological and philosophical debates about the relation of reason and feeling—and the relation of both to religion. While throughout the nineteenth century Eckhart featured for philosophers in a somewhat categorical appeal to the depth of the German speculative tradition, it is generally acknowledged that it was primarily the work of Catholic philosopher Franz von Baader that introduced Eckhart to German philosophical audiences in the mid–nineteenth century. The fact that Eckhart has come to represent for modern scholars the apogee of "speculative" mysticism also owes largely to Baader's retrieval of Eckhart as affirming the essentially (and robustly) speculative character of religion (in spite of Baader's own insistence that Eckhart be understood within the context of late medieval mysticism and his emphasis on the bridal imagery of Christian mystical literature).[14]

For Baader, the Kantian distinction of the phenomenal and the noumenal imprisons the human mind within itself, denying Reason any capacity for self-transcendence. And the Romantic alternative of Schleiermacher to locate religion in feeling (*Gefühl*) does not meaningfully challenge this confinement of thought. Both of these accounts risk collapsing the self into a merely psychological entity, reflecting only its own structure rather than a real relationship with the Other. As O'Regan puts it, "Eckhart represents a sober alternative to the seductions of feeling and affect, while offering a view of reason (*Vernunft*) that does not ignore, as calculative reason does, the depth and breadth of religious relation."[15] That is, Eckhart insists that in speculative reason lies the possibility for the profoundly real connection of the human soul to the transcendent divine.

Yet, if Baader made Eckhart available to the tradition of German idealism, he was nevertheless unwilling to endorse a complete assimilation of Eckhart's religious thought to the tenets of idealism. Hegel, with whom Baader carried out a correspondence on Eckhart, goes too far in the identification of the soul with the divine. For Baader, to efface the ontological distinction between Reason and God is not merely impious; rather, it risks collapsing altogether the soul's very capacity for transcendence. If God is in no way other to the soul, then there is no real relation entailed in their union. For all his radicality, Baader insists, Eckhart maintains an "unbridgeable difference" between beings and their ground, thus ultimately maintaining the mystery and alterity of the divine.[16] He does so, Baader explains, through the central motif of the "image of God," which, in harmony with a broader Christian mystical tradition, emphasizes both the identity and nonidentity of the soul with the divine.

Eckhart in the Mirror

Baader's presentation of Eckhart anticipates and clarifies concerns that are also very much those of Lossky—namely, to articulate a conception of divine/human relation that is neither a psychological effect nor a simple ontological identity but a dynamic transformation whereby the human person becomes a son of God by grace. And Lossky, too, emphasizes the central role of the "image of God" in this dynamic. For Eckhart, the theology of the image is thoroughly Christological, as is clearly evident throughout his commentary on the Gospel of John, which Lossky cites more than any other of Eckhart's writings.

In this way, Eckhart's deification can thus be contrasted with another Christian account of becoming God, in Boethius's *Consolation of Philosophy*. In the dialogue between the magisterial Lady Philosophy and the pathetic Boethius, Boethius confesses that, beneath the superficial grief he feels over his loss of fortune is a deeper loss: having been raised on philosophy, Boethius now finds the world devoid of justice and order, a loss that Philosophy sees as a crisis of Boethius's own self-knowledge. Philosophy repeatedly tells Boethius that he has forgotten who he is, that is, one whose beginning and end is God.[17] What Boethius knows is simply that he is miserable, seemingly incapable of finding happiness. But happiness, Philosophy shows him, is the highest good, nothing less than a state of having everything you could possibly need and want, and to have it in such a way that you could never lose it. Since nothing in this sublunary world of flux could satisfy those conditions, happiness must itself be divine, and the one seeking happiness is seeking, simply, to become God—to realize within oneself the unity of all good. Boethius admits that this follows logically, if surprisingly. But Philosophy reassures him: humans cannot become God, but there is nothing to prevent them from becoming God-like by participation.

If Boethius advances an account of becoming God here—if it can be considered an account of theosis at all—it is a decidedly non-Christological one. The *Consolation*, of course, never explicitly identifies itself with Christian revelation, and the God to whom Boethius seeks to be conformed appears primarily in the guise of Aristotle's unmoved mover, attracting, in its absolute stillness and self-sufficiency, everything in the cosmos that seeks its same quiescence. Boethius's God in the *Consolation* is also, and above all, perhaps, the Plotinian One, removed from all multiplicity in an eternal repose whose precise relationship to the world of temporal flux is so aporetic that it finally stumps even Lady Philosophy. It would seem, on some level, that to be God is to exist outside of relationality.[18]

Against the backdrop of this fundamentally Neoplatonic and seemingly solitary vision of deification, Vladimir Lossky expounds Meister Eckhart's theology of deification as an irreducibly Christological and relational dynamic, a consequence, perhaps, of a very different conception of who God is. As Charlotte Radler argues, "Eckhart's God does not reside in frozen self-sufficiency but exists and lives in and through a kenotic, relational movement."[19] But Lossky, while emphasizing the Christological character of Eckhart's thought, does not ignore or downplay his philosophical sources.

On the contrary, he carefully analyzes the Neoplatonic sources and resonances of Eckhart's account of being, but then goes on to emphasize the ways in which Eckhart's God, the Triune creator *ex nihilo* of scripture, fundamentally transforms the Plotinian dialectic of the One.

As Lossky establishes at the very beginning of his study, the central theme of his exposition is "the quest for the ineffable," but not all "ineffabilities" are the same. Rather than referring Eckhart's mysticism to a general and ill-defined concept of apophasis, Lossky demonstrates, in Rowan Williams's words, "that the use of apophasis in the history of Christian thought is anything but homogeneous," and that one must attend not only to the distinctive strategies of unsaying in a particular author but also the goal or end to which they put those strategies.[20] In the case of Eckhart, Lossky is interested primarily in the relationship of the deified creature to the uncreated and ineffable God, and he is particularly keen to demonstrate the fundamentally Christological foundation of that relationship for Eckhart. It would be foolish for me to try to summarize Lossky's massive and intricate study, but even a selective look should suffice to demonstrate what is characteristic of Lossky's interpretive strategy.

To illuminate what he calls Eckhart's "apophasis of opposition," Lossky looks to Eckhart's *Latin Commentary on the Book of Wisdom*, where Eckhart draws on Macrobius's discussion of the antithetical relationship between "one" and "number"—where the one is both transcendent to and immanent in multiplicity. Eckhart connects this dynamic to the relationship of God to creation. He establishes that God is more distinct from creation than any two created things are distinct from one another. God is opposed absolutely to creatures, so if creatures are distinct from one another, God must also be at a remove from all such distinctions. And so God is distinguished from creatures by his indistinction. Thus, Lossky explains, in God, "absolute distinction coincides with indistinction."[21] This dialectic reappears under different names in Eckhart's work—as "likeness-unlikeness" in his *Commentary on Exodus*, for example. And what Eckhart expresses dialectically in these passages he elsewhere expounds according to his doctrine of analogy, which functions as a kind of hermeneutic skeleton key in Lossky's reading of Eckhart. As Lossky explains, for Eckhart analogy is not the Goldilocks zone between equivocity and univocity, as one might understand Thomas Aquinas's account of this mode of signification. For Eckhart, rather, analogy reconciles opposite modalities into one dynamic relationship.[22] For Lossky, the analogical relationship of creator to creature expresses above all the Christian doctrine of *creatio ex nihilo*. Because God, as Being, creates the world out of nothing, there is an absolute nonidentity between God and creation which is tantamount to the difference between Being and Nothing. But precisely because creation has its being from nothing other than its cause, creation cannot *be* other than God, and one can thus speak of an absolutely univocal relation between them, as long as it is understood simultaneously as an absolutely equivocal relation.

Eckhart often puts this relationship in terms of image and likeness, as in the first of his *Parisian Questions,* where he answers the question of the identity of God's understanding and existence by arguing that God is not a being but an act of understanding. (This argument is one of the primary grounds on which Eckhart is labelled an "intellectualist" or "speculative" mystic.) As the cause of being, God cannot have being, since "nothing is formally in both a cause and its effect (*causa et causato*) if the cause is a true cause."[23] Moreover, Eckhart explains the identity of intellect and existence in God (the proposition that God's existence is nothing other than his understanding) by arguing that intellect and being are mutually referring and mutually exclusive orders. This Eckhart illustrates with reference to image and likeness (*species*): "An image, as such, is also not a being: the more we think about its entity the more it distracts us from knowing the thing whose image it is. Similarly . . . if a likeness in the soul had the nature of being, by its means we would not know the thing whose likeness it is: if it had the nature of being, as such it would make us know itself and distract us from knowing the thing whose likeness it is."[24] In angelic and human acts of understanding, beings are the cause of our knowledge, and thus our knowledge (i.e., the cognitive likeness in our understanding) is not being.[25] But God's knowledge is the cause of being, and thus God, as understanding, cannot exist.

This dialectical understanding of analogy, which is both an account of theological predication and an ontology, has been well and often noted in Eckhart's thought, no doubt reflecting the indelibility of Lossky's reading of Eckhart for subsequent scholarly treatments. But less commonplace now is the particular way that Lossky uses the lens of analogical causality to draw out an irreducibly Christological account of deification in Eckhart's thought. While, according to the dialectic of likeness-unlikeness, every created thing is in some manner indistinct from God, and while God's creative operation is the indivisible work of the Trinity, since there is only one *esse* in God, nevertheless it remains the case that only intellectual creatures are capable of "deifying transformation" through Christ that goes beyond exemplary participation. Lossky thus finds an Eckhartian doctrine of deification that is distinct from the condemned teaching of an uncreated aspect of the soul. The account of deification is thoroughly speculative, in the sense that the human capacity to become God is rooted in intellection, and it is by virtue of that intellectual capacity that human beings become a *speculum*, a mirror reflecting absolutely the image of God in Christ. "The son is the natural image of the Father, because his generation is a 'simple, formal emanation,' a 'transfusion of the total essence.'"[26] But whereas the Son is the image of the Father, the human person can be regenerated in the image of the entire Trinity, since deification "involves the habitation of Christ in the soul and the sanctifying action of the Holy Spirit, that is to say the concourse of the two divine persons sent into the world."[27] Because the Son is eternally generated, and because this eternally generated image of the Father assumed human nature, human beings can be regenerated by the grace of adoption.

The connection is purely speculative. Eckhart often has recourse to mirrors as illustrative examples: he uses it to express the relationship of created essences to their exemplars in the divine art. But here, Lossky claims, when Eckhart explains the relationship of deified human beings to God through the language of justice, the mirror image returns, charged now with a new meaning. "Now it concerns not only the formation of essences by participation in the seminal exemplarity of the Word, but of a deifying transformation which is the first fruit of the incarnation of the Son of God."[28] He cites Eckhart's Commentary on John: "Like mirrors, no matter how many are placed in front of the face of a man, all receive the form of the same numerically identical face, so too each and every one of the just are just by the same justice, entirely and absolutely, being formed, informed, and transformed into the same justice. They cannot all be univocally just, nor would each one be truly just, if justice were one thing in itself and another in the just."[29] Lossky glosses the term "univocally" here to forbid any interpretation that would identify human beings univocally with the divine justice. Rather, the mirror image expresses the univocity of the just with one another. "The connection of the just one to justice is univocal only for the Son of God," and remains so in the incarnation. Christ is a divine person in two natures—he is justice itself through his consubstantiality with the Father; and yet, in assuming human nature, Christ receives or becomes justice in the same way that all human beings can, through a transfiguration by divine grace. If this is a bit confusing, it is because Lossky is attempting to hold together two things—human beings are univocal to Christ with respect to his humanity, but equivocal with respect to his divinity. In this way, analogy not only expresses the relationship of creation to its creator: the doctrine of analogy is also Eckhart's doctrine of the Incarnation, and of the deification of human beings that it makes possible. The just man *is* justice, analogically speaking, insofar as every just person receives fully the very image of justice, as in a mirror, and has no other form than that of justice.

The figure of the mirror illustrates several things for Lossky's Eckhartian doctrine of deification. First, it establishes deification as a dynamic of distinction and indistinction. Because the mirror has no form of its own, it is capable of taking on fully the form that appears before it, and thus has no other form than that which it images. And second, just as a face remains one no matter how many mirrors reflect it, so too does God remain absolutely unique—deification does not create a legion of gods any more than the Son's natural imaging of the Father creates multiple Gods within the Trinity. And third, the mirror metaphor expresses the eternal generation of the Son and the dynamic character of deification. Justice does not take root in the soul of the just as a fixed trait or *habitus*. Rather, just as an image in a mirror depends on the continual presence of the face it reflects, so too the relationship of justice to the just one, and of the Trinity to the deified human being, is one of ongoing, intimate presence. This is the same reality that Eckhart expresses elsewhere as the eternal birth of the Son in the soul.[30] "Precisely because the divine form is not continually fixed, as a *habitus* would be, in the human subjects which it informs, the generation is a continuous act."[31]

Yet there is a problem with the mirror metaphor, namely that it implies a certain exteriority of justice to the just man—a separation between the mirror and what it images that is inappropriate to the relationship of Son of God to the deified human person. Lossky cites Eckhart's clarification at his defense at Cologne: "It should not be thought that the Son of God is something extrinsic or distant from us to which we are made analogous, like an image cast in a mirror, but inasmuch as God, one and undivided through essence, is intimate and near to each one of us, 'in whom we live, and move, and have our being.'"[32] In this respect, at least, we might see Eckhart anticipating the later German Idealist spin on the figure of the *speculum* or mirror, which gives its name to the process of "speculation." If for many medieval thinkers *speculatio* referred to an itinerary of divine knowledge whereby the natural world indirectly reflects its creator, for Eckhart, the "speculative" dynamic of deification points to something more direct, something more intimate and unified than mere "reflection."

The distinction between "speculation" and "reflection" is a Hegelian one, not an Eckhartian one, but it captures something of the dynamic Lossky finds in Eckhart's account of the distinction and indistinction of self and God. Rodolphe Gasché characterizes the Hegelian distinction between speculation and reflection this way: "In contrast to philosophical reflection, whose essence resides in opposing, and in this manner relating, one thing to another—and which therefore cannot conceptualize the unity of what is in opposition—speculative thought possesses, as Hegel puts it, the *boldness* to *think* contradiction. . . . It has the boldness to conceive of opposites in their unity."[33] Speculation is a mirroring that both "articulates what is diverse" and "exhibit[s] the totality of which this diversity is a part."[34] The subject-object relation is caught up in a constant exchange, as in a mirror, and the split between form and image overcome. Thus, speculation does not simply express a preference for the intellectual over the affective, or the philosophical over the experiential, as it has often functioned in histories of Christian thought, but rather marks a mode of belonging prior to the relations realized in ordinary forms of knowing and loving. For Lossky's Eckhart, this speculative dynamic is the human being's capacity to be made "naturally supernatural" by deifying grace. This deifying act is a "second grace"—the supernatural *gratia gratus fasciens*—given only to beings possessed of intellect and goodness, and not simply the *gratia gratis data* given to all created beings.[35] For Eckhart, these two graces correspond to the Neoplatonic *exitus* and *reditus*, the free and gracious flowing out of all things from God and the intellect's reversion to the Godhead.

Lossky stresses that the transfiguration of the human person is an additional act of grace, and that a proper understanding of the role of grace in Eckhart is crucial to avoid the misinterpretation of Eckhart as teaching a "pure and simple" identity between created persons and the second person of the Trinity.[36] By insisting on the act of grace that effects the becoming-God of the soul rather than as a simple ontological unity, Lossky reclaims Eckhart definitively from Hegelian idealism. Yet here, as in his insistence on reading analogy into Eckhart's vernacular writings, Lossky's concern to distinguish Eckhart from modern German philosophical appropriations (and his evident desire to rehabilitate Eckhart from medieval charges of heresy) leads him to smooth over points of tension in Eckhart's own thought. Grace is a tricky concept in Eckhart's writing, and as Bernard McGinn explains, the role of grace in the realization of union with God is never entirely clear: "for Thomas Aquinas, union with God in this life takes place only in and through the action of supernatural grace. Eckhart, on the other hand, sometimes affirms that grace unites us to God, but at other times speaks of grace more as a means than an end: something necessary to attain indistinct union with God, but not constitutive of union itself."[37] Lossky rejects the idea of union as an ontological given that would obviate the role of Christ in theosis (or indeed would, from Lossky's perspective, disqualify Eckhart's account of union as theosis at all). But he is equally concerned to stress that theosis is not, for Eckhart, an act that transforms the human person into something entirely new. It is, rather, the end in which and for which human beings were created, and more important, the sharing in a union that exists eternally in the Godhead. Deification is in no case simply the act of uniting that which was previously distinct, namely, the human self and God. Divine union establishes not only what human beings are capable of becoming but also reveals the fundamental truth of what they already are. On this point no medieval Christian mystic is clearer than Meister Eckhart.

Rudolf Otto and the Eckhartian Self

Thus, any account of deification raises, and perhaps more than anything seeks to answer, the question of what a "self" is in the first place. This question was central to the nineteenth-century German appropriations of Eckhart such as those of Franz Baader, and it remained central to the new articulations of the *Geisteswissenschaften* or human sciences in the early twentieth, when debates about Schleiermacher's account of religious experience continued to animate theological and religious studies. The concept of the numinous in Rudolf Otto's *Das heilige* is both dependent on and an attempted corrective to what he saw as an overly psychologistic rendering of religious *Gefühl*. Similar concerns animate his comparative study of mysticism, where he focuses on the "speculative system" of Meister Eckhart in relationship to the Vedanta philosophy represented by Adi Sankara. Otto published "Mysticism East and West: A Comparative Analysis of the Nature of Mysticism" in 1929, based on lectures he had given at Oberlin College in 1924.[38] In their published form, the lectures appear to represent Otto's attempt to vindicate German nationalist pride in its own speculative genius, while critiquing, however softly, the Indo-Germanic myth that sought to purify the German cultural inheritance, intellectually and historically, of Judaic influence. Testing the increasingly fashionable hypothesis that the mystical aspects of all religious traditions are fundamentally harmonious, Otto examines in parallel the thought of Meister Eckhart with that of Adi Sankara, the eighth-century Indian philosopher who is considered the founder of the Advaita or nondualistic Vedanta tradition. In the first series of lectures, Otto details the striking commonalities between the Indian thinker who proclaimed the nonduality of *atman* and *brahman* and the German who cleared the ground in which God and self exist without distinction. For Otto, the glowing vitality of Eckhart's mysticism, and its profoundly ethical character, derives from the Palestinian soil from which it grew, in contrast to the fundamentally cold and nihilistic character of Indian philosophy. Christian mysticism is, in the end, more Judaic than it is Indian.

In his zeal to purge Eckhart of "Eastern" influence, Otto wants to clear Eckhart not only of the charge of crypto-Hinduism; he also tries to clear the more difficult bar of showing that Eckhart's teachings are unadulterated by that other East, the Greek philosophical world of Plotinus and his successors. Curiously, then, Otto's project resonates with Lossky's own readings of the Christian mystical tradition, from Dionysius to Eckhart, as being finally distinct from Neoplatonic philosophy. As Sarah Coakley observes, Lossky maintained that the resemblances between the mystical theology of Dionysius the Areopagite and Plotinus were "only outward" and superficial, and that at the root of their systems we will find a wholly different character.[39] Otto employs this same strategy in his Oberlin lectures, which, after painstakingly pointing out the parallels between Eckhart and eastern thought, pivots halfway through and begins systematically dismantling those parallels. Beneath the surface resemblances, at the heart of Eckhart's mysticism lies a distinctively Christian teaching about the human person and his profound relation to the divine.

Though Otto was concerned to free Eckhart from alien philosophical frameworks, Otto was himself responding to and drawing on contemporary philosophical concerns. As Gregory Alles has observed, Otto loosely but explicitly adapts the Kantian notion of schematization for his appeal to the numinous as a *sui generis* experience that, at least partially, precedes conceptualization.[40] And, under the influence of his mentor at Göttingen, the systematic theologian Hermann Schultz, Otto largely followed Schleiermacher's description of this *sui generis* experience as a feeling of being in relation to a power that is qualitatively distinct from the cognitive relation to phenomenal objects of the material world. For Otto religious experience is mystical "in the measure that religious feeling surpasses its rational content."[41] But for Eckhart, Otto maintains, unlike for the Eastern mystics and philosophers, "the proper expression of the feeling of at-one-ness is not a mystical pleasure," or eros, "but agape"—what Otto identifies as "the pure Christian emotion in its elemental chastity and simplicity—"a love of a kind which neither Plotinus nor Sankara mentions or knows."[42] Here, too, Otto follows his mentor Hermann Schultz, who sought to bend Schleiermacher's account of religious experience in the direction of an ethic. For Otto, who concludes his study of Eckhart with a chapter entitled "The Ethical Content," the centrality of agape in Eckhart's thought indicates the profound connection between divine union and active, ethical care for others. The Christian mystic, typified by Eckhart, is thus delivered from the temptations of solipsism to which Eastern mystics (both the Indian and the Plotinian) are drawn.

Despite the influence of Schleiermacher and, more proximately, Schultz, Eckhart functions here, as he did for Baader, more as corrective to than as confirmation of Schleiermacher's account of religious experience. Otto finds in Eckhart and Sankara sufficient evidence that religious feeling cannot be reduced to "absolute dependence."[43] And he affirms, with Baader, the fundamentally intellectual, as opposed to emotional, cast to what he calls Eckhart's "speculative system." Apparently, as Alles has also noted, Otto understands *Gefühl* (usually translated "feeling") not to mean an emotional event or affective disposition (though it does not rigorously exclude these phenomena) but an intuition deeper than conscious, discursive reason.[44] Otto shares Wilhelm Dilthey's early insistence that the interrelated psychic activities of "thinking-feeling-willing" must be referred to some more primary capacity which, for Otto as for Dilthey, can be understood as a fundamentally religious experience.[45]

Thus, to affirm Eckhart's mysticism as "speculative" is, for Otto as for Baader, not to deny feeling or to make divine union an achievement of the intellect, but to point to a deeper unity upon which the activity of feeling and thinking rest. Eckhart's mysticism testifies to a "vast region of our unconscious life and being" within the self that lies hidden deep beneath "individual, empirical acts of imagination, will, and feeling. . . . Here,"

Otto writes, "at the core itself is the original being of man, the true center of all characteristic action and reaction. Here are the deeps which can remain unmoved and unchanged when at the surface the play of powers, thoughts, concepts, emotions, desires, cares and hopes of the moment is in full swing in time and place, changing like fleeting waves. Thither, the life of the soul can find retreat when it withdraws from the play of the outward faculties, from the divisions of discursive reflection, from the disruption of outward impulses: when, as we say also in our common speech, a man 'comes to himself.'"[46] In spite of the bombast of Otto's portrayal of Eckhart as the prophet of Germanic vigor, his account of Eckhartian speculation returns to a ground deeper than action or passion.

On this score, modern scholars such as Bernard McGinn are in agreement with Otto. Challenging the characterization of Eckhart's mysticism as intellectual rather than affective, McGinn observes that Eckhart's vision of "union without distinction" is grounded in a reality that is deeper than the activities of knowledge or love, to the groundless ground of the self.[47] Eckhart's insistence that the soul's relationship to the divine is secured not through external works (including its sacramental obligations) but rather through a more fundamental ontological relation seems to elevate the dignity of the individual soul.[48] At the same time he proclaims that this soul *is* nothing apart from God, and that union with God is the realization of this nothingness. This apparent doubleness has allowed modern readers both to credit Eckhart with the discovery of the modern self and to find in his writing a liberating alternative to modern individualism.

For an example of the former, Larry Siedentop's recent triumphalist history of Western secularism contends that Eckhart's influence on the later pietistic emphasis on "innerness" and self-relation was a critical step in the emergence of the individual as the basic unit of Western liberal society.[49] By contrast, and more originally, Ben Morgan has recently argued that it was not in Eckhart but in the efforts to restrain the radicality of his vision of theosis after the condemnation of his teachings that the modern self was brought into being.[50] With Eckhart's more circumspect followers, above all the German Dominican Henry Suso, Eckhart's radical vision of indistinction between self and God is curtailed into a regimen of constant self-policing and self-fashioning that anticipates the disciplinary self of the modern West, one whose ideal is not relationality but autonomy. With the chastising of Eckhart's mysticism, the modern world eradicated the very language with which we might articulate a self who is constituted essentially by its connectedness rather than its separateness. Or, to put it another way, we imagine that a self is fashioned by boundaries, and the difference they delineate, answering only the question of what makes me distinct. Whereas Siedentop celebrates the development of the individual as the signal achievement and enduring moral contribution of the West to the world, Morgan emphasizes what has been lost, and what, partly through the reading of Eckhart, might yet be recovered. If for Morgan the relational ontology of Eckhart is one well from which a new vision of selfhood might be drawn, Lossky's reading of Eckhart's dialectic of distinction and identity anticipates such a vision, one that cuts as well across the putative division of a "Western" individualism and an "Eastern" emphasis on relationality grounded in the ongoing reality of theosis. For Lossky's Eckhart, the distinction between the self and God was not a qualification or attenuation of theosis but a reality that coincides absolutely with the soul's identity to God, offering a vision of the human that, by virtue of its indistinction, is capable of the most profound relationship with that which is.

Notes

1. While the roots of this scholarly taxonomy may be traced to nineteenth-century German philosophical retrievals of Jacob Boehme and Meister Eckhart and contemporary debates about the nature of speculation, its influence on subsequent historians far outlasted those debates. For the former, see Cyril O'Regan, "Eckhart Reception in the 19th Century," in *A Companion to Meister Eckhart*, ed. Jeremiah M. Hackett (Leiden: Brill, 2013), 629–77. A notable example of the latter is Steven Ozment, who contrasts Eckhart with the "bridal mysticism" of Bernard of Clairvaux, in *The Age of Reform, 1250–1550* (New Haven, CT: Yale University Press,1980), 130–31.

2. Charlotte Radler, "'In Love I Am More God': The Centrality of Love in Meister Eckhart's Mysticism," *Journal of Religion* 90, no. 2 (2010): 171–98.

3. Amy Hollywood, *The Soul as Virgin Wife* (Notre Dame, IN: University of Notre Dame Press, 1995); "Inside Out: Beatrice of Nazareth and Her Hagiographer," in *Gendered Voices: Medieval Saints and Their Interpreters*, ed. C. Mooney (Philadelphia: University of Pennsylvania Press, 1999), 78–98; Patricia Dailey, "The Body and Its Senses," in *The Cambridge Companion to Christian Mysticism*, ed. Amy Hollywood and Patricia Z. Beckman (Cambridge: Cambridge University Press, 2012), 264–76; Patricia Dailey, *Promised Bodies: Time, Language, and Corporeality in Medieval Women's Mystical Texts* (New York: Columbia University Press, 2013); Sara S. Poor, *Mechthild of Magdeburg*

and Her Book: Gender and the Making of Textual Authority (Philadelphia: University of Pennsylvania Press, 2011).

4. Radler, "In Love I Am More God"; McGinn, *The Mystical Thought of Meister Eckhart: The Man from Whom God Hid Nothing* (New York: Herder & Herder, 2003), 36–37; "Love, Knowledge, and Mystical Union in Western Christianity: Twelfth to Sixteenth Centuries," *Church History* 56, no. 1 (1987): 17.

5. Jeffrey Hamburger, "Speculations on Speculation: Vision and Perception in the Theory and Practice of Mystical Devotions," *Deutsche Mystik im abendländischen Zusammenhang: Neu erschlossene Texte, neue methodische Ansäte, neue theoretische Konzepte* (Tübingen: Max Niemeyer, 2000), 353–408.

6. Cited in ibid., 358.

7. Ibid., 359.

8. Hamburger cites Hans-Georg Gadamer's contrast of Eckhartian intellectual speculation with the taste for "visual spectacle" among the uneducated masses (ibid.). This closely echoes in another idiom the distinction between speculative and experiential mysticism, the latter associated with corporeal visions, visual and tangible devotional objects, and literal-mindedness. At root is the judgment that Eckhart represents a more highly developed religious sensibility than those of the masses. This appraisal curiously recapitulates the arguments of the authorities who condemned Eckhart's teachings in 1329, worrying that his vernacular preaching, even if orthodox, was liable to be misunderstood by the simple souls who heard him. The critical edition for the *bulla* and other documents relating to the trial is by Loris Sturlese in *Acta Echardiana, Die deutschen und lateinschen Werke*, vol. 5 (Stuttgart: W. Kohlhammer, 2006). For an up-to-date and detailed examination of the historical events and documents relating to Eckhart's trial, see Walter Senner, "Meister Eckhart's Life, Training, Career, and Trial," in *A Companion to Meister Eckhart*, ed. Jeremiah M. Hackett (Leiden: Brill, 2013), 44–84.

9. Vladimir Lossky, *The Mystical Theology of the Eastern Church* (Crestwood, NY: St. Vladimir's Seminary Press, 1976), originally published in French as *Essai sur la théologie mystique de l'Église d'Orient* (Paris: Aubier, 1944).

10. In addition to the essays in the present volume, see George Demacopoulos and Aristotle Papanikolaou, eds., *Orthodox Constructions of the West* (New York: Fordham University Press, 2013). With respect to Lossky in particular, see Sarah Coakley, "Eastern Mystical Theology or Western 'Nouvelle Théologie'? On the Comparative Reception of Dionysius the Areopagite in Lossky and de Lubac," in ibid., 125–41; Goran Sekulovski, "Dionysius, Eckhart, and Vladimir Lossky: Reception, Interpretation, and Influence," *St. Vladimir's Theological Quarterly* 59 (2015): 17–28, esp. 22–26.

11. Vladimir Lossky, *Théologie négative et connaissance de dieu chez Maître Eckhart* (Paris: Librairie Philosophique J. Vrin, 1960). English translations are my own.

12. Aristotle Papanikolaou notes that the more common and literal English translation of theosis as deification "conjures up images of individual striving toward some sort of superhuman, godlike transformation. If there was one thing that deification was not meant to signify, it was the human transformation into Zeus." *The Mystical as Political: Democracy and Non-Radical Orthodoxy* (Notre Dame, IN: University of Notre Dame Press, 2012), 2.

13. Dermot Moran, "Meister Eckhart in 20th-Century Philosophy," in *A Companion to Meister Eckhart*, ed. Jeremiah M. Hackett (Leiden: Brill, 2013), 669–98, at 675.

14. O'Regan, "Eckhart Reception in the 19th Century," 635.

15. Ibid.

16. Ibid., 637.

17. Boethius, *The Consolation of Philosophy*, trans. David Slavitt (Cambridge, MA: Harvard University Press, 2008). The best Latin edition is Claudio Moreschini, *De consolatione philosophie: Opuscula Theologica*, 2nd rev. ed. (Munich: K.G. Saur, 2005).

18. It would be a mistake to attempt to derive Boethius's theology of divine union from the layers of literary artificiality in the *Consolation*. Joel Rehilan has advanced, productively though controversially, an interpretation of the *Consolation* as Menippean satire, not only in its prosimetrical form but on the basis of what he reads as a satirical presentation of Philosophy, one whose grandiloquence ultimately cannot hide her impotence in answering Boethius's questions. The only escape she offers is death, the virtuous suicide of the Stoics that Boethius cannot accept. Read in this light, Philosophy's route to becoming divine through reason's transcendence of human attachments would stand as a stark alternative to Christian perfection, rather than a classicized translation of it. Joel C. Rehilan, *The Prisoner's Philosophy: Life and Death in Boethius's* Consolation (Notre Dame, IN: University of Notre Dame Press, 2007). For a rebuttal of Rehilan's thesis, see Arco den Heijer, "Soothing Songs and the Comfort of Philosophy: The Use of Prosimetric Satire and Philosophical Dialogue in Boethius' 'Consolation of Philosophy,'" *Hermes* 142, no. 4 (2014): 431–60.

19. Radler, "In Love I Am More God," 183.

20. Rowan Williams, "Lossky, the *Via Negativa* and the Foundations of Theology," in *Wrestling with Angels: Conversations in Modern Theology* (Grand Rapids, MI: William B. Eerdmans, 2007), 1–24, at 1.

21. Lossky, *Mystical Theology*, 262.

22. "For the Thuringian theologian, analogy is not the happy medium (*le juste milieu*) between the equivocal and univocal, but reunites in some way these two contradictory modalities." Ibid., 287.

23. Meister Eckhart, *Parisian Questions and Prologues*, trans. Armand A. Maurer (Toronto: Pontifical Institute of Mediaeval Studies, 1974), 48. Latin

text in Meister Eckhart, *Werke II* (Frankfurt: Deutscher Klassiker Verlag, 1993), 21:539–53, at 548.

24. Meister Eckhart, *Parisian Questions*, 47, translation modified.

25. On the nonidentity of being and knowledge in angelic intelligence, see Meister Eckhart, *Parisian Questions*, 2.

26. Lossky, *Mystical Theology*, 360.

27. Ibid.

28. Ibid., 359.

29. Ibid., citing Meister Eckhart, *Expositio Sancti Evangelii Secundum Iohannem*, ed. J. Koch, in *Die deutschen und lateinschen Werke* (Stuttgart: W. Kohlhammer, 1936), 3:104n199.

30. As Amy Hollywood explains, in the eternal generation of the Word in the soul, "differentiation and relationship do occur, although all are equal and all are divine, for the soul takes part in the act of formal emanation and in the univocal relationship that exists between the Father and the Son. The soul takes part in what could be called a nondualistic differentiation, a form of differentiation that avoids the fall into duality and dualistic reference by reason of its univocity and eternal repetition." *The Soul as Virgin Wife*, 150. Hollywood stresses that in the birth of the Word in the soul, (reading especially his vernacular sermon *Justi vivent in aeternum*), analogical relationship is transformed into a univocal relationship. Lossky remains more circumspect about naming the relationship of the soul to the divine "univocal," reflecting (or perhaps determining) his focus on the Latin commentaries, and pointing to Eckhart's defenses at Cologne and Avignon, where he rebutted his accusers' cherry-picking of "reckless passages (*passages téméraires*) taken from the German sermons, where the Thuringian mystic speaks of transforming union without referring explicitly to analogy," Lossky, *Mystical Theology*, 369.

31. Lossky, *Mystical Theology*, 368.

32. Ibid., 361, citing the edition of Eckhart's trial documents by Gabriel Théry, "Édition critique des pièces relatives au procès d'Eckhart contenues dans le manuscrit 33b de la Bibliothèque de Soest," 129–268, *Archives d'histoire littéraire et doctrinal du moyen âge* 1 (1926): 267.

33. Rodolphe Gasché, *The Tain of the Mirror: Derrida and the Philosophy of Reflection* (Cambridge, MA: Harvard University Press, 1998), 44.

34. Ibid.

35. Eckhart draws this distinction in his *Commentary on Wisdom*, nn. 272–74 (LW 2:602–4) and in his Latin Sermon 25: "The first kind of grace is usually called 'grace freely given', that is, without merits; the second, 'saving grace'. The first is common to good and evil and to all creatures; the second is proper only to intellective and good creatures." *Meister Eckhart: Teacher and Preacher*, 218. Latin text in *Werke II*, 602. As Bernard McGinn notes, the distinction of *gratia*

gratis data and *gratia gratus fasciens* was common, but the definitions Eckhart gave these two terms were not. See *Meister Eckhart: Teacher and Preacher*, 222n16.

36. Lossky, *Mystical Theology*, 369.

37. Bernard McGinn, *The Harvest of Mysticism in Medieval Germany (1300–1500)* (New York: Herder and Herder, 2005), 161.

38. Rudolf Otto, *Mysticism East and West: A Comparative Analysis of the Nature of Mysticism*, trans. Bertha L. Bracey and Richenda C. Payne (London: Macmillan, 1932), originally published as *West-östliche mystik: Vergleich und Unterscheidung zur Wesensdeutung* (Gotha: L. Klotz, 1929).

39. Coakley, "Eastern Mystical Theology," 129. For Lossky, as Coakley notes, the distancing of Dionysius from Plotinus underwrites his claim for a distinctly Eastern Orthodox tradition stretching from the Cappadocians to Gregory Palamas. We might note here Lossky's important difference from Otto in constructing "the East." For the latter, Plotinus and Adi Sankara together constitute an eastern mystical tendency (characterized, above all, by its lack of ethical character) distinct from the spirit of Eckhart.

40. Gregory D. Alles, "Toward a Genealogy of the Holy: Rudolf Otto and the Apologetics of Religion," *Journal of the American Academy of Religion* 69, no. 2 (2001): 323–41, at 325.

41. Otto, *Mysticism East and West*, 139.

42. Ibid., 214.

43. Ibid., 146.

44. Alles, "Toward a Genealogy of the Holy," 324n1.

45. While Dilthey sought in his analysis of religion to avoid questions about the objective truth of its claims about external reality, he was also concerned to avoid the reduction of religion to subjective, non-cognitive states of feeling. In his unfinished "Critique of Historical Reasoning," for instance, he distinguishes the capacity for "re-experiencing" (*nacherleben*) religious states of the past from mere "re-feeling" (*nachfühlen*), *Drafts for a Critique of Historical Reason*, in *The Formation of the Historical World in the Human Sciences*, trans. Rudolf A. Makkreel and William H. Oman (Princeton, NJ: Princeton University Press, 2002), 236. See Benjamin D. Crowe, "Dilthey's Philosophy of Religion in the 'Critique of Historical Reason,' 1880–1910," *Journal of the History of Ideas* 66, no. 2 (2005): 265–83, esp. 273–79. In his early *Einleitung in die Geisteswissenschaften* (*Introduction to the Human Sciences*), Dilthey too portrays religious experience (and all theistic doctrines that seek to externalize it) as fundamentally a state of being in a relationship of dependence, an opening to "the other" that defines and underlies the possibility of self-reflection or self-determination (*Selbstbestimmung*). See Wilhelm Dilthey, *Introduction to the Human Sciences: An Attempt to Lay the Foundation for the Study of Society and History*, trans. Ramon J. Betanzos (Detroit: Wayne State University Press, 1988), 157–62.

46. Otto, *Mysticism East and West*, 204.
47. McGinn, "Love, Knowledge, and Mystical Union," 17.
48. On Eckhart's distinction between the interior and exterior acts, see Hollywood, *Soul as Virgin Wife*, 166–72.
49. Siedentop emphasizes, here and in his earlier writing, the Christian roots of the Western secular organization of society as an association of free, equal individuals. Though his concerns are different, Siedentop's history of the triumph of liberalism in the West reproduces in a number of respects Wilhelm Dilthey's narration of the long emergence of *Selbstbestimmung* (self-reflection or self-determination) out of Western metaphysics in his 1883 *Einleitung in die Geisteswissenschaften*. Larry Siedentop, *Inventing the Individual: The Origins of Western Liberalism* (Cambridge, MA: Belknap Press, 2014).
50. Though Morgan eschews the task of identifying a single moment or linear history of the "invention" of the self, he focuses especially on Henry Suso's deployment of late medieval mystical technologies "in the pursuit of self-control." Importantly, he sees Suso's techniques of self-mastery as prescriptively masculine, and observes in Suso's spiritual direction of the Dominican nun Elsbeth Stagel a consistent denial of self-determination to women. Lost, then, was the sense of exchange and mutual formation among beguine women and their male priest confessors that characterize earlier mystical writings such as Eckhart's. Ben Morgan, *On Becoming God: Late Medieval Mysticism and the Modern Western Self* (New York: Fordham University Press, 2012), 138–47.

Knowing through Unknowing

The Qualified Necessity of Human Reason in Dionysius

Peter Bouteneff

The modern debates around the writings and legacy of Dionysius are by now well known. In controversial cases such as these, one always hopes for a thoughtful discernment between these two—the writings and the legacy—because while we do have the writings themselves in a well-preserved corpus, we also know of their use and abuse, their appropriation and distortion, their warm and cold reception, in different sectors of church history. The situation for Dionysius is further complicated because the process of reception: the "legacy" begins immediately upon the appearance of the corpus in the early sixth century and goes on from there to exert an enormous influence on some of the church's most important and enduring theologians—Saint Maximus the Confessor, Saint John of Damascus, and Saint Gregory Palamas, to name just three of the more influential ones.

In the seminars I lead on Dionysius, after a dip into his apparent influences in middle-late Platonism we limit our reading and discussion strictly to the texts themselves. Only in the last weeks of the semester are participants given the choice of incorporating later patristic, medieval, modern, and postmodern materials into their research and writing, because even as he will necessarily appear within studies of subsequent figures, and within surveys of the relationship between Christianity and Hellenism, Dionysius deserves his own attention. When we do read the corpus by itself, limiting our prejudices, we cannot fail to be struck that we are here encountering something completely unique. We are excavating the earth's strata and finding a set of bones and fossils that makes us rethink the interrelationship of species.

We also read Dionysius with the virtual certainty that he is writing some five hundred years after the person whose name he takes, the figure identified in Acts 17:34, and so we know that he is veiling his own identity. That is only the first point of utter uniqueness. Moses cannot be the author of the Pentateuch, David cannot have written all the Psalms, and Paul did not write all the letters attributed to him. We are used to these stretched concepts of authorship and attribution. But a sixth-century author who deliberately cloaks himself in an identity with a first-century apostolic pedigree is a new one. And, as Jaroslav Pelikan quipped succinctly, "the pseudonym worked,"[1] such that from Hypatius of Ephesus, Severus of Antioch, and John of Scythopolis right on through the early Reformation period, his alleged apostolic credentials meant that—whether one liked him or not—he had to be read with solemn reverence. We may be stunned that no one thought it strange that a first-century author would use the word "τρισυπόστατον (tri-hypostatic)," not to mention numerous other anachronisms that slipped through an otherwise careful disguise. So whether he seemed to need a "Christological corrective," an adjustment to his alleged monenergism (he was in fact invoked by all sides of the post-Chalcedonian melee), he could not be ignored, and contributed a great deal to the development of these and scores of Eastern and Western Christian thinkers. Even after his Pauline-era identity was cracked wide open, his influence remained—and remains—rightfully large, but now it is due to his writing and its legacy over the ensuing 1,500 years.

Dionysius's corpus is compelling and fascinating beyond measure. Its ongoing immersion into the darkness of divine transcendence and radical nonknowability, its reflections on the distinction between names and the things named, its reflections on the Trinity, its meditation upon the nature (and ontological nonexistence) of evil—these are liable to shake our world, in a positive way. One of the main causes of difficulty, immediately and right up to the present, is his understanding of the celestial and ecclesiastical hierarchies. These may be (and I think rightly) interpreted as comprising a *taxis* that, although stratified, finally serves the *universal* enlightenment of human beings. But the hierarchies are also easily construed as a fabricated divine rationale for an elitist and clericalist church structure.

In our reflection of Dionysius's radical uniqueness, I would add that we have no other "father of the church" who is so difficult to associate in an obvious way with the gospel proclamation of Christ, the God-man, crucified for us and for our salvation. So that when it comes to the infamous "Christological corrective" that later fathers supposedly deemed necessary to levy upon Dionysius, it stems from the paucity in the corpus—unique among the "Fathers"—of direct reference to Christ, and the outsized influence of Greek pagan religious philosophy. Some, like Fr. John Meyendorff, made their peace with Dionysius on this score by seeing him as a missionary to the Greek who, rather than force Christ down pagan philosophical throats, sought to immerse himself fully within their world—such that the sheep (Greeks) would recognize the voice of the shepherd (Christ as mediated through Dionysius). In fact, Meyendorff's affirmative remarks about the Areopagite are usually overlooked from among his more condemnatory sentences. He pointed out the ways that Dionysius detached himself completely from key Neoplatonic postulates and how Dionysius succeeds in using the Greeks' own ideas to disprove them, standing on Cappadocian principles though smartly avoiding reference to them (other than "τρισυπόστατον," I guess), in order to maintain some semblance of a first-century identity.[2]

As I said at the outset, the assessment of Dionysius in our own era has been a matter of passionate debate, and among his admirers (such as myself), Fr. Alexander Golitzin (now Archbishop Alexander) is the most helpful in giving us perspective on the interrelationships among the moderns, and between them and the late-ancients.[3] When it comes to Meyendorff, what he disdained in Dionysius comes down in part to the hierarchies, but we have to recall that Meyendorff is reading Dionysius almost exclusively through the eyes of the conflict between Gregory Palamas and Barlaam the Calabrian. When we do look to the Ps.-Areopagite's legacy we see how intertwined the reception of Maximus—and more especially Palamas—is with his own. For Meyendorff there appears to be a zero-sum game, where the rise of Palamas is essentially dependent upon the demise of Dionysius. But as Fr. John Romanides points out, one cannot judge Dionysius by how badly Barlaam misunderstands him, unlike Palamas who actually derives more solid doctrine from the Areopagite.[4]

In fact, Meyendorff knows this and accounts for it. As he points out in his main monograph on Palamas, the use of Dionysius in Barlaam was unbalanced, emphasizing only the divine inaccessibility, while Palamas understood Dionysius "in his own fashion," more correctly, supporting his assertion of the communicability of the Divine energies—the uncreated, and therefore undiluted, unmitigated energies.[5] Palamas saw Dionysius as a key to understanding the human vocation of theosis. God is in fact communicable, and therefore *knowable*, and even if these assertions must be qualified, they open a question of huge importance which stands at the heart of the present essay: if theosis is the telos of the human being, what is the role of human reason in the attaining of that goal? Dionysius—so concerned with the telos of theosis as well as with the radical unknowability of God—is the one to whom we will turn as our guide.

The human person, uniquely among the whole of creation, is graced with the vocation of union with God.[6] While this is a holistic calling, in the sense of involving every faculty of human being and experience (spiritual and corporeal), ancient patristic writing will often focus on the role of the reasoning intellect (νοῦς). Not because the intellect is the sole subject of union with God, but because the noetic faculty is that by which humans are capable of the conscious—and ultimately self-transcending (*ekstatic*)—choice to enter into relationship with God. As such, the intellect is also the sole factor distinguishing humans from the rest of corporeal creation.

Readers of the Great Dionysius will know that the explicit goal of his writing is this very theosis: union with God/the Divinity.[7] It is the aim of the hierarchies, the purification/illumination/perfection, the symbology and really everything that he writes about. The conclusion of the ecstatic prayer that opens the *Mystical Theology* is that Timothy, the essay's addressee, abandon everything (and every non-thing), "be elevated as far as possible to the unity of that being beyond knowledge" (*MT* 1, 998B).[8] The ascent to that union, like Moses's ascent on Sinai, culminates with a "mysterious and dark cloud of unknowing," where,

καὶ οὐδενὸς οὔτε ἑαυτοῦ οὔτε ἑτέρου, τω παντελῶς δὲ ἀγνώστω τη πάσης γνώσεως ἀνενεργησίᾳ κατὰ τὸ κρεῖττον ἑνούμενος καὶ τω μιδέν γινώσκειν ὑπὲρ νοῦν γινώσκων.

being neither oneself nor someone else, one is supremely united by the completely unknowing inactivity of every knowledge, and knows beyond intellect by knowing nothing. (*MT* 1.3, 1001A)

These short citations remind us that even as the goal is union with God, the core assertion of the Dionysian corpus lies with the radical otherness of God and its repercussions for the radical non-knowability of God. With that in mind, it would seem that the reasoning intellect would be useless in attaining to God, unless it is somehow switched into a kind of self-destruct mode, or subjected itself to a thorough recalibration. Rather than knowing, the intellect must unknow; rather than be active, it must be inactive. This noetic reversal is definitive of apophatic theology, and few have articulated it more consistently and thoroughly than Dionysius.

But "unknowing," in and by itself, is neither the goal nor the only vehicle towards divine knowledge:

> God is known through knowledge and through unknowing (καὶ διὰ γνώσεως ὁ Θεὸς γινώσκεται καὶ διὰ ἀγνωσίας). . . . [Even though] the most divine knowledge of God is one which knows *through* unknowing (δι' ἀγνωσίας γινωσκομένη).[9] (*DN* 7.3, 872A)

Both unknowing and knowing play a role, and if anything, in this particular passage "knowing" is the main verb or activity, and "unknowing" is effectively the adverb. One can only go so far with the logic-defying language of an "active unknowing." Because we are finally talking about knowledge, though a radically qualified knowledge.

Virtually every time he writes about unknowing or unsaying, Dionysius advocates a balance (albeit uneven) between apophatic and cataphatic approaches to the Divinity: apophatic because God is essentially outside the created order of being, but cataphatic because God is the source of all being. Apophatic because created being is at a radical remove from the Divinity, cataphatic because created being has its archetype in the Divinity. So in a fairly straightforward sense, the limits and the uses of reason run exactly parallel to Dionysius's concept of God as radically other, and God as source/archetype, respectively. But even as we recall this balance between reason's use and limitation, would we not argue that human reason is necessary even to perceive this very duality, as well as to act on it? Put another way, the act of separating the intellect from itself, the work we are supposed to do with the intellect, is an act of the reasoning intellect. Managing, diverting, subverting reason is a conscious, reasoned undertaking. As Dionysius might have put it, it is an active inactivity.

As we proceed, this essay will seek to elaborate on this effective apo/cataphatic balance, and then to defend the fundamental idea of the qualified necessity of reason in Dionysius. I will here be drawing chiefly on the *Divine Names*, with some reference to the *Mystical Theology*.

In order to explore further the explicit role of reason/knowledge in Dionysius, and the ways it must be qualified, we may recall that the purview of human knowledge is limited to that which exists, the knowledge of existing things (γνῶσις τῶν ὄντων) (*DN* 1.4, 593A), by which is meant *created* things. In this sense, God is not an "existing thing;" his uncreated being is of a different order than created being. Yet—as cause of all the things that are—he is rightly known *through* (and named with reference to) created-existing things.[10] It would therefore be wrong to suggest that God's radical otherness entails an unbridgeable abyss, else union with God would be impossible. But it would be still more dangerous to suggest that God's relationship to the created order provides direct access to him, as if we could apply to the uncreated God the categories and attributes of created being, in an unqualified way. And that is precisely the trap into which we so often fall. Dionysius expresses that lament in plain language:

> We are so accustomed to speaking in an unqualified cataphatic way. We have a habit of seizing upon what is actually beyond us, clinging to the familiar categories of our sense perceptions, and then we measure the divine by our own standards, and of course are led astray by the apparent meaning we give to the divine and unspeakable logos (reason).[11] (*DN* 7.1, 865C)

I have reason to pause here in order to explore some of the identifiable sources of Dionysius's concerns about reliance on human reason. In the *Divine Names* he appears to have been rattled by several currents of thought that, despite an earlier provenance, evidently maintained their relevance during the time of his writing.[12] He was compelled to show, e.g., that God was different from the "One" of the Neoplatonists, which creates through emanations of itself that are coeternal and contiguous with itself (*DN* 10.3, 940A). Dionysius's God, as source of all of creation, was also different from the demiurges of classical pagan religions (*DN* 11.6, 953C–956A), and radically different from mythologies where gods operated as do human beings—complete with sex and violence. Belief systems descended from Plato were right to assert a divine source to all existing things, but Dionysius evidently needed to emphasize repeatedly that God is not a being within the world, nor does God create through intermediaries but is himself the source of all that is.

Although the polemic against late Arianism left less of a trace in the Dionysian writings, it too may have provided an impetus for several concerns related to those above. One is the radical nonknowability of God, as against Eunomius's argument that God is knowable—even more knowable than one's own self.[13] The other is Aetius's assertion that the names of God have a binding effect upon him—an argument that had special force for the neo-Arian argument when it came to the word "ἀγέννητος,"[14] for if God had the essential name/attribute of being "ingenerate," it could only mean that the Son, being generated by the Father, is less than God (the same being the case for the Holy Spirit, as proceeding from the Father).

These supposed motivations for Dionysius's argumentation serve my core argument. Because whether or not we understand Dionysius as a "polemicist" there is little doubt that his treatises both draw on and react to existing intellectual/philosophical traditions: nothing comes from nowhere.[15] And this means that his writings are, like all good rhetoric, efforts at *persuasion*. Their rhetorical/persuasive character is significant because it in turn means they are works of reason, aimed at reason. Dionysius's motivation for writing in the first place is to convince the reader to consider these things with the mind, and act on them with the mind, even if acting on them means short-circuiting the mind. Here, then, is another argument for the qualified necessity of reason for Dionysius.

But let us return to the dynamic he establishes in the *Divine Names*. God is both other and archetype. His identity as source and archetype gives us the possibility of knowing him through the things he has created:

> when praising the Cause of everything, we use names drawn from all the things that are caused . . . So as Cause of all and as transcending all, he is rightly nameless and yet has the names of everything that is. (DN 1.5–7, 593D–596C)

But God forbid we should apply these created categories or names to God in an unqualified way. God cannot even properly be said to *exist*, if by "existence" we are thinking—as we naturally do—about the created order. Qualification can take the form of saying that God is "supremely nonexistent," i.e., saying God exists and then unsaying it. The saying of anything about God necessitates unsaying. Divine knowledge is analogical and so is divine speaking. Of course, all language is analogical, even reference to created things, but the radical otherness of God entails a unique and radical deployment of analogy.

Dionysius establishes the way in which the names of God relate to his actual being, by positing a very clear directionality: from God to creation and not the other way around. The names of things and their qualities are derived from their source. Beginning with existence itself (which we in the created realm only experience as a derivative of divine existence) and through all the divine attributes of goodness, peace, light, love, justice, etc.—for Dionysius these can describe aspects of the created world only because their ontological origin rests entirely in God.

> God is not some kind of being. . . . He was not. He will not be. He did not come to be. He is not in the midst of becoming. He will not come to be. No. He is not. Rather, he is the essence of being for the things which have being. Not only the things that are, but also the essence of what they are, come from him who precedes the ages. (*DN* 5.4, 817D)

Therefore, "He is not a facet of being. Rather being is a facet of him. He is not contained in being, but being is contained in him. Being does not possess him, but he possesses being" (*DN* 5.8, 824A).[16] And what is said concerning "being" is the case also for the other attributes, as we see regarding the attributes of goodness, being, life, and wisdom:

> The divine name "Good" tells of all the processions of the universal Cause; it extends to beings and nonbeings and that Cause is superior to being and nonbeings. The name "Being" extends to all beings which are, and it is beyond them. The name of "Life" extends to all living things, and yet is beyond them. The name "Wisdom" reaches out to everything which has to do with understanding, reason, and sense perceptions, and surpasses them all. (*DN* 5.1, 816B)

Only in this way, from the divinity to the creation—or, as in the above citation, *extending into* (ἐκτείνεται εἰς) creation—can the names function, commensurate both with God's radical otherness and his being the archetype of all that is.

What I am here calling "directionality"—the direction from God to creation—is crucial for Dionysius as a corrective to the ruinous, idolatrous tendency to reason from creation to God that we have taken note of above, the inclination to apply to God the names of created things without *un-applying them*.[17] We are to erase our preconceptions of these categories of existence, goodness, peace, justice, at the very least by adding the prefix ὑπερ to whatever we say—as in the stunning prayer that opens the *Mystical Theology*, which addresses the Trinity as "beyond being, beyond divinity, beyond goodness" (Τριὰς ὑπερούσιε, καὶ ὑπέρθεε, καὶ ὑπεράγαθε) (MT 998A).

Going further, beyond the beyond, Dionysius advocates complete negation, where God is said to be nonexistent, nongood. Yet saying that the divinity is nongood is different from saying that it is evil, and likewise God's "nonexistence" does not mean that he has no being whatsoever. There is a difference between denial-as-negation, and what he calls "denial in the sense of superabundance" (*DN* 2.2, 640B). In that sense, the divinity is *supra*-nonexistent. Likewise, the praise of "unknowing" (ἀγνωσία) is not the praise of ignorance or stupidity (ἄγνοια). In each case, it is a matter of reconceiving—not by crude opposition, but by *de*conceiving. And this is the whole point of the oxymorons that Dionysius so loves—the sober inebriation, the active inactivity, the unknowing-knowing, the dazzling darkness. In fact, even darkness has two words associated with it—σκότος is associated in *DN* 4.5 with simple ignorance (ἄγνοια), and means obscurity, or deprivation of light, while γνόφος is the darkness of superabundant light,[18] associated with supreme unknowing (ἀγνωσία).

Once again, the language from created things entails saying and unsaying, and Dionysius asserts that the unsayings are if anything more valuable to us than the sayings, that "the preference is for the way up through negations" (*DN* 13.3, 981B). Our minds must be "halted" (*DN* 1.4, 592D) and redirected. The words we use about God must be characterized by an ek-static transcendence, so that they may be removed from their sheerly created sense.

Back to my main thesis: all of this—the use of words and their qualification, both the saying and perhaps especially the unsaying; the analogical ascent through the symbols—all of this *requires the reasoning intellect*. Non-noetic creation—the animals and the inanimate objects—are not in the business of naming anything,[19] neither do they occupy themselves with either saying or unsaying; they do not think and qualify their thoughts, because they do not have reason. Human beings do, however, and are to use it both to reason about God *and* to qualify that reasoning. Dionysius is explicit about this:

> our intellect (νοῦς) has the capability to think (νοεῖν), owing to which it can perceive conceivable things, and perceive as well a unity which transcends the mind's own nature, through which the mind is joined to things beyond itself. It follows that we ought to think on God not according to our capacities, rather we must be taken entirely out of ourselves and transcendently become of God . . . (*DN* 7.1, 865C–868A)[20]

The mind is capable of thought and of ek-static self-transcendence, and when it comes to reasoning about God, it must choose to allow itself to be taken beyond itself. By reason, we must choose to transcend reason.

That redirection may begin with a shutdown, a "reboot," if you will, something that Dionysius not only describes and recommends, but also initiates in the reader. He says it directly, e.g., in the *DN*: "The simple and unified truth of the intellectual visions of God are beyond our intellection of the divine ideas. *We call a halt to the activities of our minds . . .*" (*DN* 1.4, 592CD).[21] In a related way, Dionysius speaks in the *MT* of the active steps that Moses takes to ascend to the divine vision. What does he do? He

> *abandons* (ἀπολύεται) those who see and what is seen in order to enter the darkness of unknowing (τὸν γνόφον τῆς ἀγνωσίας), he *shuts out* (ἀντιλήψεις) every knowing apprehension, . . . united most excellently by the completely unknowing inactivity (ἀνενεργησίᾳ) of every knowledge, and knowing beyond intellect by knowing nothing (τῷ μηδὲν γινώσκειν ὑπὲρ νοῦν γινώσκων). (*MT* 1.3, 1001A)

But again, Dionysius does not only describe this active-inactivity, or inactive-activity; his writing is often constructed in such a way as to enact that very process in the reader. The Dionysian corpus is peppered throughout with profusions of double and triple negatives that deliberately force the reader to let go and be taken up out of himself.

> αὐτὸς δε ὑπὲρ νοῦν καὶ οὐσίαν ὑπεριδρυμένος, αὐτῷ τῷ καθόλου μὴ γινώσκεσθαι μηδὲ εἶναι, καὶ ἔστιν ὑπερουσίως καὶ ὑπὲρ νοῦν γινώσκεται. Καὶ ἡ κατὰ τὸ κρεῖττον παντελὴς ἀγνωσία γνῶσίς ἐστι τοῦ ὑπὲρ πάντα τὰ γινωσκόμενα.

> The more-than-founded beyond-intellect and being is beyond every way of being and is known beyond intellect by its total not-knowing and not-being. The greatest all-complete unknowing is a knowledge of that beyond all that is known. (*EP* 1, 1065A)

This is not merely a complex Greek sentence structure; it is an initiation into a process. Taking this even further, there are passages that sound almost like incantations, like the poetic and ecstatic verses of traditions that seek to reflect and even implement a release from set thought patterns.[22] There are rhythmic litanies, into which we are to be lost as if in whirlpools, such as this one which closes the *Mystical Theology*:

> As we climb higher, we say this. [The divinity] is not soul or mind, nor does it possess imagination, conviction, speech, or understanding. Nor is it speech per se. . . . It is not number or order, greatness

nor smallness, equality or inequality, similarity or dissimilarity. It is not immovable, moving, or at rest. It has no power, it is not power, nor is it light. It does not live nor is it life. It is not a substance, nor is it eternity or time. It cannot be grasped by the understanding since it is neither knowledge nor truth. It is not kingship. It is not wisdom. It is neither one nor oneness, divinity nor goodness. Nor is it a spirit, in the sense that we conceive spirit. It is not sonship or fatherhood and is nothing known to us or to any other being. It falls neither within the predicate of nonbeing nor of being. . . . It is both beyond every assertion, . . . *and free of every limitation; beyond every limitation, it is also beyond every denial.* (*MT* 5, 1045D–1048B)

By what he is saying, and sometimes even by the sheer volume of it and even the rhythm of it, he is rattling our intellects out of their habitual patterns, towards their ek-stasis.

Saint Dionysius is cognizant of the irony of his vocation as a writer, as one who reasonably reflects upon and teaches about that which is beyond all reflection, reason, and conception. In a passage characteristic of many of the church fathers, he writes,

I know well that I am not capable of comprehending those conceptual truths. I know that I lack the words to articulate such knowledge of God. I would not even listen to, let alone speak of, the divine philosophy were it not that I am convinced in my mind that one may not disregard *the received knowledge of divine things.* (*DN* 3.3, 684C)

Dionysius knows that human beings, and he among them, are imperfect, that God is inexhaustible and inexpressible, and yet is convinced that human beings are charged with the task of engaging their reasoning intellects to discern and articulate those things that God reveals about himself, namely, the "received knowledge."

To summarize: the reasoning intellect is a necessity for Dionysius in at least the following ways:

1. The corpus is aimed at persuading reasoning minds. Specifically, it is logically and supralogically convincing them to engage in a complete rethinking about the nature of the Divinity and its knowability through unknowing.

2. The discernment of God's radical otherness and his identity as archetype of existence—the principles of Dionysian unsayings and sayings, respectively—requires a reasoning mind.

3. And finally, it takes a conscious, reasoning mind to act on that discernment, to shut off and redirect the mind towards the analogical ascent through sayings and (supra-)unsayings.

In all of its richness, the Dionysian corpus is not a comprehensive or systematic theology, and those who approach it as one are consistently disappointed. Mistaken expectation is one of the main factors that has led to the widely diverse reception of his corpus, that I alluded to at the outset of this essay. In fact the corpus has a finite and relatively short list of points that it seeks to instill, all of which orbit around the core goal of divine/human communion, of theosis. It explores the *taxis* of things seen and unseen (the hierarchies), it talks of sacraments and rites, it even speaks to compassion, love, justice. And yes, it speaks of Christ. But given who God is and who we are, the journey of divine/human communion will always be one of knowing the supra- nonknowable God through an active unknowing, a radical redirection of the reasoning mind. But the mind is not only the subject of that redirection: it is its freely willing agent.

Notes

1. "The Odyssey of Dionysian Spirituality," in *Pseudo-Dionysius: The Complete Works*, trans. Colm Luibheid, ed. Paul Rorem (New York: Paulist Press, 1987), 21.

2. John Meyendorff, *Christ in Eastern Christian Thought* (Yonkers, NY: St. Vladimir's Seminary Press, 1975), 95, 99.

3. See especially "Dionysius Areopagites in the Works of Saint Gregory Palamas: On the Question of a 'Christological Corrective' and Related Matters," *Saint Vladimir's Theological Quarterly* 46 (2002): 163–90.

4. "Notes on the Palamite Controversy and Related Topics—II," *The Greek Orthodox Theological Review* 9, no. 2 (Winter 1963–64): 225–70, at 250. Meyendorff's understanding and appreciation of Dionysius is greater than that of Fr. Alexander Schmemann, who writes in his diaries that the success of the Dionysian corpus in Byzantium resulted in "the reduction of the Church to a mysterious piety, the dying of its eschatological essence and mission, and, finally, the de-Christianization of this world and its secularization." *The Journals of Father Alexander Schmemann 1973–1983* (Yonkers, NY: St. Vladimir's Seminary Press, 2000), 316–17. Schmemann was evidently not a fan.

5. See John Meyendorff, *A Study of Gregory Palamas*, 2nd ed. (Yonkers, NY: Faith Press/St. Vladimir's Seminary Press, 1974), 132–33.

6. The uniqueness of the human person with regard to this goal is classically tied to the creation of humans in the image and likeness of God (Gen 1:26–27). See Norman Russell, *The Doctrine of Deification in the Greek Patristic Tradition* (Oxford: Oxford University Press, 2006).

7. Although he uses them functionally interchangeably, Dionysius prefers the term ἡ θεότης (the Divinity) to ὁ Θεός (God).

8. All references are to the chapter headings provided in medieval manuscripts, followed by the column number in Migne, *Patrologia Graeca*, vol. 3. Translations are adapted from John D. Jones, *Pseudo Dionysius: The Divine Names and Mystical Theology* (Milwaukee: Marquette University Press, 1980) and from C. Luibheid et al., eds., *Pseudo-Dionysius: The Complete Works* (New York: Paulist, 1987).

9. I have added the italics. This passage is cited, and attributed to Dionysius, in the *Cloud of Unknowing* §70.

10. This very point is made early on in the *Divine Names*. See esp. 1.5–7.

11. I have altered Luibheid's translation. Jones's translation reads "we are deceived into following an apparently divine and ineffable logos when we receive what is beyond us in a way that is familiar to us, when we become entangled in what is native to our sensations, and when we reject what is divine for what is ours" (175).

12. This presumes that Dionysius wrote in the late fifth or early sixth century, as is commonly held.

13. See Epiphanius, *Panarion* 76.4.2. The suggestion of Eunomius's role in Dionysius's argument for divine nonknowability is also made in Rosemary Arthur, *Pseudo-Dionysius as Polemicist* (Burlington, VT: Ashgate, 2008), 155, 169.

14. *Syntagmation*, Prop. 26 (cf. *Panarion* 76.12.26).

15. See Arthur, *Pseudo-Dionysius as Polemicist*.

16. Cf. *Pseudo-Dionysius*, 101n183.

17. Dionysius speaks of the "still more uninformed, who describe the transcendent Cause of all things in terms derived from the lowest orders of being" (*MT* 2, 1000A).

18. See Daniel Jugrin, "Agnosia: The Apophatic Experience of God in Dionysius the Areopagite," *Teologia* 67 (2016): 102–15, at 109.

19. Gen 2:19–20 establishes the act of naming as a uniquely human vocation, among created beings.

20. Translation substantially altered from Luibheid.

21. I have drawn on both the Jones and Luibheid translations and have added emphasis.

22. One thinks of the Hebrew *niggun* tradition, for example.

Knowing in Theosis

A Byzantine Mystical Theological Approach

Ashley Purpura

Within Orthodox Christianity, like most religions, there exists a trajectory of deploying, creating, and even strategically dehumanizing the "other" in order to construct itself authoritatively.[1] In its ritual context, the hymning of voiceless and undifferentiated "others" provides a foil for proclaiming Orthodoxy, and yet Orthodox Christians theologically believe the people belonging to these groups are nevertheless in the image of God.[2] Proclaiming "Orthodoxy," as the true faith and one that historically developed out of a series of dogmatic and political controversies, nearly necessitates an "othering" that some might valorize as a type of apophatic definition of Orthodoxy. Despite scholarly efforts to deconstruct and complicate these false polarizations, "Orthodoxy as not 'x'" continues for many Orthodox as a mode of self-definition.[3] This way of speaking and ultimately knowing dominates the "other," in a potential erasure of the "other's" ability to participate in theosis.[4] Certainly not all Orthodox Christian discourse identifies itself, or what it asserts through a possessive and dominative "othering" of a thing or person that it is "not," but, if the Orthodox tradition at any level is marked by a normative assertive reasoning through faith that elides and "others" fellow human beings, then that model is theologically problematic. This theological dissonance manifests as Orthodox Christian authors, leaders, and sources express knowledge of the Orthodox self through the implicit domination of others—erasing their particularities and asserting limits over their possibilities for manifesting divine likeness—all the while also claiming that *every* person is capable of participating in theosis.

Although there has been some theological retrieval of "otherness" by the modern Orthodox theologian John Zizioulas, who draws on Emmanuel Levinas and others, to construct the "other" as necessary and good, Zizioulas primarily treats "otherness" in positive terms as a marker of divine-likeness without sufficiently addressing the problematic involuntary "otherness" of those subjugated by a dominating power (as the term is used in postcolonial and gender theory).[5] Thus, there is a disconnect between how modern critical and gender theorists might consider "otherness," as problematically situated amid a male or clerical-monastic discourse, and how Zizioulas as a hierarchical theologian engages and conceives "otherness" in more universal and theologically essential terms.[6]

In this essay, I primarily draw on the mystical monastic writings of Symeon the New Theologian (949–1022), and briefly reflect on liturgical resonances of this mystical tradition in the more lay-oriented commentaries of Nicholas Cabasilas (1322–1392) to argue that the Orthodox mystical tradition offers an alternative mode of knowing, speaking, and authoritatively signifying faith-based identities that is anchored by theosis. Writings oriented by a direct experience of God communicate knowledge in a way that does not necessitate the subjugation of an "other," the creation of a hierarchized opposite to know itself, or the rejection of rationality, but rather renders the seemingly privileged self voluntarily subjugated as the "other" in order to encounter the divine, the "Other" par excellence.[7] This unknowing-knowing offers a theological trajectory that might more capaciously attend to both the necessary Otherness of God, and human particularity as a form of divinely given "otherness" for relational communion, and oppose the destructive mode of "othering" that often marks religious discourse.[8]

Symeon the New Theologian

As a monastic leader, and then an ecclesial exile, Symeon gave passionate and authoritative voice to his experience of God and the perspective he acquired from it in his instructive, ascetic, and poetic writings.[9] Symeon provides bold and detailed accounts of union with God and relates how divine encounters personally transformed him.[10] The experience of divine indwelling affects the ways Symeon speaks and understands himself and those around him. He details (sometimes indirectly) the ecstatic encounter of divine light, the longing for its return, and the tears accompanying its experience—all of which are part of union with God that renders Symeon in a state of wonder and contemplation. Being humbly in a position of receptive unknowing thus gives rise to true knowledge—not as something that can be grasped and defined, but as a relational and apophatic acknowledgment of an authentic encounter with the Other.[11] Humble love, as such that defends the beloved ardently, knows the other intimately, and yet constantly admits there is infinitely more to know of the other, and longingly invites the other's self-disclosure is evidenced in Symeon's writings.[12] Such a mode of speaking reasons from within a humbled deifying relationship, rather than one of asserting oneself over another.

Knowledge, Language, and Understanding in Light of Theosis

For Symeon, the ecstatic divine experience causes a reorientation of knowledge and the act of knowing that is imbedded in an intense desire to know the God who is beyond knowing. While reflecting upon his visionary experience brought about by contemplating divine love in all creation, Symeon explains that the divine vision, "having itself filled me with divine joy, removed and snatched away my mind, and my senses, and all my worldly yearning. And my mind ran down and sought to overtake by yearning the manifested radiance."[13] Upon receiving the experience of union with God, Symeon describes his reason and sense perception are overwhelmed, and his desire transformed. In the experience of God, Symeon no longer desires to know in a "worldly" way, but rather comes to knowledge of God by yearning for His presence. Symeon prayerfully exclaims that, "those who understand your [God's] divinity in faith" are "gripped by much fear," and "do not have anything to say, for You [God] are beyond the mind, all-incomprehensible, all-unattainable are your works, and your glory, and the knowledge of You." The understanding of God that Symeon offers is precisely from a position of awestruck lowliness at the incomprehensible nature of God—a position of humble unknowing. Symeon continues in the same passage, however, by suggesting that even within this position of humble apophasis he does know "the love that [God] gave to us" by faith.[14] Indeed, by divine encounter and being in a position of humility in order to solicit divine presence, Symeon is left in a state of transfigured unknowing and silence. He is unable to sufficiently speak of God, unable to sufficiently know God—yet knows Him intimately through the union of divine love. Symeon is struck through ecstatic experience in a state of wonder.[15]

It is from this position of wonder, humility, and longing, that Symeon speaks authentically and authoritatively—offering, in almost a Pseudo-Dionysian tone—a multiplication of signifiers that are negated in the divine, and yet give indication to God through faith.[16] Knowledge is, thus, transformed from mental and sensory conclusions "about" to faithful desire to be overwhelmed in the love of the divine Other.

Symeon claims that those who encounter God through a type of apophatic faith are united to God in a divine way that transfigures knowledge. He explains that those who have experienced God have "wholly possessed Christ in themselves by action and experience, by perception, knowledge, and contemplation."[17] Divine union is both the means of perception, knowledge, and contemplation, and the end of it. Perhaps with Symeon it is better to conceive of knowledge, perception, and contemplation in relation to a unitive experience as an interior transcendent reality rather than as something that necessitates a distinct action and actor, perceiver and that which is being perceived, and a knower and the object of knowledge. Instead, there is a union without confusion, which Symeon describes in dogmatic theological terms saying, "when I participate in your flesh I participate in your nature, and I truly partake of your essence."[18] Such a union for the finite human results in a state of humble awareness of one's own infinite lowliness in relation to God, and the participant longs for and wonders at God's revelation nevertheless.[19]

Accordingly, Symeon describes divine indwelling as a knowledge-giving loving embrace. Instead of constructing hierarchized dichotomies to convey meaning, Symeon experiences knowledge of himself and God through the deconstruction of difference in divine union. The difference between God and Symeon is overcome in the experience of union and recast as nothing other than divine love that is intimately experienced and beyond full sensible comprehension. At one point, Symeon says he found God, "folding his entire self around me He tenderly kisses all of me," such that "all my members become bearers of light."[20] In the divine embrace, Symeon knows his own unworthiness and receives God who gives "his whole self" to him. Symeon perceives this union so intimately that in Hymn 15 he is able to point to each member of a deified body and say these "are Christ" as a logical consequence of divine indwelling.[21] Symeon experiences God as God united to him, as God loving and offering Godself to Symeon in such a way that Symeon's knowledge of God, and knowledge of himself, comes from a position of divine union.

The union that Symeon presents as manifesting perhaps only momentarily as light in the members of his body is ongoing in its ability to communicate spiritual knowledge through relationship. Symeon's knowledge of God, of others, comes through visionary and sacramental communion.[22] He describes knowledge through this personal union to God by saying, "the soul cannot live unless it is ineffably and without confusion united to God, who is truly the life eternal. Before this union in knowledge, vision and perception is dead, even though it is endowed with intellect and is by nature immortal."[23] According to Symeon, the union of the soul to God is life-giving and knowledge-producing, and without this personal union there is no vision or perception. Intellectual knowledge is not the same as life-giving union that manifests truth. It is not that the mind is somehow inferior to the soul, but that the mode by which knowledge is gained in the former is not founded in relation to theosis.

For Symeon, faith is a prerequisite for "full" true knowledge, such that knowledge apart from relationship, encounter, and personal union with the divine Other as dwelling in, and reshaping knowledge of, the self is insufficient.[24] Symeon makes clear that humble seeking and a longing relationship is necessary for properly expressing and possessing divine knowledge. Symeon explains, "Knowledge of these things [the Trinity] is for them whose intellect is illumined daily by the Holy Spirit on account of their purity of soul ... whose word of knowledge and word of wisdom is through the Spirit alone."[25] It is the Spirit that offers knowledge and wisdom "alone" with all else being counted as naught. The illumination, however, is synergistic, with the mystic continually striving in "purity of soul"—a purity which necessitates a rejection of not just sin, but preconceptions and knowledge aside from God. Indeed, there is a voluntary component to participating in theosis. In another instance of critical distinction, Symeon remarks that, "If Christ says: 'I am the light of the world,' those who do not see Him are outright blind," equating lack of divine recognition with inability to perceive altogether. Although for Symeon, it is fair to infer the preceding quote refers to those who do not have divine vision as he does, he further explains this assertion by saying that those who have remained "blind" have done so by lack of love, longing for God's presence, and voluntary submission to God's commandments.[26] The prerequisite for divine vision is voluntary love and an active longing which works to prepare the self (here, through obedience to the commandments) for divine self-disclosure.

Symeon's descriptions of desire for the other in a relationship of apophasis transforming knowledge, also is mirrored in his ascetic instructions and *Hymns* regarding the ability to speak. At one point Symeon reflects, "What is this spine-chilling mystery that is being accomplished in me? In no way can a word recount, nor can my miserable hand write to the praise and glory of Him Who is above praise, of Him who is beyond telling."[27] By this, Symeon acknowledges that language is insufficient to communicate the experience of God's love and adopts an apophatic style in his writing. Symeon appears intensely aware of God dwelling within his body and soul and finds himself humbled and inadequate to sufficiently praise or speak of God. The union with the Other, results in an acknowledgement of the insufficiency of language and reason to accurately convey an experience of ongoing love. Nonetheless, Symeon expresses himself in words, but from a position of admitting the awareness he has of his own lowliness and God's greatness—rather than cataphatically laying claim to the encounter he has with the divine Other.

The transformation of speech in relation to God manifests in Symeon's *Hymns* in very direct ways when Symeon writes in the voice of God.[28] While Symeon is not the first hymnographer to write in the voice of a sainted other, Symeon is distinctive because his speech in this way directly reflects and manifests as an experience of divine indwelling.[29] That is, Symeon is able to take up the voice of God in his *Hymns* not just as a pious imagining, but as an outpouring of the intense reality he knows of God dwelling within and united to him. Consequently, Symeon says in the voice of Christ such things as, "I descended from above. Being invisible in every way, I took on the thickness of flesh and assumed a soul; being God unchangeably, I the Logos became flesh."[30] Symeon does not speak as if he *were* God or as if he knows *about* God; rather, he speaks from *within* God and knowing God within him. Symeon experiences God through personal union and is therefore able to speak out of humble love authoritatively *as God*. It is only in light of voluntary self-giving union that Symeon is able to speak in the voice of God, or on behalf of God, as a type of pious outpouring of his deifying reality. Where Symeon speaks as God, he offers a proliferation of praise to boast on behalf of the Other, to share with the reader the immensity of God's condescending love as he has experienced it and provides a model of speaking that does not falsely subjugate to convey meaning—but rather speaks truthfully from within a reality modeled on, and in, celebration of divine self-giving.

Preparing to Encounter

With knowledge transformed apophatically through divine union, and desire and humility being both prerequisite and consequences of theosis, it follows also that Symeon adopts an attitude of humble and preparatory solicitation of divine self-revelation, rather than asserting knowledge via constraining assumptions about who he thinks God should be. Symeon's writings attest that in order to receive the experience of divine union, one must actively desire God's revelation in the form of self-unknowing asceticism. In one hymnic description of a divine encounter, Symeon explains that God cannot be comprehended apart from within the yearning and amazement Symeon has for Him. He says, "This is why I am wounded by his love, / insofar as He is not seen by me, I melt away in my senses, / and groaning, I burn in mind and heart." In response to the revelation of divine love, Symeon longs to see and know more. He does not lay claim over and ruminate on what he already thinks he knows about God, as a subject, but rather longs in an open position of receptivity and active desire to know Him more. Symeon continues by describing his mourning "despair" in longing after God's presence upon which, "He [God] is seen by me and He looks at me, He who looks upon all things." Symeon experiences the gift of God's gaze, and his reaction is one of astonishment at, "how the Creator stooped down when He opened the heavens / and displayed his unspeakable and strange glory to [him]." Symeon's posture of humble yearning and contemplation is a preparation for divine union, upon which he finds God dwelling within him. Such a model of awaiting self-disclosure from another by actively seeking their presence with love necessitates a humbling redirection of focus from oneself to the other.

Symeon contrasts the type of knowledge that comes from within God and through a position of humble longing relationship for God, to other false ways of knowing that lack the ascetical preparation. In Hymn 201, he juxtaposes "the heretics who have studied much / think that they know You, think that they understand You, / these all-wretched heretics suppose that they even see You, my God" against his own spiritual practice of faithful prayer and psalmody, by which he believes that he has "the summit of faith," "all knowledge of truth," and that he is united to Christ and shares in His "divine nature."[31] It may certainly be the case in this example that Symeon demonstrates a type of "othering" regarding the "heretics" in order to construct his own spiritual practice as superior, but the distinction he draws is clear. Those who are united to God do not *think* they know God or understand God, they *know* God through union. It is through an activity of faith that Symeon is united in loving union to God, and by this he shares and participates in God's nature, which becomes Symeon's nature by grace. Such a union gives Symeon "knowledge and truth," opposed to those who have "studied much" without first positioning themselves in a posture of humble prayer. The distinction Symeon sets forth, however, is not so much a positioning of divine experience in mysticism over and against intellectual study, but rather knowledge from within divine union and a position of faithful humility, opposed to false knowledge that claims to "know" aside from a mutually self-giving relationship. The assumptions of the proud, whom Symeon critiques, make the "other" an object of study rather than a person who may voluntarily bestow self-disclosure within a loving relationship. Unsurprisingly, Symeon criticizes the prideful person as unable to know, claiming, "by their own choice, they want to cover their eyes and ears, and because of this they imagine that they both see and hear."[32] Those who do not yearn after God with humility instead offer their own knowledge and reasoning in place of God's revelation.

The fostering of desire for divine union is not the only way Symeon recommends preparing and seeking out the presence of God. The apophatic posture of unknowing in order to know, Symeon yokes with intense desire to see God as he is, and to see creation as God sees it. This necessitates a letting go of preconceptions and placing oneself in a receptive posture of desire. Symeon instructs his monastic followers to "be eager to find Christ and see Him as He is" and then instructs them, saying, "let us give ourselves as slaves to Him, our Lord and God, who for our sakes 'took on Himself the form of a slave' and died for us. Come let us be humbled under His mighty hand (I Pet. 5:6)."[33] The longing Symeon has for divine union is paired with a longing for humility, and to see God's love as the perfection of humility. This desire results in a union that wherein Symeon says we may "possess" (κτησώμεθα) God "abiding in us." This possession, however, is not domination or bounded possession of a captive and complete quantity, rather in having God within, God continues to "feed our souls," with ongoing communion.[34] Thus, Symeon claims that he must allow the divine Other to continually reshape him in humility and in knowledge of Himself in order to increase in divine likeness.[35]

Even if someone does not yet vividly encounter the divine light, Symeon also suggests that Christ's indwelling is ongoing for those who cooperatively long for and purify themselves for God.³⁶ Symeon explains that by keeping commandments "day by day [one] is purified anew to the extent that he practices them. He becomes radiant, he is illuminated, there is granted to him to see revelations of great mysteries of the depth of which no one has ever seen nor is at all able to see who has not striven to attain the height of such purity." Accurate human perception of God (the Other) depends on emptying the self through humility and penitence. Symeon emphasizes the need for human purification to receive illuminative knowledge that is ultimately unknowable in its depth. Following this, Symeon explains upon receiving revelation, the person, "to the degree that he perceives, he is wounded to the quick and acquires yet greater humility, deeming himself entirely unworthy of the knowledge and revelation of such mysteries," with the result that the person is "unwounded by presumptuous thoughts, and grows daily in faith, in hope, and in love for God." The greater the divine knowledge, the greater the humility and love, to the extent that Symeon claims one who has full knowledge of Christ will "conduct himself as one who neither has nor knows anything and will consider himself as a useless and unworthy servant."³⁷ Purification of the self and humility leads to the full knowledge of God, which then leads to knowledge of the self in further lowliness, in order to accurately receive the divine Other. Such a mode of knowing does not objectify the Other through categories of assertion, nor subjugate it through a type of discursive domination, but in a position of humble faith comes to knowledge through increasing divine likeness, that is, humility.³⁸

Although, divine revelation and ecstatic visions cannot be taught or earned, Symeon teaches his disciples to train themselves in humility, detachment, purity, and obedience in order that they may invite the self-disclosure of God. Symeon depicts such ascetic efforts themselves as a type of divine-likeness because they lower and empty oneself in preparation for receiving another.³⁹ For Symeon, one can only solicit divine presence through a position of "repentance and humiliation" that is, putting on Christ's lowliness to have Christ reveal his glory. Such a position is one of detachment, penitence, and rejecting one's self apart from the self-united to Christ.⁴⁰ Symeon beseeches God to dwell in him in such a way that knowledge of God supplants and reorients Symeon's knowledge of himself.⁴¹ Detachment from the world is not only physical retreat into monasticism, but also an internal and mental unknowing in order to know oneself through faith united to Christ.

Consequences of Theosis for Knowing Others

Having presented how the immediate experience of theosis offers a transfigured mode of knowing and speaking, as well as means of soliciting and preparing for divine encounter, I turn to the consequences of the experience of theosis for knowing oneself and others. It is through divine union that one's perceptive and intellectual faculties function as they should. The result, as Symeon relates, is that "One might say that he no longer hears any human voice or voices, but only the voice of the Living Word whenever it speaks through a human voice. By its hearing the soul admits Him and no other."[42] The human person is transformed into one who recognizes God not only in a vision of light, but also in their fellow human beings.[43] Perhaps one could read Symeon as suggesting a way of knowing that only admits a longing for seeing the "other" as an icon of God, rather than a human construct, or person perceived through matrices of categorical limitations (whether based on actions, appearances, social position, etc.). Lest one think that such an approach to knowledge is restricted uniquely to human's relationship with God directly, the results of the encounter in which God condescends to disclose his love to the lowly, should likewise be extended to the knowledge of all human "others."[44] Through divine union, the human person is made to know those around them first and foremost as God has created them and called them to be, individualized in their uniqueness, but not confined by assumptions or categories created by humans that may limit human perception of them. Symeon explains that love of humankind is "to keep equally toward all, both the good and the wicked, a deep-seated love, and each day lay down your soul on behalf of all." This self-giving on behalf of the other, Symeon says, makes the person "an imitator of the Master," and "a true image of the creator . . . in every respect, of the divine perfection."[45] The giving up of the self on behalf of all others, to know them in this liberating way, is an expression of divine likeness.

Nicholas Cabasilas

Having presented ecstatic knowledge in the writings of Symeon the New Theologian, I now briefly suggest a few comparative points in the liturgical reflections of Nicholas Cabasilas in order to show that such a knowing through theosis is not limited to those with mystical visions, but also available to the worldly layperson in the pious participation of the sacraments. Cabasilas describes a reframing of knowledge and knowing the "other" through the experience of sacramental and liturgical divine union. Cabasilas thus serves as an essential foil to Symeon for thinking about how a broader nonmonastic and nonvisionary audience might "know" the divine Other in a way that is likewise consistent with the reality of theosis. Unlike Symeon, we have no evidence Cabasilas himself was any type of mystical visionary, and yet he comparably describes liturgical and sacramental participation as a means of accessing the same type of divine union and indwelling as described by the New Theologian.[46] Accordingly, Cabasilas's approach to knowledge, reason, and speaking resonates with the perspectives offered by the earlier Symeon, not because he was necessarily writing and thinking about Symeon's works but because he has a similar sense of the immediacy of experiencing the reality of divine indwelling. Consequently, Cabasilas provides an important example of liturgical encounters with God as the goal and basis by which knowledge may be expressed authoritatively and authentically. Repeatedly, Cabasilas invites his readers to contemplate the divine mysteries, and models the type of reasoning that negates its own singularity and fosters desire for personal loving participation in the other.[47] Thus, Cabasilas demonstrates that the knowing through theosis presented by the New Theologian is not only a monastic or elite mystical enterprise, but available and accessible for *all* liturgical participants.

First, much like Symeon's focus on fostering the human desire for God, Cabasilas also tries to move his readers to compunction and contemplation by describing how God longs to transform human understanding by turning it away from distractions and back instead to a unity of love.[48] Cabasilas invites his readers to marvel at God's union with the liturgical participants that transforms their minds with love for the one they encounter. Knowing God, in this way offers a model for knowing the "other" and all else through a love and knowledge of God in them—a desire to see God in all—after the experience of divine union. Cabasilas observes in the context of liturgy, participants need to put aside human preconceptions and through the experience of God's glory enter the activity of wonder. He explains, "in doxology we lay aside ourselves and all our interests and glorify the Lord for his own sake, for his power and his glory. . . . Immediately we approach God we recognize the inaccessibility and force and grandeur of his glory, and are filled with wonder and awe and similar feelings."[49]

Cabasilas suggests recognizing God in this way, as God is, leads to a type of self-humbling at the "inaccessibility" of God's glory and one's simultaneous participation in it by giving up the self to "glorify the Lord for his own sake."

Much like Symeon, Cabasilas emphasizes the mode of knowing God is not something apart from how one might know human "others," and the human potential for divinization, Cabasilas explains the need to recognize others as the Body of Christ and all Eucharistic participants as participants in divine union. He explains the need to really recognize the Eucharistic participants as united to Christ, saying, "if one could see the Church of Christ, insofar as she is united to him and shares in his sacred Body, one would see nothing other than the Body of the Lord."[50] While Symeon might claim to actually see Christ as light, Cabasilas urges his readers to have *faith* to recognize the reality they might not yet be able to see. In contrast to the emphasis Symeon gives to God's voluntary submission and self-revelation, however, Cabasilas emphasizes the need for human's to voluntarily submit their minds and knowledge to God through faith, and to be transformed in sacramental participation.[51] It is not merely a temporary indwelling or a momentary sacramental union, but an enduring union that begets true knowledge of the other. There is a mutual submission, a self-giving up from both God (that is paradoxically full) and the human to bring about unity and a new knowledge. The recognition of this divine vision and self-revelation is only limited, according to Cabasilas, by human lack of faith, purity, and love, but is offered to all in the sacraments of the Church. While not as obvious and ecstatic as that of Symeon the New Theologian, the Eucharist, Cabasilas emphasizes, is indeed the coming and appearance of Christ, and one's perception of this vision is limited only by one's own lacking spiritual preparation and purification.[52]

For Cabasilas the goal of reason is contemplation of God, or more precisely wonder, brought about through divinely participative activity—such as liturgy. This divine reflection is not merely an intellectual activity of the mind, but as Symeon would agree, a unitive fostering of love that brings about a different type of knowledge. Cabasilas explains, "One acquires right reason not merely by learning it, but also by employing it in necessary actions."[53] Reason, however, is not just something to practice independently, but something oriented toward and perfected in divine contemplation and united in divine love. Cabasilas describes divine union as surpassing "understanding" and surpassing even that which one might think they know most intimately. He thus suggests a mode of knowledge and reason that humbly acknowledges the subject as ultimately ungraspable.[54] Those who live in Christ, who are sacramentally and spiritually united to Christ know through loving Christ, they know as He does through a position of love.[55] The knowledge that comes through this type of love provides an intimacy and immediacy of participation in, and on behalf of the "other," rather than domination of it.[56] Even in liturgical participation, one cannot maintain the self as a priority above giving up the self on behalf of seeking to know the other through love.

Cabasilas, like Symeon, also speaks of Christ voluntarily "possessing" (ἐκτήσατο) humans and the human voluntary possession of Christ, but specifically, in the Eucharist. Cabasilas explains that "the Son, in inheriting us, possesses us far more highly and excellently than he did by creating us" because "we submitted (ὑπετάξαμεν) our minds in recognizing him as true God and sovereign lord of every creature; we submitted our wills in giving him our love, accepting his rule, and taking his yoke upon our shoulders with joy."[57] Divine indwelling is dependent on voluntary submission, an action that is repeatedly written into the words and actions of the liturgical service itself, such that Christ submits to human consent in sacramentally disclosing Himself to the Christian.[58] Submission as a form of love and accepting the obligations offered by the other are thus presented as modes of divine likeness and the means of divine communion.

Last, both Cabasilas and the New Theologian claim that divine experience and indwelling divine presence gives the faithful the ability to know authoritatively in a new way. For Cabasilas, by participating in and contemplating the sacraments, an individual is able to recognize and know with authority the divine likeness in others.[59] Likewise, Symeon the New Theologian polemically insists that true spiritual leaders have divine experience, so that only then are they able to guide others.[60] In this way, experience is not in lieu of rational knowledge but rather prerequisite for having knowledge transfigured into a new way of knowing. It is by divine communion (either mystically or sacramentally—of course, not that these are mutually exclusive categories) that one becomes divinely communicative. Knowing God personally through experience, encounter, and Eucharist can then make the divine presence known among others, lead those the participants share such knowledge with to their own encounter and indwelling with God, and be recognized by those around them as authentically manifesting divinity (either by words, sacraments, or embodied iconicity).

The ecstatic experiential way of knowing through unknowing, allowing the self to be transformed through relationship, asserting from a state of humble wonder rather than domination, and speaking on behalf of the other in a way that invites their continued presence without obscuring and constraining them, is one that is attested by the lofty mystical writings of Symeon the New Theologian and reflected in the liturgical commentaries of Nicholas Cabasilas. Certainly, these authors and the others who engage in a similar mode of expressing authoritative knowledge through humility do not represent this way of speaking and knowing exclusively. They engage, balance, and negotiate the more dominant way of discourse throughout their writings. Nevertheless, in their reflections on direct encounters with God—whether ecstatic or liturgical, they represent a type of divine knowing that is nondominating and non-"othering," and reflects reasoning through faith toward, and from within, an immediate awareness of the reality of theosis. Both authors historically engaged to defend Orthodoxy, and with authority grounded in their faith they taught that the human person can experience union with God. For the one who experiences this union, their knowledge and their ways of knowing themselves and others are called to be transformed in light of experiencing and desiring divine indwelling.

Despite Symeon and Cabasilas's positions of wonder and self-professed unworthiness, they express a certitude of faith through reasonable extension of their direct and bodily experience of possessing God within themselves. This boldness in faith manifests a mode of articulating Orthodoxy that humbly desires to see the "other" as created by God, knows through unifying mutually participative relationships rather than oppositional dichotomies, and embraces an apophasis of the self and its preconceptions of the other in favor of seeing and speaking more truthfully—and yet admittedly insufficiently—on behalf of, and oriented by, the priority of love. This type of approach needs to be considered for how it might be best applied to those whose knowing and identities are already forcefully shaped and subjugated by the dominate reasoning and hierarchized orders of those in ostensible positions of privilege and power. Certainly it would be problematic and theologically inconsistent to tell those upon whom kenosis and humility have been used as religious tools of oppression and valorization of abusive systematic or structural dehumanization that digging deeper into those categories for which they really have no other option is the best expression of theosis. Cabasilas especially notes how Christ awaits and desires the human voluntary submission to his commandments, and the New Theologian emphasizes not only the unknowing of the self, but also the knowing of the self infinitely loved, deified, and emboldened to speak on behalf of truth, even in opposition to established authorities.[61] For those in positions of privilege, however, who identify and have shaped the discourse of Orthodoxy, who have the ability to be recognized and speak from loci of ecclesial authority—rather than those who feel alienated, erased, or oppressed by it—this mode of knowing and discursively reasoning through a priority of humble love offers a way of encountering and embracing the other that more accurately communicates the reality of theosis.

Although the textual examples I have presented here are from only two Greek-speaking Orthodox saints, I would suggest that such ways of knowing and deconstructing otherness in favor of a desired intimate personal relationship are not just an overlooked way of expressing experience, but likely a pervasive feature of other divinely reflective and didactic texts.[62] While it remains to be seen how the mode of knowing I have presented via the New Theologian and Cabasilas finds resonances in other authors, time periods, and cultural expressions across Christianity, the possibility of this mode of knowing and speaking in relation to not only God but also fellow humans may provide a resourceful framework for unknowing those that have been traditionally "othered" and obscured by Orthodox tradition. Perhaps embracing such a trajectory necessitates a certain reframing of what and how Orthodox Christians consider Tradition. Such a reevaluation need not be considered a rejection of Tradition, but rather a rediscovering of potentially illuminating aspects of Orthodox experience and thought, which attest to its ability to express itself with greater faithfulness to a fundamental belief in theosis.

Notes

1. A brief outline of the development of Christian identity, particularly Orthodox identities vis-à-vis an "other" can be found in George Demacopoulos and Aristotle Papanikolaou, "Orthodox Naming of the Other: A Postcolonial Approach," in *Orthodox Constructions of the West* (New York: Fordham University Press, 2013), 1–22.

2. For example, the Orthodox hymnographic tradition includes an "othering" construction of "heretics," and "Jews" in order to celebrate and affirm Orthodox identity. See, for example, *The Lenten Triodion*, ed. Mother Mary and Kallistos Ware (South Canaan, PA: St. Tikhon's Seminary Press, 2002), 349, 564, 587, 589.

3. Several excellent studies critically reconsidering the ways Orthodox identity exists in relation to others can be found in Demacopoulos and Papanikolaou, *Orthodox Constructions of the West*.

4. Much of what Grace Jantzen in *Becoming Divine: Towards a Feminist Philosophy of Religion* (Bloomington: Indiana University Press, 1999), 1–59, observes regarding the trends that elide women's voices in philosophy of religion could likewise be applied to much Orthodox discourse.

5. Zizioulas, *Communion and Otherness*. Further discussion on Zizioulas's contributions to conceiving personhood, freedom, otherness, and theology can be found in Douglas Knight, ed., *Theology of John Zizioulas: Personhood and the Church* (New York: Routledge Press, 2017); Gayatri Chakravorty Spivak, "The Rani of Sirmur: An Essay in Reading the Archives," *History and Theory* 24, no. 3 (1985): 247–72; Edward Said, "Introduction," in *Orientalism* (London: Routledge & Kegan Paul, 1978), 1–30.

6. Zizioulas, *Communion and Otherness*, 52–53, does have some limited discussion on the "other" as deployed in postmodernism. For the use of the "Other" in gender theory, I have in mind Luce Irigaray's critique of the male construction of women in *Speculum of the Other Woman*, trans. G. C. Gill (Ithaca, NY: Cornell University Press, 1985), and *This Sex Which Is Not One*, trans. C. Porter (Ithaca, NY: Cornell University Press, 1985). Related discussion for how Irigaray's writings might be read sympathetically alongside negative theology and conceiving a divine Other, see Amy Hollywood, "Beauvoir, Irigaray, and the Mystical," *Hypatia* 9, no. 4 (1994): 158–85, and Ann-Marie Priest, "Woman as God, God as Woman: Mysticism, Negative Theology, and Luce Irigaray," *Journal of Religion* (2003): 1–23.

7. Related discussion can be found in John Zizioulas, *Communion and Otherness*, ed. Paul McPartlan (New York: T&T Clark, 2006), 55–91.

8. For a discussion of the theological resourcefulness of unknowing see, Charles Stang, *Apophasis and Pseudonymity in Dionysius the Areopagite: 'no Longer I'* (Oxford: Oxford University Press, 2012).

9. Symeon reflects most directly on this in his Discourses and Hymns, for which I refer to the following translations: Symeon the New Theologian, *The Discourses*, trans. C. J. deCatanzaro (Mahwah, NJ: Paulist Press, 1980), a translation of what is elsewhere called his *Catechetical Discourses*; Symeon, *Divine Eros: Hymns of Saint Symeon the New Theologian*, ed. Daniel Griggs (Crestwood, NY: St. Vladimir's Seminary Press, 2010); Saint Symeon the New Theologian,

On the Mystical Life: The Ethical Discourses: The Church and the Last Things, vol. 1, trans. Alexander Golitzin (Crestwood, NY: St. Vladimir's Seminary Press, 1995); Saint Symeon the New Theologian, *On the Mystical Life: The Ethical Discourses: On Virtue & Christian Life*, vol. 2, trans. Alexander Golitzin (Crestwood, NY: St. Vladimir's Seminary Press, 1996); references in the original Greek come from Symeon, *Opera* in *Patrologia Graeca*, vol. 120, ed. J. Migne (Paris, 1865); Symeon, *Syméon le Nouveau Théologien: Catéchèses*, ed. Basile Krivochéine, 3 vols., Sources Chrétiennes 96, 104, 113 (Paris: Éditions du Cerf, 1963–1965); Symeon, *Syméon le Nouveau Théologien: Hymnes*, ed. Johannes Koder, 3 vols., *Sources Chrétiennes* 156, 174, 196 (Paris: Éditions du Cerf, 1969–1973); Symeon, *Traités théologiques et éthiques*, ed. Jean Darrouzès, 2 vols., Sources Chrétiennes 122, 129 (Paris: Éditions du Cerf, 1966); Symeon, *Epistles of St. Symeon the New Theologian*, ed. and trans. H. J. M. Turner (Oxford: Oxford University Press, 2009). For a contextual interpretation of the Hymns and their genre as more erotic love songs than liturgical poetry, see John McGuckin, "Symeon the New Theologian's Hymns of Divine Eros: A Neglected Masterpiece of the Christian Mystical Tradition" *Spiritus: A Journal of Christian Spirituality* 5, no. 2 (2005): 182–202; for his near-contemporary Byzantine hagiography, see Niketas Stethatos, *The Life of Saint Symeon the New Theologian*, trans. Richard P. H. Greenfield (Cambridge, MA: Harvard University Press, 2013).

10. See for example, Symeon, *Catechetical Discourse* XVI (*The Discourses*, 198–202).

11. Symeon, Hymn 1 (*Divine Eros*, 36), Hymn 52 (*Divine Eros*, 366). On tears in Symeon see Hannah Hunt, *Joy-bearing Grief: Tears of Contrition in the Writings of the Early Syrian and Byzantine Fathers* (Leiden: Brill, 2004), 171–224; see the insightful studies of the impact of divine experience on Symeon's life and thought in Hilarion Alfeyev, *St. Symeon the New Theologian and Orthodox Tradition* (Oxford: Oxford University Press, 2000) and Helen Theodoropoulos, "Love of God and Love of Neighbor in the Mystical Theology of St. Bernard of Clairvaux and St. Symeon the New Theologian" (PhD diss., University of Chicago, 1995).

12. See Symeon's opening Mystical Prayer and Hymn 1 for examples (*Divine Eros*, 33–43). For discussion of the ways that Symeon uses erotic and nuptial imagery to convey his experience of divine union to others see, Derek Krueger, "Homoerotic Spectacle and the Monastic Body in Symeon the New Theologian," in *Toward a Theology of Eros: Transfiguring Passion at the Limits of Discipline*, ed. Virginia Burrus and Catherine Keller (New York: Fordham University Press, 2006), 99–118.

13. Symeon, Hymn 17 (*Divine Eros*, 102–4).

14. Ibid., Hymn 18 (*Divine Eros*, 119).

15. Symeon, *Catechetical Discourse* XVI (*The Discourses*, 200).

16. See especially Dionysius's *The Divine Names* and *The Mystical Theology* in *Pseudo-Dionysius: The Complete Works*, ed. Colm Luibhéid and Paul Rorem (New York: Paulist Press, 1987).

17. Symeon, *Catechetical Discourse VIII* (*The Discourses*, 143–44).

18. Ibid., Hymn 7 (*Divine Eros*, 57).

19. See ibid., Hymn 1 (*Divine Eros*, 35–43).

20. Ibid., Hymn 16 (*Divine Eros*, 92–93).

21. For example, see Symeon's Hymn 23 and Hymn 15 in *Divine Eros*.

22. Symeon, *Catechetical Discourse I* (*The Discourses*, 45) is also relevant here where Symeon characterizes divine-likeness in terms of humility. Symeon says "However great your zeal and many the efforts of your asceticism, they are all in vain and without useful result unless they attain to love in a broken spirit (Ps 51:19). By no other virtue, by no other fulfillment of the Lord's commandment, can anyone be known as a disciple of Christ."

23. Ibid., *Catechetical Discourse XIII* (*The Discourses*, 183).

24. Symeon, *Ninth Ethical Discourse* (*On the Mystical Life* 2:112).

25. Ibid., 113–14.

26. Ibid., *Thirteenth Ethical Discourse* (*On the Mystical Life* 2:172).

27. Ibid., Hymn 1 (*Divine Eros*, 35).

28. Examples abound, see for example Symeon's Hymns 41, 53, and 58 (*Divine Eros* 291–301, 374–82, 389–410).

29. Derek Krueger, "Writing and Redemption in the Hymns of Romanos the Melodist," *Byzantine and Modern Greek Studies* 27 (2003): 2–44. Romanos is one of the foremost Byzantine hymnographers who wrote dialogue hymns in the voice of Jesus, and as Krueger has demonstrated this was not unrelated to his own spiritual practice. Symeon, however, is rather unique as his *Hymns* are not liturgical in nature.

30. Symeon, Hymn 53 (*Divine Eros*, 378).

31. Ibid., 26 (201).

32. Symeon, Hymn 52 (370).

33. Symeon, *Catechetical Discourse II* (*The Discourses*, 49).

34. Ibid. (*The Discourses*, 50, 58).

35. Ibid., *Catechetical Discourse XVI* (*The Discourses*, 200). Regarding the vision of light, Symeon can only say "Lord have mercy" during his ecstasy.

36. For examples, see Symeon's *Hymns* 7, 13, 17, 18, and 52 in *Divine Eros*.

37. Symeon, *Ninth Ethical Discourse* (*On the Mystical Life* 2:127).

38. Ibid., Hymn 36 (*Divine Eros*, 277). Symeon elaborates that the glory of God, the divine likeness that humans might acquire is "the sharing of your [Christ's] sufferings, the imitation of your works, and your humility."

39. Ibid., *Catechetical Discourse XIII* (*The Discourses*, 182).

40. Ibid., *Catechetical Discourse XXXVI* (376). See also *The Epistles of St. Symeon the New Theologian*, ed. H. J. M. Turner (Oxford: Oxford University Press, 2009), 171.

41. Symeon, Hymn 45 (*Divine Eros*, 332).

42. Ibid., *Catechetical Discourse XIV* (*The Discourses*, 189–90).

43. Symeon, Hymn 44 (*Divine Eros*, 316). Relatedly, Symeon says, "Truly the soul of every human being, according to his image is a rational image of the Logos."

44. Ibid., *Sixth Ethical Discourse* (*On the Mystical Life* 2:79–80). Symeon's Hymn 30 (*Divine Eros*, 235) is also informative here for understanding the human person as participating in mutual divine indwelling. Symeon says, "A human being is small among visible creation, shadow and dust, yet can have all of God within, God, on whose finger creation is suspended, and from Whom everything has both life and movement, every mind, soul, and reason of all rational beings has existence from Him."

45. Symeon, Hymn 44 (*Divine Eros*, 320).

46. Related discussion of Cabasilas as a humanistic thinker and mystical hesychast supporter can be found in Marcus Plested, *Orthodox Readings of Aquinas* (Oxford: Oxford University Press, 2012), 100–108; additional historical context is given in Eugenia Russell, "Nicholas Cabasilas Chamaetos (c. 1322–90): A Unique Voice among His Contemporaries," *Nottingham Medieval Studies* 54 (2010): 122–24, and Marie-Helene Congourdeau, "Nicholas Cabasilas of Thessaloniki: The Historical Dimension of the Person," in *Personhood in the Byzantine Christian Tradition: Early, Medieval, and Modern Perspectives*, ed. Alexis Torrance and Symeon Paschalidis (New York: Routledge, 2018), 114–27.

47. Nicholas Denysenko, "*The Life in Christ* by Nicholas Cabasilas as a Mystagogical Work," *Studia Liturgica* 38 (2009): 242–60, and Constantine Tsirpanlis, *The Liturgical and Mystical Theology of Nicholas Cabasilas* (Athens: Theologia, 1976).

48. Cabasilas, *A Commentary on the Divine Liturgy*, trans. J. M. Hussey and P. A. McNulty (Crestwood, NY: St. Vladimir's Seminary Press, 2010), 48.

49. Ibid., 43.

50. Ibid., 91.

51. Cabasilas, *The Life in Christ*, trans. Carmino J. deCatanzaro (Crestwood, NY: St. Vladimir's Seminary Press, 1998), 128.

52. Cabasilas, *A Commentary on the Divine Liturgy*, 92–93.

53. Ibid., *The Life in Christ*, 171.

54. Ibid., 46.

55. Ibid., 216.

56. Ibid., 214–15. Note the Greek uses three different words to convey the power of love, the one loving, and the things loved, "Ἡ γὰρ τῆς ἀγάπης δύναμις τοῖς ἐρῶσιν οἰκεῖα τὰ τῶν φιλουμένων οἶδε ποιεῖν."

57. Cabasilas, *A Commentary on the Divine Liturgy*, 93.

58. Panayiotis Nellas, "The Spiritual Life in Christ: A Study of the Christocentric Anthropology of St Nicolas Kavasilas," in *Deification in Christ: Orthodox Perspectives on the Nature of the Human Person* (Crestwood, NY: St. Vladimir's Seminary Press, 1987), 107–55.

59. Ibid., 89. Cabasilas explains, "This therefore becomes clear: the baptismal washing has instilled into men some knowledge and perception of God . . . they are able to know more perfectly by experience than were they merely to learn it by being taught."

60. For example of this, see especially his first letter, regarding confession in *The Epistles of St Symeon the New Theologian*, 26–69; and related discussion in H. J. M. Turner, *St. Symeon the New Theologian: The New Theologian and Spiritual Fatherhood* (Leiden: Brill, 1990); for its implications in a broader context for modern Christian theological thinking, see William Abraham, *Divine Agency and Divine Action, Volume II: Soundings in the Christian Tradition* (Oxford: Oxford University Press, 2017), 118–37.

61. Cabasilas, *A Commentary on the Divine Liturgy*, 93; Symeon, *Hymn* 58 (*Divine Eros*, 398–416).

62. The following translations offer representation of several other prominent saints' most "mystical" writings: Seraphim, *The Aim of Christian Life: The Conversation of St Seraphim of Sarov with N. A. Motovilov*, trans. Maxim Nikolsky (Cambridge: Saints Alive Press, 2010); Silouan the Athonite's writings as collected in the second part of Archimandrite Sophrony, *St Silouan the Athonite* (Crestwood, NY: St. Vladimir's Seminary Press, 1999); and Isaac of Nineveh, *On Ascetical Life*, trans. Mary Hansbury (Crestwood, NY: St. Vladimir's Seminary Press, 1989).

Deification in Evagrius Ponticus and the Transmission of the *Kephalaia Gnostika* in Syriac and Arabic

Stephen J. Davis

In the spring of 2004, I participated in a conference on the Christian doctrine of deification at Drew University, entitled "Partakers of the Divine Nature." The scholars in attendance presented papers on conceptions of theosis in classical Greek philosophy, Paul's letters, 2 Peter, Irenaeus of Lyon, Origen of Alexandria, Athanasius of Alexandria, the Cappadocian Fathers, Ephrem the Syrian, Ps.-Dionysius the Areopagite, Maximus the Confessor, the thirteenth-century Christian Arabic author Būlus al-Būshī, and even Anselm, Martin Luther, John Calvin, John Wesley, and modern Catholic and Orthodox theologians from Karl Rahner to Sergius Bulgakov. Notably, none of us discussed the works of the fourth-century Christian ascetic writer Evagrius Ponticus, and he was conspicuously absent from the articles in the collected volume of essays that resulted.[1] This is consistent with a larger trend in historical scholarship on early Christianity: relatively little attention has been paid to questions related to deification in the Evagrian corpus.

Indeed, to my knowledge, there have been only two brief studies specifically focused on this topic. The first is an article by Augustine Casiday entitled "Deification in Origen, Evagrius and Cassian," published in 2003. Only seven pages long, Casiday's essay briefly surveys the theology of three major early Christian authors. As a result, he is able to devote only just over two pages to a discussion of Evagrius, focusing especially on the author's commentaries and scholia on scripture and on citations from his letters.[2] Casiday's primary concern, however, is not with Evagrius *per se*, but rather with "John Cassian's reception and interpretation of the Origenist-Evagrian heritage."[3]

The second study related to Evagrius and deification appears as a chapter subsection in Norman Russell's 2004 monograph *The Doctrine of Deification in the Greek Patristic Tradition*. In chapter 8, which takes as its principal theme the "Monastic Synthesis" inspired by Maximus the Confessor, Norman pauses for just over three pages to discuss Evagrius Ponticus's perspective on deification.[4] Most of his treatment involves a summary of Evagrius's biography and three-stage program of spiritual training. He concludes by brusquely criticizing Evagrius's "gnosticizing approach to deification," emphasizing its rejection by the Fifth Ecumenical Council and (in contrast) valorizing the "major corrective" offered by Maximus.[5]

Aside from these two brief studies, Evagrius's conception of deification—or human salvific participation in the divine—has only received glancing treatment by editors and translators of his writings. When it comes to Evagrius's masterwork, the *Kephalaia Gnostika*, Ilaria Ramelli's 2015 translation of that text is a good example.[6] In her introduction, Ramelli invokes the language of deification (theosis) fifteen times, and she peppers her verse-by-verse commentary with occasional mentions of this theme, but she does not devote any section to a sustained discussion of that topic. She also never truly pauses to point out that Evagrius did not in fact use the language of theosis himself in his extant writings. Indeed, the lack of attention to Evagrius on the subject of deification is undoubtedly due to the fact that he refrains from employing that word as a *terminus technicus*.

As a result of this rather sparsely populated scholarly landscape, the question of how Evagrius brings notions of divine participation to expression begs for further analysis, and that is the task to which I devote myself in this short article, with two main goals. First, I will survey Evagrius's writings and discuss the role his notion of the "Holy Unity" plays in his conception of how rational beings take on divine attributes and ultimately are assimilated to the Holy Trinity. Second, I will use the *Kephalaia Gnostika* and its reception in Syriac and Arabic as a case study of how such Evagrian notions of deification were transmitted into later medieval Syriac- and Arabic-speaking contexts. To that end, I will incorporate two newly catalogued Arabic manuscripts from the Monastery of the Syrians (Dayr al-Suryān) in Egypt as additional pieces of evidence for tracing this transmission history.

The Theological Logic of Deification in Evagrius

In his extant writings, Evagrius never uses the Greek term θέωσις, nor do we find a direct Syriac or Arabic equivalent in the translations of his works, but he does develop an elaborate theory of how humans are destined to ascend to unity with the Godhead. While this doctrine is already evident in his earliest documented epistle, his *Letter on the Faith*, it is a subject on which he markedly elaborates in later writings such as his so-called *Great Letter*. These two letters offer test cases to trace the evolution of Evagrius's views on the subject.[7]

Probably written on his journey from Constantinople to Jerusalem in the year 382 CE, Evagrius's *Letter on the Faith* shows how his doctrine of eschatological unity with God is motivated by readings of key passages from the Psalms and the Gospel of John.[8] In chapter 9, he cites Psalm 82:6 (LXX 81:6)—"I have said, You are gods" ('Εγὼ εἶπον θεοί ἐστε)—to affirm that human beings can be "called gods through grace" (κατὰ χάριν ὀναμάζονται).[9] He contextualizes this statement by way of a twofold contrast. On the one hand, Evagrius sets the proper designation of human beings as gods over against the demons' false claims to divinity, citing Psalm 96:5 (LXX 95:5) as a further prooftext: "The gods of the pagans are demons" (Οἱ θεοὶ τῶν ἐθνῶν δαιμόνια). On the other hand, he is careful to emphasize that while humans may be considered gods "by grace" (κατὰ χάριν), only the Godhead should be understood as divine "by essence" (κατ' οὐσίαν).[10] For Evagrius, human participation in the unity of God is made possible through the Eucharist. Here, he crucially exegetes John 6:57, connecting Christ's unity with the Father ("I live through the Father") to human unity with Christ as brought into effect by the Eucharist ("And whoever eats me will live through me").[11] Later in the letter, Jesus's prayer in John 17:21 underscores the Christological mediation of this unity in God: "Grant them that they may be one in Us, even as I and you are one, Father."[12] Evagrius interprets this verse to mean that God's own oneness serves to "unify all when he comes into each" (ἐν ἑκάστῳ γινόμενος ἑνοῖ τοὺς πάντας) and to do away with multiples and numbers "by the presence of the Unity" (τῇ τῆς μονάδος ἐπιδημίᾳ).[13] The divine unity that Evagrius invokes is also described in terms of the destiny of rational beings to "approach the unconcealed divinity" (αὐτῇ γυμνῇ προσελθεῖν τῇ θεότητι).[14] He characterizes it as a kind of "ultimate blessedness" (ἡ ἐσχάτη μακαριότης).[15]

In Evagrius's later writings, he elaborates upon his doctrine of divine Unity by way of a more fully fleshed out Trinitarian theory and an expanded repertoire of metaphors meant to envision the nature of that Unity. His so-called *Great Letter* is a case in point. Often referred to as the *Letter to Melania [the Elder]*, it may in fact have been written to Rufinus, as Evagrius addresses a male recipient (ܡܪܝ; "my lord") on three separate occasions.[16] In any case, it probably dates to the final decade and a half of Evagrius' life (ca. 385–399/400 CE), when he was living as a monk in Kellia.

In the *Great Letter*, one sees how Evagrius draws out the Trinitarian implications of his doctrine of Unity with the divine in more detail. Early on, when he writes about those who are "so receptive" (ܡܩܒܠܢ) and "so near" (ܩܪܝܒ) to God that they "become aware of their Creator's intention, wisdom and power," he notes that they "are ministered to by the Word and the Spirit . . . directly and not through the mediation of created things."[17] In that state, multiplicities and numbers pass away, and rational beings are "united (ܡܚܝܕ) to the nature of the Father . . . [and] absorbed (ܡܬܒܠܥ) into the hypostases of the Son and Spirit," such that those beings actually become "one nature in three persons" (ܚܕ ܟܝܢܐ ܒܬܠܬܐ ܩܢܘܡܝܢ) united with the Trinity.[18] Thus, this Unity is primarily described in terms of God's action of changing such rational beings "completely to his own nature" (ܡܫܚܠܦ ܠܟܝܢܗ ܕܝܠܗ), but Evagrius is still careful to emphasize that such beings will "be joined" (ܢܬܚܝܕ) and become one with the divine nature "by [God's] grace" (ܒܛܝܒܘܬܗ).[19] That process of unification is described in a plethora of other terms as well: it is said to emerge, for example, from a "concord" (ܫܠܡܘܬܐ) of wills and from a transformation of rational beings into the very "color" (ܓܘܢܐ) and "taste" (ܛܥܡܐ) of God.[20]

One key metaphor deployed by Evagrius in order to illustrate this Unity is that of rivers flowing into an endless sea. Thus, he describes the return of rational beings to God as follows:

> If this visible sea (which is one in nature, color and taste), when many rivers of different taste join it, not only is not changed to their qualities, but instead easily changes them completely to its own nature, color and taste—how much more so the intelligible, infinite and immutable sea, that is, God the Father? When like torrents to the sea, the minds return to him, he completely changes them to his own nature, color and taste: in his endless and inseparable unity, they will be one

and no longer many, since they will be united (ܚܝܕܘܗܝ‍) and joined (ܡܩܦܝܗܘܢ‍) to him.²¹

Evagrius returns to this metaphor of the ocean again toward the end his letter. He imaginatively places us, as his readers, at the seashore, where we gaze in amazement upon the "limitlessness" of the ocean, and he then prompts us to observe "how the rivers, torrents and streams that pour into it become limitless (ܠܐ ܡܣܬܝܟܝܢ) and undifferentiated (ܠܐ ܡܦܪܫܝܢ) in it." So too it is, he says, for "the end of the intellects," which unite themselves "in the one uniquely real knowledge . . . [and] become this one without end."²²

The Divine Unity in the *Kephalaia Gnostika*

Having examined two of his important letters, I now turn to Evagrius's masterwork, the *Kephalaia Gnostika*, as a comparative case study. Here, I am especially interested in the question of how Evagrius's doctrine of the divine Unity was mediated over the course of the text's complicated transmission history. Probably edited in its final form toward the end of his life while he was dwelling at the monastic settlement of Kellia (ca. 385–399/400 CE), the *Kephalaia Gnostika* became the third and final part of a monumental trilogy composed by Evagrius on the subjects of ascetic practice and contemplation.²³ While the original Greek survives only in fragments, the *Kephalaia Gnostika* is preserved in two Syriac recensions (S_1 and S_2, both translated from Greek), an Armenian adaptation, and an Arabic version derived from a Syriac *Vorlage*.²⁴

Evagrius's idea of our ultimate unification with God was "translated"—and thus reinterpreted—in and through the Syriac and Arabic versions of the text. The "unreformed" or "unexpurgated" Syriac recension (S_2)²⁵ preserves a version of the text copied before Evagrius's writings fell out of favor on account of the Origenist controversy and before they became the subject of intensive editorial censorship. By contrast, the "reformed" or "expurgated" Syriac recension (S_1) shows signs of editorial interventions designed to purge the text of certain perceived Origenist elements.²⁶ The surviving Arabic translation, attested in two manuscripts preserved at Dayr al-Suryān (the so-called Monastery of the Syrians) in Egypt is clearly based on S_1, but those copies of the text also occasionally witness variations in phrasing that provide us with glimpses of how Arabic editors and scribes further adapted Evagrius's theology to their own cultural and linguistic context.²⁷ How was Evagrius's doctrine of divine Unity reconditioned in the context of such editorial emendation and translation?

Divine Unity in the Unexpurgated Syriac Version of the Kephalaia Gnostika

My reading of how Evagrius's doctrine of Divine Unity comes to expression in the unexpurgated Syriac version of his *Kephalaia Gnostika* will focus on two main plot points in his larger cosmic narrative of salvation, a narrative that draws significantly on Origen's theology of creation/fall and ultimate return/restoration (ἀποκατάστασις).²⁸

The first plot point is the fall of rational beings away from the primordial Unity, which was occasioned by "movement" or "motion" (ܡܬܬܙܝܥ or ܡܬܬܙܝܥܢܘܬܐ).²⁹ The implication here is that the original Unity was characterized by stillness. According to Evagrius, this movement away from the divine was caused by "negligence" (ܡܗܡܝܢܘܬܐ) and a conspicuous "carelessness" or "lack of vigilance" (ܠܐ ܙܗܝܪܘܬܐ), whereby the intellect "turn[ed] its face away" (ܐܗܦܟ ܐܦܘܗܝ) from God.³⁰ The result was pluriformity: the constitution of "different worlds/eons" (ܥܠܡܐ ܡܫܚܠܦܐ), and the creation of a hierarchy of light, heavy, and heavier bodies.³¹

The second plot point is the return or restoration of rational beings to the Divine Unity through ascetic contemplation and knowledge. This happens by means of a progression from natural knowledge (which is likened to the body and associated with the contemplation of beings) to spiritual knowledge (which is likened to the soul and associated with an intimate acquaintance with God).³² When retrained through the discipline of ascetic contemplation, the intellect becomes susceptible to the Holy Trinity and shares in the ungraspable knowledge of that Divine Unity.³³ Among all beings, Christ alone possesses this knowledge of and unity with God (the Father) essentially and without interruption. He is, accordingly, the guide who leads rational beings through the eons to reunification with God.³⁴

Evagrius expends much ink in trying to describe the nature of that ultimate experience of Divine Unity. It is characterized by the removal of numbers/eons and by the vanishing of bodies.³⁵ It is marked by "an indescribable peace" (ܫܝܢܐ ܠܐ ܡܬܡܠܠܢܐ) and by the intellect's pervading of thesoul when it is mingled with the light of the Holy Trinity.³⁶ It is depicted as the creation of a "living intellect" (ܗܘܢܐ ܚܝܐ), as a form of coinheritance and mutual contemplation with Christ, as an "intelligible anointing"

(ܡܫܝܚܘܬܐ ܡܫܡܠܝܬܐ) modeled after Christ as the "Anointed One" (ܡܫܝܚܐ), and as a type of "vision" (ܚܙܘܐ) in which we gaze upon "pure souls" (ܢܦܫ̈ܬܐ ܕܟܝ̈ܬܐ) and upon "the luminous beams of the Holy Trinity" (ܙܠܝ̈ܩܐ ܡܪܘܡ ܢܘܗܪ̈ܢܐ ܣܝܡ ܕܬܠܝܬܝܘܬܐ ܩܕܝܫܬܐ).[37]

In this complete state of Divine Unity, Evagrius affirms that no one will be leaders or subject to leadership, but rather "all of them will be gods" (ܟܠܗܘܢ ܐܠܗܐ ܢܗܘܘܢ), probably an allusion once again to Psalm 82:6 (LXX 81:6).[38] Ultimately, this process of deification culminates in unity with God and a corresponding assimilation of divine attributes: by receiving "essential knowledge" (ܝܕܥܬܐ ܐܘܣܝܬܐ), the rational intellect comes to be "called God" (ܐܠܗܐ ܢܬܩܪܐ), a designation given on account of the fact that through such knowledge it is equipped with the prerogative of creation, as well as the attributes of impassibility, purity, and perfect oneness.[39]

Divine Unity in the Expurgated Versions of the Kephalaia Gnostika

In the expurgated Syriac and Arabic versions of the *Kephalaia Gnostika*, the basic outlines of these two plot points remain present, but there are some subtle (and not so subtle) changes that reframe Evagrius's conception of divine participation in important ways.

First, the narrative of a cosmic fall before creation is partially obscured. In *KG* 3.68 the editor of the unexpurgated Syriac version altogether avoids discussion of "the first rest of God" (ܢܝܚܐ ܩܕܡܝܬܐ ܕܐܠܗܐ)—i.e., the state of unity before creation—which was said to be characterized by an absence of evil, and instead focuses on God's teaching or instruction ("his primary exhortation"; ܡܪܬܝܢܘܬܗ ܩܕܡܝܬܐ) related to the elimination of evil at the consummation of all things.[40] In *KG* 1.65, the same editor, in describing the fall away from God, omits all mention of the constitution of multiple worlds or eons.[41]

Second, the process whereby human beings are reconciled to God is described with more of an emphasis on divine agency. While the expurgated Syriac version and the Arabic translation acknowledge that the fallen soul must reacquire the perfect image of the Holy Trinity through "great work" (Syr. ܥܡܠܐ ܣܓܝܐܐ) or "many works" (Ar. أعمال كثيرة),[42] the editors/translators of these texts notably place a greater focus on God's grace in facilitating this redemptive process. In *KG* 2.11, the editor of the expurgated Syriac text inserts the phrase, "the action of the grace of Our Lord" (ܡܥܒܕܢܘܬܐ ܕܛܝܒܘܬܗ ܕܡܪܢ) to underscore the role of divine agency in the intellect's receptivity to contemplation, and this is accentuated in the Arabic translation where the emphasis on "the grace of our Lord" (نعمة ربنا) is foregrounded syntactically.[43] Elsewhere the agent of that grace, called "the Wisdom of the Holy Unity" (ܚܟܡܬܐ ܕܝܚܝܕܝܘܬܐ ܩܕܝܫܬܐ), is identified as Christ, who is the doctor and guide of rational souls.[44]

The cumulative effect of these editorial moves is that the ultimate experience of the Divine Unity is crucially redefined and, in the process, markedly deemphasized. There are two changes that are particularly worthy of note, one pertaining to the status of bodies at the end of all things, and the other to a downplaying of the language of Divine Unity itself.

Regarding bodies, the expurgated Syriac version presents a different interpretation of their status at the consummation of all things. At *KG* 1.65, the revised Syriac text omits all mention of "bare intellects" and their "continual satiation" in unity with God.[45] Instead, at *KG* 2.5, there is an emphasis on the eschatological existence of "spiritual bodies" (ܦܓܪ̈ܐ ܕܪܘܚ) and "their true life" (ܚܝܝܗܘܢ ܕܝܠ ܫܪܝܪܐ).[46] The last trumpet of judgment in *KG* 3.66 is accordingly described as the "renovator" (ܡܚܕܬܢܝܬܐ) of all bodies rather than the bellwether that announces their disappearance.[47] Two verses later, at *KG* 3.68, the editor omits any mention of the "vanishing of bodies" (ܐܘܒܕܢܐ ܕܦܓܪ̈ܐ), a phrase invoked twice in the unexpurgated version: instead he characterizes God's judgment simply as "the destroyer of the totality of all evil" (ܡܚܒܠܢܐ ܕܗܘܐ ܕܟܠܗ ܒܒܝܫܘܬܐ).[48]

Regarding the language of Divine Unity, there is a concerted (albeit not completely systematic) attempt to replace it with other alternatives more familiar within the framework of Nicene Trinitarian orthodoxy. In the expurgated Syriac, the editor simply replaces the word "Unity" (Syr. ܝܚܝܕܝܘܬܐ) with "Holy Trinity" (ܬܠܝܬܝܘܬܐ ܩܕܝܫܬܐ) on two occasions.[49] Elsewhere knowledge of the "Holy Unity" (ܝܚܝܕܝܘܬܐ ܩܕܝܫܬܐ) becomes simply "holy knowledge" (ܝܕܥܬܐ ܩܕܝܫܬܐ).[50] This reticence also has implications for the way that human participation in the divine is defined. In the unexpurgated version at *KG* 5.84, the human intellect, viewed from the perspective of the present, is characterized as "God's temple" (ܗܝܟܠܐ ܕܐܠܗܐ) and "the seer of the Holy Unity" (ܚܙܝܐ ܕܝܚܝܕܝܘܬܐ ܩܕܝܫܬܐ), but in the expurgated version the intellect will only be fulfilled or completed as God's temple at some future point when it is judged to be "worthy of becoming a dwelling place" (ܕܫܘܐ ܠܡܗܘܐ ܒܝܬ ܡܥܡܪܐ) and when it is "worthy of contemplation of the Holy Trinity" (ܕܫܘܐ ܠܬܐܘܪܝܐ ܕܬܠܝܬܝܘܬܐ ܩܕܝܫܬܐ).[51] Even more notably, at *KG* 4.89, the editor of the expurgated

Syriac version rephrases the text to have Christ lead the rational nature not toward "union in the Holy Unity" (ܚܝܕܘܬܐ ܕܝܚܝܕܝܘܬܐ ܩܕܝܫܬܐ) but rather toward "the commerce of his Holy Trinity" (ܠܡܘܠܟܝܐ ܕܬܠܝܬܝܘܬܗ ܩܕܝܫܬܐ).[52] In the Arabic version, the word used to convey the sense of "commerce" is خلطة, which can also be translated as "company" or "close partnership."[53] Such a word choice suggests a certain reluctance on the part of the Arabic translator/editor to affirm a thoroughgoing state of Unity, one that would threaten to blur the boundaries between humanity and divinity.

Admittedly, both the expurgated Syriac version and Arabic translation continue to affirm the insight drawn from Psalm 82:6 (LXX 81:6) that "all of them will be gods" (Syr. ܟܠܗܘܢ ܐܠܗܐ ܢܗܘܘܢ; Ar. كلهم آلهة يكونون).[54] Perhaps contrary to expectation, there is also at least one sentence (*KG* 5.81) where the expurgated Syriac version and the parallel passage in one of the two Arabic manuscripts actually place more emphasis than does the unexpurgated text on "the contemplation of the Unity" (Syr. ܬܐܘܪܝܐ ܕܝܚܝܕܝܘܬܐ), or, more expansively, "the spiritual contemplation that belongs to the Holy Unity" (التآورية الروحانية التي للوحدانية المقدسة). In this context, both highlight the fact that such contemplation is the means by which the intellect "has attained fulfillment" (Syr. ܐܫܬܡܠܝ) or "has become perfected" (Ar. اتكمل) and thereby comes to be "called God" (Syr. ܐܠܗܐ ܡܬܩܪܐ; Ar. يدعا إلاه).[55] While the corresponding sentence in the unexpurgated Syriac version likewise discusses how the intellect will be "called God" (Syr. ܐܠܗܐ ܢܬܩܪܐ), it conspicuously lacks any mention of the "Holy Unity" and the "fulfillment" or "perfection" of the intellect.[56]

Nonetheless, even in a somewhat exceptional case like *KG* 5.81 where the expurgated Syriac version and the Arabic translation present a more clearly divinizing perspective, crucial caveats and conditions apply. First, the intellect's perfection is said to be "in the image of its Creator" (Syr. ܒܕܡܘܬܐ ܕܒܪܘܝܗ; Ar. بصورة خالقه).[57] While this statement certainly marks a form of human participation in the divine, it also draws a rather firm distinction between God as Creator and the intellect as God's creation. Second, in both texts, the intellect's divine designation is accompanied by a clause emphasizing that this status can be attributed only "by means of grace" (Syr. ܒܛܝܒܘܬܐ; Ar. بالنعمة), and not through some essential or hypostatic identification with God.[58] As a result, the overall result of the editorial and translational changes in the expurgated Syriac and Arabic versions ends up being a vision of salvation that looks less like the complete union of theosis or the eschatological Divine Unity and more like an intimate exchange in which human and divine come to be in close relation, with each retaining its own distinctiveness.

* * *

In conclusion, the Syriac and Arabic reception of the *Kephalaia Gnostika* reveals how, via processes of scribal transmission and translation, more robust and thoroughgoing conceptions of deification subtly began to be written out of the Evagrian textual record. With respect to the expurgated Syriac version (S_1), most scholars think such editorial redactions are best explained in relation to reemerging concerns about the theology of Origen in the early sixth century—concerns that gave rise to the so-called Second Origenist Controversy under the emperor Justinian I, culminating in the Second Council of Constantinople in 553 CE.[59]

But when it comes to the Arabic translators, as well as to later Syriac- and Arabic-speaking readers, another factor may also have determinably framed the importance such Christians placed on deemphasizing the language of Divine Unity and deification: namely, their participation in an increasingly Islamicate society where the oneness of God and the definitive boundary line between the human and the divine became the essential qualification for publicly palatable theology and good citizenship. Thus, in the Arabic transmission of the text, one sometimes finds hints of an implicit two-pronged apologetic program at work. On the one hand, the Arabic translators had to navigate the doctrinal strictures of Trinitarian Nicene orthodoxy, with its complicated and contested inheritance of theosis as one particular vision of human salvation. On the other hand, they also sought at points to bring Evagrius's ascetic theology into more amenable conversation with Islamic theological proclivities regarding the oneness of God, and they did so by following the expurgated Syriac version of the *Kephalaia Gnostika* in domesticating some of the work's more controversial elements. For these reasons, the two Arabic copies of the *Kephalaia Gnostika*—recently discovered in the manuscript library at Dayr al-Suryān and now edited for publication for the first time[60]—promise to facilitate further fruitful research into how Evagrius's ideas about ascetic contemplation, deification, and the Divine Unity were translated—and, in the process, reconditioned—for readers equipped with new linguistic and cultural sensibilities.

Notes

1. Michael J. Christensen and Jeffrey A. Wittung, eds., *Partakers of the Divine Nature: The History and Development of Deification in the Christian Traditions* (Madison, NJ: Fairleigh Dickinson University Press, 2007).

2. Augustine M. C. Casiday, "Deification in Origen, Evagrius and Cassian," in *Origeniana Octava: Origen and the Alexandrian Tradition. Papers of the 8th International Origen Congress, Pisa, 27–31 August 2001*, ed. L. Perrone, with P. Bernardino and D. Marchini (Leuven: Peeters, 2003), 2:995–1001, at 996–98.

3. Casiday, "Deification," 995.

4. Norman Russell, *The Doctrine of Deification in the Greek Patristic Tradition* (New York: Oxford University Press, 2004), at 238–41.

5. Ibid., 241.

6. Ilaria L. E. Ramelli, trans., *Evagrius's* Kephalaia Gnostika: *A New Translation of the Unreformed Text from the Syriac*, Society of Biblical Literature, Writings from the Greco-Roman World 38 (Atlanta: SBL Press, 2015).

7. *Letter on the Faith*: Greek text edited by Jean Gribomont, "[Ps.-]Basil, 'Epistula 8,'" in *Basilio di Cesarea: Le Lettere*, ed. M. Forlin-Patrucco (Turin: Società Editrice Internazionale, 1983), 1:84–112; German translation by Gabriel Bunge, *Evagrios Pontikos: Briefe aus der Wüste* (Trier: Paulinus, 1986), 284–302; English translation by A. M. Casiday, *Evagrius Ponticus* (New York: Routledge, 2006), 45–58. *Great Letter*: Syriac text (with a hypothetical reconstruction of the original Greek) edited by W. Frankenberg, *Euagrius Ponticus* Abhandlungen der königlichen Gesellschaft der Wissenschaften zu Göttingen, Philologisch-Historische Klasse, Neue Folge, XIII.2 (Berlin: Weidmann, 1912), 610–19 [=sect. 1–32]; see also the edition by Gösta Vitestam, *Seconde partie du traité qui passe sous le nom de 'La grande letter d'Evagre le Pontique à Mélanie l'Ancienne', publiée et traduite d'après le manuscript du British Museum Add. 17192*, Scripta minora Regiae Societatis Humaniorum Litterarum Lundensis 3 (Lund: CWK Gleerup, 1963–1964), 1–29; German translation by Bunge, *Evagrios Pontikos*, 303–28 [=sect. 17, 24, 25, and 33–68]; English translation by Casiday, *Evagrius Ponticus*, 63–77.

8. The traditional view that the *Letter on the Faith* was written by Evagrius while in the city of Constantinople, *circa* 379–380 CE, has been critiqued and corrected by Joel Kalvesmaki, "The *Epistula Fidei* of Evagrius of Pontus: An Answer to Constantinople," *Journal of Early Christian Studies* 20, no. 1 (2012): 113–39. Despite this redating, the letter still constitutes Evagrius's earliest surviving correspondence: see also Robin Darling Young, "The Role of Letters in the Works of Evagrius," in *Evagrius and His Legacy*, ed. J. Kalvesmaki and R. Darling Young (Notre Dame, IN: University of Notre Dame Press, 2016), 154–74, at 157.

9. Evagrius, *Letter on the Faith* 9: ed. J. Gribomont, "[Ps.-]Basil, *Ep.* 8," 90 [=sect. 3]; trans. Casiday, *Evagrius Ponticus*, 48. The section numbering for *On*

the Faith follows the system of Casiday's English translation, which adopted that of Bunge's earlier German translation (*Evagrios Pontikos*). The (less precise) numbering system for Gribomont's original edition is indicated in square brackets after the page number reference.

10. Ibid.

11. Evagrius, *Letter on the Faith* 14: ed. J. Gribomont, "[Ps.-]Basil, *Ep.* 8," 94 [= sect. 4]; trans. Casiday, *Evagrius Ponticus*, 50.

12. Evagrius, *Letter on the Faith* 25: ed. J. Gribomont, "[Ps.-]Basil, *Ep.* 8," 102 [= sect. 7]; trans. Casiday, *Evagrius Ponticus*, 53.

13. Ibid.

14. Evagrius, *Letter on the Faith* 23; ed. J. Gribomont, "[Ps.-]Basil, *Ep.* 8," 100 [= sect. 7]; trans. Casiday, *Evagrius Ponticus*, 53.

15. Evagrius, *Letter on the Faith* 21–23, 37: ed. J. Gribomont, "[Ps.-]Basil, *Ep.* 8," 98–100, 110 [= sect. 7 and 12]; trans. Casiday, *Evagrius Ponticus*, 52, 57.

16. Bunge, *Evagrios Pontikos*, 194; Casiday, *Evagrius Ponticus*, 63–64; Casiday, *Reconstructing the Theology of Evagrius* (Cambridge: Cambridge University Press, 2013), 64; see also Vitestam, *Second partie du traité*, 4–5. Some, however, have continued to argue for Melania as the recipient, attributing the masculine grammatical references either to a scribal error or to the fact that Melania's name was sometimes written in the neuter case as a diminutive, which (according to them) may have been misunderstood by Syriac readers: see, e.g., Michel Parmentier, "Evagrius of Pontus' Letter to Melania," *Bijdr* 46 (1985), 2–38, esp. 5–6; repr. in *Forms of Devotion, Conversion, Worship, Spirituality, and Asceticism*, ed. E. Ferguson (New York: Garland, 1999), 272–309; and Ramelli, *Evagrius's Kephalaia Gnostika*, xxix–xxx.

17. Evagrius, *Great Letter* 8: ed. Frankenberg, *Euagrius Ponticus*, 612–14 (Syriac text on even pages); trans. Casiday, *Evagrius Ponticus*, 66. As in the case of Evagrius's *Letter on the Faith*, the section numbering for his *Great Letter* follows the system of Casiday's English translation, which adopted that of Bunge's earlier German translation (*Evagrios Pontikos*).

18. Evagrius, *Great Letter* 22–23, 27: ed. Frankenberg, *Euagrius Ponticus*, 616, 618; trans. Casiday, *Evagrius Ponticus*, 68, 69.

19. Evagrius, *Great Letter* 27 and 63: ed. Frankenberg, *Euagrius Ponticus*, 618 [= sect. 27]; ed. Vitestam, *Second partie*, 27 [= sect. 63]; trans. Casiday, *Evagrius Ponticus*, 69 and 76. The verb ܚܠܛ can mean not only "to be joined to," but also "to be mixed or intermingle with," "to pour out or flow into," or "to [have a] share in." Michael Sokoloff, *A Syriac Lexicon: A Translation from the Latin, Correction, Expansion, and Update of C. Brockelmann's* Lexicon Syriacum (Winona Lake, IN: Eisenbrauns, 2009), 454).

20. Evagrius, *Great Letter* 23, 27–30: Frankenberg, *Euagrius Ponticus*, 616, 618; trans. Casiday, *Evagrius Ponticus*, 68, 69–70.

21. Evagrius, *Great Letter* 27–30, quote at 27: ed. Frankenberg, *Euagrius Ponticus*, 618; trans. Casiday, *Evagrius Ponticus*, 69–70, quote at 69 (slightly modified to conform to American English spelling).

22. Evagrius, *Great Letter* 66: ed. Vitestam, *Second partie*, 27–28; trans. Casiday, *Evagrius Ponticus*, 77.

23. His *Praktikos* and *Gnostikos* comprise parts one and two of this ascetic trilogy. For the Greek text of the *Praktikos*: see Claire and Antoine Guillaumont, eds., *Traité pratique, ou, Le moine*, SC 170–71 (Paris: Cerf, 1971); for a collation of the Greek and Syriac texts, with an English translation, see Joel Kalvesmaki, ed., "Guide to Evagrius Ponticus," http://evagriusponticus.net/cpg2430.html. For the Greek text of the *Gnostikos*, see Antoine Guillaumont and Claire Guillaumont, eds., *Le gnostique, ou, À celui qui est devenu digne de la science*, SC 356 (Paris: Cerf, 1989); for a collation of different Greek and Syriac versions, with an English translation, see Kalvesmaki, "Guide," http://evagriusponticus.net/cpg2431.html.

24. For relevant bibliography on the Syriac and Arabic versions, see my discussion to follow. For editions of the Greek fragments, see Irenée Hausherr, "Nouveaux fragments grecs d'Évagre le Pontique," *Orientalia Christiana Periodica* 5 (1939): 229–33; J. Muyldermans, *À travers la tradition manuscrite d'Évagre le Pontique: Essai sur les manuscrits grecs conservés à la Bibliothèque nationale de Paris*, Bibliothèque du Muséon 3 (Louvain: Bureaux du Muséon, 1932), 74, 85, 89, 93; J. Muyldermans, *Evagriana. Extrait de la revue Le Muséon 44, augmenté de: Nouveaux fragments grecs inédits* (Paris: Paul Geuthner, 1931), 52–59; and Paul Géhin, "Evagriana d'un manuscrit basilien (Vaticanus Gr. 2028; olim Basilianus 67)," *Le Muséon* 109 (1996), 59–65. For the Armenian adaptation, see Barsegh Sargisean, *Varkʻ ew matenagrutʻiwnkʻ: Tʻargmanealkʻ i hunē I hay barbaṛ I E. daru* (The Life and Works of the Holy Father Evagrius Ponticus in an Armenian Version of the Fifth Century, with Introduction and Notes) (Venice: S. Ghazar, 1907).

25. Antoine Guillaumont, *Les six centuries des 'Kephalaia Gnostica' d'Évagre le Pontique*, Patrologia Orientalis 28.1 (Paris: Firmin-Didot, 1958), 17–257 (odd pages).

26. Guillaumont, *Les six centuries*, 16–256 (even pages). Guillaumont's argument for the precedence of S_2 over S_1 has been accepted by the vast majority of scholars (Ramelli, *Evagrius's* Kephalaia Gnostika, xx–xxiv), but for a dissenting voice, see Casiday, *Reconstructing the Theology of Evagrius Ponticus*, esp. 64–71.

27. Dayr al-Suryān: DS Arabic Ascetic 24 (= MS 177), ff. 57b–115b; and DS Arabic Ascetic 31 (= MS 184), ff. 150b–183b. For a discussion, see Stephen J. Davis, "Evagrius Ponticus at the Monastery of the Syrians: Newly Documented Evidence for an Arabic Reception History," in *Heirs of the Apostles: Studies on Arabic Christianity in Honor of Sidney H. Griffith*, ed. D. Bertaina, S. T. Keating,

M. N. Swanson, and A. Treiger (Leiden: Brill, 2019), 349–94. These two manuscripts are now catalogued in Stephen J. Davis and Mark N. Swanson, *Catalogue of Coptic and Arabic Manuscripts in Dayr al-Suryān. Volume 4: Arabic Ascetic Discourses* (CSCO 697, Subsidia 145; Leuven: Peeters, 2022).

28. Origen of Alexandria discusses his understanding of ἀποκατάστασις in succinct and summary terms in his *Commentary on the Gospel of John* 1.16.91–92, ed. C. Blanc, 2nd ed., SC 120 bis (Paris: Cerf, 1996), 104; trans. R. E. Heine, FC 80 (Washington, DC: Catholic University of America Press, 1989), 52: "For since a 'good way is very great, we must understand that the practical . . . relates to the initial matters, and the contemplative to those that follow. I think its stopping point and goal is in the so-called restoration (ἀποκατάστασις) because no one is left as an enemy then. . . . For at that time those who have come to God because of the Word which is with him will have the contemplation of God as their only activity, that, having been accurately formed in the knowledge of the Father, they may all thus become a son, since now the Son alone has known the Father." Recent scholarly treatments on Origen's theory of ἀποκατάστασις and its reception history include the following two volumes: G. MacDonald, *"All Shall Be Well": Explorations in Universal Salvation and Christian Theology from Origen to Moltmann* (Cambridge: James Clarke & Co., 2011), esp. the article by Tom Greggs, *"Apokatastasis*: Particularist Universalism in Origen (c. 185–c. 254)," 29–46; and Ilaria L. E. Ramelli, *The Christian Doctrine of* Apokatastasis: *A Critical Assessment from the New Testament to Eriugena*, Supplements to Vigiliae Christianae 120 (Leiden: Brill, 2013), esp. 137–215 (on Origen), and 461–512 (on Evagrius).

29. Evagrius Ponticus, *KG* 1.49; 3.22 (S_2, ed. Guillaumont, *Les six centuries*, 41, 107; trans. Ramelli, 51, 153).

30. Evagrius Ponticus, *KG* 1.49; 3.28 (S_2, ed. Guillaumont, *Les six centuries*, 41, 109; trans. Ramelli, 51, 156).

31. Evagrius Ponticus, *KG* 1.65; 2.68 (S_2, ed. Guillaumont, *Les six centuries*, 47/49, 87; trans. Ramelli, 51, 153).

32. Evagrius Ponticus, *KG* 2.5 (S_2, ed. Guillaumont, *Les six centuries*, 63; trans. Ramelli, 90). Elsewhere, Evagrius writes that "the end of natural knowledge is the holy Unity" (*KG* 1.71: S_2, ed. Guillaumont, 51; trans. Ramelli, 68), but it would appear that this end can only be made possible via the intellect's spiritual (i.e., "substantial/essential") knowledge (*KG* 2.11: S_2, ed. Guillaumont, 63; trans. Ramelli, 94–95).

33. Evagrius Ponticus, *KG* 2.11, 16; 3.11, 13, 32 (S_2, ed. Guillaumont, *Les six centuries*, 65, 67, 103, 111; trans. Ramelli, 94–95, 97, 145, 146, 159).

34. Evagrius Ponticus, *KG* 3.1–3; 4.89 (S_2, ed. Guillaumont, *Les six centuries*, 99, 175; trans. Ramelli, 141–142, 243).

35. Evagrius Ponticus, *KG* 1.7; 3.66, 68 (S_2, ed. Guillaumont, *Les six centuries*, 19, 125; trans. Ramelli, 8–9, 179, 180).

36. Evagrius Ponticus, *KG* 1.65; 2.29 (S_2, ed. Guillaumont, *Les six centuries*, 47, 73; trans. Ramelli, 64, 108).

37. Evagrius Ponticus, *KG* 3.71–72; 4.4, 8, 18, 21, 90; 5.3 (S_2, ed. Guillaumont, *Les six centuries*, 127, 137, 139, 143, 145, 175, 177; trans. Ramelli, 183–84, 198, 201, 205, 207, 244, 250).

38. Evagrius Ponticus, *KG* 4.51 (S_2, ed. Guillaumont, *Les six centuries*, 159; trans. Ramelli, 227).

39. Evagrius Ponticus *KG* 5.81 (S_2, ed. Guillaumont, *Les six centuries*, 211; trans. Ramelli, 310); see also *KG* 5.82, 84, 85 (ed. Guillaumont, *Les six centuries*, 211, 213; trans. Ramelli, 310–312).

40. Evagrius Ponticus, *KG* 3.68 (S_1, ed. Guillaumont, *Les six centuries*, 124).

41. Evagrius Ponticus, *KG* 1.65 (S_1, ed. Guillaumont, *Les six centuries*, 46/48).

42. Evagrius Ponticus, *KG* 3.28 (S_1, ed. Guillaumont, *Les six centuries*, 108; DS Arabic Ascetic 24 [= MS 177], f. 65b; DS Arabic Ascetic 31 [= MS 184], f. 163 [labeled in the manuscript as *KG* 3.29]).

43. Evagrius Ponticus, *KG* 2.11; (S_1, ed. Guillaumont, *Les six centuries*, 64; DS Arabic Ascetic 24 [= MS 177], f. 67a; DS Arabic Ascetic 31 [= MS 184], f. 157b).

44. Evagrius Ponticus, *KG* 3.13; 4.18, 89 (S_1, ed. Guillaumont, *Les six centuries*, 102, 142, 174).

45. Evagrius Ponticus, *KG* 1.65 (S_1, ed. Guillaumont, *Les six centuries*, 46).

46. Evagrius Ponticus, *KG* 2.5 (S_1, ed. Guillaumont, *Les six centuries*, 62).

47. Evagrius Ponticus, *KG* 3.66 (S_1, ed. Guillaumont, *Les six centuries*, 124).

48. Evagrius Ponticus, *KG* 3.68 (S_1, ed. Guillaumont, *Les six centuries*, 124).

49. Evagrius Ponticus, *KG* 1.65; 3.32 (S_1, ed. Guillaumont, *Les six centuries*, 46, 110). See also *KG* 2.11(S_1, ed. Guillaumont, 64), where the language of "Unity" is replaced with the more generic theological phrase, "the place of [God's] indwelling."

50. Evagrius Ponticus, *KG* 3.72 (S_1, ed. Guillaumont, *Les six centuries*, 126).

51. Evagrius Ponticus, *KG* 5.84 (S_1, ed. Guillaumont, *Les six centuries*, 212).

52. Evagrius Ponticus *KG* 4.89 (S_1, ed. Guillaumont, *Les six centuries*, 174).

53. Evagrius Ponticus *KG* 4.89 (DS Arabic Ascetic 24 [= MS 177], f. 88b; DS Arabic Ascetic 31 [= MS 184], f. 171a [labeled in the manuscript as *KG* 4.92]).

54. Evagrius Ponticus, *KG* 4.51 (S_1, ed. Guillaumont, *Les six centuries*, 158; DS Arabic Ascetic 24 [= MS 177], f. 85a; DS Arabic Ascetic 31 [= MS 184], f. 169a [labeled in the manuscript as *KG* 4.55]).

55. Evagrius Ponticus, *KG* 5.81 (S_1, ed. Guillaumont, *Les six centuries*, 210; DS Arabic Ascetic 31 [= MS 184], f. 175b [labeled in the manuscript as *KG* 5.80]).

56. Evagrius Ponticus, *KG* 5.81 (S_2, ed. Guillaumont, *Les six centuries*, 211.

57. Evagrius Ponticus, *KG* 5.81 (S_1, ed. Guillaumont, *Les six centuries*, 210; DS Arabic Ascetic 31 [= MS 184], f. 175b [labeled in the manuscript as *KG* 5.80]).

58. Evagrius Ponticus, *KG* 5.81 (S_1, ed. Guillaumont, *Les six centuries*, 210; DS Arabic Ascetic 31 [= MS 184], f. 175b [labeled in the manuscript as *KG* 5.80]).

59. For a discussion of this sixth-century historical context as it pertains to Evagrius and the production of the expurgated version of his *Kephalaia Gnostika*, see Luke Dysinger, *Psalmody and Prayer in the Writings of Evagrius Ponticus*, Oxford Theological Monographs (Oxford: Oxford University Press, 2005), 199–211 (appendix 1). On the heightened opposition to Evagrius's thought during the Second Origenist Controversy, see also A. Guillaumont, "Évagre et les anathématismes antiorigénistes de 553," *Studia Patristica* 3, no. 1 (1961): 219–26; A. Guillaumont, *Les 'Kephalaia gnostica'*, 143–59; F. Refoulé, "La christologie d'Évagre et l'origénisme," *Orientalia Christiana Periodica* 27 (1961): 221–66; Daniël Hombergen, *The Second Origenist Controversy: A New Perspective on Cyril of Scythopolis' Monastic Biographies as Historical Sources for Sixth-Century Origenism*, Studia Anselmiana 132 (Rome: Pontificio Ateneo S. Anselmo, 2001), 21–23, 168n164, 270.

60. Stephen J. Davis, *The Gnostic Chapters: A Critical Edition and Translation of Evagrius Ponticus'* Kephalaia Gnostika *in Arabic* (Leiden: Brill, 2023).

The Embodied Logos

Reason, Knowledge, and Relation

Rowan Williams

The words "rationality," "embodiment," and "deification" seem about the most discordant mix one could imagine; each pulls away from the others, and it seems counterintuitive if we set out to bring them into some sort of sustained conversation, let alone harmony. But the purpose of this essay is to do something like this. If we quarry the full sense of each term within a particular kind of theological framework, in which "logos" itself, as understood in the Byzantine tradition, appears as relational, manifest in embodiment, and grounded in the self-imparting and self-reflecting life of divine love, we may be able to discover a more integral picture of human knowing as well as divine action. It hardly needs saying that the hegemony of certain models of rationality, indifferent to embodied relation, is a factor in the global crisis of human survival we presently face; it is surely a moment for exploring what the narrative and discourse of God's incarnate "reasoning" might have to say that is salutary in this situation.

The fourth chapter of Evagrius's *Gnostikos* summarizes the difference between *gnosis* from outside and knowledge that comes from God.[1] The former allows us to engage with the reality of material things and represent them to ourselves by way of *logoi*; the latter, by the grace of God, brings realities into direct contact with our intellective capacity so that this capacity receives the *logoi* themselves. Thus, to quote the text, "What stands in opposition to the former is error; what stands in opposition to the latter is anger and the spirit of aggression" (*thumos*). The chapter that follows develops this a little further, comparing the indulgence of aggressive passion with stabbing yourself in the eye, an image that recurs in other writings by Evagrius. The aggressive instinct—in other words, the passion that prompts us to push away what menaces us—is what prevents the *logos* of any object encountered from entering into the intelligent spirit, *nous*; so that the problem is not that we have *made a mistake* about the world but that in one crucial sense we have *mistaken what the world itself is*. We have acted or reacted as though the world were a separate agent or set of agencies, with an interest or agenda standing in rivalry to our own individual interest; and so, by misconstruing the very nature of our environment—as the metaphor graphically puts it—we pierce our eyes with an iron stylus, surely not an accidental image in its evocation of the world of learned writing.

This distinction between error and the effect of *thumos* is a useful point to begin from in thinking about what the anthropology of the Greek Christian tradition has to say about mind, sense, and embodiment. Evagrius is, it seems, offering a way of distinguishing between a direct and an indirect encounter with *logos*. Knowledge "from outside" is the process of making sense of the objects around us; whereas the *gnosis* given by God is a "receiving" of the *logoi*, not a process in which the rational structures of things are deployed by the human knower in constructing a coherent representation of the world. In the knowledge that comes from God, the *logoi* as activated by God act upon us, not the other way around. And if we put this brief passage alongside a couple of others later in the treatise, we can see emerging a clear picture of how passion distorts the gnostic's calling. Chapter 42 asserts that the characteristic trial or temptation of the gnostic is the kind of false apprehension that presents what is existing as if it were nonexistent, or the nonexistent as real, or the real as existing otherwise than it actually does. The chapter immediately following ascribes such "false *gnosis*" to the presence of passion or of the origins of some enquiry in something other than the quest for the good—which amounts to much the same thing.[2] A little more elaborately, the treatise *peri diaphoron logismon*, On Thoughts, spells out in chapter 8 the differences between angelic, human, and diabolical *logismoi* in a way evidently connected with the model presupposed in the *Gnostikos*.[3] Angelic thought searches for the spiritual *logoi* within what is perceived; diabolical thought proposes to the perceiving self the *acquisition* of what is perceived; and human thought simply registers the *morphe psile*, the simple form, that is there to be perceived. As such, it is neither acquisitive nor contemplative. Where angelic knowledge grasps the symbolic significance of things and how all external phenomena have something to convey from God to the *nous*, and where diabolical knowledge seeks to use the things perceived for gratification, human *logismos* is primitively just the receiving of an intelligible form. Evagrius is primarily concerned with how this works as an exegetical tool, shaping the way we make sense of passages in scripture and saving us from literalism; but the distinction is clearly of wider pertinence. If we render *logismos* as "a process of reflecting," we can see Evagrius as in effect teasing apart two kinds of *non*-egocentric thinking and one kind of thinking that is directed to the self's ambitions (as spelled out in more detail in chapter 1 of *On Thoughts*,[4] where the basic passions are named as gluttony, avarice, and vainglory). True knowledge, so this implies, is the receptivity of human *logismos* instructed and enlarged by angelic.

It is not, then, that "passion" causes us to make mistakes—as if we were simply being recommended to keep a cool head in our deliberations and our analyses of the world and ourselves. Evagrius is stating more than a prudential commonplace. And the exercise of ordinary human *logismos* is already an activity that requires grace for it to avoid the lure of diabolical selfishness. If we are genuinely able to see "humanly," to allow the simple contact of the knowing subject and the "simple form," we may also be free to see "angelically"; but the fragility of our capacity to know truly is there from the start, so that the innate freedom to grow from human to angelic perception is in no way automatic. The defensive/aggressive spirit in us will always be present, pushing us toward that refusal of the simple *logoi* in themselves that prevents genuine *gnosis*. Or, as in *On Thoughts*, it may equally be the acquisitive spirit that distorts and diabolizes our relation with what we encounter: Evagrius is not creating a single consistent system in these works but offering diagnoses of the various sources of our failure to arrive at authentic knowledge. But what these diagnoses have in common is the conviction that passion creates a particular kind of *gap* between the knowing subject and the world that is known; so that the renewal of mind and spirit entails a closing of that gap. As Evagrius's language makes plain, this does not mean that the distinctive agency of the *nous* in any one of us is somehow canceled or swallowed up in something alien to it: what is given/acquired in the state of "graced" knowledge, angelic reflection, is a habit of perceiving the world that is irreducibly linked with ethical practice. The *praktike* which has already been learned by the would-be Gnostic remains fundamental, and the Gnostic has to be faithful in generosity, material and spiritual,[5] so that there remains a clear sense of a conscious subject adopting and maintaining policies of behavior—at this stage at least with a measure of deliberateness, even if in higher states such policies become second nature. The key capacity for the gnostic is the consistent refusal to treat the world as pure object, ontologically alien (and thus as either desirable for the ego or threatening to the ego). And this is, as chapter 4 of the *Gnostikos* says, a matter of the *nous receiving* the *logoi*.

To pick up the language of another tradition, this presupposes a "nondual" basis for epistemology. Raimon Panikkar, in a dense and suggestive discussion in his book on *Mysticism and Spirituality*,[6] considers this question in the light of the way our intellect constructs a "mythos," a comprehensive stance toward reality that does not lend itself to any translation into "logos"—using this latter term in a rather different sense from Evagrius's, as denoting some kind of systematic knowledge. Panikkar's "mythos" is a pervasive perspective acknowledging that we as knowing subjects are part of a net of related agencies making up the finite world, and as such it is close in meaning to Evagrian *gnosis*. "The participative knowledge we refer to is not the knowledge of one part of reality, but the consciousness of all reality from a concrete perspective. An a-dualistic (Panikkar prefers this term to "nondualistic") consciousness is needed that relates us at the same time as it keeps us at a distance. It is the consciousness of relation as such and not that of entities that relate to each other."[7] The phrase "from a concrete perspective" is important here as clarifying that a nondual approach is not equivalent to any view that denies the reality of finite substance in any sense. Each subject begins from a distinct location; and this entails a recognition and acceptance also of beginning form a *bodily* location; we do not have any other means of specifying what makes a perspective "concrete" or distinctive. And in this light, Evagrius's phrasing about *logos* and matter needs some careful parsing. The "from outside" knowledge he describes is a knowledge of material substances, organized into a coherent system by the application of the idea of *logoi* as potentially tools for making intelligible connections between phenomena and representing them accordingly. But this is not to be identified with the action of divine grace in granting a genuine participation in the *active* intelligible structures of the material things of the world: this level of relatedness is something that, while not abolishing the particularity of our base of orientation, denies us the illusion of existing in a self-contained "elsewhere" from what we are encountering, or of somehow being "ungenerated," self-starting beings with no intricate webs of dependence shaping what we are.[8]

In other words, it is not that the *gnosis* that comes by grace allows us access to a world of *logoi* somehow *independent* of the material, a "realm of ideas" existing "somewhere" else. To recover an awareness of a place in the order of things, a position within a connected web, is necessarily to acknowledge the body. Ironically, an epistemology that knows only the operation of "from outside" knowledge applied to a material universe is in danger of occluding the reality of the body in its specific location and embeddedness in a pattern of interdependence, nurturing the fantasy that knowing is essentially the action of a disembodied subject working on embodied data—the default position of a good deal of postmedieval Western thinking about knowledge, as if the object is always somewhere and the subject is nowhere. The Evagrian interest in both detached seeing, unclouded by aggression or acquisition (the human style of *logismos* understood independently of its distortion by passion), and the difference between error and passion points us back—perhaps unexpectedly—to the possibility of a new account of *sense*, understood as first and foremost the reality of bodily connection, resonance and responsiveness, the capacity to move and adjust and improvise within a world of stimuli reaching beyond what can be grasped at any given moment. In the striking phrase used by Orion Edgar in his study of the theological implications of Merleau-Ponty's philosophy, "*nature* lies on both sides of perception."[9] For the *gnosis* that is given by God, sense (material stimulus) and intellect at the deepest level (awareness of the interconnection of reality) are inseparably bound up together. The renewal of mind and the transformation of sense go hand in hand.

It is obvious that this condition of *gnosis* is something quite other than a simple capacity for acquiring information. Evagrius approaches it as a spiritual gift because it is not a capacity that can be defined in terms of its *function* alone: it is intrinsic to a habit and quality of life as a whole that is to do with growing into adequate relation with the rest of finite reality rather than gaining tools for technical mastery. This does not mean that "technical mastery" is by definition an evil or that the task of representing the world with some degree of success is to be deplored. Evidently, Evagrius believed that knowledge from outside, a competent practice of representation, with the practically useful consequences that this entails, was a given element in human life. What is more important is what disciplines are in place to check the "diabolization" of such practices when they serve nothing but the passions that Evagrius outlines at the beginning of *On Thoughts*. Passion, in this scheme of understanding, is essentially what seeks to de-realize the material world by reducing it to whatever functions we are determined it should perform for our benefit; it is not too difficult a step from "successful representation" to this reductive picture, though there is no *necessary* trajectory. But unless our practices of organized representation are seen in the context of a prior and larger question, the question of how we attune ourselves to the rest of the finite world's energies, we yield to a model that reduces both object and subject. It reduces the object by encouraging us to "see" only in terms of our wants, and the subject by ignoring the already given dependence of our material identity on the preexisting web of agency that forms and situates our specific reality. This is why "impassioned" knowledge is more than a mistake, why it must be understood as a misapprehension of the very nature of a "world." Knowledge that is substantially determined by aggression or acquisitiveness is dangerous to the extent that it encourages a perilously inadequate recognition of the limits within which we live our lives. The "diabolical" consciousness works on the tacit assumption that my will and my interest are primordial, undefined affairs, unrelated to my history and my body, "unworldly." Hannah Arendt famously reproached classical Christian—especially Augustinian—anthropology with creating a "worldless" ideal of love,[10] but the truth is almost diametrically opposite. It is the reduction of the world to an ensemble of passive objects to be desired or avoided by an individual appetite that most lethally dissolves the sense of a world. The critique of a desire directed toward "the world" in the Augustinian (or indeed Johannine) sense is a critique of a very specific model of reality. The "world" in this context is the environment understood simply as a reservoir of objects whose significance is in their utility in satisfying an indeterminate series of desirous reactions in us, producing an indeterminate series of particular gratifications. An engagement with the actual created world that is in some measure free from passion is one that recognizes both the dependence of the knowing subject and the "excess" in the object that makes it more than simply *my* object, oriented toward my desires. What sustains my awareness in this framework is the complex of connections I have not chosen and do not wholly see; and this is how we might render in somewhat different terms the Evagrian language of receiving the *logoi* of what we encounter rather than understanding them *only* as useful tools for assembling perceptions into a coherent representational system.

Full "gnostic" awareness, then, entails the knowing subject's sense of being located in a world exceeding any account of its life that is solely focused on the functional matching of objects to desires. The renewed mind is free to share in a network of embodied interaction, which it attends to, learns from, and takes time with; the mind is not driven by the need to use its environment to find answers to its questions or satisfaction of its wants. Hence the appropriateness of calling this sort of awareness "contemplative." Contemplation might be understood as the discipline of opening the mind to a "world" in the full sense we have been discussing—a complex within which the particular subject stands but which is not to be mastered or exploited by the subject as if that subject stood "somewhere else" or, worse, "nowhere in particular," in the fictive world of ego and gratification. It is a discipline that inhabits limit, location, time, and constraint, seeking above all to allow the interaction of the "network" to happen in *this* place and time; and this in turn entails learning physical habits and disciplines that are appropriate to a life lived in accordance with *logos*. There are things we "know" in and only in physical attunement to the world. Finally, in its freedom to welcome and acknowledge this kind of engagement in the world, the mind is opened to the unifying source of every *logos*, the self-communication of God. In the classical language of the Greek contemplative tradition, this is where "natural contemplating," *phusike theoria*, becomes *theologia*, attunement with the divine Logos.

The transformation of knowledge, mental and material, is thus bound up with the education of the mind in inhabiting its location in time and space—learning to be a *creaturely* mind, we might say. To be hospitable to *logos* at any level is to encounter and acknowledge a boundary—but precisely *not* a boundary between self and world, rather the boundary of being as an embodied subject in this location over against that, in interaction with that. Transformed *sense* is what happens as we become more seriously aware of the interface between my physicality and the physicality around me; when I begin to see and sense what is there, stripped of my passionate intention toward it. When Pope Francis and Patriarch Bartholomew speak of our environmental crisis as a "sin against ourselves" and of the interconnectedness of environmental disorder with other sorts of disorder and imbalance,[11] we are reminded that the effect of "passionate intention" is a state of *irrationality*: a definition of reason only in instrumental terms produces, it seems, the corporate insanity that is the prevailing human attitude to both the material order we are part of and the societies we create. Irrationality at this level is humanity at war with itself, and this is inexorably our destination if we become incapable of asking about how we might become receptive and attentive to the *logos*-level of our universe. To quote Evagrius once again, the *gnostikos*, in being attuned to *logos*, is also attuned to the diverse levels of capacity in his/her audience and is thus able to communicate with "justice," giving each what is proper for them, direct and simple teaching for some, *ainigmata* for others.[12] So the person who has received the life of *logos* into the mind (and body) becomes the perfect communicator of what has been received because she/he understands what can be heard and received in the process of teaching in the case of each person. Attunement to the world's harmonics brings attunement to the diversity of the human world also; and this is hardly surprising since what is needed for both is freedom from passionate intention, from aggression and acquisitiveness. A world whose sanity is restored would be one in which "reason" had been rediscovered as a condition not of instrumental control and conceptual precision but of *appropriate responsiveness*, to the human and the nonhuman order alike. The key insight of the theological perspective offered by the Pope and the Patriarch is to do with this, with the recovery of the idea of an "apt" or fitting relation that is not simply translatable into comprehensively conceptual terms; absent this recovery, we remain at war with our humanity, as with our planet.

If, then, we are to talk about spiritual transformation, it must be a way of talking about how we learn to inhabit our place within a connected environment, within a world of limit and mutuality. This is not an eccentric innovation for our theology of the "spiritual": what I have so far been stressing is that the heart of the Greek Christian tradition involves a doctrine of what *logos* means and a practical diagnostic of the damage done by passion to our knowing at the most comprehensive and truthful level. And to understand this is also to open the door to a fresh understanding of the notion of theosis in the Greek Christian tradition. At first sight, it seems that the aspiration to deification is an aspiration to be freed from the limiting perspectives of materiality and passion alike. In chapter 22 of *On Thoughts*, referring also to the texts on the subject in the treatise *On Prayer*, *apatheia* entails being freed from "worldly desire" and from the concepts or representations of sense objects (*aistheta pragmata*);[13] advance in the life of the spirit toward its fullness apparently has as its condition the abandonment of any awareness of the particular, the "located." But there are two basic points which should qualify this reading of the texts and of the model derived from them. Early in *On Thoughts* (chapter 3),[14] Evagrius notes how the aggressive passion is tamed by practical charity (almsgiving), the *nous* is purified in prayer and desire is disciplined by fasting. The passion-free spirit is then able to look at the human world without making distinctions: Paul's language about there being neither male nor female (Gal 3:28), neither Greek nor Jew, slave nor free (Col 3:11) is quoted. And the point seems to be not that freedom from passion abolishes the particular but that it liberates us to love without reference to our own preference or affinity. *Apatheia* is the liberty of the mind to see and respond without what we would call an "agenda" of its own. Similarly the critical comments about sense-based concepts are specifically linked to what happens in prayer: what is going to be most destructive is the confusion of an awareness of God with the awareness of any thing in the perceptual field. Such confusion is one form—the most damaging—of precisely the sort of *misidentification of what is real* that Evagrius is diagnosing in chapter 42 of the *Gnostikos*: to see the other whom I must love primarily in terms of the identities that I can categorize (as familiar or unfamiliar, as like or unlike myself) is the reduction of the real that passion invariably generates; and the "seeing" of God as an item in the field of my routine material/intellectual perception is the most extreme case of such reduction.

So what this does *not* mean is that the spirit on its way to unity with the divine, to theosis (not itself a common Evagrian word), *itself* becomes in some way "limitless," simply identified with what it encounters, undetermined and unlocated. Such a picture of the self or spirit would in fact be another product of "passionate" thinking, seeking to remove from the world anything that I as an individual mind or spirit cannot contain. Non-passionate engagement with the world is invariably *responsive*: its dispassionate character is shown in its freedom to receive what is there to be understood and loved without asking about its use. It is a freedom to see what God gives to be seen. Growing into what God intends for us is growing into undistorted vision (to echo the original title of Fr. Sophrony's famous study of Saint Silouan of Mount Athos,[15] but it is also the prosaic business of sustaining that vision by fasting and almsgiving, by the daily business of engaging rightly or justly with what is in fact in front of our eyes. But this reminder that the Evagrian account of spiritual maturity depends on a fundamentally "responsive" dimension in our humanity opens the door to a still more important theological point, one that will take us beyond much of what Evagrius explicitly says and closer to the world of Maximus the Confessor and the tradition flowing from him. Briefly: our divinization is not the (impossible) acquisition of impersonal divine attributes, but our assimilation to the eternal Logos in the Logos's *filial* relation to the Source of Godhead. We are to become "divine" only after the pattern of the Son. The entire direction of classical Christian theology is defined by the basic conviction that we are adopted into the relation that Jesus enjoys with the Father and that we are enabled to pray with his prayer (as in the two classical Pauline texts, Rom 8:15 and Gal 4:6, and in the Farewell Discourses of the Fourth Gospel). When this is translated into the more abstract language of patristic and Byzantine trinitarianism, it evolves into a complex but closely interconnected theological vision of how the structures of all finite agencies and substances realize aspects of the fullness that is eternally in the divine Logos; the incarnation of the Logos is the means by which the diversity of finite life—a diversity that, because of sin, has become fragmentation and rivalry—is once again made coherent, mutually life-giving instead of mutually destructive.[16] And that making-coherent is realized as finite reality opens itself more fully to the creative act that sustains it; as finite reality becomes receptive and responsive, as it comes to actualize the image of the eternal Logos.

For finite *intelligence* this means the acquiring of what we could call the "filial" mind. The reality of the eternal Logos is simultaneously wholly dependent and wholly creative: it is not "receptive" in any sense that could mean simply that it was passive, yet it is not "independent" in any sense that would imply that it could be itself without receiving all that it is from an other. All created agency thus has to be seen in this context: to be created is to derive from an act that is not ours, but it is also to be the conduit of generative gift to the rest of the finite order, each finite agent giving in its own unique way the life that it has itself been given. For the human creation, characterized by love and intelligence, to actualize the life of *logos* is to exercise at whatever level and in whatever mode the human capacity for self-representation and world-representation in such a way that how we represent ourselves to ourselves and the world to ourselves is permeated by response to eternal gift. And the fundamental problem with the life of "passion" is that it drives us to representations that are detached from the awareness of gift, gift received, and gift transmitted. As we put it earlier, the passionate mind lacks *hospitality*, the readiness to give habitation to both the finite and the infinite other in their sheer non-negotiable difference from the knowing self. This is why Evagrius and the tradition stemming from him see the opposite of significant knowledge not as error but as anger or acquisitive desire. In contrast, the hospitable mind is remade in the image of eternal Logos, eternal filiation, insofar as it receives what it encounters at the level of *logos*—that is, at the level where what is "sensed," apprehended, understood is the relation of what we encounter to its maker. Our own "hospitality" to the world unites with the "hospitality" to the act of the creator that lies at the heart of the reality of this world's objects, and ultimately to the "hospitality" of the eternal Word to the gift of the eternal Father. And my own conscious and linguistic welcome to the *logoi* as a finite knowing subject—my active/contemplative knowledge of the world—becomes a means for the interactive life of the creator within creation to reach a deeper intensity and communicability; hence the familiar language about humanity as exercising a "priestly" role in creation, though the exploration of that would take us into a still wider discussion.

The balance in the "rational" creation of receptivity or dependence and generative, innovative liberty is uniquely complex and significant in the human subject—which is why a theological perspective should both welcome *and* qualify the language of Simone Weil in her retrieval of a Platonic and Christian account of our human presence in the world. "God," she writes, "has created a finite being, which says "I," which is unable to love God. Through the action of grace the "I" little by little disappears, and God loves himself by way of the creature, which empties itself, becomes nothing."[17] Well, yes and no: if the process were *only* the repetition of finite subjects learning to cancel their individual agendas, this might serve as a summary. But it does not really do justice to the supplementary idea that the act by which the individual ego gradually comes to see itself in a "converted" way, as an element in the interactive world of *logos*, is itself life-giving, and is so in a unique mode. "We have got to renounce being something," writes Weil in her notebooks:[18] we must imitate God's refusal to be an identity over against an other. Creation is the act by which God refuses to be "everything."[19] But there is a conceptual tangle here. To be a finite substance—and more particularly a finite spirit/ *nous*—is to be *located*, to be placed here and not elsewhere in the network of finite interrelation and to have a perspective that is neither universal nor freed from specificity. The life that is lived in and from that location, seeking to see truthfully and to engage dispassionately, is, in its ascetical struggle to move away from acquisition and aggression, becoming a gift to the life of other finite substances, mediating to them the liberating presence of the creator in new ways, ways that are inextricably bound up with the particularity of who and where each subject is. The creature does not *become nothing*, as if its particularity were essentially an obstacle to God being God: a theology and metaphysic of *logos* insists that the creature—and supremely the "rational," *logikos*, subject that is the human *nous*—becomes the bearer of an irreplaceable grace within the exchange of finite life. The risk of Weil's language is to give room to precisely that fiction of a "limitless" selfhood that we have seen to be alien to the central thrust of the ascetical tradition. The corrosive effect of passion is not—as Weil often seems to suggest—in remaining tied to the sheer fact of finite individuality; it is the consistent refusal to understand and inhabit that individuality in the awareness of being a means of gift, the bearer of a needed or desired element in the total of finite interaction. Orion Edgar's work on Merleau-Ponty draws this out in a somewhat different but recognizably convergent idiom. Seeing an "environment" is, he notes, necessarily an enterprise that is not to be completed or mastered in a single moment and angle of perception. "The 'incarnational' logic that we have been arguing for . . . takes account of the location of the perceiver in the world, it understands Being as given in limited aspects and not as a reality that could be best seen and ideally known from the perspectiveless position of an absolute observer or a purely transcendent God or described in terms of a pure geometry."[20] A fuller grasp of what the Evagrian and Maximian tradition implies allows us to map this with some clarity, in that it allows us to understand the interconnection of finite agency, arising as it does from the measureless plurality of possible finite perspectives, "points of orientation," as the *mimesis* in time and space of the infinite divine Logos. As such, it cannot be something whose sole purpose is self-cancelation; but at the same time, its imitation of the divine Logos entails a radical dissolution of the image of a solid selfhood with self-defined and autonomous interests; or, to use the traditional and evocative theological term, it entails a kenotic element. Passion-free perception and reception of what is real is at the heart of what we might call a "filial" mode of awareness: a Christomorphic mind (cf. Rom 12:2, I Cor 2:16, Phil 2:5) is one that understands itself as receiving and communicating the one Logos in a uniquely located mode, from where it actually sits as a material system of energy. The divine Logos is "embodied" in the entire scheme of finite "rationality" and its unique and definitive embodiment in the person of the Incarnate Word is, above all, that which restores to finite substances the capacity to function as vehicles of gift and mutuality rather than being warring elements in a fundamentally violent cosmic system.

We have learned, rightly, to be wary of appeals to "rationality"; the characteristic modern usage of the term is instrumental and focused on the reasoning skills of individuals; it stands at a fastidious distance from any kind of metaphysical, let alone spiritual, concern. And in standing at that distance, it continues to compound the increasingly deadly problem of our era, the persistent myth of our essential disembodiedness—in the sense of a belief in our capacity to determine our goals and our fate independently of any alignment with the facts of our belonging in the material world. The characteristic twin distortions of much contemporary semipopular scientism are, on the one hand, a strict mechanical model of *all* material interaction, including our own brain activity, to the extent that some can toy with the oddly self-subverting notion that consciousness is purely epiphenomenal, and, on the other, a "transhumanist" or "posthumanist" aspiration to reduce our human experience to nonorganic systems of information exchange, invulnerable to time and decay. Both assume a gulf between mind and matter, both see "reason" as a process of solving mental problems. It is incidentally worth asking about the impact of this on some kinds of philosophical anthropology for which a particular model of "reasoning" capacity becomes what we appeal to in settling the normal conditions for recognizing an agent as "personal" and deserving of the rights of a person. For some decades, the witness of the L'Arche communities, along with the generally heightened cultural sensitivity to the stigmatizing and patronizing of people with nonstandard neurological conditions, has opened new perspectives on how we think about the diversity of "rationality." The responses of gratitude, affection, emotional alertness, the ability to create and sustain relationships that are visible in such persons should make us hesitate about defining rational behavior without reference to such qualities and skills. These perspectives help us see "reasoning" as a richly analogical term, capable of being applied to any sustained ability to adjust intelligently to an environment, human or nonhuman.

It is an insight expressed with characteristic clarity by one of the twentieth century's greatest Christian writers. Flannery O'Connor, meditating on Aquinas's definition of art as "reason in making," laments the way in which "reason" has "lost ground" in modernity: "As grace and nature have been separated, so imagination and reason have been separated, and this always means an end to art. The artist uses his reason to discover an answering reason in everything he sees. For him, *to be reasonable is to find in the object, in the situation, in the sequence, the spirit which it itself.*"[21] Which is perhaps as good a definition of *logos* as modern Christian reflection has to offer.

Speaking of *logos* in this connection is therefore a way of challenging the hegemony of a profoundly inadequate account of what we mean by reason. The path to theosis is a path to rationality, counterintuitive as this may sound, once we have grasped something both of the diagnostic of passion and the metaphysics of *logos* in the patristic and Byzantine texts with which we started. We have seen that the ideal of perception assumed by these and comparable texts (in the Christian West as well as the East) is "filial" in the sense that it looks to a state in which we are receiving as fully and comprehensively as possible what God gives for our specific mode of finite existence and freely cooperating in transmitting life to the rest of the created network—thus echoing the eternal identity of dependence and initiative that is the life of the divine Logos. And whether we are thinking of the needs and dignities of human persons who may not embody the rationality we casually treat as normal and normative, or of the disastrous and suicidal folly of our policies toward the environment we inhabit, it is this filial reasoning that will provide the alternative to an increasingly narrow and life-threatening set of models and rhetorical conventions. In sum, and echoing O'Connor: "reason" is what attunes us to the reality of where we live in a way that makes possible the fullest mutual movement of life and intelligent communication; it is to be understood theologically as the embodiment in time and space of the eternal receiving and communicating/responding that is the life of the second divine hypostasis. To live consistently as human spirits within this *logos*-animated exchange is "deification" in the sense of growing into the filial identity for which we are made. From beginning to end, this is a narrative of embodied agency (as if there were in the world any other kind), and to apprehend it as such is to be delivered from the tyranny of a fantasized "elsewhere" which is the true and proper home of a detached spirit; yet it is also to reflect with sharpened intelligence on the complexities of "representation"—both the representation of the world we inhabit and the representation of the unrepresentable God. It is a commonplace that the Evagrian tradition provides a clear critique of all attempts to represent God as an inhabitant of the universe and so of all unthinking physical imagery; but this is not a scheme that simply asserts the superiority of spirit over matter as if there were two competing realms. God cannot be materially itemized simply because he is the context within which any meaningful representation makes any sense at all: God is that which eternally begets *logos* within the divine life, and gratuitously shapes a finite order in which that *logos* is imitated and participated in limited and particular material systems. But that could be taken further to imply that truthfully representing the word we inhabit means seeking representation that does at least some justice to the range of interconnection that surrounds us—which suggests some thought about the "rationality" of metaphor and symbol, and the activity of the artist as a witness to "reason" in the sense here outlined.

Thus the discussion so far will have left us with some inchoate thoughts about how the seed sown in the Evagrian texts may grow to have bearing on artistic as well as ethical and even political questions such as we wrestle with in this bleak time of the breaking of cultures and the loss of an authentic humanism. But can we press the question little further and suggest that the very idea of truthful or just representation—and so of truthful and just *reasoning*—is, for Christian theology, grounded in the divine begetting of *logos*?

Fundamental to the trinitarian vision of divine life is the conviction that it belongs to the very grammar of the divine that God's life is *generative*: it is impossible to think the divine simply as a One beyond relation or reciprocity. When Karl Barth in the twentieth century writes of God's "self-repetition" in the trinitarian life, he is giving important expression to this basic orientation.[22] God generates God, and in that sense "repeats" God. Part of the hinterland of trinitarian language is, of course, the Wisdom tradition of the Hebrew scriptures and the paracanonical texts that elaborate them. Whether we are directed to a Wisdom that is, before creation, "alongside" God (as in Prov 8), or a Wisdom that "emanates" from the divine like a breath, naming herself as God's active and glorious presence (Sir 24, Ws 7) or a mirror of divine agency (Ws 7), the underlying insight is one and the same: it is intrinsic to divine action that it "resonates" with itself, that it lives and acts in a self-generated harmonic. It gives itself to be given back again; its unity is not naked self-identity, but a moment of self-reflexivity that we could clumsily call a sort of eternal "feedback." And the elaboration of the language of *logos* in Greek Christian theology is the canonical vehicle in early Christian thought for expressing this belief: eternal reality is productive of its own reflection, inseparably moving into otherness and returning in what I have elsewhere called, in a different, Christological, context, a nondual nonidentity.[23] God is God in acting so as to be God *to* God, as reflection *and* as the generativity of that reflection itself as it returns to its source—as Source and Word and Spirit simultaneously.

The idea of eternal *logos* and *sophia* in the divine implies that we can think of the trinitarian life not simply as God's repetition of God, in Barthian terms but as God's "correspondence" with God,[24] or, in other words, the ontological basis of *truth* is God's self-relation, God's own identity in difference, an identity that can be shown/spoken in what it is not. To grasp what truthfulness means, we look to this fundamental fact of divine self-resonance or—to borrow the characteristic vocabulary of the Fourth Gospel (as in, for example, chapters 5 and 15)—divine self-*testimony*. In the Johannine account of divine action, Father, Son, and Spirit testify, bear witness to one another; each realizes and manifests what the other is, each tells the truth about its other, and about its other's relation to what is other to that other. Any language about this shows immediate strain; but the basic point is not a complicated one. If God corresponds to God and so truly reflects God, that reflection is a witness to the truth reflected. It is this self-relation and self-testimony that, for a theologian like Origen, enjoins the conclusion that God is "rational" and that the eternal Logos incarnate in Christ is witness to this rationality—rationality understood as communicable life, life that can represent itself to itself in a nonidentical fashion, as a "true and faithful"[25] repetition of divine life. And if rationality is so understood, as communicable life, nonidentically repeated, we can see more readily why, for the Greek Christian tradition, *logos* in the created order is a dimension of finite reality that shares in the eternal Logos: the very idea of intelligibility is grounded in the character of infinite act as self-giving and self-correspondence. Hence the notion we explored earlier, a theme central in Eastern Christian thought from Evagrius to Maximus and beyond: mature knowledge is a fusion of the *logos* in the knower and the *logos* in what is known, so that the paradigm of knowledge is resonance and participation. In a different idiom, the Aquinas of the *de veritate*[26] treats the eternal *verbum cordis* within the divine life as the model and source of intellection in finite minds: God's "word" is God "imaging" God, "manifesting" God to God, expressing (in a phrasing that Aquinas takes from Richard of St Victor) the *sensus Patris*, the Father's "meaning," in and through the immeasurable diversity of finite particulars considered as it were abstractly—as the modes in which divine life is imitable and participable even independently of the actual existence of finite substances. The eternal Word as the Father's infinite other is the ground of the relation of all otherness—finite otherness—to the Father. It is the ground of finite reality's sharing in divine act; it is what holds the diversity of finite existence within the otherness of God to God; it is the way in which the one God is active in the multiplicity of finite reality, not as an external agency alongside finite act but as infinite act "corresponding" to itself through the medium of finite diversity, just as divine life corresponds to itself eternally and necessarily in the purely relational otherness of the divine persons. So the *verbum* in the finite subject is the subject in harmony with itself in and through its relation with what is other, as it is also the object "repeating itself" in the knowing subject. Because in finite intellects knowing and existing are *not* the same reality, whereas in God they are the one identical eternal act that is divine life, our "word" does not *constitute* the otherness in which it is repeated; in God, the Father eternally generates the Word that is the self-correspondence of the Father's hypostatic being in another hypostasis, and also freely repeats that self-correspondence in the "uttering" of the finite world in which intelligible form is apprehended through the reception by finite intellect of forms grounded in the ultimate structure of intelligibility, the divine Word. Those who have argued that Thomas is primarily interested in the *theological* grounding of true knowledge in the *de veritate* are not wrong, though it is somewhat misleading to suggest that his explorations here are therefore not intended to be "philosophical."[27] We could more accurately say that Aquinas is arguing that certain convictions about God are basic for making sense of truth-telling, if truth-telling does indeed presuppose a genuine modification of the intellect by what is known (rather than being a simply self-generated activity with no connection to what is other)—and this is a philosophical point as far as it goes; but the convictions about God that are relevant here are convictions about the trinitarian life, not about deity in general, and this should dispose us to take seriously the claim that Aquinas is advancing a consciously theological, and specifically trinitarian, epistemology.

We could sum up what has been said so far as the argument that God's truthful or faithful correspondence with God's own divine life or act is the condition for all that we call intelligence or rationality; and since that self-resonance or self-correspondence is built in to the doctrine of the Trinity, we have a clear connection between a trinitarian ontology and the particular epistemology—centered upon the idea of knowledge as resonance with *logos*, the range of behaviors expressing and enacting attunement to the communicative and intelligible energy of what is known—that we have traced earlier in this essay. I have used the phrase, a *"range* of behaviors": as I have argued elsewhere,[28] one of the deepest cultural problems of our day is the assumption that a certain limited range of linguistic and representational behaviors, concentrating on causal analysis, repeatable manipulation, and the search for some "fundamental" level of causality is what constitutes truthful knowing. In fact, to pick up a theme developed by some phenomenologists in the tradition of Merleau-Ponty, knowing an object in our habitual and unreflective understanding may well include a diversity of sense experience and habitual physical response—the clues and prompts given by taste or touch or smell, all part of our capacity to recognize and map an environment in which we are finding our way as material agents. There is here no substitute for the time it takes to learn such habits of recognition, no timeless compact digest of criteria to be marshalled in the concept-forming mind: ask yourself, for example, what would substitute for the way the sense of smell works in identifying decayed or infected food, or incipient fire.[29] A "rational" connectedness with the material environment is one that would include appropriate awareness—even if not a conceptually refined translation—of such habits of "educated" response. To understand human knowing, we need to imagine what we might call an educated *body*. How does this relate to the picture so far sketched?

Educated sense/sensuality implies a physical, ultimately neural, capacity to connect diverse experiences and make of them a coherent pattern; it is a kind of intelligence in the sense that intelligence identifies connectable *form*, consistent patterning in diverse phenomena. Bodies gradually accumulating "reasonable" habits do just this. And this in turn means that intelligence is naturally working with a spectrum of different kinds of difference—a spectrum of ways in which one substance may be active in another, one set of coherent actions molding the shape of the act and identity of another. The point is that the way in which a material substance "repeats" itself is precisely this spectrum of impacts and transactions through bodily engagement which produce in the knowing subject a set of "apt" or congruent behaviors whose success and sustainability through changing and challenging circumstances demonstrate the reality of the contact with a real otherness. "Correspondence" to reality as a definition of truthfulness means *the range of sustainable response* activated in a knower in contact with a known object, not simply a set of checkable statements about an object.

Put this in the light of what has been discussed earlier about the trinitarian life, and what comes into focus is this: the universe that we know is a system in which coherent and durable patterns of energy (intelligible forms) characteristically generate in other levels of organized energy a version of their own pattern of life (form gives intelligibility to matter, in more conventional language); and in the case of intelligent, language-using subjects, this generated version of a received form may exist across a range of activities from physical habit to mental representation of various sorts (picturing, mathematical modeling, verbal symbolization and so on). This is how in the finite world a substance "corresponds" to itself, repeats itself; this is how it is "truly" received. In rethinking our epistemology to escape from the tyranny of a representation confined to one limited, "canonical" mode (say mathematical modeling), claimed as the fundamental form of true knowledge, we need not have only a participatory model of knowledge (as an increasing number of thinkers seem to agree) but more specifically a model that understands the shape of finite reality itself as nonidentical repetition—grounded in the truth that the source of finite reality is the nonidentical repetition that is the divine life. To speak of what is actual is always to speak of this: "what is" is always necessarily action that generates its reflection in difference.[30] As we noted earlier, difference within God can be thought only in terms of relation, since there can be no intelligible way of ascribing temporal dilation, physical distance, oppositional or exclusive confrontation to the ultimate generative act that is God's life. But, as Aquinas argues, echoing Richard of Saint Victor, God expresses the *sensus* of what God is in the begetting of the eternal Word; God "acts upon" God, the Father acts in begetting the Word, in something we can only represent as analogous to our self-reflection, the process by which we continuously *own* what is already the content of our identity, but in so doing augment and differentiate that content. We cannot *in divinis* speak of "augmentation," of course, but we can perhaps use the language as a springboard for imagining how the nonidentical repetition that is the eternal Word is also the condition of that divine dimension of action that we call Spirit, that which is irreducible to either "Father" or "Son." Divine life is not an emergence into duality and a collapse back into identity; if we pursue the "feedback" analogy mentioned earlier, we can dimly see how the primordial repetition that is the Word, in reflecting the Source's reality truthfully to the Source, posits that the Source *as* self-giving and self-corresponding is not now "caught" in a sterile self-repetition, a mere second identity, but is established as generative in a different mode.[31]

To say that these are ambitious (overly ambitious?) and speculative ideas is obvious. But it is important to try and set out how a trinitarian ontology mandates a particular approach to epistemology, so as to clarify a central and pivotal concern for any theologically inflected philosophy—the need to challenge reductive models of knowing which assume the normative status of nonrelational, descriptive, and external modes of understanding the environment and fail to deal with the mutual "implication" of knower and known. If the foundational rhythm of reality is—so to speak—utterance and resonance and enhanced utterance, then it is not merely the case that language "represents" reality: reality itself is linguistic, in the sense that intelligible communication, the giving and receiving of intelligible form, is ultimately *what there is*. And this in turn is not just to say that fundamental reality communicates what it is: mutual communication, the life of reality in what it is not and the simultaneous return of that "what it is not" to what it repeats, is the most basic characterization of "being" that we can offer. It is not a theme that has found many modern theological explorers, but the not very well known work of Sergii Bulgakov, *Chapters on the Trinity*, sketches such a "linguistic" account of trinitarian life, seeing the relation of subject, predicate and copula as a reflection of the grammar of divinity.[32] What *is* is not exhausted in its bare self-identity, it is capable of being "named," and so establishes itself as generating a kind of "tension" (in a nonpejorative sense) between its sheer exercise of being and the interwoven actuality of that being as gift and response. If all language is not to fall back into tautology ("X is what it is"), it must reflect the truth that X's being what it is involves its being in or for what it generates in action and "feeds back" into itself as part of its definition. "X is Y" states that X cannot be itself without an active exercise of being in which it is not self-identical; and, for Bulgakov, this is grounded in the ultimate "antinomy" of being which is the simultaneous absoluteness of God, God's "no-thingness," and God's self-differentiation or self-relation.[33] Recognizing this antinomy saves us from two basic errors in theology: making the "absoluteness of God a sort of exclusive conceptual definition which would render the trinitarian life (and so ultimately the engagement of God with creation) unthinkable; and reducing the divine life to a contingent plurality of instances of "divine nature"—with the implication that the foundational structure of the world is likewise a series of instances of nature, existing primitively in mutual isolation, and subsequently coming into relation. What Bulgakov is seeking, in common with many more recent theologians, is a way of affirming the irreducibility of relation; his originality is in linking this to the working of language itself, seeing language as a key to the inescapability of non-identical correspondence and being-in-the other for our understanding of the real.

I have suggested that truthful representation is a notion that should include all forms of appropriate and sustainable responses to the environment in which intelligence is at work. In this sense, a certain kind of habit may constitute for some purposes a "truthful representation": the exercise of a skill like wood carving or violin playing involves the body in *showing* how an instrument is constructed and how it can effectively operate. The skill *tells* us something. Its successful exercise is the meeting place of identities realized in each other—the tool or instrument is meaningless independently of its activation in this particular mode, and the craftsman or performer is "in-formed" by the possibilities of the tool or instrument, acquires new definition through this formative relation and in so doing exhibits both their own identity and that of the object used. But this in turn moves into a "telling" about the material worked on, whether the literally material stuff of wood being carved or the "matter" of musical relations and frequencies; another definitive frontier between identity and otherness opens up. Truth-telling comes into focus as something involving a whole history of convergence between identities, centered on what could be called a sustainable habit of engagement, an "apt" response that is effective and generative because it is fitted to the *act* of what it responds to/represents. As Klaus Hemmerle observes in his celebrated *Theses on Trinitarian Ontology*,[34] things are only what they are in action: "And this action is a constitution, a communication, a delimitation and an adaptation to an overarching context."

The present discussion has attempted, as Hemmerle himself does, to move a little further. The contention is that knowledge is like this, intelligence is like this, because of the basic character of reality as shown in the trinitarian life of God. Logos, as we all know, is more than "word"; but what theologians came to say about the eternal Logos, and then about the role of *logos* in the processes of human cognition and conscious agency allows us to say that—as Aquinas seems to assume—our speech, in the broadest sense, is both a clue to thinking about the triune God and a reality comprehensively illuminated by that God. The act of naming, representing, acknowledges the way in which identities "call out" for vehicles that will manifest their nonidentity, that will repeat them in a correspondence that is not just static "reproduction." This is why, to borrow Hemmerle's phrasing again,[35] human beings discover that they are "present in everything which [their] questioning and thinking encounter." And at the heart of this aspect of our intelligence—which is both verbal in the straightforward sense and also preverbal and paraverbal and postverbal—is the trinitarian source of finite being, which *is* only in differentiated harmony with itself. Because it corresponds to or coincides with itself in nonidentical fashion, we can understand that there is no context in which mere self-identity is the final stopping point of ontological analysis. What is, is communicable, repeatable, generative of representation. All our own intelligent life is in one way or another bound up in "cultures of representation," the search for sustainable relatedness within the complex of the finite world. But because the divine is not in any way a further or supreme instance of "being," God in "telling the truth" about the divine life through the generation of the Word simultaneously tells the truth about all finite reality, establishing that it is in relation to God that each finite identity ultimately has its ground, and so also grounding the irreducibility of mutual relation between finite identities in virtue of their common relatedness to God. If all *logoi* exist in the one eternal Logos, each distinct finite *logos* has at its root a relation it shares with every other; and thus each has a relation with an eternal Logos that is simultaneously the root and rationale of every other, so that the *multiform* relatedness of the eternal Logos is what each is related to—and thereby related to each other.

The wisdom celebrated in Hebrew scripture is therefore not just a mechanism for diffusing divine agency to an inferior level (arguably this is the position associated with Arius in the debates of the fourth Christian century). The significance of words like "mirror" and "emanation" (*katoptron* and *aporroia* or *apaugasma*) for the Origenian tradition makes a larger claim about a God whose life is intrinsically communicative—not in any sense that would "require" creation as a recipient of communication but in virtue of its own reality as intelligent and loving. We assume that God's generative life cannot be *less* than intelligent and loving, even if we cannot say what the inseparable exercise of infinite intelligence and love is *like*. That God is in correspondence with God is, for the Nicene theology of the fourth century, the condition of the reality of divine communication with the finite, both in the ongoing self-giving of creation itself and in the specific moments we identify as revelation. Karl Barth's fundamental theological insight about Trinitarian theology was that the Trinity illuminated how and why God could speak to us; God is able to speak in revelation because God is primordially the God who utters God's self to God's self. In the grammar of our talk about God's eternity, this is not—as it is in God's relation with the finite and in the relation of on finite substance to another—any kind of supplement, making up what is lacking, initiating a process of enhancement or (to use the word used here earlier) "augmentation." God does not "inform" God, activate a potentiality in God and so forth. The challenge of a thoroughgoing trinitarian scheme is to imagine a being-in-the other that is purely and simply a matter of simultaneous self-constitution in relation; and for this we have no adequate analogy. To return to Bulgakov's treatment of his "antinomies," this is where the real absoluteness of God imposes an apophatic humility. It is not that we are unable to discover an essential/conceptual definition of God; we have no tools that could finally clarify what it means to say that the Father is not Father except as Father of the Son and breather of the Spirit—that God is not God except in giving and bringing back the divine life to itself and so establishing itself as intelligent and loving.

The point about apophasis is important. None of this discussion should be taken as an attempt to anatomize the divine life "in itself." Its purpose is simply to clarify what is entailed by the claim that our own intelligence and love "image" their divine origin. What Hemmerle calls the discovery of my knowing self in all that I know is the finite echo of the truth that infinite agency is a self-differentiation, an identity in otherness. This is shown to us in the event of Jesus, the human life in which the internal reciprocity of God with God and the overflow or excess of that reciprocity is spelled out in temporal sequence—as the gift of the Father to the incarnate Son by the bestowal of the Spirit, the gift of the Son to the Father in obedient love and the gift of the Spirit to the Church, a process in which each divine agent bears truthful witness to the other(s), as the Farewell Discourses in John's Gospel explain. We are able to understand this idea of divine witness in the context of historical narrative, but we have no resource that will enable us to conceptualize what this "witness" means in eternity, except to say that it is the way in which God exercises indivisibly the love and intelligence of which we are the created shadows. And if the whole structure of this argument is correct, then our knowing of the triune God is in any case not the construction of a conceptual framework but the "aptness" of a life that fits with the constraining and defining reality of God's being—a knowing that is first the relation of self-forgetfulness in the face of the divine, the carrying of the cross, and the filial prayer of *Abba*. This is what a theologian like Vladimir Lossky meant by insisting that "negative theology" could not be understood as simply a moment in the verbal negotiation of what could and could not be said of God, a phase in the to and fro of definitional ventures; it had, rather, to be grasped as a habit of faithful living (once again, an "apt" response to divine agency).[36]

Rethinking *logos*—infinite and finite—for our times is thus a matter of thinking together God's self-correspondence, God's truthfulness to God, with our own self-discovery in what we know and our attempts not only to create truthful formulation of what we encounter but to develop a sustainable lived response to it. The more we elucidate what is meant by God's self-correspondence in the trinitarian life, the meaning of terms like Word and Wisdom and image, the more we understand how language—generously defined—is ontologically basic. The more we clarify what our own knowledge as finite intelligences involves, the more we see that intelligence and speech—again, generously defined, and including symbolic and communicative gesture—are not inexplicable or gratuitous outgrowths on the body of solidly atomistic material realities. Bringing these two intellectual exercises together is a complex business, but it is, so I have argued, a necessary task in a climate of debased accounts of human intellect and a nervousness about religiously molded metaphysics. I have tried to suggest that it is ultimately scriptural talk of God that prompts the particular metaphysical trajectory we have been considering, and that the emerging metaphysic and epistemology, so far from making our discourse more abstract, in fact reinforces the centrality of practice and of material location and temporality. Appropriately, perhaps, it is a metaphysic that proposes incarnation and kenosis to finite subjects as the ground of truthfulness—just as they are the form taken by divine truthfulness, "self-correspondence," in God's enfleshed speech to us.

Notes

1. Evagrius, *Le Gnostique, ou a celui qui est devenu digne de la science*, ed. Antoine Guillaumont and Claire Guillaumont, Sources Chrétiennes 356 (Paris: Cerf, 1989), 92–93. For a good introduction to Evagrius with some representative texts, see Augustine M. Casiday, *Evagrius Ponticus* (London: Routledge, 2006).

2. Evagrius, *Le Gnostique*, 170–71.

3. Evagrius, *Sur les pensées*, ed. Paul Gehin, Claire Guillaumont, and Antoine Guillaumont, Sources Chrétiennes 438 (Paris: Cerf, 1998), 176–79; English translation in Casiday, *Evagrius Ponticus*, 91–116.

4. Evagrius, *Sur les pensées*, 148–49, 150–51.

5. Gnostikos 7, 98–99.

6. Raimon Panikkar, *Mysticism and Spirituality, Part One: Mysticism, Fullness of Life* (Maryknoll, NY: Orbis Books, 2014), 142 ff.

7. Ibid., 144.

8. The significance in the spiritual life of accepting that ne is generated has been developed recently in the work of Luigi Giussani; see, for example, Julian Carron, *Disarming Beauty. Essays on Faith, Truth and Freedom* (Notre Dame, IN: University of Notre Dame Press 2017), 45–46.

9. Orion Edgar, *Things Seen and Unseen: The Logic of Incarnation in Merleau-Ponty's Metaphysics of Flesh* (Eugene, OR: Cascade Books 2016), 187; italics in original.

10. See Hannah Arendt, *Love and Saint Augustine*, ed. and tr. Joanna Vecchiarelli Scott and Judith Chelius Stark (Chicago: University of Chicago Press, 1996).

11. See, for example, sections 16, 34, and 56 of Pope Francis's 2015 encyclical *Laudato si'*.

12. *Gnostikos* 44, 174–75.

13. *Sur les pensées* 22, 230–31, 232–33.

14. Ibid., 160–61, 162–63.

15. Archimandrite Sofrony (Sakharov), *The Undistorted Image: Staretz Silouan 1866–1938* (London: Faith Press, 1958).

16. Antoine Lévy, O.P., *Le créé et l'incréé: Maxime le confesseur et Thomas d'Aquin* (Paris: Vrin, 2006), esp. chs. 2 and 3, is the most comprehensive and insightful of recent discussions of Maximus's Christocentric metaphysics. Lars Thunberg's older *Microcosm and Mediator: The Theological Anthropology of Maximus the Confessor* (Lund: Hakan Ohlssens Boktryckeri, 1965), remains a dependable guide.

17. *The Notebooks of Simone Weil*, vol. 1, trans. Arthur Wills (London: Routledge and Kegan Paul, 1956), 331.

18. Ibid., 193.

19. Compare the formulation of Jacques Pohier in *God in Fragments* (London: SCM, 1985), "God is God, so God is not everything" (the title of the book's third section).

20. Edgar, *Things Seen and Unseen*, 135.

21. Quoted Greg Wolfe, *Intruding Upon the Timeless. Essays on Art, Faith, and Mystery*, 2nd ed. (Baltimore, MD: Square Halo Books, 2018), 21.

22. Karl Barth, *Church Dogmatics I.1. The Doctrine of the Word of God*, trans. G. W. Bromiley, 2nd ed. (Edinburgh: T&T Clark, 1975), e.g., 348–355.

23. Rowan Williams, *Christ the Heart of Creation* (London: Bloomsbury, 2018), esp. the concluding chapter.

24. The awkwardness of speaking about God's "self-correspondence" was pointed out in discussion of this essay on its first delivery as a paper, and I grant the problem; but it is difficult to find another way of articulating the idea that God generates a form of divine life and agency that is a nonidentical repetition of its source.

25. See, for example, Origen's *Commentary on John* I.42, II.4, GCS Origenes Werke 4 (Leipzig, 1903); ET in *The Anti-Nicene Fathers*, vol. 10 (Grand Rapids, MI: Eerdmans, 1974).

26. See especially *de veritate* IV.1.

27. For some helpful discussions of this debate, see *Mental Representation*, volume 4 of the Proceedings of the Society for Mediaeval Logic and Metaphysics (Newcastle: Cambridge Scholars Publishing, 2011), especially the papers by Gyula Klima and Joshua Hochschild.

28. "Understanding Our Knowing: the Culture of Representation," paper presented at the second colloquium of the Beyond Science and Religion project in Cambridge, July 2019. See also "Appendix: On Representation," in Rowan Williams, *The Edge of Words: God and the Habits of Language* (London: Bloomsbury, 2014), 186–97.

29. See Edgar, *Things Seen and Unseen*, ch. 2, on eating as a form of perception/knowledge.

30. In discussion of this essay, the point has been made that this converges with aspects of Karl Rahner's theology of symbol; the literature is considerable, but one place to start is Stephen M. Fields, S.J., *Being as Symbol: On the Origins and Development of Karl Rahner's Metaphysics* (Washington, DC: Georgetown University Press, 2001).

31. This is the force of John Milbank's seminal essay "The Second Difference" in his collection *The Word Made Strange: Theology, Language, Culture* (Oxford: Blackwell, 1997), 171–93.

32. Sergii Bulgakov, *"Glavy o troichnosti,"* part 1, in *Pravoslavnaya Mysl* (1928): 31–88.

33. See Sergii Bulgakov, *Icons and the Name of God* (Grand Rapids, MI: Eerdmans, 2012).

34. Klaus Hemmerle, *Thesen zu einer trinitarischen Ontologie* (Einsiedeln, Switzerland: Johannes Verlag, 1992), #20; English translation, *Theses Towards a Trinitarian Ontology* (New York: Angelico Press, 2021), 36–38.

35. Ibid., #11.

36. See, e.g., Vladimir Lossky, "Apophasis and Trinitarian Theology," in *In the Image and Likeness of God* (Crestwood, NY: St. Vladimir's Seminary Press, 1974), 13–29; Rowan Williams, "Lossky, the *via negativa* and the Foundation of Theology," in *Wrestling with Angels: Conversations in Modern Theology*, ed. Mike Higton (London: SCM Press, 2007), 1–24.

Acknowledgments

Faith, Reason, and Theosis is based upon a conference that took place at Fordham University in June 2019. That conference was the fifth of the Solon and Marianna Patterson Triennial Conference on Christian Unity. We would like to thank Solon and Marianna Patterson for their visionary leadership and commitment to the cause of Christian unity. We would also like to acknowledge here members of the Advisory Council of the Orthodox Christian Studies Center at Fordham for their guidance and support.

Contributors

William J. Abraham was the Albert Cook Outler Professor of Wesley Studies at Perkins School of Theology at Southern Methodist University. After earning his BA from the Queen's University of Belfast, Northern Ireland, he completed an MDiv at Asbury Theological Seminary and a DPhil at Oxford University. He was the author or editor of more than twenty books on topics ranging from Wesleyan theology to evangelism to philosophy of religion, including the three-volume *Divine Agency and Divine Action* (Oxford University Press, 2018–2019), *Canon and Criterion in Christian Theology* (Oxford University Press, 2002), and *The Oxford Handbook of United Methodist Studies* with James E. Kirby (Oxford University Press, 2011). He was an ordained elder of the Southwest Texas Conference of the United Methodist Church. During production of this volume, William "Billy" Abraham died suddenly on October 7, 2021. In addition to this brilliant theological output, he will be remembered for his passion for theology and for his commitment to Christian unity.

Peter Bouteneff is Professor of Systematic Theology and Kulik Professor of Sacred Arts at St. Vladimir's Orthodox Theological Seminary. After taking a degree in music, he earned an MDiv from St. Vladimir's and an MPhil and a DPhil at Oxford University. He has worked for many years in theological dialogue, notably as Executive Secretary for Faith and Order at the World Council of Churches, and has written extensively on Orthodox relations with other churches. He has broad interests in theology ancient and modern and is committed to exploring the connections between theology and culture. He is editor of the "Foundations" series for St. Vladimir's Seminary Press and author of books including *Beginnings: Ancient Christian Readings of the Biblical Creation Narratives* (Baker Academic, 2008) and *Arvo Pärt: Out of Silence* (St. Vladimir's Seminary Press, 2015). His 2018 book *How to Be a Sinner* (St. Vladimir's Seminary Press) has been called "a minor classic in modern spirituality." He is founding director of the Institute of Sacred Arts at St. Vladimir's Seminary.

Carolyn Chau is Associate Professor of Systematic and Moral Theology at King's University College at Western University in London, Canada. She received her PhD from Regis College, University of Toronto, and her MDiv from Yale Divinity School. Her research examines questions at the intersection of contemporary Catholic ecclesiology, ethics, and secular culture. Her first book, *Solidarity with the World: Charles Taylor and Hans Urs von Balthasar on Faith, Modernity, and Catholic Mission* (Cascade, 2016), mines twentieth-century philosophy and theology for insights into the possible shape of dynamic and attractive Christian witness in "post-Christian" cultures. She is working on a second monograph on Christian ethics and Pope Francis. She has served as a theologian on ecumenical dialogues for the Canadian Conference of Catholic Bishops and currently directs the Centre for Advanced Research in Catholic Thought at King's.

Robert Glenn Davis is Associate Professor of Historical Theology at Fordham University. He received his doctorate from Harvard University, where he studied the history of Christian thought and practice with an emphasis on medieval Neoplatonism and mystical theology. His primary area of research is medieval Latin Christian thought and practice from the twelfth through the fourteenth centuries, with a focus on Christian mystical theology and spiritual practices of intellectual and affective transformation in late medieval Europe. His book *The Weight of Love: Affect, Ecstasy, and Union in the Theology of Bonaventure* (Fordham University Press, 2016) examines the complex embodiment of human affect and the role it plays in Bonaventure's account of ecstatic union with God and the life and death of Saint Francis of Assisi.

Stephen J. Davis is Woolsey Professor of Religious Studies and Professor of History at Yale University, specializing in the history of ancient and medieval Christianity, with a focus on the eastern Mediterranean and the Near East. His areas of teaching and research include the study of women and gender, pilgrimage and the cult of the saints, the history of biblical interpretation and canon formation, Egyptian Christianity, Arabic Christianity and its relation to Islam, early Christian art and material culture, and the application of archaeological, anthropological, sociological, and literary methods in the study of historical texts. He is author of several books, including *Christ Child: Cultural Memories of a Young Jesus* (Yale University Press, 2014), *Monasticism: A Very Short Introduction* (Oxford University Press, 2018), and *The Gnostic Chapters: A Critical Edition and Translation of Evagrius Ponticus' Kephalaia Gnostika in Arabic* (Brill, 2023). He is the founding director of the Yale Monastic Archaeology Project (YMAP), as well as a related Project to Catalogue the Coptic and Arabic Manuscripts at Dayr al-Suryān. He also currently serves as the founding editor of the Orthodox Christian Studies Center's *Christian Arabic Texts in Translation* series with Fordham University Press.

George E. Demacopoulos is Fr. John Meyendorff & Patterson Family Chair of Orthodox Christian Studies and Professor of Theology at Fordham University. Along with Aristotle Papanikolaou, he cofounded and codirects Fordham's Orthodox Christian Studies Center. He also serves as coeditor of the *Journal of Orthodox Christian Studies*. He is the author of four scholarly books, including *Colonizing Christianity: Greek and Latin Religious Identity in the Era of the Fourth Crusade* (Fordham University Press, 2019).

David Bentley Hart is an Orthodox philosophical theologian, essayist, and cultural commentator. He earned his BA from the University of Maryland, MPhil from the University of Cambridge, and MA and PhD from the University of Virginia. He has been a fellow at the University of Notre Dame's Institute for Advanced Study and the visiting Danforth Chair in Theological Studies at Saint Louis University and has held positions at the University of Virginia, Duke University, and Providence College. He is author of twenty books, including *The Experience of God: Being, Consciousness, Bliss* (Yale University Press, 2013), *The Hidden and the Manifest: Essays in Theology and Metaphysics* (Eerdmans, 2017), and *Roland in Moonlight* (2021). His translation of the New Testament was published by Yale University Press in 2017.

Philip Kariatlis is Sub-Dean and A/Professor in Theology at St Andrew's Greek Orthodox Theological College in Sydney, Australia. He earned his BA from the University of Sydney and MTh from the Sydney College of

Divinity from where he also received his doctorate specializing in ecclesiology. His research interest lies in Church doctrine, specifically its existential and salvific character. He translated the doctoral dissertation of Archbishop Stylianos (Harkianakis), "The Infallibility of the Church in Orthodox Theology" (2008) and has written in several peer-reviewed journals in Australia and abroad. His book *Church as Communion: Gift and Goal of Koinonia* (ATF Press & St. Andrew's Press, 2011) examines the church not only as a gift of God's presence among the world but also as a gracious sign oriented toward God's eschatological kingdom. Since 2010, he has been a member of the Faith and Unity Commission of the National Council of Churches of Australia.

Aristotle Papanikolaou is professor of theology, the Archbishop Demetrios Chair of Orthodox Theology and Culture, and the codirector of the Orthodox Christian Studies Center at Fordham University. He is also Senior Fellow at the Emory University Center for the Study of Law and Religion. In 2012, he received the Award for Excellence in Undergraduate Teaching in the Humanities. Among his numerous publications, he is the author of *Being with God: Trinity, Apophaticism, and Divine-Human Communion* (University of Notre Dame Press, 2006) and *The Mystical as Political: Democracy and Non-Radical Orthodoxy* (University of Notre Dame Press, 2012). He is also coeditor of *Thinking Through Faith: New Perspectives from Orthodox Christian Scholars* (St. Vladimir's Seminary Press, 2012), *Christianity, Democracy and the Shadow of Constantine* (Fordham University Press, 2016), and *Fundamentalism or Tradition: Christianity after Secularism* (Fordham University Press, 2019).

Jean Porter holds an endowed chair in the Department of Theology at the University of Notre Dame. She holds an MA and PhD from Yale University and an MDiv from Weston Jesuit School of Theology. Her focuses on the moral theology of Thomas Aquinas. She has written on scholastic theories of natural law, Thomistic virtue theory, and philosophical and theological views on legal theory. She is a member of the American Academy of Arts and Sciences and is a past President of the Society of Christian Ethics. Her books include *Nature as Reason: A Thomistic Theory of the Natural Law* (Eerdmans, 2005), *Ministers of the Law: A Natural Law Theory of Legal Authority* (Eerdmans, 2010), and *Justice as a Virtue: A Thomistic Perspective* (Eerdmans, 2016).

Andrew Prevot is Associate Professor of Theology at Boston College. He earned his BA from Colorado College and his PhD from the University of Notre Dame. He writes and teaches at the intersection of spiritual, mystical, systematic, and liberation theologies; phenomenology; and continental philosophies of religion. His publications include *Thinking Prayer: Theology and Spirituality Amid the Crises of Modernity* (University of Notre Dame Press, 2015), *Theology and Race: Black and Womanist Traditions in the United States* (Brill, 2018), and *The Mysticism of Ordinary Life: Theology, Philosophy, and Feminism* (Oxford University Press, 2023).

Ashley Purpura is Associate Professor of Religious Studies at Purdue University. She received her PhD from Fordham University in 2014 and a master's degree from Harvard Divinity School. She researches the history of Orthodox Christian thought in its Byzantine tradition and investigates how historical religious practices and ways of thinking shape power structures and complex identities for past and present religious communities. She has published articles on religious authority and conceptions of gender, and her book, *God, Hierarchy, and Power: Orthodox Theologies of Authority from Byzantium* (Fordham University Press, 2018) examines the development and maintenance of "hierarchy" as a theological concept. She is coeditor of the Orthodox Christian Studies Center's Orthodox Christianity and Contemporary Thought series published by Fordham University Press.

Kirsi Stjerna, a native of Finland, is the First Lutheran, Lost Angeles/Southwest California Synod Professor of Lutheran History and Theology at Pacific Lutheran Theological Seminary at California Lutheran University. She received her graduate education at Helsinki University and Boston University and previously served as Professor of Reformation Church History at Lutheran Theological Seminary at Gettysburg. She is author of *Lutheran Theology: A Grammar of Faith* (Bloomsbury, 2021) and co–general editor of and contributor to *The Annotated Luther*, vols. I–VII (Fortress Press, 2015–2017). Her book *Women and the Reformation* (Wiley, 2008) was followed by an edited volume, *Women Reformers of Early Modern Europe: Profiles, Texts, and Contexts* (Fortress Press, 2022). She is an ordained pastor of the Evangelical Lutheran Church of America and of the Evangelical Lutheran Church of Finland.

Michele E. Watkins is Assistant Professor of Theology and Religious Studies at the University of San Diego, where she teaches courses in early church tradition and Black and womanist theologies. Previously, she served as the Gerald L. Schlessman Assistant Professor in Methodist Studies and Assistant Professor of Theology at the Iliff School of Theology. She served as the assistant pastor at St. Mark United Methodist Church and is the immediate past dean of the Maceo D. Pembroke Institute for Ministerial Recruitment and Leadership Development and the former National College Director of PUSH Excel, an educational initiative of the Rainbow Push Coalition. She holds a PhD and MDiv from Garrett-Evangelical Theological Seminary, a BS in Psychology from Howard University, and a Certification in Non-Profit Management from the Kellogg School of Management at Northwestern University. She is a Provisional Elder in the Northern Illinois Conference of the United Methodist Church.

Rowan Williams was Archbishop of Canterbury from 2002 to 2012 and then Master of Magdalene College, Cambridge, until 2020. He is now retired and living in Wales. His books include studies of Teresa of Avila, Fyodor Dostoevsky, and Sergii Bulgakov, as well as *The Edge of Words* (Bloomsbury Continuum, 2014) and *Christ the Heart of Creation* (Bloomsbury Continuum, 2018). His *Looking East in Winter: Contemporary Thought and the Eastern Christian Tradition* (Bloomsbury Continuum, 2021) brought together numerous essays on Eastern Christianity. He is also known as a poet and translator of poetry.

INDEX

Abraham, William J., 159–73
Action, L' (Blondel), 18
Acts of the Apostles, 219
Adam, 45–46, 86, 91n49, 161
Aeterni Patris (Leo XIII), 18
Aetius, 224
Against Heresies (Irenaeus of Lyon), 135
aggression, 267–68
Albert of Cologne, 46
alienation, 46, 110n29
Alles, Gregory, 209–10
analogia entis, 94–96, 101
analytic philosophy, 171–73
ancestral mimesis, 145–48
Anglicanism, 166
Anselm of Canterbury, 2, 139
Anselm of Laon, 71n22
Apollinarianism, 82
apophasis, 203, 233, 236, 244, 289–90
apotheosis, 73, 78, 88n3
Aquinas, Thomas, 2, 6; being in, 42–43; creation in, 33n8, 69n10; deification in, 37–38, 69n7; doctrine of God and, 40–44; glory in, 38, 40, 43, 62; grace in, 29–30, 38–39, 43–44, 47–49, 53–55, 57–68, 70n19; Incarnation in, 70n16; intellect in, 19–20, 34n10; nature in, 20–21; sin in, 46–47, 58–59; theosis in, 37–68, 179; truth-telling and, 283; virtue in, 38–39; Word and, 285; work of Christ and, 44–49
Arendt, Hannah, 272
Arianism, 223
Aristotle, 17, 20–21, 95, 202

asceticism, 65, 83, 85, 178, 193, 237, 248n22, 256
Athanasius of Alexandria, 76, 82, 91n59, 178, 187
Atheological Summa (Bataille), 183
Augustine, 2, 18, 47, 98
Ayer, A. J., 171, 175n17

Baader, Franz von, 200–1, 208
Baker, Matthew, 82
Balthasar, Hans Urs von, 93–108, 182
baptism, 83–84, 92n65, 162, 171, 185, 187, 250n59
Barlaam, the Calabrian, 220
Barth, Karl, 2, 96, 289
Bartholomew I of Constantinople, 273
Basil of Caesarea, 150
Bataille, Georges, 183–84, 193
Beatific Vision, 38, 40, 51, 54, 60, 66
Becoming Divine (Jantzen), 183–84
Behr, John, 73, 82, 88n10, 91n49
being: in Aquinas, 42; God and, 42–43, 225; God as, 172–73, 204
Beloved (Morrison), 138, 140–48, 150, 152–53, 190
Blackness, 134
Black women, 141–45
Blondel, Maurice, 18, 25
Boehme, Jacob, 212n1
Boethius, 202, 214n18
Bonaventure, 2, 179
Bondage of the Will (Luther), 124–25
Bornkamm, Heinrich, 128n10
Bouteneff, Peter, 218–45

Bowne, Borden Parken, 174n13
Bradley, F. H., 171
Braine, David, 24–25, 35n13
Bulgakov, Sergei, 18, 285

Cabasilas, Nicholas, 76–77, 84, 90n35, 91n55, 92n63, 232, 240–44
Cajetan, Thomas, 20, 23
Calvin, John, 2, 134, 165
Carter, J. Kameron, 135
Casiday, Augustine, 251–52, 262n9
Catholicism, 1
causality, 17, 21, 57–58, 69n10, 204, 284
Certeau, Michel de, 183–84
Chapters on the Trinity (Bulgakov), 286
charity, 38, 54, 66, 275
Chau, Carolyn, 93–108
Chiles, Robert E., 173n2
Christ. *See* Jesus Christ
Christian Life, The: A Study (Bowne), 175n13
Christification: baptism and, 83–84; deification as, 74–80, 104; Eucharist and, 84–85; gift of, 83–86; grace and, 86; as human becoming, 80–83; living out of, 83–86; origin of term, 74; rationality, 80–83; sacraments and, 84–85, 92n63; salvation and, 79–80
Ciraulo, Jonathan, 93–108, 110n36
Coakley, Sarah, 106, 209, 216n39
Coleman, Monica A., 148
colonialism, 141
Colossians, Epistle to, 76, 275
Commentary on Exodus (Eckhart), 203
communion, 79–80, 140–41, 185
Communion and Otherness (Zizioulas), 135–36
Compendium (Aquinas), 33n8, 34n10
Cone, James H., 137, 174n8
Consolation of Philosophy (Boethius), 202, 214n18
Constantinople, 1
contemplation, 66, 99, 188–93
Copeland, M. Shawn, 149–51
Corinthians, First, 76, 79, 85, 278
cosmology, 75
Crainic, Nichifor, 9n1
creation: in Aquinas, 33n8, 69n10; deification and, 32, 45; directionality and, 225; God and, 43; likeness and, 105
creatures, God and, 42–43, 55
Crenshaw, Kimberlé, 192
Cross, 46, 63, 178
Cyril of Alexandria, 4, 187

Dailey, Patricia, 198
David, 219
Davis, Robert Glenn, 198–212
Davis, Stephen J., 251–60
De caelo (Aristotle), 20
deification, 3–4; apotheosis and, 88n3; in Aquinas, 37–38, 69n7; as Christification, 74–80; Christification and, 104; Christology and, 5; creation and, 32, 45; destiny and, 44; in Evagrius Ponticus, 253–55; God and, 25; grace and, 18, 73; Holy Spirit and, 5, 205; as human becoming, 72–87; Jesus Christ and, 5; minimalist definition and, 5; prosopocentric approach to, 72–73; salvation and, 75; sin and, 74. *See also* theosis
Deification in Christ (Nellas), 75
"Deification in Origen, Evagrius and Cassian" (Casiday), 251–52
de Lubac, Henri, 18, 24–25, 35n13, 35n15
Demacopoulos, George E., 1–9
demonarchy, 137–39, 144–45, 152–53, 190
Denis the Carthusian, 20
Denysenko, Nicholas, 92n63
Derrida, Jacques, 184
desacralization, 134, 137, 141–45
Descartes, René, 180
desire: God as object of, 29; knowledge and, 26; in Symeon, 235–36
Desmond, William, 181–82
Dilthey, Wilhelm, 210, 216n45, 217n49
Dionysius the Areopagite, 78, 180, 186, 209, 218–45, 230n12, 230n17
directionality, 224–25
Divine Names (Dionysius the Areopagite), 221–23
Doctrine of Deification in the Greek Patristic Tradition, The (Russell), 3–4, 252

Ebeling, Gerhard, 125–26
Eckhart, Meister, 2, 179, 198–212, 212n1, 213n8, 215n35
Edgar, Orion, 271
Edwards, Jonathan, 167
Ellacuría, Ignacio, 191
Ephesians, Epistle to, 74, 76, 79, 104
Ephraim the Syrian, 159
epistemology, 163–64, 168–72, 270–71, 283–86, 290. *See also* knowledge
eschatology, 75, 93, 151, 161–63
Eschatology of Hans Urs von Balthasar, The (Healy), 93
Eucharist, 243, 253; asceticism and, 187; in Cabasilas, 242; Christification and, 83–85; Gnosticism and, 135–37; Holy Spirit and,

102; knowledge of God and, 243; participation and, 107, 253; perfection and, 92n65; salvation and, 84, 141; solidarity and, 148–52; theosis and, 185; Trinity and, 101, 193
Eunomius, 223, 230n12
Evagrius Ponticus, 172, 251–60, 267–72, 274–77
experientialism, 189

faith, 6; certitude of, 244; Christ and, 99, 119–20, 126–27; contemplation and, 66; as divine action, 119–22; in Ebeling, 125; freedom in, 130n28; Gnosticism and, 136; God and, 99, 101, 112–27, 131n47; Holy Spirit and, 99, 120, 163; justification and, 116, 119–20; knowledge, 100; knowledge and, 100–1; likeness and, 101; love and, 123–25, 132n58; in Luther, 112–27; mercy and, 118, 125; power of, 132n58; reality and, 118, 126; reason and, 101, 123–25, 176; salvation and, 6; sin and, 117–18, 120; that united with Christ, 122–23; theosis and, 177–84; in Wesley, 166
fallenness, 21–22
Fall of Man, 19, 45–46, 75, 94, 170
"Fathers, the Scholastics and Ourselves, The" (Balthasar), 94
feminism, 106. *See also* womanism
Fichte, Johann, 181
Fiddes, Paul S., 88n2
Finch, Jeffrey, 186–187
FitzGerald, Constance, 189
Florovsky, Georges, 133
Forde, Gerhard, 113, 128n6
Fourth Lateran Council, 96
Francis, Pope, 273
Freud, Sigmund, 189
friendship, 38, 58, 107

Gadamer, Hans-Georg, 213n8
Galatians, Epistle to, 72, 84, 104, 114–15, 119, 275–76
Gasché, Rodolphe, 207
Gavrilyuk, Paul, 5–6, 133
Genesis, Book of, 76, 118
German idealism, 200, 206–7
Gilson, Etienne, 200
glory: in Aquinas, 38, 40, 43, 62; grace and, 49, 62; knowledge of God and, 29, 233; light of, and divinization, 49–66; light of, intellect and, 106; love and, 108; soul and, 53; Word and, 29
Gnosticism, 135–37, 153

Gnostics, 135
Gnostikos (Evagrius Ponticus), 267–268
God: *analogia entis* and, 96; apophasis and, 289–90; as being, 172–73, 204; being and, 42–43, 225; as cause of grace, 56; creation and, 43; creatures and, 42–43, 55; deification and, 5, 25; desire to see, 21–22, 29; destiny and, 44; directionality and, 225; doctrine of, 40–44; engagement with world, 40–44; essence of, 50–51; existence of, 223, 225–26; faith and, 99, 101, 112–27, 131n47; Fall and, 19; friendship with, 38; grace and, 201; Incarnation and, 90n43; indwelling and, 116, 232; as intelligible, 61; justice and, 225; as knowable, 221, 223–24; knowledge of, 20, 28, 34n11, 35n25, 49–53, 62, 98–100, 239, 242; as light, 77–78; likeness to, 37, 51–52, 204–5, 238; love from, 85, 105–6, 132n58; love of, 62; mercy and, 109n15, 125; names of, 224–25; as object of desire, 29; otherness of, 221, 224, 232; participation in, 95, 101–2, 253; personal, 95–96; philosophy and becoming, 202; rationality and, 101; as rational spirit, 28; reason and, 124; self-correspondence of, 282–83, 286, 290, 292n24; sin and, 110n29; transcendence of, 28, 78; union with, 18, 38, 41, 45, 53, 56, 59, 75, 78, 94, 112–27, 221, 235, 238, 242–43; as unknowable, 223–24; vision of, 50–52
Golitzin, Alexander, 220
grace: in Aquinas, 29–30, 38–39, 43–44, 47–49, 53–55, 57–68, 70n19; bestowal of, 57–58; Christ and, 47–48, 62–63; Christification and, 86; Christology and, 97; created, 43–44; deification and, 18, 73; divinization and, 58, 60–61; in Eckhart, 201, 207–8, 215n35; Eucharist and, 102, 150; in Evagrius Ponticus, 257–58; first, 63; glory and, 49, 62; gnosis and, 271; God and, 201; God as cause of, 56; Holy Spirit and, 59–60, 63; life and, 64–65; life of, 54–66; in Lossky, 73; manualism and, 18; mercy and, 162; nature and, 18, 20, 22–23, 184–88; piety and, 162; salvation and, 48, 60, 70n19, 162; sin and, 58–59, 64, 70n14; soul and, 19, 48–49, 53, 59, 207; theosis and, 67–68, 184–88; uncreated, 43–44; virtue and, 56; virtue *vs.*, 55–56; in Weil, 111n42; world-order and, 35n17
Great Catechism, The (Gregory of Nyssa), 136
Great Letter (Evagrius Ponticus), 254
Gregory of Nyssa, 32, 109n15, 136
Gross, Jules, 3, 87n1
Grosshans, Hans, 124, 131n44

Hadewijch of Antwerp, 178, 198
Hadley, Chris, 110n29
Hallonsten, Gösta, 42–43, 61–62, 71n20, 71n23
Ham (Biblical figure), 134
Hamburger, Jeffrey, 199, 213n8
Harnack, Adolf von, 4–5
Hart, David Bentley, 15–32
Healy, Nicholas, 35n13, 93, 100, 106
Hebrews, Book of, 104
Hegel, Georg Wilhelm Friedrich, 181–82, 193, 207
Heidegger, Martin, 182, 184
Hellenization, 2, 4
Henry, Michael, 182–84
Hirsch, Emanuel, 128n10
historical theology, 6
History of Dogma (Harnack), 4
Hobbes, Thomas, 190
holiness, 65, 149, 160, 163–64, 168–70, 187, 192
Holiness Movement, 159
Holl, Karl, 128n10
Hollywood, Amy, 198, 215n30
Holy Spirit: in Balthasar, 107; baptism and, 162; communion and, 150; deification and, 5, 205; divinization and, 150; Eucharist and, 102; faith and, 99, 120, 163; grace and, 59–60, 63; indwelling of, 97, 192; intellect and, 235; justification and, 118; love and, 102; mercy and, 192; participation and, 98, 101, 192; Trinity and, 102–3; in Wesley, 161; witness of, 164–67
human becoming, 80–83
Humani generis (Pius XII), 18, 25, 35n15
humanism, 85, 133, 281
humility, 48, 104, 108, 233–34, 237–39, 244, 248n22, 289
Hymns (Symeon the New Theologian), 235–36, 248n29, 249n44
Hypatius of Ephesus, 219

idealism, German, 200, 206–7
identitarianism, 199
Ignatius of Antioch, 82, 93, 110n36
imperialism, 141, 177, 193
Incarnation, 30–31, 33n8, 37, 44, 46–47, 70n16, 90n43, 103, 206
individualism, 4, 57, 177, 190, 193, 199, 211–12
indwelling, 86, 97, 104, 116, 192, 232, 234, 238–39
Interior Castle (Teresa of Avila), 180
intersectionality, 192
Irenaeus of Lyon, 4, 76, 88n6, 135
Irigaray, Luce, 183–84
Itinerarium (Bonaventure), 179

James, William, 189
Jantzen, Grace, 183–184
Janz, Denis, 125
Jay, Martin, 199
Jesus Christ: baptism and, 83–84; Catholic Church and, 63–64; in Christification, 78–79; communion and, 79–80; deification and, 5; denial of humanity of, 135; divinity of, 30; Eucharist and, 150; faith and, 99, 119–20, 126–27; faith that united with, 122–23; grace and, 47–48, 62–63; humanity and, 81–82, 89n24; humanity of, 30, 135; Incarnation and, 30–31, 33n8, 37, 44, 47; indwelling of, 86, 238–39; as justice, 205–6; kenosis and, 93–94; life in, 98–99; likeness of, 45–46; love and, 91n55; as meeting point of God and humanity, 63; mission and, 93–94; Passion of, 44, 271–72; reality and, 101; Resurrection of, 46, 81, 149, 151–52; righteousness of, 126–27; as sacrament, 98; Second Coming of, 150; sin and, 104, 152; theosis and, 37; Trinity and, 99; unity with, 75–76; work of, 44–49
John, First, 49, 51
John, Gospel of, 104, 120–21, 201, 253
John of Damascus, 3, 218
John of the Cross, 178, 182, 189
Judaism, 3
Jugie, Martin, 87n1
Julian of Norwich, 179
justice: communication with, 274; deification and, 205; divinity and, 179; faith and, 113; God and, 225; salvation and, 48; soul and, 206; Trinity and, 206; womanism and, 151
justification, 112–14, 116–23, 126, 132n49, 161

Kariatlis, Philip, 72–87
Kavasilas, Nicolas, 90n35, 91n55
kenosis: Christ and, 93–94; defined, 93–94; Incarnation and, 103; of love, 97; theosis as, 93–108
Kephalaia Gnostika (Evagrius), 252, 255–60
knowledge: awareness and, 272–73; desire and, 26; in Evagrius Ponticus, 268–69; existence and, 223; faith, 100; faith and, 100–1; of God, 20, 28, 34n11, 35n25, 49–53, 62, 98–100, 221, 239, 242; holiness and, 168–70; nature and, 29–30; quest for, 82–83; soul and, 256; theosis and, 28, 231–45
Kristeva, Julia, 189
Krueger, Derek, 248n29

Lacan, Jacques, 189
language, 14, 112–14, 200, 233–36

Latin Commentary on the Book of Wisdom (Eckhart), 203
Leontius of Byzantium, 3
Leo XIII, Pope, 18
Letter on the Faith (Evagrius Ponticus), 253, 261n8
Levinas, Emmanuel, 232
Life in Christ, The (Cabasilas), 92n63
likeness: of Christ, 45–46; creation and, 105; in Eckhart, 203–4; faith and, 101; to God, 37, 51–52, 204–5, 238; holiness and, 169; humility and, 239; nature and, 188; otherness and, 183, 232; soul and, 204
Logos, 33n8, 79, 82, 87, 91n59, 236, 273, 276–79, 287
Lonergan, Bernard, 34n11, 35n17, 35n25
Lorde, Audre, 151–52
Lossky, Vladimir, 3, 41, 73, 77–78, 182, 199–208, 216n39, 290
Louth, Andrew, 1, 39–40, 44–45, 61, 68, 74–75
love: Christ and, 91n55; deification and, 77; faith and, 123–25, 132n58; glory and, 108; from God, 85, 105–6, 132n58; of God, 62; Holy Spirit and, 102; kenosis of, 97; mercy and, 125; reason and, 123–125; Trinity and, 108
Luibheid, Colm, 230n11
Luther, Martin, 2, 6; faith in, 112–27; justification in, 112–14, 116–23, 126, 132n49, 161; mercy in, 121; reason in, 124, 131n44; sin in, 118; vocabulary in, 116–19

Macrobius, 203
Mannermaa, Tuomo, 112, 114–16, 122–23, 125–26, 128n10, 129n16, 129n18, 129n20
Mantzaridis, Giorgios, 73
manualist traditions, 2, 18, 25, 31
marginalized persons, 106
Marx, Karl, 181
materiality, 94, 138, 181, 274
Matthew, Gospel of, 160
Maximus the Confessor, 3–4, 15, 28, 96–97, 187, 218, 275, 291n16
McGinn, Bernard, 198, 208, 211, 215n35
McGrath, Alister, 113, 128n6
McGuckin, John, 73, 88n3
McInerny, Brendan, 101
McInroy, Mark, 110n25
Mechthild of Magdeburg, 198
mercy: faith and, 118, 125; God and, 109n15, 125; grace and, 162; Holy Spirit and, 192; love and, 125; in Luther, 121
Merleau-Ponty, Maurice, 284
Meyendorff, Jean, 70n12, 220
Middle Passage, 141

Mielle de Prinsac, Annie-Paule, 143
Milbank, John, 35n15
Mirror of Simple Souls (Porete), 180
mission, 93–94, 107–8
Mitchell, Basil, 171
Moltmann, Jürgen, 190
Moore, G. E., 171
moral agency: theosis and, 153
Morgan, Ben, 211–12, 217n50
Morris, Susana M., 143
Morrison, Toni, 138, 140–48, 150, 152–53, 190
Moser, Matthew, 100
Moses, 38–39, 57, 65, 219, 227
mystical theology, 9n1
Mystical Theology (Dionysius the Areopagite), 180, 186, 222, 225, 227–28
Mystical Theology of the Eastern Church (Lossky), 199
mysticism, 65, 165, 183, 189, 198–200, 209–12
"Mysticism East and West: A Comparative Analysis of the Nature of Mysticism" (Otto), 208–9

names, of God, 224–25
nature: in Aquinas, 20–21; in Aristotle, 21; in Braine, 24–25; creation of, 89n24; divinity and, 23; grace and, 18, 20, 22–23, 184–88; knowledge and, 29–30; pure, 31; reason and, 26; sin and, 185–86; theosis and, 184–88
Nellas, Panayiotis, 73–82, 84–87, 89n14, 89n17, 89n24, 90n35, 90n43, 91n55, 92n63, 92n74
Neoplatonism, 94, 180, 202–3, 207, 220
Nicholas of Cusa, 32, 172
Nicomachean Ethics (Aristotle), 21
Nietzsche, Friedrich, 181, 183

O'Connor, Flannery, 279
Omero, Oscar, 191–92
On Prayer (Evagrius Ponticus), 274
On the Incarnation (Athanasius of Alexandria), 76, 178
On Thoughts (Evagrius Ponticus), 268–69, 271–72, 274–75
Ordinary Gloss, 58
O'Regan, Cyril, 182, 200–1
Origen, 139, 255, 260, 264n28, 282
otherness, 73, 90n26, 95, 135, 182–85, 223–25, 229, 232
Otto, Rudolf, 200, 208–12

paganism, 3
pain, suffering *vs.*, 152
Palamas, Gregory, 3, 41–42, 70n12, 71n20, 87n1, 90n35, 107, 216n39, 218, 220–21

Palamite synthesis, 3
Panikkar, Raimon, 270
Papanikolaou, Aristotle, 1–9, 73, 77–78, 90n27, 152, 200, 214n12
Parisian Questions (Eckhart), 204
participation, 125; in God, 95, 101–2, 253; Holy Spirit and, 98, 101, 192; as mission, 107–8
Passion, 44, 271–72
patristic tradition, 19–20, 38–39, 87n1, 89n14, 94–96, 109n11, 112, 136, 138, 150, 165, 187, 221, 280
Paul, 38–39, 57, 65, 79, 84, 114, 129n18, 180
Pelagianism, 22, 161
Pelagius, 98
Pelikan, Jaroslav, 219
Pentecostalism, 159, 162
perception, 166–67
Perkinson, James W., 134
Peter, First, 238
Peter, Second, 38, 78, 104
Peura, Simo, 114–16, 129n16, 130n22, 130n28
phenomenology, of Christian experience, 161–63
Philippians, 278
Pius XII, Pope, 18, 25, 35n15
Plantinga, Alvin, 171
Plato, 95, 223
Platonism, 42, 109n11, 176, 190, 218, 277
Plotinus, 203, 209, 216n39
Political Theology (Schmitt), 190
Poor, Sara, 198
Porete, Marguerite, 180, 192, 198
Porter, Jean, 37–68
post-Pentecostalism, 159
potency, 21–22, 24, 30–31, 33n6, 34n12
Prayer (Balthasar), 98
predication, 17, 204
Prevot, Andrew, 176–94
Protestantism, 1–2, 5, 159–60, 175n13, 181
protology, 75
Przywara, Erich, 96
Psalms, Book of, 120, 253, 257, 259
Pseudo-Dionysius, 172, 234
Pseudo-Macarius, 159
Purpura, Ashley, 231–45

Radler, Charlotte, 198, 202
Rahner, Karl, 185
Ramelli, Ilaria, 252
rapture, 27, 65–66
rationality, 80–83, 101, 133, 278–83
reason, 6; contemplation and, 66; cooption of, 138; in Dionysius the Areopagite, 218–45;

faith and, 101, 123–25, 176; Fall of Man and, 124; God and, 124; love and, 123–25; in Luther, 124, 131n44; nature and, 26; salvation and, 82; self-transcendence and, 201; soul and, 124; theosis and, 15–32, 177–84; virtue and, 55–56; will and, 27–28, 59
reflection, 142, 207, 211, 269, 282, 285
Rehilan, Joel, 214n18
ressourcement, 18
Resurrection, 46, 81, 149, 151–52
revelation, 33n8, 35n19, 95–96, 100–1, 160, 163–64, 173, 202, 237, 239, 289
revivalism, 159–60
Richard of St. Victor, 282, 285
righteousness, 115–23, 126–27, 129n18, 130n21, 130n28, 132n49
Ritual: Power, Healing, and Community (Somé), 147–48
Roman Catholicism, 2
Romanides, John, 2, 220
Romanos the Melodist, 248n29
Romans, Epistle to, 120, 134, 164, 276, 278
Rückert, Hanns, 128n10
Russell, Bertrand, 171
Russell, Norman, 3–5, 74, 87n1, 252
Russia, 1

salvation: Christ and, 163; Christification and, 79–80; deification and, 75; Eucharist and, 84, 141; in Evagrius, 256; faith and, 6; grace and, 48, 60, 70n19, 162; justice and, 48; reason and, 82; survival and, 139; theosis and, 72; in Zizioulas, 150
sanctification, 61, 117, 161–62, 170, 173
Sankara, Adi, 208
Schelling, Friedrich, 181
Schleiermacher, Friedrich, 2, 10n7, 165, 181, 201, 210
Schmemann, Alexander, 229n4
Schmitt, Carl, 190, 193
Schultz, Hermann, 210
"Scripture Way of Salvation, The" (Wesley), 162
Second Coming, 150
Seeberg, Erich, 128n10
self, 208–12
self-correspondence, 282–83, 286, 290, 292n74
Sermons on Several Occasions (Wesley), 160
Severus of Antioch, 219
Showings (Julian of Norwich), 179
Siedentop, Larry, 211, 217n49
sin: alienation and, 110n29; in Aquinas, 46–47, 58–59; Christ and, 104, 152; deification and,

74; faith and, 117–18, 120; freedom from, 49; grace and, 58–59, 64, 70n14; justification and, 117; in Luther, 118; nature and, 185–86; original, 75; in Wesley, 161; in Western tradition, 46
slavery, 141–43, 145–48
Social Gospel, 162
solidarity, 63, 105, 148–52
Somé, Malidoma Patrice, 147–48
Song of Songs, 184
Sophrony, 275
soul: deification and, 205; dignity of, 211; glory and, 53; grace and, 19, 48–49, 53, 59, 207; individualism and, 190; justice and, 206; knowledge and, 256; likeness and, 204; mind and, 235; reason and, 124; in Symeon, 235; theosis and, 179; transcendence and, 201; Word and, 215n30
Speculum of the Other Woman (Irigaray), 183
spiritualization, 94–96
Stagel, Elsbeth, 217n50
Stjerna, Kirsi, 112–27
subjectivism, 167–68
suffering, 137–39, 152
Summa contra gentiles (Aquinas), 19–20, 33n8
Summa theologiae (Aquinas), 33n8, 52–53, 58, 67, 69n7, 70n20
supernatural, 18–19, 24
Surnaturel (de Lubac), 18, 25
Suso, Henry, 211
Swinburne, Richard, 171
Symeon the New Theologian, 3, 166–67, 174n12, 232–80, 247n12, 248n22, 248n29, 248n38, 249n44

Teresa, My Love (Kristeva), 189
Teresa of Avila, 180, 187, 190
Theologic I (Balthasar), 100
Théologie négative et connaissance de dieu chez Maître Eckhart (Eckhart), 199
theology: epistemology of, 172; grace and, 43–44; historical, 6; of incarnation, 30; mystical, 9n1; New Theology, 18
theosis: ambiguous meanings of, 176–94; in Aquinas, 37–68, 179; in Balthasar, 96–103; centrality of, 9n1; challenging of, 94–96; conditions of, 184–93; disambiguated, 193–94; effects of, 184–93; faith and, 177–84; grace and, 67–68, 184–88; as kenosis, 93–108;

knowing others and, 240; knowledge and, 28, 231–45; Luther and, 112–14; moral agency and, 153; nature and, 184–88; reaffirmations of, 6; reason and, 15–32, 177–84; salvation and, 72; soul and, 179; theology and, 1; Trinity and, 89n26; understanding and, 233–36; will and, 28. *See also* deification
thumos, 267–68
Tillich, Paul, 113
Townes, Emilie, 151–52
Townsend, Luke Davis, 69n7
transcendence, 28, 78, 201, 226
Transfiguration, 136
Trinity, 41; asceticism and, 256; economic, 177, 185; Eucharist and, 101, 193; Holy Spirit and, 102–3; Jesus Christ and, 99; justice and, 206; love and, 108; theosis and, 89n26
Truth, Sojourner, 191–92
truth-telling, 283
Turner, Denys, 189
Two Kinds of Righteousness (Luther), 119

verification, 171
vision, 50–52
Vision of God, The (Lossky), 3
Vogelsang, Erich, 128n10

Watkins, Michele E., 133–53, 190
Watkins-Ali, Carroll, 140
Weil, Simone, 111n42, 277
Wesley, John, 2, 159–73
whiteness, 134–35
white racial narcissism, 138
white supremacy, 135
Williams, A. N., 68n2, 70n20
Williams, Delores S., 137–39, 190
Williams, Rowan, 96–97, 182, 203
Wolski Conn, Joann, 189
Wolterstorff, Nicholas, 171
womanism: evil and, 137–39; neopatristic synthesis and, 133–34. *See also* feminism
women, Black, 141–45
Word, 29, 33n8, 78, 215n30, 278, 283, 285
world-order, 35n17

Yannaras, Christos, 182

Zizioulas, John, 73, 77–78, 89n26, 135–36, 139, 150–51, 190, 232

ORTHODOX CHRISTIANITY AND CONTEMPORARY THOUGHT

SERIES EDITORS
Aristotle Papanikolaou and Ashley M. Purpura

A. G. Roeber, *Orthodox Christianity and the Rights Revolution in America.*

Bryce E. Rich, *Gender Essentialism and Orthodoxy: Beyond Male and Female.*

Kristina Stoeckl and Dmitry Uzlaner, *The Moralist International: Russia in the Global Culture Wars.*

Sarah Riccardi-Swartz, *Between Heaven and Russia: Religious Conversion and Political Apostasy in Appalachia.*

Thomas Arentzen, Ashley M. Purpura, and Aristotle Papanikolaou (eds.), *Orthodox Tradition and Human Sexuality.*

Christina M. Gschwandtner, *Welcoming Finitude: Toward a Phenomenology of Orthodox Liturgy.*

George E. Demacopoulos, *Colonizing Christianity: Greek and Latin Religious Identity in the Era of the Fourth Crusade.*

Pia Sophia Chaudhari, *Dynamis of Healing: Patristic Theology and the Psyche.*

Brian A. Butcher, *Liturgical Theology after Schmemann: An Orthodox Reading of Paul Ricoeur.* Foreword by Andrew Louth.

Ashley M. Purpura, *God, Hierarchy, and Power: Orthodox Theologies of Authority from Byzantium.*

Aristotle Papanikolaou and George E. Demacopoulos (eds.), *Faith, Reason, and Theosis.*

Aristotle Papanikolaou and George E. Demacopoulos (eds.), *Fundamentalism or Tradition: Christianity after Secularism.*

George E. Demacopoulos and Aristotle Papanikolaou (eds.), *Christianity, Democracy, and the Shadow of Constantine.*

George E. Demacopoulos and Aristotle Papanikolaou (eds.), *Orthodox Constructions of the West.*

George E. Demacopoulos and Aristotle Papanikolaou (eds.), *Orthodox Readings of Augustine.*

John Chryssavgis and Bruce V. Foltz (eds.), *Toward an Ecology of Transfiguration: Orthodox Christian Perspectives on Environment, Nature, and Creation.* Foreword by Bill McKibben. Prefatory Letter by Ecumenical Patriarch Bartholomew.

Lucian N. Leustean (ed.), *Orthodox Christianity and Nationalism in Nineteenth-Century Southeastern Europe.*

Georgia Frank, Susan R. Holman, and Andrew S. Jacobs (eds.), *The Garb of Being: Embodiment and the Pursuit of Holiness in Late Ancient Christianity.*

John Chryssavgis (ed.), *Dialogue of Love: Breaking the Silence of Centuries.* Contributions by Brian E. Daley, S.J., and Georges Florovsky.

Ecumenical Patriarch Bartholomew, *In the World, Yet Not of the World: Social and Global Initiatives of Ecumenical Patriarch Bartholomew.* Edited by John Chryssavgis. Foreword by Jose Manuel Barroso.

Ecumenical Patriarch Bartholomew, *Speaking the Truth in Love: Theological and Spiritual Exhortations of Ecumenical Patriarch Bartholomew.* Edited by John Chryssavgis. Foreword by Dr. Rowan Williams, Archbishop of Canterbury.

Ecumenical Patriarch Bartholomew, *On Earth as in Heaven: Ecological Vision and Initiatives of Ecumenical Patriarch Bartholomew.* Edited by John Chryssavgis. Foreword by His Royal Highness, the Duke of Edinburgh.

www.ingramcontent.com/pod-product-compliance
Lightning Source LLC
Chambersburg PA
CBHW020354080526
44584CB00014B/1017